THE WORLD'S GREAT RELIGIONS

TIME INCORPORATED

Editor-in-chief
HENRY R. LUCE
President
ROY E. LARSEN

———————

"The World's Great Religions" Series and Book were produced
under the general direction of

EDWARD K. THOMPSON, *Managing Editor*
PHILIP H. WOOTTON JR., *Assistant Managing Editor*
JOSEPH KASTNER, *Copy Editor*
MARIAN A. MACPHAIL, *Chief of Research*

by the following editorial staff:

Editor
SAM WELLES

Art Director
CHARLES TUDOR
BERNARD QUINT, *associate*; ALBERT KETCHUM, ROBERT YOUNG, *assistants*

Assistant Editor
OLIVER E. ALLEN

Writers
LINCOLN BARNETT, RALPH GRAVES, HENRY ANATOLE GRUNWALD,
EMMET JOHN HUGHES, PAUL HUTCHINSON, LIN YUTANG,
HENRY MOSCOW, WINTHROP SARGEANT,
DOROTHY SEIBERLING, CLAUDE STANUSH

Head Researcher
MONICA HORNE

Text and Picture Research by
JANE NELSON, JANE WILSON, VALERIE VONDERMUHLL; BARBARA ELLIS,
JOZEFA STUART, SUSAN NEUBERGER, MAYA PINES, WARREN R. YOUNG

Photographs and Illustrations by
DMITRI KESSEL, HOWARD SOCHUREK, GORDON PARKS, LYND WARD,
LEONARD MCCOMBE, ALFRED EISENSTAEDT, DAVID DOUGLAS DUNCAN,
CORNELL CAPA, FRANK LERNER, ANTONIO PETRUCCELLI,
BORIS ARTZYBASHEFF
(The names of other photographers and illustrators whose work appears
in this book will be found in the Picture Sources, pages 309–10)

Editorial Assistants
ALBERT J. DUNN, ADRIENNE FOULKE, EDWARD PUCCIA,
KAY CAMPBELL, LOIS RHOADES

———————

Publisher
ANDREW HEISKELL

Assistant Publisher
ARTHUR R. MURPHY JR.

"The World's Great Religions" series appeared in LIFE in six parts
during 1955: Hinduism (February 7), Buddhism (March 7), Chinese
faiths (April 4), Islam (May 9), Judaism (June 13), and the double
Special Issue on Christianity (December 26). Two years of intensive research and photography throughout the world were devoted to the combined project. A third year has been spent in expanding the series into
book form, with 160 pages of additional material both on the religions
themselves and in selections from their scriptures. An introduction, in-
dex, and lists of credits and of picture sources have also been added.
   Working closely with the above staff were also the following individuals and departments of the magazine: Ray Mackland, Picture Editor;
Irene Saint, LIFE Newsbureau Chief; Helen Deuell, Copy Chief; LIFE's
foreign and domestic correspondents, picture bureau and copy desk.

THE WORLD'S GREAT RELIGIONS

TIME INCORPORATED · NEW YORK · 1957

CREDITS

LIFE is indebted to many authorities and institutions, notably those listed below, for their generous assistance in the preparation of "The World's Great Religions" Series and Book. However, LIFE assumes responsibility for the selection and arrangement of all the material in the book and the viewpoints expressed.

ALBRIGHT, DR. WILLIAM F.—W. W. Spence Professor of Semitic Languages, Johns Hopkins University

ARKUSH, RALPH MONTGOMERY—Jurisconsult, Russian Orthodox Greek Catholic Church of North America, New York

AUNG, U. HPE—New Buddhist Institute, Rangoon

BAINTON, DR. ROLAND H.—Titus Street Professor of Ecclesiastical History, Yale University Divinity School

BARNES, DR. C. RANKIN—Secretary, National Council of The Protestant Episcopal Church, New York

BARR, ALFRED H., JR.—Director of Collections, Museum of Modern Art, New York

BASS, RALPH—Director of Magazine and Feature Section, American Jewish Committee, New York

BELKIN, DR. SAMUEL—President, Yeshiva University

BEZSMERTNY, ALEXANDER E.—Secretary to Metropolitan, Russian Orthodox Greek Catholic Church of North America, New York

BISAR, DR. MOHAMED—Director, Islamic Center, Washington, D.C.

BRAUDE, RABBI WILLIAM G.—Temple Beth El, Providence, R.I.

BUSHY, DOUGLAS A.—National Council of The Protestant Episcopal Church, New York

CAMPBELL, JOSEPH—Professor of Literature, Sarah Lawrence College

CHAN, DR. WING-TSIT—Professor of Chinese Culture and Philosophy, Dartmouth College

COHEN, RABBI GERSON D.—Librarian, Jewish Theological Seminary of America

CROSS, DR. FRANK M., JR.—Professor of Old Testament, McCormick Theological Seminary

DAS, DR. TARAKNATH—Adjunct Professor of Public Affairs, New York University

DOANE, ROBERT R.—President, World Assets Audit Association, Inc.

DODGE, DR. BAYARD—President Emeritus of American University, Beirut

DWYER, S.J., REV. JOHN S.—Chairman of Department of Theology, Fordham University

EDWARDS, DEANE—President, Hymn Society of America, New York

EISENDRATH, RABBI MAURICE N.—President, Union of American Hebrew Congregations, New York

ETTINGHAUSEN, DR. RICHARD—Associate in Near Eastern Art, Freer Gallery of Art, Washington, D.C.

EWING, S.J., REV. J. FRANKLIN—Assistant Professor of Anthropology, Director of Research Services, Fordham University

FATEMI, DR. N. SEIFPOUR—Professor of Social Science, Fairleigh Dickinson University

FLANAGAN, O.S.M., REV. NEAL—Stonebridge Priory, Lake Bluff, Illinois

FLOROVSKY, THE RT. REV. GEORGES—Professor of Church History, Harvard Divinity School

FRIESS, DR. HORACE L.—Professor of Philosophy, Columbia University

GELLER, VICTOR B.—Director, Field Activities, Yeshiva University

GHINE, U OHN—Editor, *The Light of The Dhamma*, Rangoon

GINSBERG, DR. H. L.—Professor of Biblical History and Literature, Jewish Theological Seminary of America

GLUECK, DR. NELSON—President, Hebrew Union College-Jewish Institute of Religion

GOODRICH, DR. L. CARRINGTON—Dean Lung Professor of Chinese, Columbia University

GORDON, MRS. ANTOINETTE—Tibetan and Oriental Collections, American Museum of Natural History, New York

GOTWALD, DR. LUTHER A.—Executive Secretary, Division of Foreign Missions, National Council of the Churches of Christ in the U.S.A., New York

GRANT, DR. F. C.—Edward Robinson Professor of Biblical Theology, Union Theological Seminary

HALVERSON, DR. MARVIN P.—Executive Director, Department of Worship and the Arts, National Council of the Churches of Christ in the U.S.A., New York

HAMILTON, DR. CLARENCE H.—Professor Emeritus of Philosophy of Religion, Oberlin College

HAMILTON, DR. GEORGE HEARD—Professor of the History of Art, Yale University

HANDY, DR. ROBERT T.—Associate Professor of Church History, Union Theological Seminary

HARDING, G. LANKESTER—former Director, Department of Antiquities, Government of Jordan, and former Curator, Palestine Archaeological Museum

HARRIS, DR. ERDMAN—Lecturer in Religion and the Fine Arts, Yale University Divinity School

HILLS, MARGARET T.—Librarian, American Bible Society, New York

HOENIG, DR. SIDNEY B.—Director of Adult Education and Professor of Jewish History, Yeshiva University

JACQUET, CONSTANT H. J.—Research Assistant, Bureau of Research and Survey, National Council of the Churches of Christ in the U.S.A., New York

JEFFERY, DR. ARTHUR—Executive Officer, Department of Near and Middle East Languages, Columbia University, and Union Theological Seminary

KAYSER, DR. STEPHEN S.—Curator of The Jewish Museum, New York

KAZANAS, REV. CONSTANTINE J.—Dean, Hellenic Cathedral of the Holy Trinity, New York

KNOX, DR. JOHN—Director of Studies, Union Theological Seminary

KRAMRISCH, DR. STELLA—Professor of Eastern Art, University of Pennsylvania

LIEBERMAN, DR. SAUL—Dean of Rabbinical School, Jewish Theological Seminary of America

LIU, DR. WU-CHI—Editor, Human Relations Area Files, Inc., Yale University

MARCUS, DR. JACOB R.—Adolph S. Ochs Professor of Jewish History, Hebrew Union College-Jewish Institute of Religion

MAUNG, THE HON. JUSTICE U THEIN—Chief Justice, Union of Burma, Vice-President, Union of Burma Buddha Sasana Council

MCDONALD, O.S.B., ABBOT CUTHBERT—St. Benedict's Abbey, Atchison, Kansas

MOREY, DR. CHARLES R.—late Marquand Professor of Art and Archaeology, Princeton University

MUNSHI, DR. K. M.—Governor, Uttar Pradesh State, Republic of India

MURRAY, S.J., REV. JOHN COURTNEY—Editor, *Theological Studies*, Woodstock College

NIEBUHR, DR. H. RICHARD—Sterling Professor of Theology and Christian Ethics, Yale University Divinity School

NIEBUHR, DR. REINHOLD—Graduate Professor of Christian Ethics, Union Theological Seminary

NIKHILANANDA, SWAMI—Director, Ramakrishna-Vivekananda Center, Inc., New York

PARKER, DR. PIERSON—Professor of New Testament Literature and Interpretation, General Theological Seminary

PRIEST, ALAN—Curator of Far Eastern Arts, Metropolitan Museum of Art, New York

QURESHI, DR. I. H.—Visiting Professor of History, Columbia University

RADHAKRISHNAN, DR. SARVEPALLI—Vice-President, Republic of India

RATHBONE, PERRY T.—Director, Boston Museum of Fine Arts

RICHARDSON, DR. CYRIL C.—Washburn Professor of Church History, Union Theological Seminary

SAMARASEKARA, DHANAPALA—Social Affairs Officer, United Nations

SCHMEMANN, REV. ALEXANDER—Dean, St. Vladimir's Orthodox Theological Seminary

SICKMAN, LAURENCE—Director, The William Rockhill Nelson Gallery of Art and Atkins Museum of Fine Arts, Kansas City

SILVER, RABBI SAMUEL M.—Union of American Hebrew Congregations, New York

SKEHAN, MSGR. PATRICK W.—Professor of Semitics and Egyptian Languages and Literature, Catholic University of America

SMITH, DR. MYRON R.—Honorary Consultant in Islamic Archaeology and Near Eastern History, Library of Congress, Washington, D.C.

SOLOVEITCHIK, DR. JOSEPH—Professor of Talmud and Philosophy, Yeshiva University

STOODY, DR. RALPH—General Secretary and Executive Director of the Commission on Public Relations and Methodist Information, The Methodist Church, New York

TAO, FRANK—Editor, Chinese News Service

TILLICH, DR. PAUL J.—University Professor, Harvard Divinity School

TRAGER, DR. FRANK N.—Research Professor of Government, New York University

WALSH, MSGR. CHARLES M.—Director, Confraternity of Christian Doctrine, New York

WIKGREN, ALLEN—Associate Professor, New Testament Language and Literature, University of Chicago

WOLFSON, DR. HARRY A.—Nathan Littauer Professor of Hebrew Literature and Philosophy, Harvard University

YOUNG, DR. T. CUYLER—Garrett Professor of Persian Language and History, Princeton University

ACKNOWLEDGMENTS TO INSTITUTIONS

AMERICAN BIBLE SOCIETY—New York

ARAB STATES DELEGATION TO THE UNITED NATIONS

COLUMBIA UNIVERSITY—New York

JEWISH THEOLOGICAL SEMINARY OF AMERICA—New York

METROPOLITAN MUSEUM OF ART—New York

NATIONAL COUNCIL OF THE CHURCHES OF CHRIST IN THE U.S.A.

NEW YORK PUBLIC LIBRARY

REPUBLIC OF INDIA INFORMATION SERVICES

ROMAN CATHOLIC ARCHDIOCESE OF NEW YORK

UNION THEOLOGICAL SEMINARY—New York

WILLIAM ROCKHILL NELSON GALLERY OF ART—Kansas City, Missouri

Special acknowledgment is also made to the following publishers for their permission to quote copyrighted material used in this book, especially in the selections of religious writings of the various faiths. In some instances, different translations have been combined or the wordings slightly changed for accuracy or clarity. Spellings in the book conform with common Western usage.

ABHEDANANDA, SWAMI (compiler)—*The Sayings of Sri Ramakrishna.* New York: The Vedanta Society, 1903.

BREWSTER, EARL H. (editor)—*The Life of Gotama the Buddha.* London: Routledge & Kegan Paul Ltd., 1926.

BROWNE, LEWIS (translator)—*The Wisdom of Israel.* New York: Random House, Inc., 1945.

BURNELL, A. C. (translator)—*The Ordinances of Manu.* London: Routledge & Kegan Paul Ltd., 1891.

BURTT, E. A. (editor)—*The Teachings of The Compassionate Buddha.* New York: The New American Library of World Literature, Inc., 1955.

CAMPBELL, W. L. (translator)—*The Tree of Wisdom.* Calcutta: Calcutta University at the Baptist Mission Press, 1919.

CARUS, PAUL (translator)—*The Gospel of Buddha.* La Salle, Illinois: The Open Court Publishing Company, 1917.

CATHOLIC STUDENTS' MISSION CRUSADE, U.S.A.—"Catholic Students' Mission Crusade World Mission Map." Cincinnati: Catholic Students' Mission Crusade, U.S.A., National Center, 1956.

CONZE, EDWARD (editor)—*Buddhist Texts Through the Ages.* Oxford: Bruno Cassirer Ltd., 1954.

DAVIDS, C. A. F. RHYS (translator and editor)—*Psalms of the Early Buddhists.* London: The Pali Text Society, 1909.

DAVIDS, T. W. RHYS (translator) and C. A. F. Rhys (editor)—*Buddhist Birth Stories* (Jataka tales). London: Routledge & Kegan Paul Ltd., 1925.

DAVIDS, T. W. RHYS and C. A. F. Rhys (editors)—*The Sacred Books of the Buddhists.* London: The Pali Text Society, 1910, 1921.

DUTT, MANMATHA NATH (editor)—*The Garuda Purana.* Calcutta: Society for the Resuscitation of Indian Literature, 1908.

EVANS-WENTZ, W. Y. (editor)—*Tibetan Yoga and Secret Doctrines.* London: Oxford University Press, 1935.

GODDARD, DWIGHT (editor)—*A Buddhist Bible.* New York: E. P. Dutton & Co., Inc., 1938.

GRIFFITH, RALPH T. H. (translator)—*Hymns of the Atharva-Veda.* Benares: E. J. Lazarus & Company, 1895.

GRIFFITH, RALPH T. H. (translator)—*Hymns of the Rig-Veda.* Benares: E. J. Lazarus & Company, 1896.

GRUBB, KENNETH G. (editor) and E. J. BINGLE (associate editor)—*World Christian Handbook, 1952 Edition.* London: World Dominion Press, 1952.

HAMILTON, CLARENCE H. (editor)—*Buddhism. A Religion of Infinite Compassion.* New York: The Liberal Arts Press, 1952.

HERTZ, RABBI JOSEPH H.—*The Authorized Daily Prayer Book.* New York: Bloch Publishing Company, 1955.

JEWISH PUBLICATION SOCIETY OF AMERICA—*The Holy Scriptures According to the Masoretic Text.* Philadelphia: 1955.

LANDIS, BENSON Y. (editor)—*Yearbook of American Churches for 1957.* New York: National Council of the Churches of Christ in the U.S.A., 1956.

LIN YUTANG (translator and editor)—*The Wisdom of Laotse.* New York: Random House, Inc., 1948.

MADHAVANANDA, SWAMI (translator)—*The Brihadaranyaka Upanishad.* Almora: Advaita Ashrama, Third Edition, 1950.

MORGAN, KENNETH W. (editor)—*The Religion of the Hindus.* Translations from Sanskrit by V. Raghavan. New York: The Ronald Press Company, 1953.

MÜLLER, F. MAX (translator)—*Lectures on the Science of Religion.* New York: Charles Scribner's Sons, 1872.

MÜLLER, F. MAX (editor)—*The Sacred Books of the East.* Oxford: The Clarendon Press, 1879-1910.

NEWMAN, RABBI LOUIS I. (translator), with the collaboration of Samuel Spitz—*Talmudic Anthology.* New York: Behrman House, Inc., 1945.

NIKHILANANDA, SWAMI (translator)—*The Upanishads.* Volume I. New York: Harper & Brothers, 1949.

PICKTHALL, MOHAMMED MARMADUKE (translator)—*The Meaning of the Glorious Koran.* London: George Allen & Unwin Ltd., 1930.

PRABHAVANANDA, SWAMI, AND ISHERWOOD, CHRISTOPHER (translators)—*Bhagavad-Gita: The Song of God.* Hollywood, Calif.: Marcel Rodd, Inc., 1944.

REICHELT, KARL LUDVIG—*Truth and Tradition in Chinese Buddhism.* Translated by Kathrina van Wagenen Bugge. Shanghai: The Commercial Press, Ltd., 1927.

STEINBERG, MILTON—*Basic Judaism.* New York: Harcourt, Brace and Company, Inc., 1947.

THOMAS, E. J. (translator)—*Buddhist Scriptures.* London: John Murray (Publishers) Ltd., 1913.

WALEY, ARTHUR (translator)—*The Analects of Confucius.* London: George Allen & Unwin Ltd., Second Edition, 1945.

WARREN, HENRY CLARKE (translator)—*Buddhism in Translations,* Vol. 3, *Harvard Oriental Series.* Cambridge, Mass.: Harvard University Press, 1947.

WOODWARD, F. L. (translator)—*Minor Anthologies of the Pali Canon. Part II.* London: Oxford University Press, 1935.

TABLE OF CONTENTS

GOD THE CREATOR WAS PAINTED BY MICHELANGELO ON SISTINE CEILING

HOW MANKIND WORSHIPS

by PAUL HUTCHINSON

The late Dr. Paul Hutchinson, who died suddenly soon after writing this introduction, was a distinguished Methodist minister and for many years editor of The Christian Century *magazine. Before his untimely death he gave* LIFE's *editors much helpful advice and counsel on the planning and execution of this book on the great religions of the world.*

Dr. Hutchinson intended this article not only as an opening statement for the entire book but as a brief discussion of comparative religion. For this reason the illustrations on the following six pages have been chosen for the purpose of showing the religious practices of various groups which are not treated at any length in the book itself.

ENDLESS are the forms man's religion has taken. The names of his gods and goddesses will never be completely catalogued. The rituals through which he has sought protection or blessing run the gamut from the horrible to the sublime. The explanations of his rites may fill ten thousand volumes, and many of them disagree violently. Such young and fascinating sciences as anthropology, archaeology and paleontology are constantly uncovering new evidence concerning the life of our paleolithic ancestors. The evidence brings to light infinite variations, but on one thing it agrees. Man is a religious being.

However and wherever he developed, from the time he became man, man has worshiped, and has often shown a belief that he possesses an immortal soul. His irresistible urge to worship has been explained by a leading American anthropologist, William Howells, who says that man, unlike other animals, is "the creature who comprehends things he cannot see and believes in things he cannot comprehend."

It is not the purpose of this book to present a history of man's religious evolution. We are not here dealing with the magic, the myths, the hunting rites, the planting rites, the puberty rites, the burial rites or the myriad incantations by which our primitive ancestors sought to protect themselves against the wiles and fury of a capricious nature, to ensure food and shelter, to coalesce into enduring tribes, or to speed the dead into happiness beyond their carefully attended graves. This is a story so enthralling that it is hard not to yield to temptation and sketch it, at least in outline, again. But we leave it for others.

Neither will we attempt to trace the record of the religions which flourished while past civilizations and nations flourished, and died when they died. In this book we seek rather to consider the principal religions which are alive today, molding our own lives and the lives of our contemporaries, seeking to impress their image on the history of our times. This book deals with religion as a living element in today's culture, not as a museum piece. Man has always worshiped. Man still worships. What does he worship? And how? These are our questions.

TO BE SURE, these living religions in which we can observe our fellows seeking contact with the Infinite did not materialize suddenly without ancestry. Sometimes their followers speak of them as unique, so utterly set apart from all other faiths—past and present—as to be a spontaneous and self-contained spiritual manifestation, something akin to the biblical figure Melchisedec, "without father, without mother, without descent, having neither beginning of days, nor end of life." But it is not so. Religions have their genealogy, just as have the men who gain sustenance and assurance from them.

As this is being written, for example, there is considerable commotion because the recently discovered Dead Sea Scrolls furnish evidence that some ideas, rites and terminology of the New Testament are similar to those of the Qumran community which dwelt in the Jordan wilderness a century before Christ. The natural inference is that there was a relationship between this community and the early Christians. Yet what does this indicate other than that Christianity, whose Jewish origins have not only been acknowledged but insisted on from its birth, owes a particular debt to the spiritual legacy of one Jewish reforming sect? The extent of this particular inheritance is not likely to be determined for many years. Scholarship has scarcely begun its examination of the scrolls.

All religions trace back; all have in their lore likenesses to the lore of other faiths. Jewish and Christian scholars, reading the 4,000-year-old Babylonian epic of Gilgamesh, find—in its striking parallels to the Genesis story of Noah, with an ark covered by pitch, the rain, sending out the raven and the dove, the ark landing on a mountain—simply added evidence of the extent to which Hebrew culture emerged out of, and was influenced by, that of the Tigris and Euphrates valleys. The gods and goddesses of the Roman pantheon were often the same divinities of whom Homer sang, having been captured and renamed when Roman legions overran Greece. Buddhism came out of Hinduism, and Hinduism in its bewildering variety shows the influence of the primitive village worship from which it emerged. Mohammed explicitly acknowledged his indebtedness to Judaeo-Christian sources. For the Jewish and Christian faiths, the Bible is a superb record of the way in which, out of a nomad beginning, influenced by the civilizations of the Nile and the Middle East, challenged and at times seduced by the deities of the land, the Hebrew tribes which settled in Palestine finally came to worship the majestic, yet forgiving, monotheistic God of the prophets and Jesus.

In our contemporary world, while there are many religions, by far the most influential, reckoning by the extent of their followings, are the six with which this book mainly deals—Hinduism, Buddhism, the religions of the Chinese, Islam, Judaism and Christianity. The affinities between some of them are many; the differences are also many—in some instances they are fundamental. But all of them obviously have supplied answers to many of the great questions roused in every human mind by the mystery of life, all have brought strength to bear its sorrows, all have shed light on the path of conduct, all have furnished assurance in the presence of death. They have done this with varying effectiveness, and the present writer, a Christian, would not conceal his belief that Christianity has been the most effective of all. But all have brought answers to men's prayers. If it were not so, they would not be living religions. They all deserve our study and our respectful understanding.

THERE IS a tendency, a product of the egotism in all of us, to mock the unfamiliar in other men's faith and worship. Such words as "heathen," "idolatry," "superstition," are used more often as smear words or in derision than in their legitimate meanings. They are words we hurl at others; seldom do we apply them to ourselves. Yet every man should command respect in the moment when he bows before his god. We may believe that his conception of the Divine lacks valuable, even essential, elements. His forms of worship may appear to us bizarre, sometimes repellent. But in that moment of prayer, every man is at his best; if we are as wise as we like to think ourselves, it is then that we will try to understand him. This book is an approach to such understanding.

One difficulty in discussing these living religions lies in knowing precisely what is being discussed. If one says "Buddhism," the immediate question is: What Buddhism—Hinayana, Mahayana or the Lamaism of Tibet? If one says "Islam," is the reference to the Sunni or the Shiite versions, with their deep divergences? By "Judaism" do we mean the tradition-bound faith of Orthodox Jews, or the modernized beliefs of Reform congregations, or the middle-of-the-road teachings of Conservative rabbis? What are we talking about when we say "Hinduism," the soaring mysticism of the sadhus, the profound speculations of Hindu philosophers, or the animism of the unlettered millions in India's teeming villages? And as for "Christianity," how can one with candor speak as though the Roman, the Eastern Orthodox, the Anglican and the hundreds of Protestant churches were all one and the same thing?

Then, there is the difficulty of distinguishing between a religion's highest teachings and what that religion seems to be in the thought and practice of most of its followers. Another aspect of this same difficulty

ORNAMENTAL GATEWAYS called *torii* form a stately entranceway to Japanese Shinto shrine at Fushimi, Kyoto. The presiding deity, Inari, is said to use foxes as messengers and, in return for gifts, to provide patrons for geishas.

CARVED LANTERNS guide tourists and pilgrims to Kasuga Shrine, begun in 768 A.D. by the Fujiwaras, a clan that dominated Japan between 8th and 11th Centuries. The temple was once center of an anti-Buddhist movement.

is the gap, not to say the discrepancy, which frequently appears between the original teaching of a religion's founder (as nearly as it can be ascertained) and what that faith has become after centuries of being worked over and interpreted by the subtle minds of thousands of translators, commentators and reformers. Sir James G. Frazer, in his classic *Golden Bough*, a study of religious origins, argues that the watering down of a founder's teaching to accommodate it to "the prejudices, the passions and the superstitions of the vulgar," is not only inevitable, but that in the case of Buddhism and Christianity, it was this rejection of the "ethereal stuff" and the introduction of "baser elements" that saved them from an asceticism whose logical end would have been human extinction. Not all these distinctions can be made explicit at every stage of our story. Yet the reader should always bear them in mind.

Scholars sometimes seek to increase understanding of the living religions by trying to put them in various large categories. An interesting example is the suggestion of the Swiss psychologist, C. G. Jung, amplified by Arnold Toynbee, which sees the religions of the East as basically introverted and those of the West as extrovert. This is really stating in another way the familiar claim of a division between Buddhism and Hinduism as life-denying and Islam, Judaism and Christianity as life-affirming faiths. This is to say, one is asked to contrast the underlying belief held by followers of the Eastern faiths that man's salvation rests in his escape from the torments of life with the contention held by the Western faiths that man finds in this life a field for spiritual attainment and preparation for life in the hereafter.

Such generalizations must be received with caution. The exceptions are almost as numerous as the examples used to support the hypothesis. Buddhism, for example, does indeed seek to show man ways by which he may be delivered from the pain which permeates life, or from the ceaseless turning of the Wheel of Rebirth. But that vast portion of Buddhism known as Mahayana ("the Greater Vehicle") finds its focus not in the *Arhat*, the enlightened one who has attained Nirvana, but in the *Bodhisattva* who, at the very moment when he is about to attain Nirvana, turns back out of his devotion to the salvation of his fellows to show them the way of salvation which he has found.

Hinduism has been accused of having a view of the world, even in its great epic *Bhagavad-Gita*, that is indifferent to the passions and sorrows of this life. But contemporary Hinduism at its best shows concern here and now for the unfortunate. And if Confucianism is to be named a religion and not a philosophy, is there one in the West as life-affirming in its concentration on the search for a satisfying way of life in this world? On the other hand, as we are all aware, a taunt frequently leveled against Christianity has been that it is a "pie in the sky" religion.

IN THIS presentation of the great living religions, therefore, there is no attempt to force the faiths into ideological compartments that can be more deceptive than informative. What is here being sought is to show them as their followers know and practice them, with enough reference to the contents of the holy books, the sacred legends and myths and the traditional teachings which lie behind these practices to make them intelligible. Thus we see in Hinduism a religion that in Philip Ashby's words "is awakening from the sleep of the last centuries as it finds itself a central part of a new nation which is dreaming great dreams. Faced by the onslaughts of the West in the spheres of material civilization, culture and religion, it is stirring and searching within itself for resources by which it can resist these pressures. And, most important of all from the perspective of both the East and the West, it is discovering resources which are not only suitable for defense but also adaptable for offense against Western religion." One may question Ashby's prediction that "it may well be that within the foreseeable future it will be Hinduism which will be challenging Christianity not only in India but in the West as well." But Hinduism indeed has new currents of vitality.

This new vitality is in part a product of reform movements which began within Hinduism when Ram Mohan Roy founded the Brahma Samaj in 1830. In part it is a response to the changes in communal life that are being forced on India by the spread of a machine-based industrialization (bear in mind the revolutionary effects on Western religion of the rise of capitalism and the triumph of the Industrial Revolution). And in part it is a reflection of the eagerness of a young nation, vibrantly ambitious for a place of great influence in world affairs, to achieve a religious base for its society—a base rid of the gross aspects of animism and image-worship which other nations have seen in Indian culture, while exalting the loftiest spiritual concepts of that culture.

What is true of Hinduism today is in large measure true of its offspring, Buddhism. Over the centuries Buddhism, developing along the diverging lines of the Hinayana Buddhism of southeast and Mahayana Buddhism of northeast Asia, has become almost two separate religions. The two are compared on pages 41, 54, 64-65 and 67-69. In both, allegiance to Buddha has more tradition than vitality. Under impact of the tremendous forces which today are bearing on the East, however, there are

ANCIENT MASK worn by a Shinto temple dancer represents a black-nosed demon with a scaly monster in his hair. The costume, now regarded as an art treasure, is used in performing the ceremonial *bugaku* in the main hall of the Inner Shrine of Ise at Uji-yamada, Japan. Here, Shinto tradition says, the Sun Goddess Amaterasu Omikami, ancestress of the imperial family, first descended from heaven. For centuries royalty served in the temple priesthood.

many stirrings within Buddhism. In India, the land of its birth, from whence it has all but vanished, some 250,000 Hindu untouchables recently became Buddhists in a mass ceremony at Nagpur. The northern branches, especially in Japan, are trying to make it the spiritual base for an industrialized and scientifically trained society. Demand is felt for inner purification from the gross elements picked up as Buddhism spread across Asia. The 1954–56 conference in Rangoon—a world council of Buddhists to which representatives went from Europe and the West as well as from the East—beneath its announced preoccupation with the canon of Buddhist scriptures was in reality largely an effort to give all the expressions of Buddhism a sense of unity in faith, and to fire them to a new surge of missionary endeavor.

Yet along with these new stirrings in Hinduism and Buddhism there has come a parallel development of disquieting portent. This is the estrangement in a changing Asia between so many of the best-educated youth and their parent faiths. As Professor Ashby observes: "Anyone who has lived in the East even for a limited period has been struck by the number of young men and women who have not only given up the religion of their fathers, but who in this process have declared their independence of the total heritage of their native land. The fact that total separation from their heritage is impossible has only increased the tragedy, for it has created individuals who in their desire to become Western have only succeeded in being neither Western nor Eastern."

Here is a condition for which none of the East's religions has yet discovered a remedy, except to a limited degree in India where some ultranationalists have been wooed back toward Hinduism by its presentation as the religious vehicle of aggressive Indian patriotism. But such an appeal, whatever its present strength, involves abandonment of the universalism which has been Hinduism's boast.

WITH INCREASING frequency comes a proposal that mankind's future spiritual welfare would be insured if the major religions would recognize their essential unity of purpose and drop their differences to merge in a synthesis of the beliefs on which they can agree. Arnold Toynbee is perhaps the most influential Westerner who hopes for some such "syncretism." "The four higher religions" now alive, he writes, are "four variations on a single theme . . . If all the four components of this heavenly music of the spheres could be audible on Earth simultaneously, and with equal clarity, to one pair of human ears, the happy hearer would find himself listening, not to a discord, but to a harmony."

This call for a union of the faiths comes most frequently, however, from the East, especially from India, which has often been called, and thinks of itself, as the most religious nation on earth. Ever since Shri Ramakrishna, India's most influential religious reformer (he died in 1886) proclaimed that all religions are true, that they are simply different paths leading to one goal, the Indian passion for a universal toleration

DANCING DEVILS in the Andes, their evil eyes bulging, cavort below the hills of Cuzco, Peru, as the old Inca capital re-enacts its annual, week-long pageant of thanksgiving for the sun's warmth. These weird ceremonies, which

and synthesis has been a recurring theme. Perhaps it has never been better expressed than by that great Hindu philosopher, S. Radhakrishnan, who taught religion at Oxford and became Vice-President of the Republic of India: "In a restless and disordered world which is unbelieving to an extent which we have all too little realized, where sinister superstitions are setting forth their rival claims to the allegiance of men, we cannot afford to waver in our determination that the whole of Humanity shall remain a united people, where Moslem and Christian, Buddhist and Hindu shall stand together, bound by a common devotion not to something behind but to something ahead, not to a racial past or a geographical unit, but to a great dream of a world society with a universal religion of which the historical faiths are but branches. . . . Believers with different opinions and convictions are necessary to each other to work out the larger synthesis."

It is not surprising that such suggestions evoke a favorable response from men and women of generous spirit who are aware of the threat to any spiritual conception of life which is inherent in the spreading of the modern secularist outlook, and particularly in the missionary enthusiasm with which it is being proclaimed by world Communism. "Believers of the world, unite; it is time to close ranks!" But the glibness of such exhortations betrays a failure to recognize the basic nature of the differences by which the great faiths are sundered.

How can faiths which hold salvation to be a reward of man's own striving merge with faiths which insist that salvation reaches man as the unmerited gift of God? How can there be a flowing together of the Eastern belief that truth is to be found at the end of a human quest with the belief of the three Western faiths that truth has been revealed by a supreme act of revelation in the lives that are facts of history? Among the three faiths of the West, how can there be a synthesis of Christian conviction that the revelation of Divine truth reached its culmination in Jesus, with Moslem conviction that a more complete

CONTEMPLATIVE SIKHS sit by Pool of Immortality before the Golden Temple at Amritsar in West Punjab. Sikh faith contains Islamic elements but its followers hate Moslems, whose rulers martyred their great teacher Arjun.

blend pagan and Christian rituals and figures, commence with the traditional Indian salute to the sun god. At one point the celebrants sacrifice a black llama, mix its gushing blood with sacred corn flour and consume the result.

publication of Charles Darwin's historic *Origin of Species* and the first arresting conclusions of the "higher critics" on the nature and the inspiration behind the Christian and Jewish Scriptures.

Moreover, Islam is caught in the political hurricane sweeping over Africa and Asia. From Morocco to Indonesia, almost every country with a predominantly Islamic population is undergoing drastic political change. Pakistan, for example, proclaims itself an "Islamic Republic." But what is an Islamic republic? This is something new to history; it is up to Pakistan to show the world what the words mean. In the same way, the political changes under way in other Moslem countries are bound to have a challenging effect on Islam's own situation in these countries. Sometimes, and this is psychologically expectable, concern inside Moslem communities over what is happening or may happen to the faith erupts in regrettable measures to impose orthodoxy.

One illustration is the recent brutal persecution of the Baha'is in Iran. It is true, of course, that the Baha'i faith emerged in the last century as a reform movement within Persian Islam, and that it thus—insofar as it occurs within Persia—represents a refusal to submit to compressing the Persian populace into one unified body of Islamic doctrine. But that would not justify or explain the ruthless treatment of the little Persian portion of what has by now become the Baha'i world brotherhood seeking peace among all races, peoples, nations and faiths. The explanation lies in the Persian mullahs' inner sense of insecurity.

Islam will also be affected by the struggle in which the Arab nations are involved with Israel, by the rivalries among the Arab states for leadership, and by the decisions which Arab states make concerning where to sell their oil and where to place their political bets in the cold war between Communism and the West. On the other hand, it need not be pointed out that Judaism is already being even more deeply influenced than Islam by the struggle over Palestine. If the young state of Israel wins permanence as the homeland of the Hebrew faith, the compromises which will have to be worked out between the secularist outlook of its dominant political elements and the dogmatic traditionalism of Orthodoxy will ultimately affect Jewish synagogues and congregations throughout the world. The state of Israel has thus far permitted only one Reform synagogue in the entire country.

IN THE FOREGOING it will be noted little has been said about the religions of China. There are two reasons for this omission. The first grows out of the question as to whether Confucianism and Taoism, usually considered along with Buddhism as the religions of the Chinese, are religions at all. The second springs from our lack of knowledge about them since the Communists took over the mainland.

Certainly neither Confucius nor Lao Tzu dreamed of founding religions, and the rites which have been spoken of as "religious," both Confucian and Taoist, have only slight connection with anything the

revelation came later through Mohammed, and Jewish belief that neither surpassed the revelation of truth in "the law and the prophets"?

The living religions can all respectfully study and appreciate the spiritual values which each has brought to its followers. They can stand unitedly against an alien view which finds nothing in existence but the play of material forces. They can acknowledge their need to view their own shortcomings with penitence and to regard their neighbor-faiths with charity. But the idea that they could sink their differences in unity without consenting to what each would hold a betrayal of religious fundamentals—this is a dream, an illusion. It is an illusion because the man who calls for syncretism always has in view, however unconsciously, syncretism around the essential core of what is already his own faith.

IF HINDUISM and Buddhism are being profoundly affected by the revolutionary excitement of these times in which we live, the same is true to no less degree of the great Western faiths—Christianity, Judaism and Islam. Western readers know how deeply Roman, Anglican and Protestant Christianity have been influenced by the political and cultural changes that have come in the West in the past hundred years, and how Communism has challenged long-somnolent Eastern Orthodoxy.

It is sometimes not sufficiently appreciated in the West, however, that Islam is passing through the same crisis and readjustment. The action of the reborn Turkey in disestablishing Islam and ending the caliphate was the signal gun for a debate on the future of the faith which now goes on throughout Moslem intellectual circles. Where that debate will come out it is too early to foresee, but at least it is clear that if Islam is to continue to hold the active allegiance of the scientifically trained young men and women who are moving into leadership in the awakening Moslem world, there will have to be some sort of accommodation to the Koran's rigidities of doctrine. Here is a source of inner turmoil with which Western Christianity became familiar following the

THOUGHTFUL SYNCRETISTS who honor all faiths hear a Hindu monk by the Ganges lecture on oneness of religion. Pictures include one of Jesus in center. Mohammed is missing in deference to Islamic ban on portraits of him.

BALINESE CREMATION of Hindu corpses concealed in great gilded papier-mâché cattle is example of the way invading religions often adapt themselves to native customs such as animism. In India, destruction of sacred cows even in effigy would be considered sinful but Hindus living in Bali believe the practice confuses evil spirits. Because ceremonies may cost up to $25,000, the poor keep their dead buried until a rich man dies whose family will pay for mass funeral.

great masters taught. Both Confucius and Lao Tzu were philosophers. The former was as mundane and pragmatic a thinker as ever lived, the latter an idealist and mystic whose teachings are so elusive and intangible that it is hard to reduce them to coherence, at least for Western minds.

Insofar as Confucianism is regarded as the right method of observing national rites, such as formerly were performed by the emperor as father of his people at the Altar of Heaven in Peking on the winter solstice, and family rites connected with the veneration of ancestors, it is not much more of a religion than Memorial Day appearances of the President of the United States at the tomb of the Unknown Soldier or the annual meeting of the Society of Mayflower Descendants. As for what has become of Taoism, with its hordes of nearly illiterate, rapacious priests, one can hardly improve on the summary of Edmund Davison Soper: "Taoism today . . . is a mass of puerile superstitions. It is the worst side of Chinese religion. . . . Theoretically, the business of the ignorant priests is to help the people live in accord with Tao, *i.e.*, the Way, but practically it is magic run mad. Soothsaying in every imaginable form . . . is carried on by a priesthood which has become skillful in working on the superstitious fears of the people."

So tangential are both Confucianism and Taoism to the spiritual life of the Chinese people that, in the old days, a single Chinese often would regard himself in his ethics as a Confucianist, in his cultivation of the occult (something rarely indulged in by the educated) a Taoist, and in his religion (as we use the term) a Buddhist. Yet all the time he probably remained a good deal of a skeptical, earthy materialist. But these are not "the old days." Logically, it would seem that the Communists, with their scorn for all religion and their belief in the adequacy of Marxist-approved science to answer all men's questions and needs, would make short shrift of Confucian reverence for the past or the animistic placation of gods, spirits and demons which has been the stock-in-trade of Taoism and much popular Buddhism. Perhaps the Communist rulers who hold China in such a relentless grip are following the Moscow example, leaving the inexorable processes of nature to deal with the eradication of traditional rites and beliefs, confident that future generations of Chinese trained in Communist schools will slough off all religious faith. Communist policy anywhere, everywhere, never boggles at accommodation today if this promises to achieve Communist ends tomorrow.

THERE ARE, of course, other living religions which, because of the limited area of their influence, or the limited number of their adherents, cannot be treated in the body of this book. Their existence, however, should be borne in mind. Three of the most remarkable—the religions of the Jains, Sikhs and Parsees—are found in India.

Jainism, like Buddhism, was a revolt in the 6th Century B.C. against unworthy characteristics of Hinduism. Its million-and-a-half followers form a tight community, the prosperity of whose members contrasts strangely with their extremely ascetic practices which seek liberation from the cycle of transmigration. If Jain teaching were to be summed up in one word, it would be *ahimsa*, nonviolence, a rule which, in their determination to do no harm to any creature, the Jains often carry to what seem to Westerners absurd lengths. It is easy to understand how Gandhi has been claimed for the Jains. More of an ethic than a religion, though it has its temples and its Tirthankaras (guides across the "troubled ocean of life") who are worshiped in them, Jainism is today experiencing a new surge of vigor, presenting itself as the way to universal brotherhood and the end of war.

The Sikhs are among the most picturesque inhabitants of the Indian subcontinent. Every traveler in the port cities of the East has seen them, tall, turbaned, bewhiskered, directing traffic and policing their beats with imperturbable confidence in their ability to subdue anyone or anything needing subduing. They are another tight community, of about 6 million, dwelling mainly in the Punjab, their center in the holy city of Amritsar. They are Aryans, and theirs is one of India's youngest religions, having originated around 1500 A.D. Nanak, the founder, was succeeded by 9 generations of gurus who compiled the Sikh scriptures. But their main significance in modern India is that, as a community limited by birth, they constitute a sort of nation within the nation, a warrior race whose consciousness of mission consists largely in implacable, and at times ferocious, enmity to the Moslems.

Finally there are the Parsees, who form a tiny community, not much over a hundred thousand in size, with half their number concentrated in Bombay. They exert an influence, however, out of proportion to their size, for they are the wealthiest bankers and industrialists of the new India. They are followers of Zoroaster, the Persian religious genius who lived in or before the 6th Century B.C. Zoroaster's opposition to the idea of any deity appearing in human form, his worship of Ahura Mazda, the source of truth (symbolized by the pure light of the sun), and his war against Ahriman, the spirit of evil, has fascinated many Western minds. Parseeism entered India as a refugee faith, its followers fleeing before the Moslem conquerors of their Persian homeland. It has

ANOINTING A COLOSSUS, Jain priests pour paste and powder on 57-foot statue of Gomateswara, Indian king who became a naked ascetic. The ceremony draws hundreds of thousands to small town of Sravana Belgola in India.

HONORING A TEACHER, Sikhs crowd a tent in New Delhi for tribute to the guru Har Krishen, their leader from 1656 to 1664 A.D. Under the canopy a priest reads from scriptures. Portrait is of guru Nanak, religion's founder.

7

closed its ranks to all outsiders; today it shows none of the missionary spirit which is manifesting itself in Hinduism, Buddhism and Jainism. Its ethics are high, its dogmas almost nonexistent. So far as the other peoples of India are concerned, if they know the Parsees at all, they know them as men of probity, as conscious of their social superiority as the Hindu Brahmins. Parsees follow the custom of disposing of their dead by exposing the corpses in "Towers of Silence" where their bones are swiftly picked clean by the hovering vultures.

Something should be said of Shinto, although—as with the religions of China—it is extremely difficult to speak with confidence at present either about what Shintoism now is or about the direction in which it is moving. In the period before the war in the Pacific it became customary to distinguish between religious and state Shinto. Religious Shinto, "the Way of the Gods," grew from early Japan's animistic nature rites into the quiet worship in shrines and before ancestral tablets (a Confucian influence). State Shinto, a nationalistic cult, focused on the divinity of the emperor. Most Japanese contended that state Shinto was essentially an expression of patriotism rather than a form of worship. The emperor or high officials would visit the shrine at Ise to report to Amaterasu, the sun goddess who, in terms of official mythology, was the great-great-grandmother of Jimmu Tenno, founder in the 7th Century B.C. of the imperial line. It was held that they were doing no more than discharging a duty of office which any Buddhist, Confucianist or even Christian might perform without disloyalty to his faith.

Meanwhile, religious Shinto had been so overshadowed by the vigorous Buddhism which crossed from China, by way of Korea, in the 6th Century A.D., that the deities worshiped by the two became almost indistinguishable. Shinto gods were Buddhist bodhisattvas—and sometimes the other way round. About the only clear current of Shinto in the combined stream of the two popular religions was worship of the emperor. In the modern era, what has gathered under the general name of Shinto has been—aside from worship of the imperial family—a conglomeration of sects, many of the faith-healing variety, with teachings so eccentric that it is impossible to say just what Shinto is.

As for state Shinto, the ground seemed cut out from under it when on January 1, 1946, after Japan's shattering defeat, the present emperor formally disavowed his divinity. For a time state Shinto, frowned on by the Occupation, all but disappeared. But now that Japan has regained her sovereignty, the fortunes of state Shinto are rising. What place a de-deified imperial house will have in the reborn ceremonials is hard to foresee. But that Japanese nationalism will maintain state Shinto in some form is suggested by the fact that already a post-Occupation Christian prime minister has led a ceremonial visit of his government to report his accession to office at the great shrine of Ise!

There are other living religions, but most of them are the animistic (or in some cases the devil-worshiping) beliefs of such peoples as the Indian tribes of North and South America, the native tribes of Africa, the primitives of Australia, or the island dwellers of the Pacific and Indian oceans. Their worship is in some cases a hopeful evocation of beneficent gods, but more often it is an effort to placate vengeful deities or ward off the bad fortune to be feared from evil spirits and demons. Most of them likewise have rites intended at once to distinguish and to bind together the tribe; it is in their cremation ceremonies that the Balinese become most excited. Religion at this level has much to teach the anthropologist and the psychologist. Too often it is an enslaving rather than a liberating factor in the lives of whole peoples. But its infinite varieties cannot be treated in such a book as this.

NO GREAT new religion has swept into world prominence since Islam some 1,300 years ago. Does this mean that the foregoing list completes the roll call of living religions? Yes, and no.

Through the centuries men have died for the right to believe, but other men equally sincere have died for the right to disbelieve. However we may rate their wisdom, we must credit them with a kind of religious fervor in defense of their faith. For atheism too is a faith, in the sense that it is based on belief rather than scientific proof.

In its narrowest sense the term atheist means one who denies the existence of any and all gods. But it has come to apply to those, including skeptics, materialists and positivists, who do not acknowledge that the world was created by a being or beings of incomprehensibly magnified human intelligence and form, and also an uncounted number of people the world over who would consider that they fit the word's broader implications. In this connection, it is worth recalling the theory of the Catholic philosopher Jacques Maritain that many such folk are merely *pseudo-atheists* "who believe that they do not believe in God but who in actual fact unconsciously believe in Him, because the God whose existence they deny is not God but something else."

In the Western world outright atheism, *i.e.*, atheism in its narrowest sense, has been unfashionable since the 19th Century, having yielded to the agnosticism which Robert Ingersoll summed up thus: "Is there a

God? I do not know. Is man immortal? I do not know. One thing I do know and that is that neither hope nor fear, belief nor denial, can change the fact. It is as it is, and it will be as it must be. We wait and hope." Believers such as the present writer may draw their own conclusions about the significance of that final sentence.

Since pure atheism and agnosticism obviously do nothing toward answering the ultimate riddles of life, some nonbelievers have turned to humanism—a term which has had many varying meanings, but which today, according to Corliss Lamont in *Humanism as a Philosophy*, "is the viewpoint that men have but one life to lead and should make the most of it in terms of creative work and happiness; that human happiness is its own justification and requires no sanction or support from supernatural sources; that in any case the supernatural, usually conceived of in the form of heavenly gods or immortal heavens, does not exist; and that human beings, using their own intelligence and cooperating liberally with one another, can build an enduring citadel of peace and beauty upon this earth."

And finally there has emerged in contemporary history another great power over men's minds and acts—indeed, a faith—which is at once the denial of all religion and the most potent expression of secular religion ever to challenge the other faiths.

When Communism, after it had captured Russia, proclaimed its world mission, an English archbishop identified it as a "Christian heresy." It is more than that. Repudiating the ancient religions as, in Marxist phraseology, "the opium of the people," Communism is a burning faith which is developing with amazing speed the structural outlines and apparatus of a church. It is a faith proclaiming the coming triumph of man over adversity and evil, and man's eventual entrance into earthly paradise. If, as a writer in the New Testament claims, faith is "the substance of things hoped for, the evidence of things not seen," then Communism, with its promise of a classless social order and an equal sharing by all mankind in all the benefits of life, surely is a faith.

As for the apparatus, what familiar ecclesiastical feature does Communism lack? It has its Revealers, Marx and Lenin. It has its infallible scriptures, its orthodoxy and its heresy, its martyrs and its apostates, its hagiography and its holy office, its initiation rites and its consecrated burial grounds; it has its missionaries and its hierarchies. All it does not have today is its divinities. But give the processes of human adulation another century or two to work—and the cynical gentlemen at the party controls as much time to manipulate them—and who can say that Marx and Lenin and perhaps Mao Tse-tung may not find themselves, to their amazement, among the gods? The same has happened to other agnostics.

In assessing Communism's brother pseudo-religions and cults such as nationalism, fascism and national socialism, Arnold Toynbee writes: "Religion is manifestly one of the essential faculties of human nature. No individual human being and no human community is ever without a religion of some kind; and, when people are starved of religion, the desperate spiritual straits to which they are reduced by being deprived of this necessity of life can fire them to extract grains of religious consolation out of the most unpromising ores."

To the degree to which the secular faith of Communism proclaims the eventuality of human triumph in this world, and to the degree to which the theistic faiths thrust man's fulfillment beyond this world and beyond history, the challenge of Communism will be felt through the whole world of religion. Perhaps the very abundance of its promises will prove its undoing, unless within another generation it proves that its promises are within the reach of human performance. Until that day comes, however, the fervor of the Communist devotee will be a rebuke and a competition to every other religion which aspires to world acceptance.

IN THEIR religious aspirations men do not differ much from one another, no matter where they live, or when. They seek assurance of the favor of their gods, protection against the dangers of life, community with their fellows, courage in the hour of conflict, comfort in the hour of grief, guidance in their daily concerns, release from the pangs of conscience and, for most but not all of them, hope for some sort of immortality. The ways by which followers of the different faiths pursue these common ends vary beyond all telling, though within all the great faiths there have been mystics who have risen above the level on which most of us live to a sense of the Divine which has made them much akin.

These are critical days for religion. The enormous changes being wrought by technology in every life on every continent and at every level of social advancement, and the even more enormous changes which we can foresee with our dawning perception of the forces of the atomic age, make it imperative that man be saved from that most demonic and destructive of all idolatries—self-worship. Each great religion portrayed in this book attempts to save man from following the road of self-worship to the City of Destruction. All will accomplish that purpose to the extent that, in the words of the prophet Micah, they inspire man "to do justly, and to love mercy, and to walk humbly with [his] God."

THE SPIRIT
OF
HINDUISM

THE SPIRIT OF HINDUISM

THOUSANDS of years ago, before Moses or Buddha or Christ, sages stood on India's riverbanks and sang songs inspired, the Hindus say, "by the breath of God." Out of these chants and out of the wisdom and spirituality of the sages in the centuries since has grown the religion known today as Hinduism, the faith of more than 300 million human beings in India, and of about 15 million more in neighboring Pakistan, Ceylon and Burma and in such island outposts as Bali and even Trinidad. Its followers believe that Hinduism, the origins of which go back 4,000 years, is not only the oldest of all religions but the fountainhead of all; without question it has influenced Western thought indirectly for centuries. Pythagoras and the Neo-Platonists apparently studied it; Schopenhauer and Emerson were certainly stimulated by it; the Mahatma Gandhi won world-wide reverence for his practice of Hindu nonviolence. Yet for all its age and influence, Hinduism has remained very much of a puzzle to the West.

In theory, Hinduism is the simplest of religions; it boasts no central authority, no hierarchy, no direct, divine revelation, no rigid, narrow moral code. In practice it is so complex that on the street corners of the cities, on the bypaths of the villages all over India, countless gurus—religious teachers—sit for hours each day, surrounded by disciples and profoundly interested bystanders, endlessly dissecting its subtleties. A measure of its seeming contradictions: it has one God, it also has 330 million gods. One observance in honor of these gods is pictured on page 9, where Gita Mehta in Jaipur, India, guards the candles that traditionally frighten away demons during the festival of Dewali, which begins at dusk on the night of the new moon of Karttika (October-November).

The ancient Hindu sages pondered the fact that all things—even the granite of the mountains and the mountains themselves—eventually disappear. They were struck, too, by the eternal recurrence of life—by the caterpillar that became a butterfly and the butterfly egg that became a caterpillar. Individual bits of life, the sages reasoned, must be born again and again, passing from vegetable to animal, from animal to man, from one human body to another, up the scale, down the scale. And behind the impermanent material world, like the face behind the mask, the sages concluded, must be the invisible source of these individual bits of life and of all things—pure and unchanging spirit.

The sages came to one other, inevitable conclusion. Since the physical world is temporal, all our worldly desires are doomed to frustration and this frustration is the cause of all human suffering. Real peace can therefore be found only in the control of desire, by turning the mind to the one enduring, everlasting reality—God.

Thus the sublime objective of Hinduism is to achieve union with God—the eternal spirit which the Hindus usually call Brahman and which is not to be confused with one of Brahman's facets, Brahma the god, or with Brahmin, the priestly caste. This union is achieved not only through ritual but through the common ideals of Hindu ethics: purity, self-control, detachment, truth, nonviolence, charity and the deepest of compassion toward all living creatures.

Hindu theology strives to define Brahman and though Hindus believe that Ultimate Reality can neither be described nor debated, they have made vast efforts to explain the divine and its relationship to the world. Just one epic, the *Mahabharata*, is three times as long as the King James

Bible and contains many passages of profound philosophical poetry. (Selections from the Hindu sacred writings start on page 31.)

The efforts have not produced a monolithic body of dogma. Like India itself, which seems more like a dozen countries than one, Hinduism has so many dozens of sects that it seems more like a congress of religions than a single faith. Some Hindus regard the 330 million gods as separate deities; many philosophic Hindus merely look upon them as the infinite aspects of the one Brahman. Yet beneath the seeming anarchy and chaos lies unity.

The why of this unity is explained by Sarvepalli Radhakrishnan, the philosopher who became vice president of the Republic of India. In his book, *The Hindu View of Life*, he says: "Hinduism requires every man to think steadily on life's mystery until he reaches the highest revelation. While the lesser forms [including idols and images] are tolerated in the interests of those who cannot suddenly transcend them, there is all through an insistence on the larger idea and purer worship. . . . Every man has a right to choose that form of belief and worship which most appeals to him. . . . Hinduism is not a sect but a fellowship of all who accept the law of right and earnestly seek for the truth."

One 19th Century mystic, Ramakrishna, carried the earnest seeking so far that he became successively a follower of various Hindu sects, of Islam and of Christianity. He found, he said, that he was able to realize God in every one of the faiths; therefore he considered all equally valid. This is a tenet widely held in India. Philip Ashby, of Princeton University, writing in *The Christian Century*, reports: "A respected and eminent Indian Christian, high in the councils of world Christianity, recently said to me that he is convinced the Hindu . . . argument that all religions are equally valid may well sweep the world in the next twenty-five years." But there are critics of Hinduism who reply that in trying to stand for everything, it can really stand for nothing.

Hinduism, however, has shown great capacity for absorbing ideas and adapting to conditions. When Buddha challenged it, in the Sixth Century B.C., the Brahmins simply added him to their pantheon and accepted certain Buddhist concepts. Thereafter, Buddhism virtually disappeared from India. Christianity reached India at least 1,600, perhaps even 1,900 years ago, and during three centuries of British, French and Portuguese occupation, conditions favored Christian evangelism, yet Christians constitute only 2% of India's population today. As it had done with Buddhism, Hinduism absorbed much of the Christian message; gurus began to teach the Sermon on the Mount and many of them made a place for Christ as the tenth incarnation of the god Vishnu. Though fanatical Moslems swept into India in the 11th Century, destroying the most beautiful Hindu temples and sculpture, the Hindus were still willing to accept them as another sect. While 71 million Moslems now live in their own state, Pakistan, which was carved out of India in 1947, some 35 million Moslems still remain in India where their prophet Mohammed is on the long list of holy men honored by the Hindus. Yet always the essential message of Hinduism remains: "Thou [Brahman] art woman. Thou art man," the *Upanishads* declare. "Thou art the dark-blue bee and the green [parrot] with red eyes. Thou hast the lightning as thy child. Thou art the seasons and the seas. . . . Thou dost abide with all-pervadingness, Wherefrom all things are born."

SACRED THREAD, signifying that he has now assumed full religious duties, is accepted by Hindu boy from a priest wearing mark of the god Vishnu.

NON-BRAHMIN CASTES mingle in the village and use the same well. Some non-Brahmins have their own farms. Others work on Brahmin farms but do not enter Brahmin homes, which are grouped together on two streets.

A BRAHMIN AT HIS WORSHIP, C. N. Krishnaswami Aiyengar, prays at home before images. He uses beads to count the Hindu names for God.

CASTE Society is divided by merits earned in past lives

As Hindu thought divides life into higher and lower forms, Hindu society divides its people into higher and lower castes. The subtlety of caste divisions and subdivisions makes the social structure of Hindu society as complicated as its theology. The caste system is best revealed in a village like Kayar Colathure in southern India where these pictures were taken. There it can be seen, if not completely, at least clearly.

At the top in Kayar Colathure, enjoying many privileges, are the Brahmins or priestly caste. Below them, in descending order, are the warriors, merchants and laborers. So low that they are "out-caste," not even a part of the caste system, are the "untouchables."

In Sanskrit, the classical language of India, the word for caste is varna, meaning color. In ancient times light-skinned Aryans from the north swept down through the valley of the Indus River (from which the word Hindu comes) and proceeded to impose their authority upon the dark-skinned inhabitants. However, caste also marked a division of labor within the community and in time, for many complex reasons, the traditional four castes subdivided until today there are in India more than 3,000 subcastes. In Kayar Colathure only a few Brahmins are actually priests. Most own farms and one is the village schoolteacher. Non-Brahmins, like the village goldsmith, grocer, milkman and snake charmer, all belong to separate subcastes of the merchants and laborers.

For the religious Hindu, however, caste is not primarily social or economic. It is the functioning of karma and of reincarnation. Hindu and Buddhist ideas on these two spiritual concepts are considered on pages 30, 34-35, 37, 63 and 64. Briefly, human inequalities result from man's own doing, not from the actions of the gods. One is born into this life—into a higher or lower caste, or even into a nonhuman form—as one has lived in a past life; one will be reborn into a future life as one behaves in this one. Though the higher castes have greater privileges, their status imposes greater responsibilities. The Brahmins have heavier religious duties than non-Brahmins and their misdeeds are considered to be far more serious. A Brahmin who is greedy, for example, may theoretically drop as low as a pig in his next reincarnation.

Over the centuries, probably because they have had privileges so long, the orthodox Brahmins have come to believe themselves only one step removed from the gods. Many consider themselves polluted if approached too closely by an untouchable, and most subscribe to a rule that Brahmins eat only with Brahmins and marry only Brahmins. Taboos, however, are not exclusively Brahmin. Members of most castes eat and marry only with their own kind, and the majority of orthodox Hindus, Brahmins or not, eat separately from their wives. The taboos are tolerated partly out of respect for custom and partly because the Hindus regard caste, like society and indeed all of worldly life, as a temporary arrangement. Only spirituality is ultimate and final.

THE UNTOUCHABLES, who live segregated from the main village, worship with a sword and a trident, the symbol of the god Shiva. They do not use the village temples, even though Indian law now permits them to do so.

A CASTE FIGHT starts when a defiant non-Brahmin sacrilegiously waters his oxen where Brahmins bathe at dawn and worship the rising sun. Angry Brahmin at left finally won the battle by jerking the oxen out of the water.

A BRAHMIN LANDLORD, wearing the mark of Vishnu to whose sect he belongs, directs a laborer plowing in one of his paddies. When Krishnaswami Aiyengar wakes up in the morning, he chants in Sanskrit, "Bhooma kshamami" (O Earth, excuse me), a prayer in which he asks the Goddess of Earth to forgive him for walking on her. As all good Brahmins should, he spends several hours each day praying, meditating and studying the scriptures.

ASPECTS OF THE GOD SHIVA, which were carved 19 feet high out of the raw rock in the Elephanta Caves near Bombay, are among the greatest pieces of the world's sculpture. They were created in the 8th Century, A.D. In the center, according to one interpretation, is Shiva as the impersonal Absolute. Emerging on the left is Shiva as male and on the right Shiva as female, the opposing forms in which life is manifested in the universe.

14

TRUTH BEHIND A VEIL

Hindus use myths, symbols and an elaborate theology to explain many sides of oneness

Evolving together, entwined like the vines in the Indian jungle, Hindu philosophy and the roster of Hindu deities are like a museum of religion, presenting almost every stage in the evolution of man's thinking about God. The early gods, as in all primitive religion, personified the various forces of nature: a sun god, a wind god, a god of fire. In the awakening of the moral consciousness the god of the cosmic order began to show signs of an ethical nature. He watched over men's actions with his "eye," the sun, rewarding the good and punishing those who lied or cheated at cards. Still later, as morality advanced into metaphysics, the seers became dissatisfied with the notion of many gods and they resolved all the diversities of nature into one common source. "Reality is One," the Vedas declare. "Sages call it by different names."

By the time this monumental concept had been reached, the Hindus were worshiping a multitude of nature gods, family gods, tribal gods. In the tolerant Hindu religion, the worship was both permitted and encouraged. Today the Hindu supernatural world, like a vast and wonderful fairyland, swarms with gods resembling humans and animals, accompanied by demons, heroes, ghosts and heavenly dancing girls. This proliferation, growing out of the fantastic Indian imagination, extends down to the very forms which the gods and godlings take. Indra has a thousand eyes. Brahma is usually shown with four heads. Some statues of Ganesha have sixteen arms.

Because even upper caste Hindus accept these gods and the stories about them, Hinduism is often looked upon by outsiders as a mass of fables and superstitions. But Hinduism operates on two different levels, one popular and devotional, while the other is philosophical. Behind each god and fable is some abstract idea or allegory. The numerous arms of Ganesha, for example, symbolize the overwhelming power of God, the four heads of Brahma, the tremendous breadth of his intellect.

Though in practice the masses of the Hindus pay homage to many gods or worship just one of them as a personal god, this is fundamentally a matter of no real theological import, since Hindu religious thought is dominated by the concept of monism—the oneness of all things, of gods as well as of all living things. Though the complexity of the philosophy can be staggering to Western minds, Hindus feel the essentials can be clearly stated this way. To them all is Brahman, including our own selves. Only through ignorance and deception do we see life as multiplicity instead of oneness, and our salvation consists in dispelling the illusion of "I" and "thou" and realizing that we and all the world are part of the divine One. When we have achieved God-realization or Self-realization, as the Hindus often call it, we flow back into Brahman, losing our egos and individualities even as rivers lose their names and forms when ultimately they flow into the ocean. For the Westerner who treasures his individuality, monism is not a very comforting philosophy. But to the Hindu, to merge with Brahman means only the giving up of a finite, limited personality for an infinite one. To him, it is pure bliss.

Some knotty questions arise. If God is in the world, then is not the world God? The monists reply that God is *within* the world but is also transcendent or above and infinitely more than the world.

But if part of God is in the world and part outside, then is not God capable of being divided? How can he be one, the skeptic asks.

Hindu cosmology attempts to answer these last questions thus: Brahman, being the Absolute, is one, indivisible, unchangeable, beyond action and inaction, beyond good and evil. But latent within Brahman, as within a seed, is the power of life. When this power is manifested in the creation of a universe, it takes the form of maya, the material world that we perceive with our senses. Maya, emerging from Brahman, is like heat arising from a fire: the heat is not the fire and yet it comes from the fire and cannot

A SHAIVITE, or worshiper of Shiva, wears sect marks and a dot on his head. In meditating he focuses on dot.

exist without it. Since in this physical world we see Brahman only vaguely, as though through a veil, maya often deceives us, but it is not pure illusion. Hindu philosophers, seeking to explain the abstruse concept of maya, have compared it to a dream whose images are perfectly real to the dreamer—though only to him and only for a short time.

Maya is a projection of the Real though it is not the Real. In Hindu cosmology a universe projected from Brahman endures only for a cycle, approximately 4,320,000,000 human years, and then it is destroyed either by fire or water, and maya returns once again into the heart of Brahman.

This process is repeated over and over again, forever. In Hindu mythology Brahman appears in the form of the god Brahma to create each universe, the form of Vishnu to sustain it, and the form of Shiva to be its eventual destroyer. Unlike the Christian God, Brahma creates each universe from eternally existing material, not out of nothing as God does according to the Judaeo-Christian tradition. For the Hindus nothing which really exists is ever destroyed absolutely; things merely change form.

Brahman the Absolute, being one and impersonal, is usually referred to as It or That rather than He or She. Maya, on the other hand, takes many forms. It is differentiated as men, animals, plants and minerals and as opposites: male and female, good and evil, pleasure and pain, hot and cold. The opposites of the world are left behind in moksha, the state of peace and quiet within Brahman. When one has reached moksha, the world dissolves and people in this state are called "the silent ones." They cannot tell about their experiences, for to speak at all is to speak in terms of opposites.

Because of Brahman and maya, a Hindu has a concept of spirituality somewhat different from the Westerner's. To the West spirituality generally includes practical morality. But to the Hindu spirituality means literally to return to the spirit, to divest one's self of the world of both men and matter, to be beyond good as well as evil. When a man has reached this state, he may be physically alive in this world, but spiritually he has returned to Brahman, he has merged himself into the oneness of all things.

Though morality is implicit in the doctrine called karma, it is not the same kind of ethics which applies equally to all men, as in the West. It is rather the duty imposed by one's caste (called dharma), each caste having different duties. Even though both this duty and Western ethics serve the same purpose, the harmony of society, the religious Hindu is less concerned with society, which he considers only a temporary arrangement, than he is with his individual progress back to Spirit or Brahman.

The Hindu also has a different concept of reality. The realistic Westerner, from the Hindu point of view, is usually preoccupied with maya, the world of appearances, and in the end his realism will lead him only to the bitterness of disillusionment. In maya, though there is the progress of the individual back to Brahman, there is no final purpose toward which the whole world appears to be moving. There is no "social progress" as Westerners like to think, but only endless repetitions. Unlike Westerners, Hindus do not see time as an arrow or a flowing river, but as a pool of water. At intervals there are waves or ripples in the pool; the pool itself, however, remains unchanged.

With their concept of reality Hindus look for truth more in myths and symbols than in history or science. To the discomfiture of occidental students of man's origins, they have almost ignored their own history and very little of it is known except what Western archaeologists and historians have dug up and pieced together. However, even illiterate Hindus can readily recite voluminous details about their mythological gods and superhuman kings. For Hindu myths are truer than so-called historical facts, about which, they point out, even the historians do not usually agree. For example, they say

SUN WORSHIP is performed by Brahmin looking at the sacred orb through hole in his interlaced fingers.

Westerners make too much fuss about the details of Christ's life. They do not see what difference it makes; Jesus' words are true even if he never lived; Westerners, they feel, are too literal.

Some of their own people, particularly among the lower castes, are also too literal about their religion, the Hindus admit. In worshiping and taking care of images of the gods, these Hindus treat the images as if they were living beings with all of the needs, weaknesses and passions common to humans. The worshipers give food to the images, bathe them, put dresses, jewelry and wreaths of flowers on them, tuck them in bed at night. In at least one temple the goddess is even brought into the god's bedroom at dusk to spend the night with him. In another temple the image catches a cold after he has been bathed and then has to spend several weeks in convalescence.

Though the educated Hindu rejects such practices for himself, he nevertheless looks on them with a kindly tolerance because to him every form of worship, no matter how crude it may be, is a stepping stone to a higher form. "We see little girls with their dolls," said the mystic Ramakrishna. "But how long do they play with them? Only so long as they are not married. . . . Similarly, one needs images and symbols so long as God is not realized in His true form. It is God Himself who has provided these various forms of worship . . . to suit . . . different stages of spiritual growth and knowledge."

In popular worship the Hindus seem to have forgotten Brahma the Creator. Most Hindus, even though they may at the same time worship personal, family and village deities, become devotees of either Vishnu or Shiva who, as preserver and destroyer of all things, have more to do with their daily lives. The Vaishnava and Shaiva cults are really the two mainstreams of modern Hinduism and their different emphases and approaches to God are typical of Hindu attempts to provide adequate answers for different temperamental needs.

In Shaiva temples Shiva is often pictured doing a rapturous dance, which seems a curious posture for the god of destruction unless one remembers that the world of maya is a world of opposites. Since death for devout Hindus is practically synonymous with rebirth, not only is Shiva a destroyer but a creator, and the rhythm he dances to is that of a world perpetually forming, dissolving and reforming. The god's reproductive powers are usually represented even more concretely in Shaiva temples as Nandi the bull and the lingam, or phallic symbol. The British, when they conquered India, found the lingams positively shocking. But as a people the Hindus are not obscene and, of all the sects, the Shaiva is the most dedicated to self-discipline, asceticism and intellectualism. Salvation for most Shaivites is won primarily by knowledge, by overcoming their ignorance until they identify themselves with God.

Vishnu is more a god of love. For a Vaishnavite salvation is usually won by bhakti, a loving devotion to God as preserver. Like Christ, Vishnu took on physical form—became incarnate—to overcome evil. It is in one of the forms of his incarnations, or avatars, of which there have already been nine chief ones, that he is usually worshiped. Of the nine, the two most important are Rama and Krishna. A tenth, Kalki, is scheduled to appear in 425,000 years.

Rama's life is the subject of the classical *Ramayana*, which together with the fantastically long *Mahabharata* is one of the two great Indian epics. In this story Rama, heir to the throne of a kingdom in north India, is unjustly banished to a forest by his father. He wants to go alone but his loyal wife, Sita, in a speech which is memorized by almost every young Hindu bride, insists on following him:

> Car and steed and gilded palace,
> vain are these to woman's life;
> Dearer is her husband's shadow
> to the loved and loving wife.

Subsequently Sita is kidnaped by the demon Ravana, symbol of lust, and taken to Ceylon. Rama raises a large army with the help of the monkey god Hanuman, who becomes a symbol of loyalty. Hanuman's

PRAYING FOR FERTILITY, Hindu women circle a sacred tree, reciting the scriptures. Circumambulation is a popular form of devotion which is also performed around temples.

monkeys build a causeway from India to Ceylon over which the army marches to give battle to Ravana and rescue Sita. It is in gratitude to Hanuman that Hindus today consider monkeys to be virtually sacred, and permit them to live lives of ease, devouring fruits in the temples.

To Hindus, Rama, who nearly always acts with righteousness and nobility, is the ideal man. Sita is the ideal woman. All sects reverence Rama, no name is more commonly given to Hindu children, and all Hindus would like to die with his name on their lips. When the Mahatma Gandhi fell, mortally wounded by a fanatic assassin, he murmured, "*Ai Ram, Ai Ram*" (O Rama, O Rama).

Krishna, however, is even more popular and lovable. He is the subject of countless stories and legends. As a young man Krishna flirts with the Gopi milkmaidens and even has an affair with one of them, Radha. These erotic experiences the Hindus interpret in symbolic terms. Individual souls are drawn to God as the milkmaidens were attracted to Krishna and one should give one's self to God in complete, unquestioning surrender even as Radha did to Krishna.

Educated Hindus are the first to admit that popular Hinduism contains vulgar features intolerable to the 20th Century mind. But such features are only tolerated, never condoned, the Hindus say. This tolerance can, quite correctly, be seen as a weakness within Hinduism; it can also be a source of strength, because within the infinite latitude of its tolerance it provides a place for just about everybody. The Hindus may well be the most religious-minded people on earth. Religion not only determines the Hindu social structure, it is the theme of nearly all Indian literature, art and drama—including more than half of the motion pictures. Religious ritual marks virtually every act of the orthodox Hindu's daily life—be it getting up in the morning, bathing, eating or lovemaking.

"Religion is not like a house or a cloak which can be changed at will," Gandhi has been quoted as saying. "It is more an integral part of one's self than one's body. Religion is the tie that binds one to one's Creator and whilst the body perishes, as it has to, religion persists even after death."

Yet Gandhi's political disciple, Prime Minister Nehru, though born a high-caste Brahmin, has eschewed the practice of Hinduism; the government of India prides itself on its secularism, the Indian constitution prohibits the expenditure of government money for the promotion of any religion whatsoever, and the teaching of religion is forbidden in state-controlled or state-aided schools. The constitution outlaws "untouchability" and makes any discrimination by reason of caste, color or creed a criminal offense. But Hinduism, far from being weakened, is stronger among the ordinary people than it has been for several centuries. Whole communities which had previously been Christian have been reconverted, Hindus report. Many Hindus contend that this is because Hinduism is not only the oldest religion but also the most modern and the one best suited to solve today's problems. Much of the resurgence is undoubtedly part of the general swelling of Indian nationalism, from which it sometimes cannot be distinguished. But there is another factor which must not be overlooked; Hinduism, though it was long scornful of proselytizing and careless of social reform, has turned to both in recent years.

Through such progressive organizations as the Ramakrishna Mission, it is becoming increasingly involved in philanthropy, public health and education; at the same time it is taking pains to spread its message. The Ramakrishna Mission now has centers in most of the world's large cities, including twelve in the United States. To the Westerners whom it attracts, Hinduism's appeal generally lies in its philosophy and, perhaps, its mysticism. To the Indian, Hinduism has something additional to keep him among the faithful or to win him back if he has strayed. For though its goal is the soul's release from the world, Hinduism—with its theatrical festivals, temple ceremonies and marriage feasts, with its drums, cymbals, blazing camphor fires and caparisoned elephants—is a religion rich in life, color and emotion. The world, says the Hindu, is God's joyous creation, his lila, his sport, and it should be enjoyed, provided one remembers that the beginning and the end of all things is pure spirit or Brahman.

A MULTITUDE
SHEDDING SINS

Every 12 years, on auspicious days chosen by astrologers, pilgrims come to the junction of the Ganges and Jumna Rivers to bathe away their sins. At the appointed moment the throng surges forward into the waters. In 1954 a February day was selected as the most favorable in 144 years and four million Hindus (*above*) came to the holy spot. In the onrush about 500 persons were crushed to death. But relatives consoled themselves with the thought that of all times and places to die this was the best.

ORNATE TEMPLE
OF SHIVA

Built about the 13th Century, the luxuriantly decorated towers of a temple dedicated to Shiva rise at the edge of a village on the plains of South India. Worship of images in the Hindu temples is generally individual rather than communal. Priests who live in the temples are generally Brahmins though they may be members of other castes. Many marry and pass their offices on to their sons. They live by offerings left by worshipers and on the income from lands given to the temples by rich Hindus.

THE GODS AND DEMONS

Charged with superhuman energy, the Hindu gods posture, proliferate and dash about the universe in a frenzy of activity. Many gods in the innumerable host are obscure, worshiped only by a few devotees. In the painting at left are the best known and most popular. The trinity, Brahma, Vishnu and Shiva, are shown at the top. Four-headed Brahma the Creator (*center*), who holds sacrificial implements, prayer beads and a manuscript, presides from the mythical Mount Meru, where he lives with his peacock-riding wife, Sarasvati, the goddess of the creative arts. Vishnu the Preserver (*right*), who carries a lotus, conch shell and a mace, also lives on Meru with his wife Lakshmi. He is sometimes seen lying on Ananta, a multiheaded serpent, with the god Brahma issuing from his navel to symbolize the deities' interdependence. Vishnu rides through the heavens on Garuda, a man-bird, but periodically he has incarnated himself on earth as a fish, a tortoise that helped the gods in a struggle with demons, a man-lion (shown here disemboweling a demon), a boar, a child-dwarf who frustrated a king's plot against the gods, and finally as Rama and Krishna. Radha, lover of young Krishna, is an ordinary mortal; Rama's wife, Sita, is an incarnation of Lakshmi. Rama's chief helper is the monkey god Hanuman.

Shiva the Destroyer (*left*), third member of the trinity, lives on Mount Kailas. Sometimes he rides a bull, holding his wife Parvati with one arm. He also dances elegantly on a dwarf's back or sits meditating with the holy Ganges River spouting out of his head. Shiva's wife, who has many forms, is graceful and womanly as Parvati or Uma, but as Durga she is fierce, and as Kali she is bloodthirsty, holding a decapitated head and wearing a garland of skulls. Shiva's sons are the warlike Karttikeya, leader of the gods' armies, and the gentle Ganesha, remover of obstacles, who has a rat for a helper. These gods above the irregular horizontal line are the chief deities of the modern Hindu pantheon.

On a level lower than the trinity are (*left to right*) the twin Ashvins, physicians to the gods; Ushas, the dawn goddess, who drives seven cows symbolizing the seven days of the week; Surya, the sun god, who drives seven horses; Agni, god of fire, who rides a ram; Indra, thousand-eyed god of the firmament; Chandra, the moon, pulled by an antelope; Vayu, the wind god, and the Maruts, who are in charge of storm clouds and whose weapons are thunderbolts.

Other supernatural beings on a still lower level are the Yakshinis (female) and Yakshas (male), the demon followers of Kubera, god of wealth; Ravana, the demon king, who abducted Rama's wife Sita in the epic *Ramayana:* Ravana's followers, the Rakshasas, malevolent imps; Manu, an ancestor of the human race who, like Noah, survived a world flood; Soma, a god who is the intoxicating juice of the sacred soma plant; Varuna, god of the cosmic order, who rides Makara, a monster fish; the serpent Vritra, a chief enemy of the gods; Yama, king of death who is followed by two dogs as he drags souls into heaven and hell; the Kinnaras, heavenly musicians, half human, half birds; the Apsarases, water nymphs who tempt ascetics; the Nagas, or snake gods, and the Vrikshadevatas, or tree goddesses, who kick trees to show that nature has to be stimulated before procreation. The worship of Hindu gods and goddesses takes varying forms, some of which are shown on the following pages.

A BANQUET FOR ANTS, consisting of wet rice flour, is spread out in a complex design before a temple. In South India, Hindu women create these designs in front of their homes on holidays as good luck symbols.

PRIVILEGED MONKEYS, living in a temple dedicated to Hanuman, the monkey god, hover around the priests who feed them peanuts. Monkeys get favors because of Hanuman's aid to Rama, as told in the *Ramayana*.

LOVE OF ALL Even the lowliest creatures are sacred

Seeing God in everything, the Hindus have a reverence for everything, trees and rivers, cows and ants. This reverence is expressed in one form as ahimsa, or nonviolence to animals as well as humans, and as a result most pious Hindus are vegetarians.

The Hindu affection for the cow is something special, probably because throughout their history Indians have depended so heavily on the cow for pulling plows and carts, for milk and for fuel (dried dung is still India's principle domestic fuel). For a Hindu to consume beef is a sacrilege, tantamount to cannibalism. "All that kill . . . cows," the scriptures warn, "rot in hell for as many years as there are hairs on the body of the [slain] cow." Some Hindus bow respectfully to all cows that they pass, and wealthy men endow hostels to take care of old and decrepit cows. "The cow is a poem of pity," said Mahatma Gandhi in a lyrical outburst. "She is mother to millions of Indian mankind."

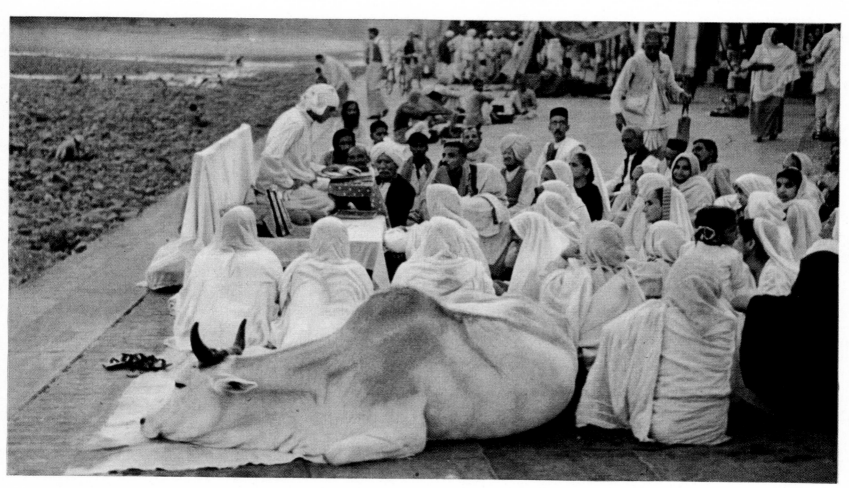

A FESTIVE FACE is painted on an elephant for Dewali holiday because Hindus like animals to take part in their celebrations. At Pongal festival cows are bathed and their heads decorated with turmeric and vermilion.

AN HONORED BEAST sits beside a dry riverbed with a group of Hindus who are listening to a sage expound on the *Ramayana*. Cows wander freely through most Indian cities and people feed them tidbits as a religious act.

BLOODTHIRSTY ASPECT of Shakti is the goddess Kali. Here, impersonated by a man, she bares her tusks and sticks out her long, red tongue. Crown is made of peacock feathers.

SHAKTI Fire and blood
honor a kind but grisly goddess

Besides the major Hindu sects of Vishnu and Shiva, there are many minor ones. The strongest, in numbers and influence, is the cult of Shakti whose followers worship "God in the aspect of mother." The cult is divided into two main groups, the Dakshinamargis, or followers of the right-hand way, and Vamamargis, or left-handed worshipers. The first take the usual path of renunciation of the world, the second the unusual path toward enjoyment of life. The Dakshinamargis do openly what they profess, the Vamamargis keep their rituals secret. Some of Hinduism's greatest saints and sages, Shankara, Ramakrishna and Vivekananda among them, have been devotees of Shakti, the Divine Mother.

Philosophically the Shaktas regard spirit as male, matter as female. Creation takes place when there is a union between the two. In popular worship Shakti is Shiva's wife and as such is given many names—Durga, Kali, Parvati, Uma, Bhavani, Devi and a thousand others.

As creator and giver of life, the Divine Mother is kindly, benevolent, smiling; she holds out her hands to all creatures, asking them to come to her as they would to their earthly mothers. But like her husband Shiva, Shakti destroys as well as creates. In dealing out tragedy and death with an impersonal hand, she can be as cruel as she is tender. To honor and please her the Bengalis hold their biggest and most elaborate festival, the Durga Puja, each autumn.

As Kali (*above*), the goddess of epidemics and earthquakes, of floods and storms, Shakti is even more terrible. Temple images of her have blood dripping from the mouth, and one portrait shows her carrying a pair of scissors to snip the thread of life. Though the macabre, blood-smeared portrayals of Kali are shocking to many Westerners, a respected Hindu teacher, in explaining his devotion to Shakti, said that it would be foolish to think that the terrible aspects of nature were not as much a part of God as those that were pleasant.

The lower classes, in their fear of the dreadful Kali, have sometimes gone to morbid extremes to please her. From the 13th to the 19th Centuries, devotees known as *thugi*, from which the English word thug comes, went around the countryside strangling human victims in the belief that a human sacrifice would satisfy Kali's thirst for blood for a thousand years. Even with approval of the Brahmins, who discouraged blood sacrifices, the British authorities had great difficulty in suppressing the *thugi*, and some Kali votaries (*right*) still kill animals in her name.

PURIFICATION BY FIRE is performed during the Durga Puja. Since evil is conceived by the mind and executed by the hands, this young aristocrat holds two flaming saucers while a priest rests another on her head.

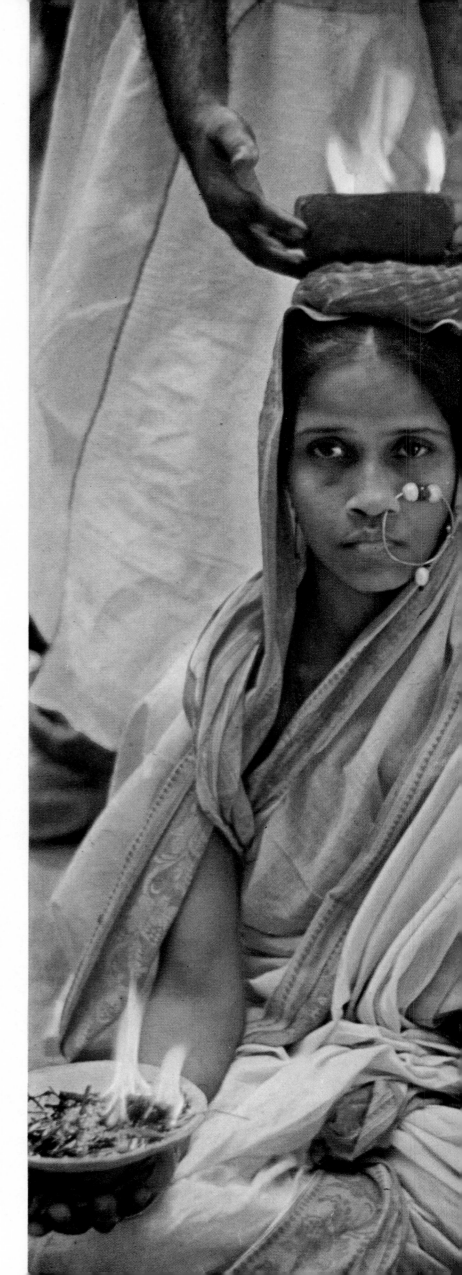

A DANCE FOR DURGA goes on for hours until the dancer, waving two incense pots, drops from exhaustion. At end of the Durga Puja thousands of the goddess' images are taken from homes and dropped into the Ganges.

A GOAT FOR KALI is decapitated at a temple. After the curved sword falls, cutting the neck in one stroke, the priests beat their drums wildly and shout "*Jai ma Kali, Jai ma Kali*" (Glory to Mother Kali, Glory to Mother Kali).

25

PHYSICAL CONTROL is practiced by a yogi as he worships the sun on the bank of the holy Ganges River. Such posturing is only a preliminary to more important disciplines, renunciation of desires and control of the mind.

ISOLATED FROM WORLD, this young sadhu meditates in a cave in the foothills of the Himalayas. He and other sadhus living in caves nearby eat one meal a day, which they get from a kitchen supported by public contributions.

YOGA Ascetic discipline is the path to union with God

Though the rearing of a family and the enjoyment of personal wealth are permitted to a Hindu, the really religious man "pants after God as a miser after gold." His one burning desire is withdrawal from the world and single-minded preoccupation with Brahman. Nowhere else in the world is asceticism considered a national ideal as it is in India. Its lure is so strong that even small children sometimes run away from home to become sadhus, *i.e.*, "those who have renounced."

This ascetic and athletic discipline is called yoga, the yoking of the mind to God. One who practices yoga is a yogi. Yogis deny their appetites and some are said to have such control over their bodies that they can stop their heartbeats for as much as one minute and hold their breath for hours. Most of India's revered heroes have been ascetics, but the ideal is so exalted that even a hero like Gandhi was not considered by the orthodox a real "holy man" because he involved himself with Indian nationalism and therefore worldly affairs. In the highest state, when the meditating yogi has cut off all sense perceptions, he is beyond family, caste, country, religious devotions, good and evil, time and space, and even beyond himself because he is one with God.

BREATH CONTROL is taught to a group of young Hindus in a school in the holy city of Hardwar. Students are also shown how to put themselves in trancelike states by concentrating on the navel or the tip of the nose.

A WANDERING SADHU, only 16, stops in the wilderness for a drink. His only possessions are a water pot and a trident. Hindus are supposed to feed all sadhus but custom is waning because many are shiftless impostors.

A CHORUS OF WIDOWS foregathers in the early morning on a ghat in Benares and chants, "Ram, Ram, Sita-Ram," before one of the thousands of images in the city. In the past some widows lay on the funeral pyres of their husbands and were burned so they could quickly join their loved ones. This custom was outlawed in the last century. Now many widows simply shave off their hair and wait patiently for death, hoping it will come soon.

SHROUDED CORPSES, carried by the mourners through the streets of Benares, are laid on a ghat where they will be burned on the pyre at left. Red shrouds are for wives, white for widows, unmarried girls and males.

DEATH The old and sick come to holy city for liberation

Since moksha, or release from the long series of incarnations, is the goal of every Hindu, the biggest event in his life is really his death. When a Hindu thinks he is about to die, his first thought is to travel if possible to the holy city of Benares where, by bathing in the sacred Ganges, he can become free of his sins. Benares has thus become a vast, bustling city of death. It teems with old and sick people and widows, and the cremation pyres on the ghats, or waterfront stairways, blaze day and night as a steady stream of corpses is brought there to be burned. The atmosphere appears grim only to a Westerner. For Hindus who regard Benares as the end of a tiresome journey, the atmosphere is almost that of a holiday.

By Hindu custom the bodies of ordinary mortals must be burned. Only the holiest of the "holy men," the sannyasis, those who have theoretically been reunited with Brahman, need not be burned. When a sannyasi dies, his body is garlanded by his disciples and tenderly carried down to the ghats where it is weighted with stones and reverently saluted before being dropped into the river. As the body slowly sinks, the disciples blow the conch shell and chant hymns, thereby marking the joyous occasion of another human soul's re-entering into union with God.

ASHES OF THE DEAD, reverently carried from the pyres in cloth sacks, are scattered with flower petals at a holy spot near Allahabad, where the Ganges' brown waters meet and mingle with the blue waters of the Jumna.

PRAYING FOR THE DEAD, two Hindu women kneel on the shores of the Bay of Bengal while water buffalo and cows cool themselves in the pounding surf. They are attempting to expedite their ancestors' rebirth. After his death, the ordinary Hindu goes to a heaven or a hell, depending on whether he has led a good or bad life; there he will await reincarnation. It is believed by the devout that the process can be accelerated if the survivors pray sufficiently.

HINDU BELIEFS

The essential quality or spirit of a religious faith is often best revealed through the writings of its major prophets or philosophers. Some of the greatest texts of Hinduism appear on the following pages; similar selections accompany the other faiths on subsequent pages. Each section is illustrated with drawings by Lynd Ward of the important symbols or attributes of that particular religion.

Devout Hindus, because they regard the Supreme Being, Brahman, as both the creator of all and the totality of all creation, believe that their most ancient scriptures are of divine origin. The oldest Hindu sacred writings are the Vedas; the Sanskrit word veda, ancestor of the English word wit, can be freely translated as "knowledge." The bards who first recited the Vedas ages ago were rishis, inspired seers who were said to have received them direct from Brahman. Although never given official canonical status, some of the Vedas are acknowledged even by skeptical historians to date back four thousand years. To orthodox Hindus they have existed since the very beginning of time.

The hymns of the early Vedas are largely animistic, the gods described in them being personifications of natural phenomena like the sun, the sky and the wind. But even the Hindus who consider there are millions of gods also believe there is one supreme God, namely Brahman, who includes all of these lesser deities. At least twenty-five hundred years ago Hindu priests were teaching that Brahman personifies and constitutes the entire universe, that Brahman came into existence before anything else and is still the omnipresent essence of everything. For this reason Hindus believe that Brahman is not only the subject but also the author of their renowned Hymn of Creation, which is given below in a translation from the original Sanskrit.

THE HYMN OF CREATION

AT that time there was neither nonexistence nor existence; neither the worlds nor the sky, nor anything that is beyond. What covered everything, and where, and for whose enjoyment? Was there water, unfathomable and deep? Death was not there, nor immortality; no knowing of night or day. That One Thing breathed without air, by its own strength; apart from it, nothing existed. Darkness there was, wrapped in yet more darkness; undistinguished, all this was one water; the incipient lay covered by void. That One Thing became creative by the power of its own contemplation. There came upon it, at first, desire which was the prime seed of the mind, and men of vision, searching in their heart with their intellect, found the link to the existent in the nonexistent. . . . There were begetters, there were mighty forces, free action here and energy up yonder. . . . The gods are later than this creative activity; who knows, then, from where this came into being? Where this creation came from, whether one supported it or not, He who was supervising it from the highest heaven, He indeed knows; or He knows not!
—RIG-VEDA X, 129

Sanskrit OM symbolizes
Hinduism's divine principle

To the early Hindu sages, "self" was that universal soul which is in each divinely created creature. Accordingly, the "self" in the next selection—another Hindu account of the creation—is not an individual but represents the god Brahman, who is the source of all existence.

THE UNIVERSAL SELF

IN the beginning this universe was Self alone, in the shape of a person. He, looking round, saw nothing but his Self. He first said, "This is I"; therefore he became I by name. Therefore to this day, if a man is asked, he first says, "This is I," and then says the other name which he may have. And because before all this, he, the Self, burnt down all evils, therefore he was a person. Verily he who knows this, burns down everyone who tries to be before him.

He feared, and therefore any one who is lonely fears. He thought, "As there is nothing but myself, why should I fear?" Thence his fear passed away, for what was there to fear? Truly fear arises from a second one only.

But he felt no delight. Therefore a man who is lonely feels no delight. He wished for a second. He became as big as a man and wife embracing each other. He then made this his Self to fall in two, and thence came husband and wife. "We two are thus, each of us, like one of the two halves of a split pea." Therefore the void which was there is filled by the wife. He embraced her, and men were born.

She thought, "How can he embrace me, after having produced me from himself? I shall hide myself."

She then became a cow, the other became a bull and embraced her, and hence cows were born. The one became a mare, the other a stallion; the one a she-ass, the other a he-ass and embraced her, and hence one-hoofed animals were born. The one became a she-goat, the other a he-goat; the one became a ewe, the other a ram and embraced her, and hence goats and sheep were born. And thus he created everything that exists in pairs, down to the ants. He knew, "I indeed am the creation, for I created all this." Hence he was called the Creation. . . .

One should meditate upon the Self alone as dear. . . . They say: Men think, "Through the knowledge of Brahman we shall become infinite." Well, what did Brahman know by which It became all? This Self was indeed Brahman in the beginning. It knew only its Self as, "I am Brahman." Therefore It became all. . . . One should meditate only upon the world of the Self. He who meditates only upon . . . the Self never has his work exhausted. From this very Self he projects whatever he wants. . . . In the beginning this was Self alone, one only. He desired, "Let there be a wife for me that I may have offspring, and let there be wealth so that I may offer sacrifices." Truly this is the whole desire, and, even if one wishes, one cannot get more than this. Therefore to this day, a man, being single, desires, "Let there be a wife for me that I may have offspring, let there be wealth that I may offer sacrifices."
—BRIHADARANYAKA UPANISHAD
ADHYAYA I, BRAHMANA IV

Another Hindu version of the creation, the famous Hymn: To Purusha, *is also an attempt to express the final, universal divine principle behind the gods, men and the entire universe. Purusha means not only literally "person" or "man," but also Brahman—the highest personal principle, the supreme spirit, "all that hath been." The hymn also uses the ancient religious concept according to which the god is offered up as a sacrificial victim. It presents an epitome of the essential ideas of Hinduism; it is also the classic religious description of the origins of Hindu castes. To this day, it is one of the most popular Hindu hymns, forming an essential part of worship in both homes and temples at the time that images are bathed. The recital of this hymn is also prescribed to the faithful for the expiation of sins.*

HYMN: TO PURUSHA

A thousand heads hath Purusha, a thousand eyes, a thousand feet.
  Covering the world all around, he yet exceeds it on all sides.
This Purusha is all that yet hath been and all that is to be;
  The lord of immortality as well as of creatures who grow by food.
So mighty is his greatness; yea, greater than all creation is Purusha.
  All creatures together are but one-fourth of him, three-fourths of him is eternal and in heaven.
With three-fourths Purusha went up: one-fourth of him again was here.
  Thence he extended on all sides into the animate and inanimate.
From him the Self was born; again Purusha from the Self was born.
  As soon as he was born, he spread eastward and westward o'er the earth.
When gods prepared the sacrifice with Purusha as their offering,
  Its oil was spring, the holy gift was autumn; summer was the wood.
From that great general sacrifice the dripping fat was gathered up.
  He formed the creatures of the air, and animals both wild and tame. . . .
When they divided Purusha, how many portions did they make?
  What do they call his mouth, his arms? What do they call his thighs and feet?
The priests were his mouth, of both his arms were the warriors made.
  His thighs became the merchants, from his feet the workers were produced.
The moon was gendered from his mind, and from his eye the sun had birth. . . .
  Storms and fire from his mouth were born, and wind from his breath,
From his navel came mid-air; the sky was fashioned from his head;
  Earth from his feet, and from his ear the regions. Thus they formed the worlds. . . .
                                                    —RIG-VEDA X, 90

Strikingly similar to many tales in other ancient scriptures, the Hindu legend of Manu describes a semidivine hero who survived a primeval deluge. Manu by tradition is both a Noah and a Moses, as he founded a new human race and was its archetype. Manu is also the Hindu lawgiver; to him are ascribed twelve highly revered books of ordinances. Scholars now believe that these were written by many authors, probably between 500 and 200 B.C.

MANU'S ESCAPE

IN the morning they brought to Manu water for washing, just as now also they are wont to bring water for washing the hands. When he was washing himself, a fish came into his hands. It spoke to him the word, "Rear me, I will save thee!" Manu asked, "Wherefrom wilt thou save me?" The fish replied, "A flood will carry away all these creatures: from that I will save thee!"

Then Manu asked, "How am I to rear thee?"

It said, "As long as we are small, there is great destruction for us: fish devours fish. Thou wilt first keep me in a jar. When I outgrow that, thou wilt dig a pit and keep me in it. When I outgrow that, thou wilt take me down to the sea, for I shall be beyond destruction."

It soon became a large fish. Thereupon it said, "In such and such a year that flood will come. Thou shalt then attend to my advice by preparing a ship; and when the flood has risen, thou shalt enter into the ship, and I will save thee from it." So, after he had reared it in this way, he took it down to the sea. And in the same year which the fish had indicated to him,

*Snakes are semidivine
and even have own god*

he attended to the advice of the fish by preparing a ship; and when the flood had risen, he entered into the ship. The fish then swam up to him, and to its horn he tied the rope of the ship, and by that means he passed swiftly up to yonder northern mountain.

It then said, "I have saved thee. Fasten the ship to a tree, but let not the water cut thee off, whilst thou art on the mountain. As the water subsides, thou mayest gradually descend!" Accordingly he gradually descended, and hence that slope of the northern mountain is called "Manu's descent." The flood then swept away all these creatures from the earth, and Manu alone remained upon the earth.

Being desirous of offspring, he engaged in worshiping and austerities. During this time he also performed a paka-sacrifice: he offered up in the waters clarified butter, sour milk, whey and curds. Thence a woman was produced in a year: becoming quite solid, she rose; clarified butter gathered in her footprint. The gods Mitra and Varuna met her on the way.

The two gods, turning their gaze upon her, said to her, "Who art thou?" "Manu's daughter," she replied. "Say thou art ours," they said. "No," she said, "I am the daughter of him who begat me." They desired to have a share in her. She neither agreed nor disagreed, but passed by them.

She came to Manu. Manu said to her, "Who art thou?" "Thy daughter," she replied. "How, illustrious one, art thou my daughter?" he asked. She replied, "Those offerings of clarified butter, sour milk, whey, and curds, which thou madest in the waters, with them thou hast begotten me. I am the blessing: make use of me at the sacrifice! If thou wilt make use of me at the sacrifice, thou wilt become rich in offspring and cattle. Whatever blessing thou shalt invoke through me, all that shall be granted to thee!" He accordingly made use of her as the benediction in the middle of the sacrifice; for what is intermediate between the fore-offerings and the after-offerings, is the middle of the sacrifice.

With her he went on worshiping and performing austerities, wishing for offspring. Through her he generated this race, which is this race of Manu; and whatever blessing he invoked through her, all that was granted to him. . . . He thereby in a mysterious manner invokes the blessing of life on this sacrifice; for as he sacrificed heretofore, so, while living, he will sacrifice hereafter. Moreover, he thereby in a mysterious manner invokes the blessing of offspring for himself and whosoever has offspring. . . . Future worship of the gods means offspring.

—SATAPATHA-BRAHMANA, KANDA I, ADHYAYA VIII, BRAHMANA I

White bull Nandi, Shiva's vehicle, is guardian of all quadrupeds

THE CODE OF MANU

WOUND not others, do no one injury by thought or deed, utter no word to pain thy fellow creatures.

He who habitually salutes and constantly pays reverence to the aged obtains an increase of four things: length of life, knowledge, fame and strength.

A believer may receive pure knowledge even from an Untouchable, and a lesson in virtue even from a loose woman. . . .

Depend not on another, but lean instead on thyself. . . . True happiness is born of self-reliance. . . .

By falsehood a sacrifice becomes vain; by self-complacency the reward for austerities is lost; by boasting the goodness of an offering is brought to naught. . . .

One should speak truth, and speak what is pleasant; one should not speak unpleasant truth; one should not speak unpleasant falsehood. This is fixed law. . . .

One should cease from eating all flesh. There is no fault in eating flesh, nor in drinking intoxicating liquor, nor in copulation, for that is the occupation of beings, but cessation from them produces great fruit.

The learned become pure by tranquillity; those doing what is not to be done, by gifts; those with concealed sin, by muttering sacred texts; the most learned in the Vedas, by austerity. By earth and water what is to be purified is made pure; a river becomes pure by its velocity; a woman defiled by her mind becomes pure by her courses; a Brahmana, by renunciation of the world. The limbs become pure by water; the mind becomes pure by truth; the self of beings by knowledge and austerity; the intellect becomes pure by knowledge. . . .

No act is to be done according to her own will by a young girl, a young woman, or even by an old woman, though in their own houses. In her childhood a girl should be under the will of her father; in her youth, of her husband; her husband being dead, of her sons; a woman should never enjoy her own will. She must never wish separation of her self from her father, husband, or sons, for by separation from them a woman would make both families contemptible. She must always be cheerful and clever in household business, with the furniture well cleaned, and with not a free hand in expenditure.

The good wife of a husband, be he living or dead, if she desire the world where her husband is, must never do anything disagreeable to him. But she may at will, when he is dead, emaciate her body by living on pure flowers, fruits and roots. She may not, however, when her husband is dead, mention even the name of another man. She must be till death subdued, intent, chaste, following that best law which is the rule of wives of a single husband. But the woman who, from desire of offspring, is unfaithful to her dead husband, meets with blame here and is deprived of her husband's place in the next world. She who, being restrained in mind and speech and body, is not

unfaithful to her husband, attains the abode of her husband, and is called virtuous by the good. A twice-born man must burn a wife of such behavior and of the same caste, if dying before him, by means of the sacred fire and sacrificial vessels, according to rule.

Having used the fires for the last rites to his wife dying before him, he may marry again, and again establish the sacred fires also. . . .

He who addressed the wife of another at a watering place, in a forest or wood, or at the union of rivers, would incur the sin of adultery. Attendance upon her, sporting with her, touching her ornaments or clothes, sitting upon a bed with her, all this is called adultery. If any man touches a woman upon an improper part of her body, or being thus touched by her, submits to it with patience, this is all called adultery, if done by mutual consent. One who is not a Brahmana deserves capital punishment for committing adultery. The wives of all the four castes must always be most carefully guarded. . . .

Wife, son and slave, these three are said to be without property: whatever property they acquire is his to whom they belong.

—THE ORDINANCES OF MANU

The most sacred single syllable in Hinduism is OM. This word is on the lips of devout Hindus from the cradle to the grave. It stands for Brahman, both as personal and impersonal God. The following passage is one of the clearest of the countless references to OM in the Hindu scripture.

OM

THE goal which all the Vedas declare, which all austerities aim at, and which men desire when they lead the life of continence, I will tell you briefly: it is OM. This syllable OM is indeed Brahman. This syllable is the Highest. Whosoever knows this syllable obtains all that he desires. This is the best support; this is the highest support. Whosoever knows this support is adored in the world of Brahma.

—KATHA UPANISHAD I, ii, 15–17

From earliest times, Hindu ritual was essentially primitive, consisting largely of sacrifices, flatteries and spells. The two charms, still used, that follow are both from early Vedas.

A CHARM TO GROW HAIR

BORN from the bosom of wide earth the goddess, godlike plant, art thou: So we, Nitatni! dig thee up to strengthen and fix fast the hair. Make the old firm, make new hair spring, lengthen what has already grown. Thy hair where it is falling off, and with the roots is torn away, I wet and sprinkle with the plant, the remedy for all disease.

—ATHARVA-VEDA VI, 22

A CHARM AGAINST STERILITY

FROM thee we banish and expel the cause of thy sterility. This in another place we lay apart from thee and far removed. As arrow to the quiver, so let a male embryo enter thee. Then from thy side be born a babe, a ten-month child, thy hero son. Bring forth a male, bring forth a son. Another male shall follow him. The mother shalt thou be of sons born and hereafter to be born. With that auspicious genial flow wherewith bulls propagate their kind, do thou obtain thyself a son: be thou a fruitful mother-cow. I give thee power to bear a child: within thee pass the germ of life! Obtain a son, O woman, who shall be a blessing unto thee. Be thou a blessing unto him. May those celestial herbs whose sire was heaven, the earth their mother, and their root the ocean . . . assist thee to obtain a son.

—ATHARVA-VEDA III, 22

One of the strengths of Hinduism has been its repeated and emphatic insistence, from earliest times right up to the present, that Hindus should learn the holy scriptures orally from a guru (teacher). Even in the 20th Century, a Hindu who wishes to steep himself in the faith of his fathers is not supposed to do so by reading and thus has less time than the man of any other modern country to learn other subjects. The sacred texts are so diverse, numerous and complicated that their proper transmission by word of mouth through the teacher-pupil relationship takes a long time. But from earliest times the Hindus have made notable contributions to various fields of learning: for example, the zero, that essential concept in mathematics, is Hindu in origin. And the teacher-pupil dialogues that have developed over the millennia of this oral teaching are among the noblest spiritual discourses known to mankind.

Thus the Upanishads record how Uddalaka taught his son Svetaketu.

SVETAKETU'S EDUCATION

THERE lived once Svetaketu Aruneya, grandson of Aruna. To him his father, Uddalaka, the son of Aruna, said, ". . . In the beginning, my dear, there was that only which is, one only, without a second. . . . It thought, may I be many, may I grow forth. It sent forth fire. That fire thought, may I be many, may I grow forth. It sent forth water. And therefore, whenever anybody anywhere is hot and perspires, water is produced on him from fire alone. Water thought, may I be many, may I grow forth. It sent forth earth [food]. Therefore, when it rains anywhere, most food is produced. From water alone is eatable food produced. Of all living things there are three origins only, that which springs from an egg, that which springs from a living being, and that which springs from a germ. . . .

"The red color of burning fire [*agni*] is the color of fire, the white color of fire is the color of water, the black color of fire the color of earth. . . . Now learn from me, my friend, how those three beings, when they reach man, become each of them tripartite. The earth [food] when eaten becomes threefold; its grossest portion becomes feces, its middle portion flesh, its subtlest portion mind. Water when drunk becomes threefold; its grossest portion becomes water, its middle portion blood, its subtlest portion breath. Fire [*i.e.*, in oil, butter, etc.] when eaten becomes threefold; its grossest portion becomes bone, its middle portion becomes marrow, its subtlest portion speech.

"For truly, my child, mind comes of earth, breath of water, speech of fire."

"Please, Sir, inform me still more," said the son.

"Be it so, my child," the father replied. . . . "As the bees, my son, make honey by collecting the juices of distant trees and reduce the juice into one form. And as these juices have no discrimination, so that they might say, I am the juice of this tree or that, in the same manner, my son, all these creatures, when they have become merged in the True [either in deep sleep or in death], know not that they are merged in the True. Whatever these creatures are here, whether a lion, a wolf, a boar, a worm, a midge, a gnat, a

mosquito, that they become again and again. Now that which is that subtle essence, in it all that exists has its self. It is the True. It is the Self, and thou, O Svetaketu, art it. . . ."

"Please, Sir, inform me still more," said the son.

"Be it so, my child," the father replied. "Fetch me thence a fruit of the banyan tree."

"Here is one, Sir."

"Break it."

"It is broken, Sir."

"What do you see there?"

"These seeds, almost infinitesimal."

"Break one of them."

"It is broken, Sir."

"What do you see there?"

"Not anything, Sir."

The father said, "My son, that subtle essence which you do not perceive there, of that very essence this great banyan tree exists. Believe it, my son. That which is the subtle essence, in it all that exists has its self. It is the True. It is the Self, and thou, O Svetaketu, art it."

"Please, Sir, inform me still more," said the son.

"Be it so, my child," the father replied. "Place this salt in water, and then wait on me in the morning." The son did as he was commanded. The father said to him, "Bring me the salt which you placed in the water last night." The son, having looked for it, found it not, for, of course, it was melted. The father said, "Taste it from the surface of the water. How is it?" The son replied, "It is salt." "Taste it from the . . . bottom. How is it?" The son replied, "It is salt." The father said, "Throw it away and then wait on me." He did so; but salt exists forever. Then his father said, "Here also, in this body, forsooth, you do not perceive the True, my son; but there indeed it is. That which is the subtle essence, in it all that exists has its self. It is the True. It is the Self, and thou, O Svetaketu, art it."

—CHHANDOGYA UPANISHAD,
PRAPATHAKA VI

To Hindus, all the inequalities of life (including those of the caste system) can be explained by the doctrine of karma. Such inequalities are not divine whim; karma teaches that they are a result of man's own doing. Karma is cause-and-effect applied to morals. Karma literally means "action," and every action a man takes—including those in his previous incarnations—has inevitable moral consequences, in this life or the next. In extreme cases it can affect a man through several cycles of life.

KARMA

A MAN is the creator of his own fate, and even in his foetal life he is affected by the dynamics of the works of his prior existence. Whether confined in a mountain fastness or lulling on the bosom of a sea, whether secure in his mother's lap or held high above her head, a man cannot fly from the effects of his own prior deeds. . . . A person's karma is the principal factor in determining his happiness or unhappiness in life. . . . A man reaps that at that age, whether infancy, youth or old age, at which he had sowed it in his previous birth. . . . A man gets in life what he is fated to get, and even a god cannot make it otherwise. Thus neither do I wonder nor mourn my lot, O Sounaka. What is lotted cannot be blotted. A frightened mouse runs to its hole; a scared serpent, to a well; a terrified elephant, to its stake—but where can a man fly from his karma? . . . A man dies not before the appointed time, even if he is riddled with shafts. A wound from the tip of a

Lotus is legendary wellspring of god Brahma the Creator

Kusa sprout proves fatal at the right moment. A man receives that which he is fated to receive, goes only there where fate leads him to, and finds only that much pleasure or pain which he is destined to meet in this life: what is there to mourn for in this life? . . .

The shadow of a cloud, the love of the malicious, an intimacy with another man's wife, youth and opulence are the five equally transitory things in the world. Life is transitory. Transient are the youth and opulence of a man. Wives, children, friends and relations are but passing shadows in the phantasmagoria of life. Only virtue and good deeds endure. Even a centenarian has but a short space of life, the one half of which is covered by the night, the other half being rendered fruitless by disease, grief, imbecility and toil. Night covers the one half of the hundred years allotted to man and is spent in sleep. Infancy and boyhood cover the half of the other moiety, a part of its remaining half being clouded by grief, misery and service. The rest is but changeful and transient like a wave of the ocean. Ah, what is the end of life? What does glory, fame or honor signify? Death with his attendants Day and Night is perpetually traveling the world in the guise of Old Age, and is devouring all created beings, as a serpent gulps down a gust of wind.

—GARUDA PURANA, 113, 115

Hypocritical water animal Makara is emblem of Kama, god of love

For devout Hindus, there is an appropriate "mantra" from holy writ to be recited on almost every conceivable occasion. A mantra is not a mere formula or a magic spell or a prayer; it is an embodiment in sound of a particular deity's power. Hindus believe that when a mantra is repeated a hundred times, or a thousand times, or even more, and the worshiper makes an effort to identify himself with the worshiped, the power of the deity will come to his help. The following are among the mantras that are still most commonly used by followers of Brahman.

ALL NAMES OF GOD
(used in daily prayers)

O GODS! All your names [and forms] are to be revered, saluted, and adored; all of you who have sprung from heaven, and earth, listen here to my invocation.
—RIG-VEDA X, 63, 2

MORNING PRAYER
(used as a preliminary in daily worship)

SUN, Anger, and the deities presiding over Anger, save me from the sin committed through anger. What sin I did at night, by mind, word and hands, by feet, stomach, or the organ of sex, may the deity presiding over the night destroy it. Whatever remains in me as sin, that and my own Self [its doer] here, I am offering as an oblation in the light of the Sun, the source of immortality.

—TAITTIRIYA ARANYAKA X, 35

MARRIAGE
(used in the wedding ceremony)

I TAKE hold of your hand for good fortune, so that with me, the husband, you may attain to old age; the solar deities give you to me for conducting domestic life. . . . I am the words

and you are the melody; I am the melody and you are the words. . . . (*To the Two*): May you not be separated; may you reach your full years, sporting with sons and grandsons and delighting in your house. (*To the Bride*): Flourish thou, without fierce looks and without harming your husband, be good to animals, be of amiable mind and of great splendor; be the mother of heroes, be devoted to gods and the bringer of happiness; be propitious to our men and our women and to our cattle. Bounteous Indra! Endow this bride with excellent sons and fortune; give her ten sons and make her husband the eleventh [*i.e.*, the husband should always be attended with love and care as if he were the youngest child].

—RIG-VEDA X, 85

A NATIONAL PRAYER
(used at many types of gatherings)

AMONG the Brahmans, may the Brahman be born with spiritual luster; in this country, may the king be born a warrior, a capable archer and chariot-fighter; may the cow be born a milch cow; the ox a good draught ox; the horse a fleet one; the damsel the object of the city's admiration; the fighter victorious; and the youth fit for the assembly; may a hero be born to the performer of the sacrifice; whenever we wish may the cloud rain; may our vegetation ripen with fruits; may there be for us acquisition and conserving [of prosperity].
—KRISHNA YAJURVEDA VII, 5, 18, I

DESIRE
(recited to expiate sins committed through lust)

DESIRE did it, Desire does it, I do not do it. Desire is the doer, I am not the doer. Desire is the agent, I am not the agent. O Desire, here, this oblation to you!
—TAITTIRIYA ARANYAKA X, 41–42

CREMATION
(addressed to the dead person)

LET your eye go to the Sun; your life to the wind; by the meritorious acts that you have done, go to heaven, and then [for rebirth] to the earth again; or, resort to the Waters, if you feel at home there; remain in the herbs with the bodies you propose to take.

—RIG-VEDA X, 16, 3

No part of the Hindu scriptures is more spiritual—or more popular—than the Bhagavad-Gita. *It is a section of the* Mahabharata, *an enormous epic of 100,000 verses said to be one of the longest poems in the world. The various sections of the* Mahabharata *narrate episodes of a long feud between members of an ancient royal family.*

The best and the best-known book of this huge epic, the Bhagavad-Gita, *is sometimes called "the Gospel of Hinduism" for its exalted philosophy and wide appeal. It consists of a dialogue between the virtuous warrior Arjuna, sick at heart at the prospect of slaying his own kinsmen during a battle in which they threaten his kingdom, and the god Krishna, who is acting as Arjuna's charioteer in the battle. They stay between the two armies as Krishna resolves Arjuna's varied religious and ethical quandaries.*

THE BHAGAVAD-GITA

("Song of God")

THEN the prince looked on the array, and in both armies, he recognized fathers and grandfathers, teachers, uncles, sons, brothers, grandsons, dear friends, and many other familiar faces. When he saw all those ranks of kinsmen, he was filled with deep compassion, and he spoke despairingly:

> Krishna, Krishna
> Now as I look on
> These my kinsmen
> Arrayed for battle,
> My limbs are weakened,
> My mouth is parching,
> My body trembles. . . .
> What can we hope from
> This killing of kinsmen? . . .
> Rather than this
> Let those evil men
> Come with their weapons
> Against me in battle:
> I shall not struggle,
> I shall not strike them.
> Now let them kill me,
> That will be better.

Having spoken thus, Arjuna threw aside his arrows and his bow in the midst of the battlefield. He sat down on the seat of the chariot, and his heart was overcome with sorrow. . . .

Then to him who thus sorrowed between the two armies, Krishna spoke, smiling, "Your words are wise, Arjuna, but your sorrow is for nothing. The truly wise mourn neither for the living nor for the dead. . . . That Reality which pervades the universe is indestructible. No one has power to change the Changeless. Bodies are said to die, but That which possesses the body is eternal. It cannot be limited, or destroyed. Therefore you must fight. . . .

"He who dwells within all living bodies remains forever indestructible. Therefore, you should never mourn for anyone. . . . Realize that pleasure and pain, gain and loss, victory and defeat, are all one and the same: then go into battle. Do this and you cannot commit any sin. . . . Poise your mind in tranquillity. . . . You have the right to work, but for the work's sake only. You have no right to the fruits of work. Desire for the fruits of work must never be your motive in working. Never give way to laziness, either. Perform every action with your heart fixed on the Supreme Lord. Renounce attachment to the fruits. Be even-tempered in success and failure; for it is this evenness of temper which is meant by yoga. Work done with anxiety about results is far inferior to work done without such anxiety, in the calm of self-surrender. Seek refuge in the knowledge of Brahman. They who work selfishly for results, without self-surrender, are miserable." . . .

And Arjuna said, "But, Krishna, if you consider knowledge of Brahman superior to any sort of action, why are you telling me to do these terrible deeds? Your statements seem to contradict each other. They confuse my mind. Tell me one definite way of reaching the highest good."

So Krishna declared, "Aspirants may find enlightenment by two different paths. For the contemplative is the path of knowledge; for the active is the path of selfless action. Freedom from activity is never achieved by abstaining from action. Nobody can become perfect by merely ceasing to act. In fact, nobody can ever rest from his activity even for a moment. . . ."

Now Arjuna said, "You speak so highly of the renunciation of action, and yet you ask me to follow the yoga of action. Now

Divine footprints recall era when Vishnu measured the sky

tell me definitely: which of these two courses is the better?" And Krishna answered:

> Action rightly renounced brings freedom:
> Action rightly performed brings freedom:
> Both are better
> Than mere shunning of action. . . .
> The wise see knowledge and action as one:
> They see truly.
> Take either path
> And thread it to the end:
> The end is the same. . . .

Then Arjuna said:

"Krishna, you describe this yoga as a life of union with Brahman. But I do not see how this can be permanent. The mind is so very restless." . . .

And Krishna answered:

"Yes, Arjuna, the mind is restless, no doubt, and hard to subdue. But it can be brought under control by constant practice, and by the exercise of dispassion. Certainly, if a man has no control over his ego, he will find this yoga difficult to master. But a self-controlled man can master it, if he struggles hard, and uses the right means. . . .

"At the hour of death, when a man leaves his body, he must depart with his consciousness absorbed in me. Then he will be united with me. Be certain of that. Whatever a man remembers at the last, when he is leaving the body, will be realized by him in the hereafter, because that will be what his mind has most constantly dwelt on during this life. Therefore you must remember me at all times, and do your duty. If your mind and heart are set upon me constantly, you will come to me. Never doubt this.

"Make a habit of practicing meditation, and do not let your mind be distracted. In this way you will come finally to the Lord, who is the light-giver, the highest of the high. . . . I am the Atman that dwells in the heart of every mortal creature: I am the beginning, the lifespan, and the end of all. . . . Whatever in this world is powerful, beautiful or glorious, that you may know to have come forth from a fraction of my power and glory. But what need have you, Arjuna, to know this huge variety? Know only that I exist, and that one atom of myself sustains the universe." . . .

And when he had spoken these words, Shri Krishna, Master of all yogis, revealed to Arjuna his transcendent, divine Form, speaking from innumerable mouths, seeing with a myriad eyes, of many marvelous aspects, adorned with countless divine ornaments, brandishing all kinds of heavenly weapons, wearing celestial garlands and the raiment of paradise, anointed with perfumes of heavenly fragrance, full of revelations, resplendent, boundless, of ubiquitous regard.

Suppose a thousand suns should rise together into the sky: such is the glory of the Shape of Infinite God. . . .

Then was Arjuna, that lord of mighty riches, overcome with wonder. His hair stood erect. He bowed low before God, and clasped his hands, and spoke:

> Ah, my God, I see all gods within your body;
> Each in his degree, the multitude of creatures;
> See Lord Brahma throned upon the lotus;
> See all the sages, and the holy serpents. . . .

Krishna then continued, seeking to make clear the most veiled of mysteries. And finally he said:

"I have taught you that wisdom which is the secret of secrets. Ponder it carefully. Then act as you think best. These are the last words I shall say to you, the deepest of all truths. I speak for your own good. You are the friend I chose and love. . . .

"You must never tell this holy truth to anyone who lacks self-control and devotion, or who despises his teacher and mocks at me. But the man who loves me and teaches my devotees this supreme truth of the *Gita*, will certainly come to me. . . . And if any man meditates upon this sacred discourse of ours, I shall consider that he has worshiped me in spirit. Even if a man simply listens to these words with faith, and does not doubt them, he will be freed from his sins and reach the heaven of the righteous.

"Have you listened carefully, Arjuna, to everything I have told you? Have I dispelled the delusions of your ignorance?"

Whereupon Arjuna answered, "Yea, by your grace, O Lord, my delusions have been dispelled. My mind stands firm. Its doubts are ended. I will do your bidding.

"Om! Peace! Peace! Peace!"

—BHAGAVAD-GITA

The prayer that Hindus use at the end of all public recitals of their epics, including the Bhagavad-Gita, *follows.*

Half-mythical creature, Garuda, is the sun conceived as a bird

BENEDICTION

MAY there be welfare for the people; may rulers follow the righteous path and protect the world; may there always be good to cows and Brahmins; may the entire universe be happy.

—ANONYMOUS

Reincarnation is a basic belief of Hinduism. Every creature that dies goes to a heaven, hell or purgatory—depending on the life it has led—and is later born again. The form into which each creature is born in its present life depends on what it did in past lives, and the form it will receive next time around depends on what it does this time. But anyone can suffer for ages in hell or purgatory before obtaining rebirth, and Hindus also believe that a quicker, better rebirth for their ancestors can be achieved by suitable rites and pilgrimages. The following passage is an instruction on how to ease the woes of ancestors, collateral relatives or even former friends who have died in years past.

THE WORSHIP OF ANCESTORS

SAID the God Brahma: "The city of Gaya is a sacred sanctuary. . . . A man, by simply making a pilgrimage to Gaya, stands absolved from all debts due by him to his forefathers. . . .

"By passing through the hill crevice or the natural tunnel known as the Brahma-Yoni, with his mind absorbed in the contemplation of his forefathers, a man is exempted for good from the trouble of passing through the uterine canal of any woman in the shape of a child. Libations of water, offered by a man to his departed spirits at the shrine of Kakajangha, give them infinite and perpetual satisfaction. . . .

"Having performed a ceremonial ablution . . . the pilgrim should offer obsequious cakes to his departed spirits at the sanctuary of the hill of spirits and invoke them as follows:

"'On the blades of Kusa grass extended in my front, and with this libation of water containing sesamum, I invoke the presence of the souls of those who have been born in my family and subsequently died without any means of succor from the shades of the infernal region. I offer these obsequious cakes for the liberation of those spirits who have once been born in flesh in the family of my father or mother. . . . I offer this obsequious

cake for the liberation of those spirits who have been kept confined within the dark walls of the hells known as the Raurava and the Kalasutra. I offer this obsequious cake for the liberation of those spirits who are at present doomed to the tortures of those divisions of hell which are known as the Kumbhipaka [hell of whirling eddies] and Asipatra Vanam [forest of sword blades.] I offer this obsequious cake for the liberation of spirits who are tortured in other quarters of hell. I offer this obsequious cake for the emancipation of those spirits who have been reincarnated as serpents, birds, or other lower animals, or have been consigned to the voiceless agonies of vegetable life. . . . I offer this obsequious cake for the elevation of those spirits in the astral plane who, for their countless misdeeds in successive rebirths, and through the workings of the propulsions of ignoble passions turned into dynamics of fate, are perpetually getting down in the graduated scale of life, and to whom a working upward to the plane of human existence has become a thing of rarest impossibility. . . .

"'May the gods and Brahma and Isana, in particular, bear testimony to the fact that I have come to Gaya, and effected the liberation of my fathers from the confines of the nether world.'"

—GARUDA PURANA, 83–85

The modern renaissance of Hinduism is highlighted by the teachings of Shri Ramakrishna (1836–1886). Gandhi wrote of him: "His life enables us to see God face to face. . . . Ramakrishna was a living embodiment of godliness."

Ramakrishna made a profound study of other religions, notably Christianity and Islam, but he lived and taught in the precincts of a Hindu temple. Hindus by the million have followed Ramakrishna because he clearly spoke from the depths of profound religious experience. His teachings have not only helped revivify Hinduism in India. The Ramakrishna Mission, founded by his followers in his name, now has more than one hundred teaching centers throughout the world, including twelve missions in the U.S., which are active not only in spiritual affairs but in medicine, education and charity.

RAMAKRISHNA'S SAYINGS

YOU see many stars at night in the sky but find them not when the sun rises; can you say that there are no stars in the heaven of day? So, O man! because you behold not God in the days of your ignorance, say not that there is no god. As one and the same material, water, is called by different names by different peoples, one calling it water, another calling it eau, a third aqua, and another pani, so the one Sat-chit-ananda, the everlasting-intelligent-bliss, is invoked by some as God, by some as Allah, by some as Jehovah, by some as Hari, and by others as Brahman. As one can ascend to the top of a house by means of a ladder or a bamboo or a staircase or a rope, so divers are the ways and means to approach God, and every religion in the world shows one of these ways. Different creeds are but different paths to reach the Almighty. . . .

Men weep rivers of tears because a son is not born to them; others wear away their hearts with sorrow because they cannot get riches. But how many . . . weep and sorrow because they have not seen God? He finds who seeks him; he who with intense longing weeps for God has found him. Verily, verily, I say unto thee, he who longs for him, finds him. Go and verify this in thine own life; try for three consecutive days with genuine earnestness and thou art sure to succeed. . . .

The Avatara or Saviour is the messenger of God. He is like the viceroy of a mighty monarch. As when there is some disturbance in a far-off province, the king sends his viceroy to quell it, so whenever there is a decline of religion in any part of the world, God sends his Avatara there. It is one and the same Avatara that, having plunged into the ocean of life, rises up in one place and is known as Krishna, and diving down again rises in another place and is known as Christ. The Avataras [like Rama, Krishna, Buddha, Christ] stand in relation to the Absolute Brahman as the waves of the ocean are to the ocean. On the tree of absolute existence-knowledge-bliss [Sat-chit-ananda] there hang innumerable Ramas, Krishnas, Buddhas, Christs, etc., out of which one or two come down to this world now and then and produce mighty changes and revolutions. . . .

What is true preaching like? Instead of preaching to others, if one worships God all that time, that is enough preaching . . . . As many have merely heard of snow but not seen it, so many are the religious preachers who have read only in books about the attributes of God . . . . And as many have seen but not tasted it, so many are the religious teachers who have got only a glimpse of divine glory, but have not understood its real essence. He . . . alone can describe the attributes of God who has associated with him in his different aspects, now as a servant of God, then as a friend of God, then as a lover of God, or as being absorbed in him. . . . The sunlight is one and the same wherever it falls, but only bright surfaces like water, mirrors and polished metals can reflect it fully. So is the divine light. It falls equally and impartially on all hearts, but only the pure and clean hearts of the good and holy can fully reflect it.

Every man should follow his own religion. A Christian should follow Christianity, a Mohammedan should follow Mohammedanism, and so on. For the Hindus the ancient path, the path of the Aryan Rishis, is the best. People partition off their lands by means of boundaries, but no one can partition off the all-embracing sky overhead. The indivisible sky surrounds all and it includes all. So common man in ignorance says, "My religion is the only one, my religion is the best." But when his heart is illumined by true knowledge, he knows that above all these wars of sects and sectarians presides the one indivisible, eternal, all-knowing bliss.

As a mother, in nursing her sick children, gives rice and curry to one, and sago arrowroot to another and bread and butter to a third, so the Lord has laid out different paths for different men suitable to their natures.

Dispute not. As you rest firmly on your own faith and opinion, allow others also the equal liberty to stand by their own faiths and opinions. By mere disputation you will never succeed in convincing another of his error. When the grace of God descends on him, each one will understand his own mistakes. So long as the bee is outside the petals of the lily, and has not tasted the sweetness of its honey, it hovers round the flower emitting its buzzing sound; but when it is inside the flower, it noiselessly drinks its nectar. So long as a man quarrels and disputes about doctrines and dogmas, he has not tasted the nectar of true faith; when he has tasted it, he becomes quiet and full of peace. . . .

Although in a grain of paddy the germ is considered the only necessary thing [for germination and growth], while the husk or chaff is considered to be of no importance; still if the husked grain be put into the ground, it will not sprout up and grow into a plant and produce rice. To get a crop one must needs sow the grain with the husk on. But if one wants to get at the kernel itself, he must remove the husk of the grain. So rites and ceremonies are necessary for the growth and the perpetuation of a religion. They are the receptacles that contain the kernel of truth, and consequently every man must perform them before he reaches the central truth. . . .

A young plant should be always protected by a fence from the mischief of goats and cows and little urchins. But when once it becomes a big tree, a flock of goats or a herd of cows may find shelter under its spreading boughs, and fill their stomachs with its leaves. So when you have but little faith within you,

you should protect it from the evil influences of bad company and worldliness. But when once you grow strong in faith, no worldliness or evil inclination will dare approach your holy presence, and many who are wicked will become godly through your holy contact. . . .

The spiritual gain of a person depends upon his sentiments and ideas, proceeds from his heart and not from his visible actions. Two friends, while strolling about, happened to pass by a place where Bhagavat [the word of God] was being preached. One of them said, "Brother, let us go there for a while and hear the good words spoken." The other replied, "No, friend, what is the use of hearing the Bhagavatam? Let us spend the time in yonder public house in amusement and pleasure." The first one did not consent to this. He went to the place where the Bhagavatam was being read and began to hear it. The other went to the public house, but did not find the pleasure that he had anticipated there and was thinking all the while, "Alas, me! Why have I come here? How happy is my friend hearing all the while the sacred life and deeds of Hari [Lord]." Thus he meditated on Hari even though in a public house. The other man who was hearing the Bhagavatam also did not find pleasure in it. Sitting there, he began to blame himself, saying, "Alas! Why did I not accompany my friend to the public house? What a great pleasure he must be enjoying at this time there!" The result was that he who was sitting where the Bhagavatam was

Temple bells are rung as devotional act

preached meditated on the pleasure of the public house and acquired the fruit of the sin of going to the public house because of his bad thoughts, while the man who had gone to the public house acquired the merit of hearing the Bhagavatam because of his good heart.

It is the mind that makes one wise or ignorant, bound or emancipated. One is holy because of his mind, one is wicked because of his mind, one is a sinner because of his mind, and it is the mind that makes one virtuous. So he whose mind is always fixed on God requires no other practices, devotion, or spiritual exercises.

The faith-healers of India order their patients to repeat with full conviction the words, "There is no illness in me, there is no illness at all." The patient repeats it, and thus mentally denying the illness, goes off. So if you think yourself mortally weak, sinful and without goodness, you will really find yourself to be so in time. Know and believe that you are of immense power and the power will come to you at last. . . .

When a man is on the plains, he sees the lowly grass and the mighty pine tree and says, "How big is the tree and how small is the grass!" But when he ascends the mountain and looks from its high peak on the plain below, the mighty pine tree and the lowly grass blend into one indistinguishable mass of green verdure. So in the sight of the worldly there are differences of rank and position—one is a king, another is a cobbler, one a father, another a son, and so on—but when the divine sight is opened, all appear as equal and one, and there remains no distinction of good and bad, high and low. . . .

Man is like a pillowcase. The color of one may be red, of another blue, of a third black, but all contain the same cotton. So it is with man: one is beautiful, another is black, a third holy, a fourth wicked, but the divine One dwells in them all.

If you fill an earthen vessel with water and set it apart upon a shelf, the water in it will dry up in a few days; but if you place the same vessel immersed in water, it will remain filled as long as it is kept there. Even so is the case of your love for the Lord God. Fill and enrich your bosom with the love of God for a time and then employ yourself in other affairs, forgetting him all the while, and then you are sure to find within a short time that your heart has become poor and vacant and devoid of that precious love. But if you keep your heart immersed always in the ocean of divine love, your heart is sure to remain ever full to overflowing with the water of the divine love.

—THE SAYINGS OF SHRI RAMAKRISHNA

THE PATH
OF
BUDDHISM

MAKING A PILGRIMAGE, disciples of Buddha climb the 7,760-ft. peak of Shri Pada in Ceylon to venerate the legendary footprints of Gautama enshrined at the top. As many as 300,000 Buddhists a year converge on the spot. Shri Pada means "sacred footprint," but the mountain is sacred for other reasons to the Hindus, who call it Siva's Peak; to some Eastern Christians, who link it to St. Thomas the Apostle, and to Moslems, to whom it is Adam's Peak.

THE PATH OF BUDDHISM

FROM the island of Ceylon to the islands of Japan, and throughout large sections of the Asian mainland, hundreds of millions of people—perhaps as many as 500 million—believe in a gentle and peaceable religion called Buddhism. Many Western thinkers, who have come to know its yellow-robed monks and have investigated the vast libraries of their quiet monasteries, deem it one of the noblest edifices of thought ever created by the human spirit. Unlike some other great religions, it preaches a system of human conduct based primarily on rationality and relying very little on the supernatural.

In its history, which stretches back 2,500 years, Buddhism has been one of the greatest civilizing forces the Far East has ever known, having stimulated the arts and contributed profound ideas to the great Tang Dynasty culture of China in the Seventh to Tenth Centuries, A.D. and brought civilization to Japan. Today it is the dominant religion of Burma, Thailand, Tibet, Cambodia, Laos and Ceylon, and a vast spiritual influence elsewhere in Asia.

Buddhism has two great schools of doctrine: Hinayana Buddhism, which is followed by southern Asians, and Mahayana Buddhism, which is followed in China, Japan, Korea, Tibet and Mongolia. The Hinayana, literally "the Lesser Vehicle," exalts individual austerity and salvation by personal example; its followers call themselves Theravada Buddhists, Theravada meaning "the teaching of the elders." The Mahayana or "the Greater Vehicle" stands for salvation by faith and good works. Both these doctrines owe their basic teachings to one of history's great religious leaders, a man named Siddhartha Gautama who was born near the town of Kapilavastu in what is now Nepal, near the border of India, in about 563 B.C. Buddha's life became a profound example to millions of his fellow men in the centuries that followed.

Stripped of the poetic oriental legends with which centuries of Asian imagination have surrounded it, the life of Gautama, or "The Buddha," as he was later called, is one of the great and simple biographies of religious literature. The son of an aristocratic Hindu chieftain of the second, or warrior caste, the young Gautama was brought up in princely luxury and splendor. "I had," one of the sutras, the ancient scriptures of the Buddhist faith, quotes him as saying, "three palaces, one for the cold season, one for the hot and one for the season of rains. Through

AWAITING THE DAWN, Shri Pada pilgrims expect to see the rising sun dip up and down for a moment in deference to Gautama. Pilgrimages are generally made by whole families and a favorite time is at the full moon of March.

GOLDEN BUDDHA in Bangkok's great Wat Bovornives monastery watches over a group of yellow-robed monks during a ceremony in which they confess their sins. Over the head of the image another larger Buddha gazes downward in meditation. Both of these images are in the position with right hand pointing earthward that Gautama the Buddha is supposed to have taken during his ordeal, when he sat unmoved before both the onslaughts and temptations.

the four rainy months, in the palace for the rainy season, entertained by female minstrels, I did not come down from the palace. . . ."

Like the other aristocratic boys of his time, the young Gautama excelled in sports, notably archery, and in an archery contest he won the hand of a beautiful wife by whom he had a son. This life of luxury and domestic happiness, however, was not enough for Gautama. Despite his father's orders that he remain in his palaces, he mounted his chariot and rode out into the world where, for the first time, he saw the spectacle of human suffering. After observing an old man, a sick man, a dead man and an ascetic, Gautama returned to his palaces profoundly troubled by the misery that lay around him. Then, one night, in the spirit of Indian renunciation, he left his sleeping wife and child and departed from his luxurious home to take up the life of a wandering mendicant. He shaved his head and put on the distinctive saffron robes of a monk.

Gautama at this time was a young man of 29 and he had made up his mind to solve the riddle of life. For six years he sought a solution. He tried various methods of meditation. He tried mortification of the flesh in the company of five Hindu "holy men" until, through starvation, he became dreadfully emaciated. But this taught him nothing. Soon he began to eat normally again and the "holy men" left him in disgust. Finally he seated himself under a tree—the sacred Bodhi tree—to think and vowed that he would not move until he attained the secret of enlightenment. In a vision the armies of Mara, evil tempter of the world of passion, attacked him with storms, rain, rocks and blazing weapons, and Mara himself offered him the wealth of the world if he would desist from his purpose. But Gautama sat unmoved, calling on the earth beneath him to witness the steadfastness of his aim. The armies of Mara fled.

After 49 days of meditation under the tree, Siddhartha Gautama achieved the enlightenment he was seeking and thereafter became known as the Buddha, or "the Enlightened one." He arose and made his way to the holy city of Benares where, in a park outside the town, he met again the five ascetics who had been his former companions and preached to them his first sermon on the meaning of life. Thereafter, for 45 years

WHEEL OF DOCTRINE, or Wheel of the Law, is symbol of Buddhism. Spokes represent the Eightfold Path.

the Buddha traveled up and down northern India, preaching and making converts to his religion. One day after eating some indigestible food, Buddha became very ill, and, calling his disciples around him, pronounced his last words on the impermanence of all things, exhorting them to work out their salvation with diligence. Having said these words, he passed on to the Nirvana which his religion describes as the ultimate end of all aspiration.

What the Buddha learned during his long meditation under the Bodhi tree and later taught as the basis of his doctrine must be considered against the background of traditional Hindu beliefs that surrounded him, for Gautama was born a Hindu, and Buddhism itself was a protestant revolt against orthodox Hinduism. From Hinduism, Buddha inherited and accepted certain age-old concepts and these were taken for granted in Buddhist thought. One of these was the idea that all living beings go through countless cycles of birth, death and rebirth. Another was the doctrine of karma, the cosmic law of cause and effect by which virtuous conduct is rewarded in future reincarnations and bad conduct leads to retribution. Another was the conception of the world as an abode of ignorance and sorrow from which wise men should seek release. Still another was the idea of renunciation: that the path of wisdom lay in taming the appetites and passions of the flesh.

But while he agreed with the Hindus on these concepts and objectives, Buddha disagreed about the methods by which the objectives were to be achieved. His experiments with violent austerity had convinced him that the spectacular mortifications of the body practiced by many Hindu ascetics of his time were vain and useless. He preferred what he called the Middle Way between asceticism and self-indulgence and believed that the wise man avoided both these extremes in a life of calm detachment. He also disapproved of the Hindu caste distinctions, believing that all men were equal in spiritual potentiality.

The kernel of his teaching lay in two great pronouncements which formed the subject of his first sermon at Benares and which have since been known throughout the Buddhist world as the Four Noble Truths and the Noble Eightfold Path. The Truths deal with the cause and cure

NIRVANA, into which Gautama the Buddha entered at his death in about 483 B.C., is symbolized by this reclining Buddha statue carved from the living rock in the famous Ajanta Caves in central India. The Ajanta Caves, an aggregation of Buddhist shrines and monastery halls dug into a rocky hillside in the mountains of Hyderabad province northeast of Bombay, are filled with magnificent sculptures and frescoes done between 200 B.C. and 600 A.D.

of human suffering, and the Path is the practical technique of action, the detailed prescription, by means of which the cure can be achieved.

The Four Noble Truths, which Buddha enunciated in his opening sermon to his disciples at the deer park Isipatana, are: 1) Suffering is universal; 2) The cause of suffering is craving, or selfish desire; 3) The cure for suffering is the elimination of craving; 4) The way to achieve the elimination of craving is to follow the Middle Way, the technique of which is described in the Noble Eightfold Path.

The Noble Eightfold Path consists of 1) Right knowledge, 2) Right intention, 3) Right speech, 4) Right conduct, 5) Right means of livelihood, 6) Right effort, 7) Right mindfulness, 8) Right concentration.

For Buddhists the practice of the virtues indicated in these short phrases forms a method of self-discipline that will lead to a life of good works and inner peace of mind. For all Buddhists the third and fourth of these phrases have been extended, in more specific form, to comprise a practical code of conduct which is known as the Five Precepts. These are: 1) To abstain from the taking of life, 2) To abstain from the taking of what is not given, 3) To abstain from all illegal sexual pleasures, 4) to abstain from lying, 5) To abstain from consumption of intoxicants because they tend to cloud the mind. Ultimately, for the good Buddhist who has finally achieved enlightenment, lies Nirvana, the spiritual goal.

Nirvana is, strictly speaking, a permanent state toward which Buddhists of all persuasions aspire. It can be defined as impersonal ultimate reality.

In developing these basic ideas, Buddhists formed a unique doctrine about the self. The self is not, as many Hindus believe, a part of an all-pervading entity or Absolute which Hindus call Brahman. It is impermanent and made up of states of mind and matter which are in a continual process of change. If a man frees himself from all worldly craving and physical desires, he comes to a true realization of self and can turn toward the ineffable, or Nirvana.

This realization, however, can come only after long and laborious effort. Through good and self-denying deeds and thoughts one is purified through successive lives. The road is hard, and one is bound for many lives to the cosmic merry-go-round which is called the Wheel of Rebirth—the Buddhists believing in reincarnation, as distinguished from the Hindu belief in transmigration. But in the end, by perseverance, one's insight leads to the sudden discovery of the truth and final release from the Wheel, which is Nirvana.

The principle of the changing self which, for unworldliness and pure idealism, is matched in very few of the world's other great religions, causes the good Buddhist to renounce all attachment to passing phenomena of the world. Even Buddha himself, among Hinayana Buddhists, is not worshiped as a man or a god but as the embodiment of a principle of enlightenment. There were, they believe, many Buddhas before Gautama, and there will be many more after him until the end of time. He was merely one human vehicle for an eternal spiritual concept. This is one of the reasons why the thousands of images of Buddha which stand in temples throughout Asia are not realistic portraits of an individual human being but idealized symbols, and this is what gives them, to Western eyes, a rather exotic and impersonal appearance.

Buddhism generally stands aloof from the affairs of the world. It has no overall authority, no pope, no elaborate ceremonies of conversion. One can become a Buddhist by practicing the principles of the Eightfold Path. It demands no adherence to legalistic requirements, as does Orthodox Judaism, and no act of submission, as does Islam. Buddhism is not so much a set of rules as a technique of action by which the individual can gradually divest himself of his worldly desires and finally achieve the spiritual tranquility of selflessness.

Because the practice of Buddhism in its ideal form demands detachment from the turmoil of daily life, it has become to a great extent a monastic religion. Though the majority of Buddhists are laymen who practice few austerities and who live and worship as simply as the laity of other religions, the ideal Buddhists are the monks who follow its path more strictly and who live either in solitude or, more often, in the great monasteries which are scattered throughout the Buddhist world. In some countries, like Thailand and Burma, virtually all Buddhist males spend at least a few weeks of their lives as monks, regarding this period as a part of their education. Almost all go back to a lay life, though in Tibet, where Buddhism has taken a somewhat adulterated form called Lamaism, monks constitute about one third of the male population and make up a priestly order which rules the state politically.

Nearly everywhere the Buddhist monk performs certain acts for the layman. He officiates at funerals, performs ceremonies in the monastery temples and takes over the religious education of the young. But his main function where the layman is concerned is to serve as an example of the Buddhist way of life and to point the way toward Nirvana. The Buddhist monk lives a life of the utmost simplicity and spends much of it in meditation. He owns almost no personal property and is supposed to get his food only by begging. His belongings include only his robe, an alms bowl to beg his food with, a needle, a string of 108 beads which he counts while meditating on the qualities of the Buddha, a razor to shave his head with, and a filter to strain insects from his drinking water, lest he inflict suffering on living things.

The three essentials for the Buddhist monk are poverty, inoffensiveness and celibacy, though certain Buddhist sects permit their monks to marry. They are permitted meals only before noon, made up of the food they have been given. Their diet is usually vegetarian, though they are expected to eat whatever is offered to them and may consume flesh if they have had no hand in or foreknowledge of the slaughter of the animal; they follow strictly the Buddhist rule against harming any living thing.

In begging, the monks practice self-discipline; they may make no distinction, for example, between the homes of rich and poor. At the same time, they confer a favor, in the form of "merit," on those from whom they accept gifts, and it is the giver who says "thank you." If the donor is a woman, the monk must not speak to her or notice her.

With the exception of a few powerful and violent priests who fought against factions of nobles during the feudal era of medieval Japan, Buddhist monks have usually been among the strictest of pacifists. The international brotherhood of Buddhist monks which has guarded the traditions of the faith for 2,500 years throughout vast areas of Asia is one of the oldest established religious institutions in the world.

SEEKING THEIR FOOD at dawn on a main thoroughfare of Bangkok in Thailand, Buddhist monks carry a large begging bowl, incense sticks and a lotus flower. Donors of the food acquire merit by giving it to the monks.

VIRTUE OF INOFFENSIVENESS, traditionally practiced by every good Buddhist, is represented in the shy behavior of monks in Ceylon who carry palm-leaf umbrellas to hide faces from passers-by as well as from sun. These monks, like those of Burma and Thailand, wear saffron robes, usually go about barefoot and carry begging bowls (here covered by their garments) into which pious Buddhist laymen put offerings of rice, vegetables and other food.

FEAST, to which relatives and friends of Buddhist family are invited, precedes the initiation of youngsters into their role as young monks. Occasion is the most expensive and most solemn event in the social life of a Burmese Buddhist family. A special pavilion is built to house the numerous guests; food, music and presents for the participating monks are provided. Ceremony depicted on these pages cost the host, a Mandalay pediatrician, about $2,000.

RENUNCIATION Children learn message of Buddha

The boys of devout Buddhist families learn at a very early age of their religious ideals of humility and monasticism. The 4-year-old Burmese boys on these pages are re-enacting, in a ceremony in Mandalay, Gautama's renunciation of the world and its pleasures for a life of meditation and poverty. For the boys the ceremony is the most impressive of their lives, exceeding in importance and expense even Burmese marriages and funerals. All participants in it, including the adult visitors,

acquire merit from the ceremony which helps them to approach their next incarnation with increased good karma, their fund of virtue. When the ceremony is over, the boys will spend at least one night in a nearby Buddhist monastery where they will get their first taste of the monkish life that is thought by all good southern Asian Buddhists to be the ideal earthly existence. Most of them at the age of 20 will enter a monastery for about three months. A few of them will permanently become monks.

PRINCELY DRESS, symbolizing the luxurious youth of Gautama, is worn by Burmese boy at the beginning of his initiation ceremony. Boy's father puts the finishing touches to the elegant garments which will shortly be discarded.

SHAVED HEAD, symbolizing Gautama's decision to forgo the pleasures of the world, is next step in the initiation. Princely garments have been removed, and the child is impressed by his elders with the vanity of all earthly frivolity.

IN A MONK'S ROBES, which replace the elegant clothing with which the initiation started, the boy carries a begging bowl. His grandfather, who has sponsored the entire ceremony, adjusts the robe's folds about the youngster's small shoulders. Next step is for a Buddhist monk to say solemnly with the boy the sacred "Three Refuges": "I seek the refuge of the Buddha; I seek the refuge of the Dharma (law); I seek the refuge of the Sangha (order of monks)."

RELICS Gautama's remains

Ever since the death of Gautama the Buddha in about 483 B.C., relics of his physical body, including his teeth and hairs from his head, have been carefully preserved and enshrined. This custom, which might not seem in accord with the comparatively rational tenets of Buddhism, involves homage to Gautama's person, not in itself but as a symbol of the Buddhist way. To house the relics, Buddhists have built dome- or towerlike shrines which are found in cities and in the countryside throughout the Buddhist world. These shrines are known generically as stupas, or pagodas, and monks and laymen alike, especially in south Asia, flock to them to walk around them in the practice known as circumambulation, to make offerings of food and flowers and to meditate on the doctrines taught by Buddha.

Since there are only a limited number of authentic relics, some of the millions of stupas in Asia contain other reminders such as images, sacred writings and prayers. In some places, like the ancient holy city of Pagan

DOME-SHAPED STUPA, housing sacred Buddhist relics on the outskirts of Mandalay, is guarded by a colossal white statue of the mythical lion-like animal called Chinthe past which monks walk on their way to worship.

are enshrined in sacred stupas

in central Burma (*below*), stupas are so numerous that they seem to dominate the entire landscape. Pagan, built in the 11th Century by a devout and benign Buddhist king named Anawrahta, originally consisted of some 1,000 buildings and was one of Buddhism's great outposts. Withering away after its conquest by the great Kublai Khan in the 13th Century, it now contains the still impressive ruins of some 850 stupas, monasteries, shrines and temples.

Buddhist stupas are the center of many of the activities practiced by laymen in order to acquire merit that leads to rebirth in a better life and thus constitutes a step toward final achievement of nirvana. Building stupas is in itself an act of merit, but there are other, simpler ways in which a layman may acquire merit: through offerings (*right*), through pilgrimages, through meditation, through helping feed the monks, through assisting in the upkeep of the stupas (*next page*). Merit may also be acquired by participating in public ceremonies (*below, right*).

OFFERINGS OF FLOWERS are placed by a family in Ceylon on a shelf at the base of a large whitewashed stupa during ceremony commemorating the legendary visit of Gautama to Ceylon. Act will gain merit for entire family.

HOLY CITY of Pagan, on Irrawaddy River in Burma, is a forest of stupas, many ruined but some still kept up and the goal of pilgrimages.

HOLY REMINDERS of Gautama are enshrined in miniature stupa in Ceylon, which is reverently carried by an important layman at a ceremony.

PUTTING ON GOLD LEAF which they have bought, laymen clamber over the outside of the Shwe Dagon Pagoda's central tower. This act of merit can be done only by men. Women may buy gold leaf but must hire men to apply it.

SWEEPING THE PAVEMENT of the Shwe Dagon Pagoda, Burmese government officials perform an act of merit. The pagoda, which covers hilltop in Rangoon, consists of spired shrines surrounding a central tower (*above*).

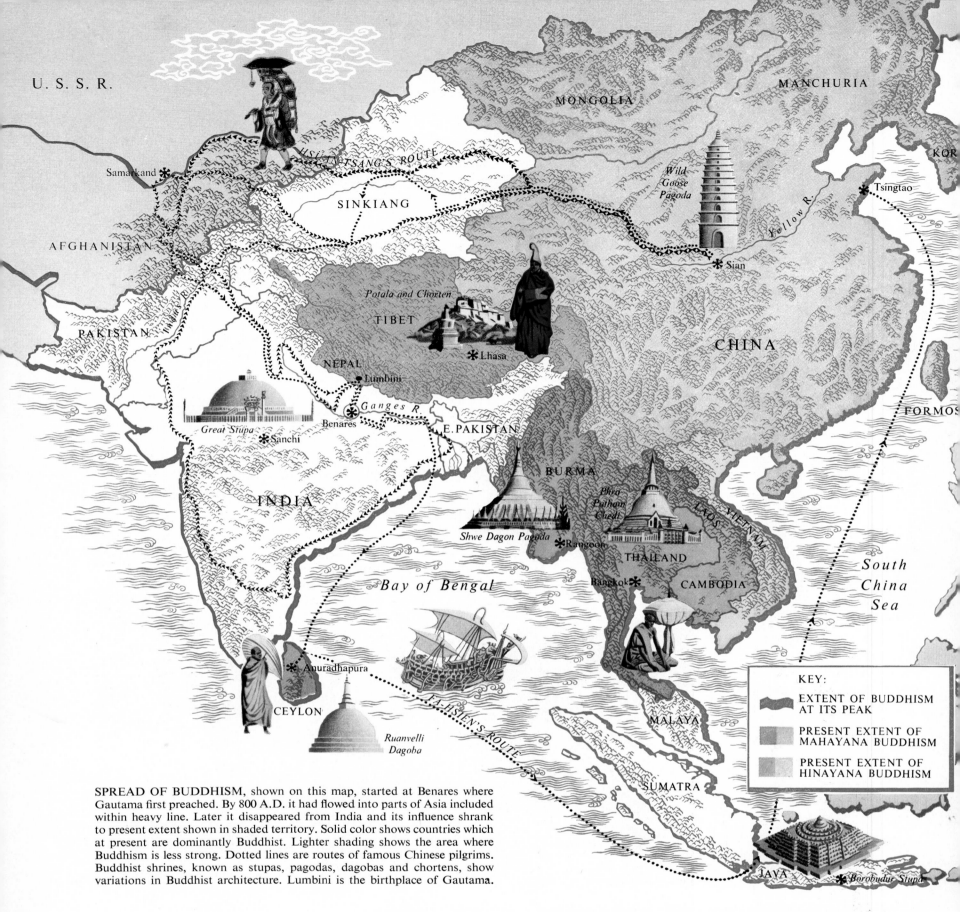

SPREAD OF BUDDHISM, shown on this map, started at Benares where Gautama first preached. By 800 A.D. it had flowed into parts of Asia included within heavy line. Later it disappeared from India and its influence shrank to present extent shown in shaded territory. Solid color shows countries which at present are dominantly Buddhist. Lighter shading shows the area where Buddhism is less strong. Dotted lines are routes of famous Chinese pilgrims. Buddhist shrines, known as stupas, pagodas, dagobas and chortens, show variations in Buddhist architecture. Lumbini is the birthplace of Gautama.

KEY:
EXTENT OF BUDDHISM AT ITS PEAK
PRESENT EXTENT OF MAHAYANA BUDDHISM
PRESENT EXTENT OF HINAYANA BUDDHISM

THE CONVERSION

A doctrine of salvation through faith was added to Buddhism as it swept north,

During the first 300 years after the death of Gautama, Buddhism spread throughout India and to Ceylon. The great Indian emperor, Asoka, who reigned from 269 to 237 B.C., was so impressed by its doctrines that, after a career of bloody conquest, he forswore war and made the peaceful tenets of Buddhism into a state religion. For a while it was dominant over Hinduism. In time men from northern Asia, following the trade routes across the Himalayas, learned about the new religion of enlightenment and brought back reports to the cities of China.

About 65 A.D. a Chinese emperor, according to a legend, dreamed that a golden image of the Buddha appeared from out of the west and dispatched messengers beyond the Himalayas to find out about the mysterious source of this dream. Indian Buddhist monks gradually made their way northward across the mountain passes as missionaries, and Chinese pilgrims traveled in the opposite direction, seeking information and opportunities to worship at the shrines where Gautama had lived and taught. Two of these pilgrims became as spectacular figures in the annals of travel as Marco Polo (see routes on map above). One of them, Fa-Hsien, left China in 399 A.D. and after incredible hardships in central Asia, spent 15 years in India compiling an eyewitness account of that country which is still studied by historians. The other traveling monk, Hsüan-Tsang, left China in 629 A.D., crossed the Gobi desert, Sinkiang and what is now Afghanistan, spent 16 years in India and returned laden with books and manuscripts. Hsüan-Tsang subsequently translated Buddhist literature so extensively that what is

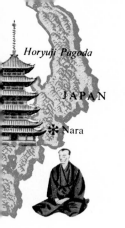

Horyuji Pagoda

JAPAN

* Nara

OF ASIA

bringing consolation to the common man

ascribed to him and his pupils in Chinese amounts to more than a thousand volumes. The court of the great Tang Dynasty, during which he lived, became filled with converts to Buddhism. Some of the greatest artists in Chinese history were devoting themselves to Buddhist subjects, and in the streets of the old Tang capital of Changan (modern Sian), Buddhist scholars could be found discussing their doctrine with Confucianists, Taoists, Zoroastrians, Manichaeans and even the Nestorian Christian missionaries from the Near East. Buddhism itself proved to be one of the hardiest of them all, and its teachings ramified into many different sects, some of which exist down to the present day.

Meanwhile, in the Seventh Century A.D., the great Japanese Prince Shotoku Taishi was converted to Buddhism, which had reached Japan

AMITABHA BUDDHA, redeemer of northern Buddhism, is symbolized in this 42-foot "Daibatsu" who sits in meditation at Kamakura, Japan. Long ear lobes denote aristocratic birth. Mark on forehead is symbol of spiritual insight.

KUAN YIN, the Goddess of Mercy depicted in this Chinese statue, is known in Japan as Kwannon. Originally an Indian male deity, she took on female attributes among the Chinese, who later carried her to Japan. Lotus recalls her Indian past.

TEMPLE ELEPHANT, bearing a shrine containing relics of Buddha's disciple, Moggaliputta, parades through Kandy, Ceylon, on Gautama's 2500th anniversary. Relics had been brought from Colombo in a bright red Plymouth.

through the sea routes from Korea, and established it as a national religion. The Japanese, who had been largely a nation of primitive fishermen and farmers, accepted the new doctrines along with the whole culture of Tang Dynasty China. Shortly afterward, about 750 A.D., an Indian Buddhist monk named Padma-Sambhava crossed the mountains into Tibet, where Buddhism already existed in scattered monasteries, and preached there a different and peculiar form of the doctrine known as Tantrism. Tantrism was a mixture of Mahayana Buddhism and certain magical and mystical doctrines derived from Hinduism. This, together with the age-old sorcery and demonolatry practiced in Tibet, made up Tibetan Lamaism. In its more popular aspects it involved prayers, ritual dances and the exorcism of devils. Out of it, in Tibet, grew a theocratic state dominated by the Dalai and Panchen Lamas, who are believed to be living incarnations of Buddhist holy beings of the past.

Wherever it penetrated, Buddhism brought with it high ethical concepts: tolerance, nonviolence, respect for the individual, love of animals and nature, and belief in the fundamental spiritual equality of all human beings. It also stimulated the production of much of the greatest art Asia has known. The superlative art of Gupta period India, still preserved in the frescoes of the Ajanta Caves northeast of Bombay, was predominantly Buddhist in inspiration. So was the art of the Tang Dynasty, the golden age of Chinese civilization, and much of the tradition of literature and art that Japan learned from the Chinese and finally made its own. In the south, helped by vigorous Indian trade, these concepts of ethics and art spread to Indonesia and to what are now Burma and Thailand. Then, after having helped spread its high culture to eastern Asia, Buddhism died out in India, the country of its origin.

From early times the type of Buddhism practiced in China, Japan and Tibet differed from that of the South Asian Buddhists. The difference was due to some extent to variations in national temperament, but it can be traced back to about 200 years after Gautama's death, when a group of his disciples adopted a new interpretation of his teaching. They

preached a doctrine based on Gautama's personal example of selfless devotion in sharing his discovery after his enlightenment, which became an interpretation with wide appeal to the common man. This doctrine became known as Mahayana, or "the Greater Vehicle," and its members referred to orthodox southern Theravada Buddhism as Hinayana or "the Lesser Vehicle." Mahayana Buddhism spread in the north and its popular aspects differed so greatly from those of Hinayana Buddhism in Ceylon, Thailand and Burma that it has constituted in many ways an entirely different religion.

Where the ideal Buddhist of the Hinayana groups remained the "arhat" or holy man who attained enlightenment for himself alone, the ideal Buddhist of the Mahayana became a saintly figure known as a "bodhisattva," a holy man who vowed that he would not enter Nirvana until the whole human race had achieved salvation with him. For the common man monasticism was obviously too demanding and for him, a majority of the Mahayanists taught, faith and devotion were enough. The austere figure of Gautama became superseded by a glorious redeemer, a god known as the Amitabha Buddha or the "Buddha of Infinite Light," to whom prayers of the faithful were addressed. Unlike Gautama, the Amitabha Buddha was not an actual historical person. It is the Amitabha Buddha, and not Gautama himself, who is represented in many of the great Buddha images of China and in the famous gigantic Buddha of Kamakura, Japan. His dominant virtue is not philosophical detachment or discipline, but compassion. He inhabits a heaven known as the "Great Western Paradise" or the "Pure Land" to which all good Buddhists can hope to go.

One ancient Buddhist text describes this paradise as a place "surrounded by radiant beams and brilliant jewels of untold price. In every direction the air resounds with harmonious tunes, the sky is full of radiance, large heavenly birds of paradise are flying to and fro. . . . [Amitabha] Buddha sits on a lotus seat like a gold mountain in the midst of all glories, surrounded by his saints."

All this was a far cry from the simple philosophical teachings of Gautama, but its rich imagery and message of hope had enormous power over the masses of northern Asia. Though Gautama continued to be reverenced in Mahayana monasteries as the great teacher, prayers to the Amitabha Buddha resounded hundreds of times a day from millions of lips, from Siberia to the Himalayas and eastward to Japan. Some Mahayana sects also elaborated a conception of hell to which the souls of evildoers passed at death. Meanwhile a goddess of compassion known as Kuan Yin (Japanese, Kwannon) developed to guide the faithful to the promised land. Kuan Yin, who is sometimes compared to the Catholic Madonna, eventually came to occupy a place equal to the great Amitabha Buddha in the affections of the Mahayanists, and statues of her were set up in temples throughout China and Japan.

An old, old prophecy says that Buddhism after 2,500 years will either fade away or enjoy a renascence; the fateful time, as Buddhist historians reckon, came with the full moon that shone on the night of May 24, 1956. In actuality, a supreme test for both Mahayana and Hinayana Buddhism had begun in 1949 with the Communist victory in China.

In conquering that ancient land, the Communists took over the area where Mahayana Buddhism had had its greatest growth and claimed its greatest number of adherents. Perhaps a third of China's 600 millions

might then have been counted as Buddhists. Communism, in doctrine the foe of all religion, promptly deprived monasteries of their lands and revenues, drove old monks to work in fields and factories and young ones to the Korean war as "volunteers." Stories filtered out of Red China of nuns compelled to marry, and of others who drowned themselves *en masse* rather than obey the order.

The Communists themselves gave the outside world one of the few clues to the reaction of the mass of Chinese people: a directive from the provincial authorities in Kwangtung in 1951 forbade Communist party workers to use sacred images for target practice or to wreck temples. Such behavior, the directive explained, "antagonized the masses" and "played into the hands of the enemy."

Other tactical retreats by the Communists followed. Soon the government of Mao Tse-tung was restoring and preserving war-damaged Buddhist temples—though as national monuments rather than as religious shrines—and Buddhist scholars, carefully screened for political purity, were contributing philosophical dissertations to international Buddhist journals and attending international Buddhist conventions.

In Tibet, where, at the time of Red China's occupation in 1950, a third of the male population was in Buddhist monasteries and where Buddhist piety was deeper, the Communists adopted the soft approach from the start. In neither China nor Tibet, of course, had Buddhism won the war; it was clear to all but the most naive that what the Communists had learned not to try to take by force, they expected to win by brainwashing, subtle bribery and outward benignity.

Outside China and Tibet, in the countries of Southeast Asia, the contest between Buddhism and Communism had even greater import for the free world. Aside from nationalism, Buddhism appeared to many Westerners to be the sole great positive force around which opposition to Communism could be built in that part of the globe. But Buddhism, abjuring compulsion, is one of the gentlest of religions. Gautama Buddha himself once rebuked some of his disciples who had been angered to violence by a physical attack on the saint, Sariputta: "Shame on him that strikes, greater shame on him who, stricken, strikes back."

Might not such gentleness prove fatal weakness?

One answer lay in the behavior of a deeply religious, smiling Burmese Socialist statesman named U Nu. As Prime Minister of Burma, he was convinced that it was futile to fight the Communists with arms alone, and, in furtherance of that idea, he sponsored a meeting of the World Buddhist Council in 1954. The first of its kind in 500 years, and only the sixth since the death of Buddha, it drew to Rangoon 2,500 monks and thousands of devout Buddhists from all over southeast Asia; and after it had dispersed, a body of scholars labored on for two years, purifying and translating the age-old Pali texts which form the bible of Hinayana doctrine. The meeting was insistently nonpolitical in outward purpose, but even before it had convened, observers realized that U Nu saw in it a chance to build a Buddhist ideological front in Southeast Asia.

Just two years later, with the dawn of the Year of the Lord Buddha—the 2500th anniversary of Gautama's birth and the year of decision by the ancient prophecy—there were signs not only that U Nu might have succeeded, but that Buddhism was on the eve of a renascence. In celebrations all over Southeast Asia, millions meditated and avowed their faith. As one Western observer commented: "In 1956 there will be few

UNDER SACRED BO TREE pilgrims from Ceylon meditate at Bodh-Gaya, India, where Buddha's Enlightenment occurred in the shade of present tree's ancestor. Ceylon's Buddhists wear white only on highly religious occasions.

things that will touch the lives of more people." But realists, Buddhist and non-Buddhist, knew it was no time for easy optimism and there might be scant cause for optimism for many years to come. A salient characteristic of Communism is persistence, and the Communists had not only persistence but—despite some costly mistakes—shrewdness. They had won some converts among Buddhist monks by such devices as discovering basic similarities between Marxism and Buddhism. Did not Buddhism, in its monkish order, endorse a classless society and was not that the very goal of Marxism? Did not Buddhism and Marxism look at some basic tenets of modern science in much the same way?

Most intelligent Asians continued to believe that Buddhism and Communism were basically opposed. To Buddhists man is not primarily an economic creature. His purpose is spiritual. The Buddhist attitude toward both war and revolution is that they are based on greed and violence and hence are wrong. Like all great religions, Buddhism postulates a life of the spirit that transcends the human span. It teaches that this life of the spirit is the only true reality. Finally, it teaches that the good life is to be attained only through an act of free will and reason.

Which would carry the more weight in the struggle against Communism: Buddhist passivity, or Buddhist insistence on liberty of thought? Perhaps the decisive factor would be the words of Buddha: "Believe nothing, O monks," he said, "merely because you have been told it . . . or because it is traditional or because you yourselves have imagined it. Do not believe what your teacher tells you merely out of respect for the teacher. But whatsoever, after due examination and analysis, you find to be conducive to the good, the benefit, the welfare of all beings—that doctrine believe and cling to, and take it as your guide."

MONKHOOD *EN MASSE* is attained by 2,700 young Burmese at end of the World Buddhist Council in Rangoon in 1956. Their heads freshly shaved, their robes donned—at a signal—for the first time, they listen to official speeches.

55

CHILDREN'S FESTIVAL (*opposite*), honoring Gautama as a child, brings youngsters into courtyard of Kyoto's Nishi Hongwanji temple. They wear costumes handed down for generations and carry artificial lotus blossoms.

SACRED BIRTHDAY of Buddha is honored in court—where children on opposite page stand—by pouring tea over image borne by papier-mâché elephant. By Japanese legend it rained tea the day that Gautama was born.

RITUAL Buddha's birthday
is observed by Japanese children

Of the world's many millions of Buddhists, 46 million live in Japan where their ancient religion competes with the national cult of Shinto, with Christianity and the secular scientific ideas found in any great modern industrial nation. Nevertheless, Japanese Buddhists are very devout, and Japanese Buddhism, reinvigorated by numerous revival and reform movements, holds a stronger position in the life of the people than Buddhism does in China and adjacent areas of the mainland. Like all Mahayana Buddhism, that of Japan is divided into numerous sects with variations in doctrine. Most of these sects have a long history in China whence they were imported at an early date by the Japanese. Their doctrines range from those of the vastly popular and pageant-loving Shin sect, one of whose ceremonies is shown on these pages, to the austere, aristocratic, contemplative sects of the Zen Buddhists (*next page*).

Shin shu is the most powerful sect, counting the greatest number of temples, monks and teachers. It believes in the Amitabha Buddha and the madonna-like Kuan Yin. Its priests, unlike those of some other sects, are permitted to marry, and the functions of the Shin clergy are often hereditary. Education and other social service work make up an important part of its duties. Shin shu Buddhists also revere Gautama, whose birthday celebration is shown in these pictures. He is known to Japanese Buddhists as Sakyamuni, or the sage of the Sakya clan, a reference to the rich and aristocratic Indian family into which he was born.

GAUTAMA AS A CHILD enshrined amid pink flowers is reverenced by a young Japanese boy carrying a tasseled rosary. After bowing before the small image, boy will pick up ladle and pour a libation of sweet tea on its head.

ZEN Austere sect seeks out truth by meditation and intuition

Once during the life of Gautama the Buddha a disciple approached him with a gift of a golden flower and asked him to preach the secret of the doctrine. Gautama took the flower, held it aloft and looked at it in silence, indicating that the secret lay not in words, but in the profound contemplation of the flower itself. From this mystical and legendary act descended the famous doctrine of Zen which is regarded by many scholars as the noblest in Buddhism. It was brought to China at the end of the Fifth Century by the Indian mystic missionary Bodhidarma, a man who is reported to have spent nine years of his life continuously meditating with his face to a wall, saying nothing to anyone. From China, Zen spread in the 12th Century to Japan where its austere disciplines appealed greatly to the stern warriors of the restless medieval period. Today it is still practiced by Japan's second largest (nine million monks and laymen) and most rigorous Buddhist sect.

Except for certain details of conduct, Zen bears a much closer resemblance to the austere Buddhism of southern Asia than it does to the other branches of northern Mahayana belief. Followers of Zen believe that enlightenment comes, not from the study of the scriptures or from metaphysical speculation, but from a sudden flash of intuition which occurs during disciplined meditation. Not until after at least ten years of meditation and rigid discipline can a monk hope to experience this revelation. Accordingly they set little store by books, preaching, discussion or theories. Zen monks train their disciples not primarily with words but with acts, whacking their heads, shouting at them, setting them difficult tasks and often propounding to them obscure conundrums designed to nudge their minds into a perception of the truth. This perception, they believe, is not to be achieved by logical explanations or by readings of the scriptures, but rather by an intuitive revelation somewhat similar, on a spiritual plane, to the laugh that spontaneously occurs when one has suddenly seen the point of a joke.

Zen Buddhism is not a theory but a technique of action, and accordingly it envelops with religious significance such simple daily acts as tea drinking, gardening and the enjoyment of nature, teaching that they, in some way, contain the essential mystery of life and that taking part in them becomes a means to understanding. Zen monks lead lives of extreme simplicity, working in the fields, begging for their food, eating a spare diet and meditating. Zen monasteries are severe and simple in appearance, and such ornament as they possess is noted for understatement rather than flamboyance. Much of the simple eloquence of Japanese art and much of the formal frugality characteristic of Japanese life are directly inspired by Zen. Recently Zen has attracted a great deal of attention from Western intellectuals and artists who have been drawn to, and stimulated by, its ideas of simplicity and intuitive inspiration.

ZEN MONK Shinichi Hisamatsu, of Kyoto's Myshinji monastery, is a revered master in the sect, and author of books on its way of life. He teaches at a Zen college in Kyoto whose name, Hanazono, means "Flower Garden."

TEA CEREMONY, being performed by Hisamatsu, is typical of the simple Zen rituals which link religion to everyday life. Here Hisamatsu manipulates ladle in the precise position prescribed for dipping boiling water out of the pot.

IN DEEPEST THOUGHT, Hisamatsu assumes on his mat the posture of meditation in which Zen monks find enlightenment. The Zen sect does not greatly value books, preaching or metaphysical speculation, but Hisamatsu, who has long since experienced the prized flash of intuition, holds several degrees and lectures on literature, religion and philosophy. His life, nevertheless, is as bare of worldly adornments as that of any other monk of the sect.

PARISH PROBLEM is posed for Fujiwara by fumes from the Mitsubishi copper and zinc smelter. One third of Naoshima's soil is now barren and the islanders have become more and more dependent on plant for their livelihood.

PRIEST Temple's keeper assumes worldly cares for islet

In Japanese villages, the priests of Buddhism abjure monastic austerity and perform duties that in many ways resemble those of parish priests in Christendom. Zosho Fujiwara, whose activities are pictured on these pages, maintains a one-priest temple of the Shingon Buddhist sect on Naoshima, a 10-sq.-mi. dot in the Inland Sea. Fujiwara conducts daily religious services, officiates at funerals, offers spiritual healing when the island's four doctors fail, teaches English and social studies in the high school and serves on the island welfare committee. Originally Fujiwara —who is married and the father of a small son—hated becoming a priest and ran away to study law. But eventually he yielded to the wishes of his father, who had served 42 years as the island's priest. Now, one of the island's most respected personages, Fujiwara says he loves his work.

MAKING HIS ROUNDS, Fujiwara is put ashore by an 80-year-old fisherman, Ei Iwakichi, who insists on wheeling priest's bicycle himself. Fujiwara's parishioners include rice farmers and factory workers as well as fishermen.

DEVOTIONAL NAP concludes one-day pilgrimage around Naoshima which the island's older ladies delight in making several times a year. They visit 48 hallowed spots such as graveyards and roadside shrines. At nightfall, they

PREPARING A MEMORIAL for an islander dead some fifty years, Fujiwara brushes ink characters on a pine slab to make a tablet. The little girl holds another. Memorials average twenty a month and augment priest's income.

change kimonos and lie down to sleep on the temple floor in the fashion that the Japanese call *Zakone*—meaning "miscellaneous fish lying in rows." A major attraction of the pilgrimage is the opportunity to swap gossip.

SWEEPING THE TEMPLE after breakfast is one of chores which the priest performs daily, though his wife helps with other duties. Fujiwara gets no salary, but fees, donations and teacher pay add up to more than $100 a month.

61

WAR DANCE, performed by monks dressed in terrifying masks and costumes in honor of nature gods thought to inhabit the peaks of the Himalayas, is one of the numerous primitive rites which have become mixed with Buddhism among the lamas or monks of Tibet and adjacent mountain regions. Tibetan Lamaism spends a good deal of its energies warding off evil, including war. Mask, with tiara of skulls, is designed to scare particularly menacing spirits.

BUDDHIST DOCTRINES

Although it began as a revolt by Siddhartha Gautama, the Buddha, against orthodox Hinduism, Buddhism to this day derives some of its doctrine from Hindu concepts. One such concept is that of the endless cycles of the universe: a huge fire destroys all life at the end of each cosmic cycle, then a flood puts the fire out, and later life resumes. The following account of the earth's restoration after the last cosmic cycle is attributed to Gautama himself and shows some of his debt to the faith of his fathers.

THE GODS ON EARTH

AFTER the floods receded and the earth came back into being, there was upon the face of the earth a film more sweet-smelling than ambrosia. Do you want to know what was the taste of that film? It was like the taste of grape-wine in the mouth. And at this time the gods of the Central Heaven said to one another, "Let us go and see what it looks like ... now that there is earth again." So the young gods of that Heaven came down into the world and saw that over the earth was spread this film. They put their fingers into the earth and sucked them. Some put their fingers into the earth many times and ate a great deal of the film, and these at once lost all their majesty and brightness. Their bodies grew heavy and their substance became flesh and bone. They lost their magic and could no longer fly ... and cried out to one another in dismay, "Now we are in sad case. We have lost our magic. There is nothing for it but to stay here on earth, for we cannot get back to Heaven." So they stayed and fed upon the film that covered the earth, and gazed at one another's beauty.

Pagoda's origin was roof over Buddha's remains

Then those among them that were most passionate became women, and these gods and goddesses fulfilled their desires and pleasure in one another. And this was how it was, brethren, that when the world began, love-making first spread throughout the world; it is an old and constant thing. . . .

And the gods who had returned to Heaven looked down and saw the young gods that had fallen, and they came down and reproached them, saying, "Why are you behaving in this unclean way?" Then the gods on earth thought to themselves, "We must find some way to be together without being seen by others." So they made houses that would cover and hide them. Brethren, that was how houses first began.

Now the people . . . hated and despised such couples and . . . hit them or pelted them with sticks, clods of earth, tiles or stones. . . . That is why today, when a girl is married, she is pelted with flowers or gold or silver . . . and the people, as they pelt her, say, "May peace and happiness, new bride, be yours!" Brethren, in former times ill was meant by these things that were done, but nowadays good is meant.

—EKOTTARA-AGAMA XXXIV, TAKAKUSU II, 737

Reincarnation, the belief that all living beings undergo cycles of birth and death, was one of the Hindu doctrines Buddha accepted—though he modified it to fit other aspects of his teaching. He believed that at death the soul passes into another body, place or condition, usually human but sometimes animal. The following passage from the Buddhist scriptures is also, in some senses, a harbinger of Freud.

REINCARNATION

WHEN a human being dies and is going to be reincarnated as a human being ... when the time of his death is approaching, he sees these signs: he sees a great rocky mountain lowering above him like a shadow. He thinks to himself, "The mountain might fall down on top of me," and he makes a gesture with his hand as though to ward off this mountain. His brothers and kinsmen and neighbors see him do this; but to them it seems that he is simply pushing out his hand into space. Presently the mountain seems to be made of white cloth and he clambers up this cloth. Then it seems to be made of red cloth. Finally, as the time of his death approaches, he sees a bright light, and being unaccustomed to it at the time of his death, he is perplexed and confused. He sees all sorts of things such as are seen in dreams, because his mind is confused. He sees his future father and mother making love, and seeing them, a thought crosses his mind, a perversity arises in him. If he is going to be reborn as a man, he sees himself making love with his mother and being hindered by his father; or if he is going to be reborn as a woman, he sees himself making love with his father and being hindered by his mother. It is at that moment that the Intermediate Existence is destroyed, and life and consciousness arise, and causality begins once more to work. It is like the imprint made by a die; the die is then destroyed but the pattern has been imprinted.

—SADDHARMA-SMRTYUPASTHANA SUTRA XXXIV

Many of the tales of Buddha's eighty years on earth are a blend of history and myth. The following selection, however, was told by Buddha himself and has a ring of personal experience. Buddha's father, trying to hide the woes of the world from his beloved son, built special palaces and gardens to shelter him from all sorrow. Although Buddha had every opportunity for sensuous pleasure, the thought of human misery moved him to spiritual action.

BUDDHA'S CONVERSION

I WAS tenderly cared for, brethren. . . . At my father's home lotus pools were made for me—in one place for the blue lotus flowers, in one place for white lotus flowers, and in one place for red lotus flowers—blossoming for my sake. . . . Day and night a white umbrella was held over me, so that I might not be troubled by cold, heat, dust, chaff or dew. . . . Endowed, brethren, with such wealth, being nurtured with such delicacy, there came this thought: Verily the unenlightened worldling subject to old age, without escape from old age, when he sees another grown old, is oppressed, beset and sickened. I too am subject to old age and cannot escape it. . . .

While I thought thus, brethren, all pride of youth left me.

Verily the unenlightened worldling subject to sickness, without escape from sickness, when he sees another sick, is oppressed, beset and sickened. I too am subject to sickness and cannot escape it. . . .

While I thought thus, brethren, all pride in health left me.

Verily the unenlightened worldling subject to death, without escape from it, when he sees another dead, is oppressed, beset and sickened. I too am subject to death and cannot escape it. . . .

While I thought thus, brethren, all pride in life left me.

—ANGUTTARA-NIKAYA I, 145

After having attained Enlightenment, Buddha was strongly tempted to keep his illumination to himself and remain in the Nirvana he had attained. But after some inner argument, he decided to tell others, hoping that his great discovery could guide all living creatures to happiness and fulfillment. For forty-five years he traveled about India, teaching, preaching and gathering many followers. At eighty he died in the arms of his beloved relative and disciple, Ananda.

THE DEATH OF BUDDHA

THERE fell upon the Lord a dire sickness . . . even unto death. . . . And the Lord addressed Ananda . . . "I am grown old, O Ananda, and full of years; my journey is drawing to its close, I have reached the sum of my days. . . . Just as a worn-out cart can only with much difficulty be made to move, so my body can only be kept going with much additional care. . . .

"Therefore, O Ananda, be ye lamps unto yourselves. Rely on yourselves, and do not rely on external help. Hold fast to the truth as a lamp. Seek salvation alone in the truth. . . . Those who, either now or after I am dead, shall be a lamp unto themselves, relying upon themselves only and not relying upon any external help, but holding fast to the truth as their lamp . . . it is they . . . who shall reach the very topmost height!" . . .

Buddha's Enlightenment came under Bodhi tree

Then the Lord addressed the brethren, "It may be that even a single brother may be in doubt or uncertainty about Buddha, or the Doctrine, or the path, or the course of conduct. Ask, brethren; do not with regret say afterwards, 'The Master was face to face with us, and we could not ask the Lord face to face.' " At these words the brethren were silent. . . .

Then Ananda addressed the Lord, "Wonderful, reverend sir . . . in this assembly of brethren there is not even a single brother who is in doubt or uncertainty about the Buddha, or the Doctrine, or the path, or the course of conduct." . . .

Then the Lord addressed the brethren, "Well then, brethren, I now exhort you. Impermanent are compound things; strive with earnestness." These were his last words. Then the Lord reached the first Ecstasy, and ascending from the first he reached the second, from the second he reached the third, and from the third he reached the fourth. From the fourth he reached the abode of infinite space. . . . When the Lord attained Nirvana, at the time of Nirvana, there was a great shaking of the earth, terrifying and frightful, and the drums of the gods resounded. . . .

—MAHA-PARINIBBANA-SUTTA

Buddha taught men a way to serenity and poise of spirit in their present life, as well as a means to liberate themselves at some time in the future (perhaps only after aeons of reincarnations) from all craving for things that perish—such

desires being what bind men meanwhile to the endless cycle of birth and death. Most men require myriad lives to achieve Nirvana. Only a few souls, such as Buddha himself, become sufficiently pure to attain Nirvana in a few lives.

The subtle differences between the spiritual philosophy that Buddha taught and the actual example of his own life indirectly but significantly caused the subsequent schism of the two great schools of Buddhist history: Hinayana and Mahayana Buddhism. Both schools of thought were in existence by 200 B.C. Hinayana means "the Lesser Vehicle" of salvation, and this form of Buddhism flourishes in Ceylon, Burma and Southeast Asia. Mahayana means "the Greater Vehicle" of salvation; it flourishes in China, Korea, Japan, Tibet and Mongolia. Specific differences between the two will be shown later in these texts. But the two schools do agree on many of the most glorious of Buddhist scriptures, among these the narrative of Buddha's first sermon after his Enlightenment.

THE SERMON AT BENARES

NOW the Blessed One thought, To whom shall I preach the Law first? Who will understand this Law readily? . . . And the Blessed One thought, The five brethren have done many services to me; they attended on me during the time of my ascetic discipline. . . . And the Blessed One . . . came to Benares, to the deer park Isipatana, to the place where the five brethren were. . . . And the Blessed One thus addressed them:

"There are two extremes, brethren, which he who has given up the world ought to avoid. What are these two extremes? A life given to pleasures, devoted to pleasures and lusts—this is degrading, sensual, vulgar, ignoble and profitless. And a life given to mortifications—this is painful, ignoble and profitless. By avoiding these two extremes, brethren, I have gained the knowledge of the Middle Path which leads to insight, which leads to wisdom, which conduces to calm, to knowledge and to Supreme Enlightenment. . . . It is the Noble Eightfold Path, namely: right views, right intent, right speech, right conduct, right means of livelihood, right endeavor, right mindfulness, right meditation. . . .

"This, brethren, is the Noble Truth of Suffering: birth is suffering; decay is suffering; illness is suffering; death is suffering; presence of objects we hate is suffering; separation from objects we love is suffering; not to obtain what we desire is suffering. In brief, the five aggregates which spring from grasping are painful.

"This, brethren, is the Noble Truth concerning the Origin of Suffering: verily, it originates in that craving which causes the renewal of becomings, is accompanied by sensual delight, and seeks satisfaction now here, now there; that is to say, craving for pleasures, craving for becoming, craving for not becoming.

"This, brethren, is the Noble Truth concerning the Cessation of Suffering: verily, it is passionlessness, cessation without remainder of this very craving; the laying aside of, the giving up, the being free from, the harboring no longer of, this craving.

"This, brethren, is the Noble Truth concerning the Path which leads to the Cessation of Suffering: verily, it is this Noble Eightfold Path, that is to say, right views, right intent, right speech, right conduct, right means of livelihood, right endeavor, right mindfulness and right meditation. . . .

"As long, brethren, as I did not possess with perfect purity this true knowledge and insight into these Four Noble Truths . . . I knew that I had not yet obtained the highest absolute Enlightenment . . . in Brahma's world. . . . Then I knew, brethren, that I had obtained the highest, universal Enlightenment in the world of men and gods. . . . And this knowledge and insight arose in my mind: the emancipation of my mind cannot be shaken; this is my last birth; now shall I not be born again."

Thus the Blessed One spoke. The five brethren were delighted, and they rejoiced at the words of the Blessed One. . . . And as the Blessed One had set going the Wheel of the Law, the earth-inhabiting gods shouted, "Truly the Blessed One has set going at Benares, in the deer park Isipatana, the Wheel of the Law, which may not be opposed . . . by any being in the world." . . . Thus in that moment, in that instant, in that second the shout reached the Brahma world; and this whole system of ten thousand worlds quaked, was shaken and trembled; and an infinite, mighty light was seen through the world. . . .

—THE MAHA-VAGGA OF THE VINAYA TEXTS

Hinayana theology is based on Buddha's teaching, Maha-yana theology on his personal example. The Hinayana stress is on each individual's mastering himself so that he may gain his own entry to Nirvana, thus emphasizing the self-purification that Buddha taught. The Mahayana stress is a broader one; those achieving self-purification, who are bodhisattvas, delay entering Nirvana—as Buddha delayed doing so for forty-five years in his own life—so that they may help others to reach the final goal. The two ideals do not necessarily conflict. But their emphasis is quite different.

The following selection shows a Hinayana viewpoint; Buddha's famous "Fire Sermon" emphasizes the need for each man to avoid everything which is on fire with craving, so that he may achieve the "coolness" of Nirvana.

THE FIRE SERMON

THE Blessed One addressed the priests, "All things, O priests, are on fire. . . . The eye, O priests, is on fire . . . impressions received by the eye . . . that also is on fire. And with what are these on fire? With the fire of passion, say I, with the fire of hatred, with the fire of infatuation; with birth, old age, death, sorrow, lamentation, misery, grief and despair are they on fire. The ear is on fire; sounds are on fire . . . the nose is on fire . . . the tongue is on fire; tastes are on fire . . . the body is on fire . . . the mind is on fire; ideas are on fire. . . .

"Perceiving this, O priests, the learned and noble disciple conceives an aversion for the eye . . . for forms . . . for the ear . . . for the nose . . . for the tongue . . . for tastes . . . for the body . . . for the mind . . . for ideas. . . . And in conceiving this aversion, he becomes divested of passion; and by the absence of passion, he becomes free; and when he is free, he becomes aware that he is free; and he knows that rebirth is exhausted, that he has lived the holy life, that he has done what it behooved him to do, and that [therefore] he is no more for this world." . . .

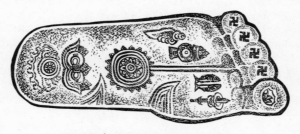

Buddha's footprint represents him symbolically as a human being

—THE MAHA-VAGGA OF THE VINAYA TEXTS

Mahayana Buddhists believe that the loving compassion of the Bodhisattva Ti-ts'ang will lead him to share even the fires of hell in order to bring its inmates to salvation.

THE BODHISATTVA
Who Saves Even From the Depths of Hell

AT that time those beings who had been saved from perdition . . . met together with Ti-ts'ang in the Central Heaven for a great assembly. In every section there were countless millions. They all came with incense and flowers, which they offered before the face of Buddha. . . . These multitudes who have passed through endless epochs of birth and death . . . now stand in the Central Heaven with the proof of experience, for Ti-ts'ang's solemn pledges and his great all-embracing mercy have proved themselves effective. . . . The "World-Honored One" stretches out his golden arms and blesses the various forms in which the Bodhisattva Ti-ts'ang has incarnated himself through the endless epochs. . . . At this time all the various bodily incarnations of Ti-ts'ang were gathered together from the different worlds into one body. Tears ran from Ti-ts'ang's eyes and nose, as with heartfelt longing and deep sadness he looked up to Buddha and said:

"For endless epochs I have been under Buddha's special guidance, so that I have received unspeakable divine strength and wisdom. This has prepared me to enter into the most varied physical forms. . . . Every single incarnation has saved millions of people and led them . . . into the state of joy of Nirvana. Moreover, if there should still be anything lacking in the way of good works, be it but a hairbreadth, a grain of sand, or a speck of dust, I will carry it all on to completion." . . .

Then Buddha lifted up his voice and praised Ti-ts'ang, saying, "Good, good—I share your joy! When you shall have fulfilled this great promise and after endless epochs shall have finished this work of salvation, then will you truly have shown yourself . . . in the most widely different worlds . . . to be the possessor of the tenderest heart and the highest wisdom."

—ANONYMOUS

In the Buddhist scriptures, especially those of Hinayana, Buddha's preaching is primarily ethical. It teaches victory over self as the greatest of all conquests, and as the indispensable, first step to spiritual achievement. The following sermon, attributed directly to Buddha, shows the ethical nature of his religion with vivid clarity.

ETHICAL TEACHINGS

BRETHREN, whatsoever grounds there be for good works undertaken with a view to rebirth, all of them are not worth one sixteenth part of that goodwill which is the heart's release; goodwill alone, which is the heart's release, shines and burns and flashes forth in surpassing them. Just as, brethren, the radiance of all the starry bodies in the heavens is not worth one sixteenth part of the moon's radiance. . . .

"Brethren, there are two ethical teachings. . . . What two? 'Look at evil as evil' is the first teaching. 'Seeing evil as evil, be disgusted therewith, be cleansed of it, be freed of it' is the second teaching. . . . Brethren, there are these three persons found existing in the world. What three? The one who is like a drought, the one who rains locally, and the one who pours down everywhere.

"And how, brethren, is a person like a drought?

"Herein, brethren, a certain person is . . . no giver of food and drink, clothing and . . . bed, lodging and lights to . . . the wretched and needy beggars. In this way, brethren, a person is like a drought.

"And how, brethren, is a person like a local rainfall? In this case a person is a giver to some, but to others he gives not. . . .

"And how, brethren, does a person rain down everywhere? In this case a certain person gives to all. . . . So these are the three sorts of people found existing in the world.

"Brethren, even if one should seize the hem of my garment and walk behind me step for step, yet if he be covetous in his desires, fierce in his longing, malevolent of heart, of mind corrupt, careless and unrestrained, not quieted but scatterbrained and uncontrolled in his sense, that monk is far from me and I am far from him. . . . Brethren, do ye live perfect in virtue, do ye live perfect in the performance of the obligations . . . perfect in the practice of right behavior; seeing danger in the slightest faults. . . . For him who so lives . . . who undertakes the training of the precepts, what else remains to be done?" . . .

—ITIVITTUKA

The best known of all the Buddhist scriptures is called the Dhammapada *or* Way of the Law. *Some of its 423 verses are thought to have been composed by Buddha himself; all show the depth and wisdom of his doctrine. It is one of the great classics of the world's religious literature.*

THE WAY OF THE LAW

ALL that we are is the result of what we have thought: it is founded on our thoughts, it is made up of our thoughts. If a man speaks or acts with an evil thought, pain follows him, as the wheel follows the foot of the ox that draws the carriage. . . . If a man speaks or acts with a pure thought, happiness follows him, like a shadow that never leaves him. . . .

Hatred does not cease by hatred at any time; hatred ceases by love—this is an old rule. . . . As rain breaks through an ill-thatched house, passion will break through an unreflecting mind. . . . If you see a man who shows you what is to be avoided, who administers reproofs, and is intelligent, follow that man as you would one who reveals hidden treasures. . . .

Irrigators lead the water wherever they like . . . carpenters fashion wood; wise people fashion themselves. As a solid rock is not shaken by the wind, wise people waver not amidst blame and praise. Wise people . . . become serene.

If one man conquer in battle a thousand times a thousand men, and if another conquer himself, he is the greatest of conquerors. One's own self conquered is better than all other people conquered; not even a god . . . could change into defeat the victory of a man who has vanquished himself. . . .

Let no man think lightly of evil, saying in his heart, "It will not come nigh unto me." Even by the falling of water drops a water pot is filled; the fool becomes full of evil, even if he gather it little by little. . . . He who has no wound on his hand may touch poison with his hand; poison does not affect one who has no wound; nor does evil befall one who commits no evil. . . .

By one's self the evil is done, by one's self one suffers; by one's self evil is left undone; by one's self one is purified. The pure and the impure stand and fall by themselves; no one can purify another. . . .

Victory breeds hatred, for the conquered is unhappy. He who has given up both victory and defeat, he is contented and happy. There is no fire like passion; there is no evil like hatred; there is no pain like this bodily existence; there is no happiness higher than peace. Hunger is the worst of diseases, bodily demands the greatest evil; if one knows this truly, that is Nirvana. . . .

Let no man ever cling to what is pleasant, or to what is unpleasant. Not to see what is pleasant is pain, and it is pain to see what is unpleasant. Let, therefore, no man be attached to anything; loss of the beloved is evil. Those who are attached to nothing, and hate nothing, have no fetters. . . . Kinsmen, friends and lovers salute a man who has been long away and returns safe from afar. In like manner, his good works receive him who has done good and has gone from this world to the other—as kinsmen receive a friend on his return. . . .

He who holds back rising anger like a rolling chariot, him I call a real driver; other people are but holding the reins. . . . Let a wise man blow off the impurities of himself, as a smith

Lotus symbolizes flowering of the human spirit

blows off the impurities of silver, one by one, little by little, and from moment to moment. . . . The fault of others is easily perceived, but that of one's self is difficult to perceive; a man winnows his neighbor's faults like chaff, but his own fault he hides, as a cheat hides an unlucky cast of the die. If a man looks after the faults of others and is always inclined to be offended, his own passions will grow. . . .

What ought to be done is neglected, what ought not to be done is done; the desires of unruly, thoughtless people are always increasing. But they whose whole watchfulness is always directed to their body, who do not follow what ought not to be done, and who steadfastly do what ought to be done, the desires of such watchful and wise people will come to an end. . . .

If a man find no prudent companion to walk with him, is wise and lives soberly, let him walk alone, like a king who has left his conquered country behind—like an elephant in the forest. . . .

A man who has learned little, grows old like an ox; his flesh grows, but his knowledge does not grow. . . . Earnestness is the path of Nirvana, thoughtlessness the path of death. Those who are in earnest do not die; those who are thoughtless are as if dead already. . . . The scent of flowers does not travel against the wind, nor that of sandalwood, or of Tagara and Mallika flowers, but the odor of good people travels even against the wind; a good man pervades every place. . . .

—DHAMMAPADA

Buddha taught that men should not demand an eye for an eye, but rather return good for evil. He further believed that human desires and frustrations can be solved only by love—not a limited or selfish love for particular people or things, but unlimited, unselfish love for all creation.

RETURNING GOOD FOR EVIL

THE Buddha observed the ways of society and noticed how much misery came from malignity and foolish offences done only to gratify vanity and self-seeking pride. And the Buddha said, "If a man foolishly does me wrong, I will return to him the protection of my ungrudging love; the more evil comes from him, the more good shall go from me; the fragrance of goodness always comes to me, and the harmful air of evil goes to him."

A foolish man, learning that the Buddha observed the principle of great love which commends the return of good for evil, came and abused him. The Buddha was silent, pitying his folly.

When the man had finished his abuse, the Buddha asked him, saying, "Son, if a man declined to accept a present made to him, to whom would it belong?" And he answered, "In that case it would belong to the man who offered it."

"My son," said the Buddha, "thou hast railed at me, but I decline to accept thy abuse, and request thee to keep it thyself. Will it not be a source of misery to thee? As the echo belongs to the sound, and the shadow to the substance, so misery will overtake the evildoer without fail."

The abuser made no reply, and Buddha continued, "A wicked man who reproaches a virtuous one is like one who looks up and spits at heaven; the spittle soils not the heaven, but comes back and defiles his own person. The slanderer is like one who flings dust at another when the wind is contrary; the dust only returns on him who threw it. The virtuous man cannot be hurt, and the misery that the other would inflict comes back on himself."

The abuser went away ashamed, but he came again and took refuge in the Buddha. . . .

—THE SUTRA OF FORTY-TWO SECTIONS

The spiritual warmth and radiance, vigor and brilliance which drew thousands of followers to Buddha in his own lifetime—and have drawn millions to him since—is nowhere better shown than in his parables. Two of the best appear below. What Is an Elephant? *has become a true folk tale known all around the earth. It may have been told for the first time by Buddha himself.*

WHAT IS AN ELEPHANT?

ON one occasion a number of disciples went to the Blessed One and said, "Sir, there are living here in Savatthi many wandering hermits and scholars who indulge in constant dispute. . . . What, Sir, would you say concerning them?"

The Blessed One answered, "Brethren, those disputatious fellows are like unto blind men. . . . Once upon a time there was a rajah in this region who called to a certain man and said . . . 'Gather together in one place all the men in Savatthi who were born blind . . . and show them an elephant.'

" 'Very good, sire,' said the man, and did as he was told and said to them, 'O blind, such as this is an elephant'—and to one man, he presented the head of the elephant, to another its ears, to another a tusk, to another the trunk, the foot, back, tail and tuft of the tail, saying to each one that that was the elephant. . . .

"Thereupon, brethren, that rajah went up to the blind men and said to each . . . 'Tell me, what sort of thing is an elephant?' Thereupon those who had been presented with the head answered, 'Sire, an elephant is like a pot.' And those who had observed an ear only replied, 'An elephant is like a winnowing-basket.' Those who had been presented with a tusk said it was a plowshare. Those who knew only the trunk said it was a plow; they said the body was a granary; the foot, a pillar; the back, a mortar; the tail, a pestle; the tuft of the tail, just a broom.

"Then they began to quarrel, shouting 'Yes, it is!' 'No, it is not!' 'An elephant is not that!' 'Yes, it's like that!' and so on, till they came to fisticuffs over the matter. Then, brethren, that rajah was delighted with the scene. Just so are these wanderers holding other views, blind, unseeing, knowing not the profitable, knowing not the unprofitable. They know not the Law. They know not what is not the Law. In their ignorance of these things they are by nature quarrelsome, wrangling and vastly disputatious, each maintaining it is thus and thus." . . .

—UDANA IV, 6

THE MONKEY

IN the Himalaya, brethren, there is a region that is . . . the range of both monkeys and human beings. It is here, brethren, that a hunter sets a trap of pitch in the monkeys' tracks so as to catch them. Now, those monkeys that are not stupid and greedy, on seeing that pitch-trap, keep far away from it. But a stupid, greedy monkey comes up to the pitch and handles it with one of his paws, and his paw sticks fast in it. Then thinking to free his paw, he lays hold of it with the other paw—but that too sticks fast. To free both paws he lays hold of them with one foot, but that too sticks fast. . . . To free both paws and both feet he lays hold of them with his muzzle, but that too sticks fast.

So that monkey, thus trapped in five ways, lies down and howls, thus fallen on misfortune and ruin, a prey for the hunter to work his will on him. . . . Even so it is with one that goes in wrong pastures. . . . Therefore, brethren, do you not so walk. To those that do, Mara the Evil One gets access, Mara

gets a chance over them. And what, brethren, is the wrong pasture? . . . It is the fivefold set of pleasures of the senses. What are the five? Material shapes cognizable by the eye, sounds cognizable by the ear, scents cognizable by the nose, tastes cognizable by the tongue, objects cognizable by the body, desirable, delightful, pleasant, dear, passion-fraught, inciting to lust.

—SAMYUTTA-NIKAYA V, 148–49

Just as many Christian thinkers differ in their views about the afterlife, so do the Hinayana and Mahayana schools differ in their concepts of what Buddha meant by Nirvana. They agree that it means rooting all desires and delusions out of one's heart. The four selections below show various Hinayana views on Nirvana. In general, Hinayana thinkers believe that it means the end of any continued separate existence, with each individual's conscious awareness merged in the Universal. Some Hinayana extremists hold that those who attain Nirvana, even Buddha himself, pass at their death into "Paranirvana," which means utter extinction. The fourth selection, however—a dialogue between King Milinda and the Buddhist monk Nagasena—insists that we can know Buddha was real by the teachings he left.

THE HINAYANA NIRVANA

THAT monk of wisdom here, devoid of desire and passion, attains to deathlessness, peace, the unchanging state of Nirvana. . . . The steadfast go out like this lamp. . . . Where is no-thing, where naught is grasped, this is the Isle of No-beyond. Nirvana do I call it —the utter extinction of aging and dying.

—SUTTANIPATA

THE stopping of becoming is Nirvana. . . . It is called Nirvana because of the getting rid of craving. . . . The good life is lived for the plunge into Nirvana, for going beyond to Nirvana, for culmination in Nirvana.

—SAMYUTTA-NIKAYA

NIRVANA is the Noble Truth of the stopping of suffering. But because when [it] is reached, craving detaches itself, besides being stopped, it is therefore called Dispassion and it is called Stopping. And because, when it is reached, there is renunciation and so on, and there does not remain even one sensory pleasure . . . it is called Renunciation, Surrender, Release. . . .

Is Nirvana extinction? No. . . . Because it is without source; it is unaging and undying. Because there is no source, no aging or dying, it is permanent. . . . Because it is attainable by means of the special cognition perfected by unfailing effort, because it was spoken of by Buddha, because it has existence in the ultimate meaning, Nirvana is not nonexistent. . . .

—VISUDDHIMAGGA, 507–509

THE BUDDHA'S NIRVANA

KING MILINDA asked, "Is it possible, revered Nagasena, to point to the Buddha as being either here or there?" . . . The Monk Nagasena asked the king in turn, "When some flame in a great burning mass of fire goes out, is it possible to point to the flame as being either here or there?"

"No, revered sir. It has ceased to be, it has disappeared."

"Even so, sire, the Lord has attained Nirvana. . . . The Lord has gone home. It is impossible to point to him as being here or there. But it is possible, sire, to point to the Lord by means of the Body of the Law; for the Law, sire, was taught by the Lord."

—MILINDAPANHA, 70–73

Buddha's word and the sun combine in Wheel of Fire

The selection below, from the Lankavatara Sutra, *is considered the best account of what the Mahayana Buddhists mean by Nirvana. It rejects the doctrine of extinction and affirms that Nirvana is a state of passionless peace which the bodhisattvas, those saviors who refuse Buddha-hood, help all living beings to attain by their saintly sacrifices.*

A MAHAYANA NIRVANA

THEN said Mahamati to the Blessed One, "Pray tell us about Nirvana." The Blessed One replied, "The term Nirvana is used with many different meanings by different people.... Those who are suffering or who fear suffering, think of Nirvana as an escape and a recompense. They imagine that Nirvana consists in the future annihilation of the senses and the sense-minds. They are not aware that Universal Mind and Nirvana are One, that this life-and-death world we are now in and Nirvana are not to be separated.

"These ignorant ones ... cling to the notion of Nirvana that is outside what is seen of the mind and, thus, go on rolling themselves along with the wheel of life and death.... Some philosophers conceive Nirvana to be ... a state where there is no recollection of the past or present, just as when a lamp is extinguished, or when a seed is burnt, or when

Two fishes are the sign of conjugal happiness

a fire goes out.... But this is not Nirvana, because Nirvana does not consist in simple annihilation and vacuity. Again, some philosophers ... conceive being to be Nirvana, some non-being.... Some, thinking that time is the creator and that the rise of the world depends on time, conceive that Nirvana consists in the recognition of time as Nirvana.... Nirvana is not to be found by mental searching....

"As to the notion of Nirvana as held by disciples and masters who still cling to the notion of an ego-self, and who try to find it by going off by themselves into solitude: their notion of Nirvana is an eternity of bliss ... *for themselves....* They forsake social relations and ... in solitude seek self-realization of Noble Wisdom by self-effort.... Clinging to the bliss of the ecstasies, they pass to their Nirvana, but it is *not* the Nirvana of the bodhisattvas."

Then said Mahamati to the Blessed One, "Pray tell us, what is the Nirvana of the bodhisattvas?"

The Blessed One replied, "Mahamati, this assurance is not an assurance of numbers nor logic; it is not the mind that is to be assured but the heart.... There is no more thirst for life, no more sex-lust, no more thirst for learning, no more thirst for eternal life; with the disappearance of these fourfold thirsts ... the defilements on the face of Universal Mind clear away, and the bodhisattva attains self-realization ... that is the heart's assurance of Nirvana."...

—LANKAVATARA SUTRA

Both the Hinayana and Mahayana schools affirm Buddha's deep compassion toward humanity. But they approach Buddha in different ways, since in Hinayana thought he is primarily human and in Mahayana thought primarily divine. The Hinayana emphasis is on a dedicated personal life; the Psalms of the Early Buddhists *characterize the aspiring devotion of the monks and nuns who forsook ordinary life. The* Psalm of Sister Subha *below tells how a nun's zeal for spiritual progress away from worldly concerns led her to pluck out her eye.*

PSALM OF SISTER SUBHA

In Jivaka's pleasant woodland walked Subha
   The Sister. A gallant met her there
And barred the way. To him thus spake Subha.
   "What have I done to offend thee, that thus in my path thou comest?
No man, O friend, it beseemeth to touch a Sister in Orders...."
   "Young art thou, maiden, and faultless—what seekest *thou* in the holy life?
Cast off that yellow-hued raiment and come! in the blossoming woodland
   Seek we our pleasure. Filled with the incense of blossoms the trees waft
Sweetness. See, the spring's at the prime, the season of happiness! ...
   Sweet overhead is the sough of the blossoming crests of the forest
Swayed by the Wind-gods...."
   "What now to thee, in this carrion-filled, grave-filling carcase so fragile
Seen by thee, seemeth to warrant the doctrine thou speakest?" ...
   "Eyes hast thou like the gazelle's, like an elf's in the heart of the mountains—
'Tis those eyes of thee, sight of which feedeth the depth of my passion.
   Shrined in thy dazzling, immaculate face as in calyx of lotus...."
"O thou art blind! Thou chasest a sham, deluded by puppet shows....
   What is this eye but a little ball lodged in the fork of a hollow tree,
Bubble of film, anointed with tear-brine, exuding slime-drops,
   Compost wrought in the shape of an eye of manifold aspects?"
Forthwith the maiden so lovely tore out her eye and gave it him:
   "Here then! take thou thine eye!" Nor sinned she, her heart unobstructed.
Straightway the lust in him ceased and he her pardon imploring:
   "O that thou mightest recover thy sight, thou maid pure and holy!
Never again will I dare to offend thee after this fashion.
   Sore hast thou smitten my sin; blazing flames have I clasped to my bosom;
Poisonous snake have I handled—but O! be thou heal'd and forgive me!"
   Freed from molesting, the Sister went on her way to the Buddha....
There in his presence, seeing those features
   Born of uttermost merit, straightway her sight was restored to her.
         —PSALMS OF THE BRETHREN AND SISTERS

The Mahayana emphasis is on worship of images in temples rather than on a retired life of devotion. The Buddha is not merely a man who lived and died on earth. The historical Buddha was only one of many manifestations of a transcendent cosmic Buddha dwelling in the universe, which *are working towards the salvation of everyone in all places and in all ages. Buddha's gospel becomes less one of salvation by works and more one of salvation by faith. The* Hymn to the Buddha of Infinite Compassion, *below, represents the Mahayana principles of prayer and devotion.*

HYMN TO THE BUDDHA OF INFINITE COMPASSION

How can there be a likeness to your virtues, untouched by foe or obstacle,
    Everlasting, unlimited, and which cannot be surpassed? . . .
This form of yours, calm yet lovely, brilliant without dazzling,
    Soft but mighty—whom would it not entrance? . . .
It was your compassion, given free course, which made you pass your time
    Among the crowds, when the happiness of seclusion suited you so much better. . . .
Your birth gives joy to people, and your growth delights them;
    While you are there they benefit, on your departure they feel lost.
To praise you takes all guilt away, to recollect you lifts up the heart,
    To seek you brings understanding, to comprehend you purity. . . .
Other men do not as much study the welfare of those who mean them well,
    As you study that of those who seek you harm.
To an enemy intent on ill you are a good friend intent on good.
To one who constantly seeks for faults you respond by seeking for virtues. . . .
        —Satapancasatka of Matrceta

The spiritual ideal of Hinayana Buddhism is the "arhat," or perfected disciple who has conquered all the cravings of his nature and thus gained the blessed release of Nirvana for himself. His only help to others is as a shining but distant example of what a few of them may eventually achieve.

The first of the two following selections tells of a king who achieved Nirvana after abandoning his kingdom for seclusion. The second expounds the doctrine that Buddha devotes his first concern to those most worthy of it.

THE BRACELETS

THERE was a king of Benares. One summer when the weather was very hot, he lay down in an upper room on a couch adorned with gold, silver and many precious stones, and made a servant massage him with ointment of sandalwood. . . . The servant was wearing a great many bracelets on her arms, and they jangled together while she massaged the king. The sound irritated him and he asked her to take one of the bracelets off. She did so, and there was a little less noise. She took off another . . . and there was only one left, and then there was no jangling at all. When the noise stopped, the king had a sudden awakening. "That is just what I ought to do with my kingdom, my ministers, subjects, concubines and attendants," he said to himself. "In fact, with all business and bother." From that moment onward he had no further worldly desires, but spent his time meditating in complete seclusion, and became a Solitary (Pratyeka) Buddha.
    —Takakusu XV, 281

Conch shell, for Buddha's voice, is blown during church services

THE THREE FIELDS

A VILLAGE headman spoke thus to the Lord, "Is a Buddha compassionate towards all living breathing creatures?" "Yes, headman," answered the Lord. "But does the Lord teach the Law in full to some, but not likewise to others?" The Lord replied, "Now, what do you think, headman? Suppose a farmer had three fields, one excellent, one mediocre, and one poor with bad soil. When he wanted to sow the seed, which one of these three fields would he sow first?"

"He would sow the excellent one first, then he would sow the mediocre one. When he had done that, he might or might not sow the poor one with the bad soil. And why? Because it might do, if only for cattle-fodder."

"In the same way, headman, my monks and nuns are like the excellent field. It is to these that I teach the Law that is lovely at the beginning, lovely in the middle and lovely at the ending, with the spirit and the letter, and to whom I make known . . . the completely fulfilled, utterly pure. And why? It is these that dwell with me for light, me for shelter, me for stronghold, me for refuge. Then my men and women lay followers are like the mediocre field. To these too I teach the Law. . . . Then recluses, Brahmins and wanderers of other sects than mine are like the poor field with the bad soil. To these too I teach the Law. . . . And why? Because if they were to understand even a single sentence, that would be a happiness and a blessing for them for a long time."

". . . Brethren, a competent herdsman of Magadha in the last month of rains at harvest time, having considered both the hither and the farther bank of the river Ganges, drove his cattle across to the farther bank in Suvideha at a place where there was a ford. First of all he drove across those bulls who were the sires and leaders of the herd, next the sturdy bullocks and young steers, then the half-grown bull-calves and heifers, and then the weaker calves. All cut across the stream of the Ganges and went safely beyond. . . . Even so, brethren . . . these, having cut across the stream of craving, have gone safely beyond." . . .
    —Samyutta-nikaya IV, 314–16
    Majjhima-nikaya I, 225–26

In Tibet, Buddhism took a form so different from those elsewhere that it goes by the name of Lamaism. This fuses Hinayana Buddhism, which first entered Tibet from India around 700 A.D., with a native animism that used magic and nature worship. The Tibetan lamas developed an ethical wisdom literature of a rather high calibre, which appears in collections under titles such as The Voice of

69

the Silence *and* The Ocean of Delight for the Wise. *The following selection of Tibetan religious proverbs is taken largely from* The Tree of Wisdom.

TIBETAN APHORISMS

In the same place where the great Lord Buddha is present
Who would acknowledge any other man?
When the sun hath arisen, though there be many bright stars in the sky,
Not one of them is visible. . . .

Eating, sleeping, fearing and copulating—
Man and the brutes are alike in these.
By the practice of religion mankind is elevated.
If religion is not understood, is man not on a level with the brutes? . . .

Whenever the mean find a little wealth,
They despise everybody and are filled with pride;
But the virtuous, although they may attain the possession of wealth,
Remain bowed like ripe rice. . . .

The swan does not look well in an assemblage of hawks,
Nor the horse among the donkeys,
Nor the lion among the foxes,
Nor the clever man among fools. . . .

All desires should be abandoned,
But if you cannot abandon them,
Let your desire be for salvation.
That is the cure for it. . . .

Whoever gives alms which do not harm others—
His resulting pleasures will neither be carried away by water,
Nor burned by fire, nor stolen by thieves.
Such possessions will never be utterly destroyed.

Let all hear this moral maxim,
And having heard it, keep it well:
Whatever is not pleasing to yourself,
Do not that unto others.

The God of Death does not wait to ask whether
Your works are completed or not.
Therefore do tomorrow's work today,
And the evening's work in the morning. . . .

Intimacy in the society of the holy,
Conversation in the society of the learned,
And the friendship of the unselfish—
These will cause no regrets.

Although a thing may afford you mental enjoyment,
Yet, if the full fruition is to be injurious, how can it be right?
If anything upsets your health,
How can it be right to eat such a sweet dish? . . .

An excellent man, like precious metal,
Is in every way invariable;
A villain, like the beams of a balance,
Is always varying, upwards and downwards.

Relinquish an evil custom even though it be of thy fathers and ancestors;
Adopt a good custom even though it be established among thine enemies:
Poison is not to be taken even though offered by one's mother;
But gold is acceptable even from one who is inimical. . . .

—SHE-RAB DONG-BU

Among the divine incarnations revered by the Mahayana Buddhists, the chief figure is the Amitabha "Buddha of Infinite Light." Not an actual person, Amitabha by legend achieved Buddha-hood on the stipulation that he could receive at death all who called on his name, so he could take them to his "Pure Land" or "Western Paradise." His realm, situated in the Western Quarter of the universe, combines the perfections of all other paradises.

The first of the following odes is offered at burial services. The second describes Amitabha's paradise in terms reminiscent of the hymn "Jerusalem the Golden."

ODE TO AMITABHA BUDDHA

Thou perfect master,
Who shinest upon all things and all men,
As gleaming moonlight plays
Upon a thousand waters at the same time!
Thy great compassion does not pass by a single creature.
Steadily and quietly sails
The great ship of compassion across the sea of sorrow.
Thou art the Great Physician for a sick and impure world,
In pity giving the invitation to the Paradise of the West.

—MASSES FOR THE DEAD

THE WHITE LOTUS ODE

What words can picture the beauty and breadth
Of that pure and glistening land?
That land where the blossoms ne'er wither from age,
Where the golden gates gleam like purest water . . .
The land where there are none but fragrant bowers,
Where the Utpala lotus unfolds itself freely.
O hear the sweet tones from hillside and grove
The All-Father's praise from the throats of the birds!

And the ages fly by in an endless chain,
Never broken by summer's or winter's change.
The burning sun can never more frighten.
The icy storms' power long ago is subdued.
The clouds full of light and the green mantled forests
Now cradle all things in their endless peace.
Now the soul is set free from the haunts of darkness
And rests secure in the dwelling of truth.
See, all that was dim and beclouded on earth
Here is revealed, appropriated, secured.

There ne'er was a country so brightened with gladness
As the Land of the Pure there far off to the West.
There stands Amitabha with shining adornments,
He makes all things ready for the Eternal Feast.
He draws every burdened soul up from the depths
And lifts them up into his peaceful abode.
The great transformation is accomplished for the worm
Who is freed from the body's oppressive sorrows.
It receives as a gift a spiritual body,
A body which shines in the sea of spirits.

And who indeed is it with grace in his tones,
Who sends his smile out to the dwellings of the suffering,
And who indeed is it whose glance is like the sun
Who shows his compassion on life and is victor?
Yes, it is God himself, who sits on the throne
And by his Law, redeems from all need.
With gold-adorned arm, with crown of bright jewels,
With power over sin, over grief, over death.
None other is like to our God in his greatness,
And none can requite his compassion's great power!

—HUI YUAN

THE PHILOSOPHY
OF
CHINA

THE PHILOSOPHY OF CHINA

ONE day nearly 2,500 years ago the great Chinese sage Confucius was asked by a disciple, "Great teacher, tell us about the life after death." Confucius replied, "We have not yet learned to know life. How can we know death?" In these words he epitomized the Chinese attitude toward the deepest enigmas of human existence and the unknown.

For, unlike the Hindus, the Chinese are not a passionately religious people, preoccupied with a spiritual quest. They have concerned themselves less with the hereafter than with the proper conduct of affairs and attainment of happiness in the here and now. The foundations of their social system rest not on revealed religion but on the ethical teachings of Confucius. The idea of God which has enkindled so much of Western literature, art and music does not permeate the native Chinese arts, which are inspired primarily by a reverence for nature. The Chinese, indeed, are not very specific about God; for them God is not so clearly defined a personality as he is to the Christian, the Jew and the Moslem. There have been no great apostles in Chinese history, no martyrs, no saviors and only a very few who could be called religious leaders. The most venerated personage in the average Chinese community has not been the priest but the scholar. Confucius himself was no monklike figure but a merry companion who delighted in lute playing, group singing, hunting, fishing and riding about in a chariot.

A modern cynic has said that the Chinese were the first people to "outgrow" religion. Yet this is misleading, for prior to the present Communist drive against traditional beliefs, China was, throughout its long existence, notably tolerant of religious systems of every kind and despite some unhappy periods, generally free from religious wars and persecutions. For this reason, perhaps, the Chinese have never engendered a single, close-knit faith like Christianity or Islam. Religion in China represents a coalescence of many elements, native and foreign, rational and naive. There is, moreover, a horizontal cleavage between the religion of the common people and that of the educated upper classes—the former characterized by a heritage of superstition and animism passed down from the dawn of Chinese civilization, the latter by strict adherence to Confucian ethics and a rigorous if faintly skeptical observance of traditional forms.

Within this complex edifice, however, rise three soaring pillars of thought: Confucianism, Buddhism and Taoism. The first of these is less a religion than a formal ethical system defining personal relationships in an ideal moral order. Outlined by Confucius in the Sixth Century B.C., its precepts have dominated every aspect of China's thought and culture; Chinese society, solidly founded upon the unity of the family, has been a Confucian society. The second element, Mahayana Buddhism, was imported from India, probably in the First Century A.D., introducing to China for the first time the appurtenances of formalized religion —among them a priesthood, prayer, a pantheon or hierarchy of gods in human form and the use of images (*opposite page*). The third element, Taoism, is less easily defined. In its original sense, Taoism refers to the philosophy of Lao Tzu, supposedly a contemporary of Confucius, who preached a retreat from civilization to nature in order to attain harmony with Tao, the "eternal way" or supreme governing force behind the universe. In its broader connotation, Taoism defines a mixture of magic and religion, dating from the Second Century A.D., within

which elements of Lao Tzu's mysticism have been submerged beneath borrowed or imitative aspects of Buddhism and primitive nature worship. A Taoist priest propitiating "water spirits" is shown on page 71.

The essential character of religion in China is that, apart from priests and other functionaries, the Chinese have never considered themselves exclusively "Confucianists," "Buddhists" or "Taoists." In 497 A.D., the court official Chang Jung was buried holding in his left hand the writings of Confucius and Lao Tzu, and in his right hand the Buddhist *Lotus Sutra*. He died, it is said, "a typical Chinese." Chinese literature is filled with references to "the harmony of the three religions . . . three roads to the same destination." The three share several doctrines in common; all teach the original goodness of man, and all hold that man can attain salvation through the realization of his essential nature. The scholar Mencius, who was born a little more than a hundred years after Confucius' death and became the greatest of the Confucian school's writers, says: "The tendency of man's nature to good is like the tendency of water to flow downwards. There are none but have this tendency to good, just as all water flows downward." And "if men become evil, that is not the fault of their original endowment. The sense of mercy is found in all men; the sense of shame is found in all men; the sense of respect is found in all men; the sense of right and wrong is found in all men. . . . Charity, righteousness, propriety and moral consciousness are not something that is drilled into us: we have got them originally. . . ."

But Mencius preaches economics together with ethics, urging the conservation of fisheries and forests and diversification in farming. This combination of vigorous pragmatism and mild mysticism which Mencius, like Confucius, epitomizes is one major Confucian contribution to Chinese national thought which can be sharply distinguished from the parallel contributions made by Buddhism and Taoism.

Undergirding all three systems is China's primitive folk religion. Centuries before Confucius, Chinese along the Yellow River expressed their religious feelings through worship of their departed ancestors. Along with ancestor worship has come down, too, a reverence for mountains, rivers and the soil. Long before Lao Tzu, every Chinese village raised a mound of earth symbolizing the fertility of the land. Each spring the mound saw dancing and heard ceremonial songs designed to cajole the gods into granting good crops; each autumn the mound was the scene of thanksgiving for the harvest. Today, on Formosa and wherever they can on the mainland of China, villagers still propitiate the Jade Emperor, god of earth and water, with gifts and ceremonies.

In the old Chinese concept, the interrelationship between man and nature is not external but organic and inseparable. If man misbehaves, heaven is upset and earth does not prosper. As if to emphasize this interdependence, the revered dead in China to this day are buried beneath mounds like those that once were dedicated to the gifts of the soil. Moreover, both graves and houses must be placed with the greatest care so that they may be in harmony with the rhythm of the universe. Otherwise, evil will befall their occupants.

It is this profound preoccupation with the unity of man and his environment, this veneration for nature, that endow Chinese religion with color and pageantry and impart to its multifold observances an exuberance and gaiety that are characteristic of few other faiths on earth.

A GUARDIAN IMAGE, designed to repel evil spirits, stands outside a Chinese Buddhist temple near Peking. Image-making was brought to China with Buddhism.

FESTIVALS Ancient rites pay homage to the spirit world

For millions of Chinese who know nothing of Confucian philosophy, Taoist mysticism or Buddhist metaphysics, the most vital component of religion lies in the recognition of powerful forces that abide on land and sea and in the supernatural world. From earliest times they have sought, through varied rites, to propitiate and give thanks to the spirits with which nature abounds and which antecede in folklore the gods of the formal faiths. It is the beneficent spirits (*shen*) and the malevolent spirits (*kuei*) which govern the fortunes and misfortunes of man. Everywhere lies danger—in the shape of animal demons, bird demons and fish demons which, if disturbed, can induce terrible disaster. No marriage or birthday should be celebrated without considering them; no building should be erected, no grave dug, without the advice of experts versed in the laws of *fêng-shui* (literally "wind-water").

For countless centuries before Confucius and Buddha these ancient spirits were appeased by sacrifice. The Chinese being a practical people, offerings have now become symbolic—betokened by the burning of paper images or the proffering of food later consumed by the donors themselves. Where the purpose of a ceremony is to invoke the patronage of friendly spirits rather than to exorcise evil ones, the occasion may take on a joyous, carnival aspect more recreational than devout. But in every instance the ritual must be correctly performed, for tradition attaches huge importance to the strict observance of forms.

While the Communist regime in China has permitted the major festivals—New Year's, the Dragon Boat Festival, the Festival of the Eighth Moon—it has made massive attempts to eradicate old traditions and beliefs. For this reason the photographs for this section had to be taken around the periphery of China—in Formosa, Singapore, and wherever the Chinese remain free and the vivid drama and color of the ancient ceremonies still endure. The festival shown on this page took place in the Formosan village of Liu-Yen in honor of an emissary of the Jade Emperor, top deity of the Taoist pantheon, and certain other gods of earth and water. Observed triennially, the rites celebrated here are to give thanks for past benefits and win divine favor for the next three years.

A PAINTED ENTERTAINER waits his turn to perform. Features of every village festival, such performers fill the intervals between religious rites with plays or short acts designed to amuse the gods as well as the worshipers.

SACRIFICIAL OFFERINGS of rice, fruits, cakes, vegetables and meat are laid out for the gods in thanksgiving and hope of future protection. Since the gods absorb only the essence of such offerings, the villagers ate them later.

A BOAT FOR THE GODS is made ready to receive its celestial passengers. The small figures lining the rail form a guard of honor. At the end of the festival the boat is burned, thus transporting the gods back home to heaven.

A RITUAL OF EXORCISM is performed by a Taoist priest (*right*) and a masked assistant who represents an evil spirit. Its purpose is to cleanse the temple of malign forces in preparation for the arrival of the beneficent gods. In his right hand the priest holds a sword, in his left a small metal bowl containing water which he takes into his mouth and blows aloft, thus purifying the atmosphere. The ceremony ends with the vanquishing and expulsion of the evil spirit.

MEMORIAL BIRTHDAY RITES in honor of a saintly feminine ancestor are attended by devout descendants, members of a Formosan family who ask blessings on her from their patron goddess. On the table in background they have placed offerings of incense, flowers, fruit and tea. Robed priests invoke the goddess's presence and solicit her good auspices. Though the ceremonial is Taoist in ritual, it is taking place in a rented room in a Buddhist temple.

AN ETERNAL HARMONY

Reverence for the natural order underlies both Confucian and Taoist philosophy

In Chinese thought man does not occupy quite the ascendant role he enjoys in Western philosophy, where he is viewed as protagonist of the natural order and prime object of creation. He is envisaged instead as but a single part, though a vital one, of the complex of nature in which he stands. Whereas Western man has sought to conquer nature for his material ends, the Chinese has aspired to attain harmony with nature for his spiritual satisfaction. And whereas many Hindus regard the world of nature as a transitory phenomenon, the Chinese have never doubted its reality and have viewed its sublime beauty and order as esthetic entities to be cherished and savored in life.

From the dawn of China's primitive folk religion, the relationship between man and nature has been conceived as a deep, reciprocal involvement in which each can affect the other. As the forces of nature can bring prosperity or disaster to man, so can man disrupt the delicate balance of nature by his misdeeds, for Heaven, Earth and man constitute a single, indivisible unity, which is governed by cosmic law (Tao). No boundaries may be drawn between the supernatural world, the domain of nature, and that of man. Hence, if this sensitive organism is to function easily, man must do his part; when he conforms to natural law, society enjoys peace and tranquillity; when he transgresses it, both Heaven and nature are disturbed, the intricate machinery of the cosmos breaks down, and calamities ensue.

Characteristically Chinese, this attitude toward nature pervades all of China's poetry, art and religion, and underlies the thinking of its great sages whose philosophy is dominated by the notion of Heaven and man functioning in unison. It shines through Confucian ethics where the rules for preserving harmonious relations between man and man are seen as measures to attain deeper harmonies between man and universe. And it is epitomized in the precepts of Lao Tzu who taught that only by subordinating himself to nature's ways could man lead a meaningful existence.

The deep desire for harmony with nature derives from prehistoric times when the ancestors of the race, experiencing the terrors and splendors of nature, saw in them the activities of good and evil powers. With the development of agriculture they became even more aware of their dependence on the regularities of nature and their helplessness before its caprices. On the one hand they discerned the order of the celestial movements, the predictable cycle of seasons, the growth of plants, the stately flow of rivers; and on the other, they were confronted by the unforeseeable violence of such natural disasters as floods, tempests and drought.

From these observations ancient unknown philosophers evolved a cosmology and philosophical interpretation of the natural order. The time may have been as early as 1000 B.C.—at about the same era when the great Hindu thinkers were formulating the concepts of the Vedas. The new Chinese ideas first appear in writing in the Fourth Century B.C. In them the sages reported the existence in the universe of two interacting forces or principles, the yang and the yin, and concluded that everything that exists is constituted by the interplay of these forces and possesses in varying degree the characteristics of both. Each represents a constellation of qualities. Yang is the positive or masculine force—inherent in everything active, warm, hard, dry, bright, procreative and steadfast; it is the essence of sunlight and fire, it is the south side of a hill, the north bank of a river. Yin is the negative or feminine principle—immanent in everything passive, cold, wet, soft, dark, mysterious,

secret, changeable, cloudy, dim and quiescent; it is the essence of shadow and water; it is the shade on the north side of a hill and the south bank of a river. Through their eternal intercourse all things have come into being, including Heaven (which is predominantly yang in character) and Earth (which is predominantly yin). In the same object one principle may prevail at one time, another later—as in the case of a piece of wood which, when cast into a fire, changes character from yin to yang. But everything in the universe—the five elements, men and women, events (success and failure, rise and fall, flowering and decay) contain within themselves these primeval energy modes.

The essential difference between the Chinese conception of yin and yang and other classic philosophical dualisms—*i.e.*, light and darkness, good and evil—lies in the fact that the latter are involved in eternal conflict, whereas yin and yang are basically in accord. Both the feminine yin and the masculine yang are necessary to the order of the universe; they are complementary; together in harmony they are always good.

But how is one to ensure this harmony between two opposites? How can they work together, abandoning their disparate identities, to produce the miraculous order in nature? The answer of the Taoists is: the source of their harmony, the origin of all the order in the world, is Tao.

The concept of Tao lies at the very heart of Chinese philosophical speculation; generations of scholars have expended lifetimes endeavoring to define it. In its narrowest sense Tao means literally "a way," "a road," "a channel"; and so, by extension, it may connote "the proper way to go," "the way of nature," "the law of life," "universal law." From the beginning of time, when the Great Ultimate or first primordial unit of the cosmos began to divide into the differentiated elements yin and yang, the Tao was operating as the force for integration, for it transcends both the world of nature and the unseen world. Even Heaven itself works through Tao; the gods act always in accordance with its way.

While it appeared in the earliest philosophical writings of ancient

YANG AND YIN, two basic forces in cosmos, are traditionally depicted as entwined in a sphere which symbolizes the Great Ultimate or Absolute. Yang (*red*) is the active or male element; yin is the passive, female element.

China, the concept of Tao reached its apogee in the *Tao Tê Ching*, the collection of arcane and mystical poems attributed to the philosopher Lao Tzu. The *Tao Tê Ching* treats Tao as the great, all-controlling principle of the universe. Yet from the beginning the author states that it is impossible to define Tao: the Tao that can be named is not the real eternal Tao; no word or name can define nature's deepest mystery—the mystery of creation and of life. Although Tao is the ultimate source of all things, "I do not know whose Son it is, an image of what existed before God." Through Tao all things have been given life and form. "Before the Heaven and Earth existed, there was something nebulous: silent, isolated, standing alone, changing not, eternally revolving without fail, worthy to be the Mother of All Things. . . ."

Following this prelude, the book goes on to develop the thesis that knowledge of Tao is the secret of life; the aim of human existence is to attain harmony with Tao and thereby find peace and enlightenment. The concord of Heaven and Earth is achieved only when Tao is allowed to take its natural course. Unhappily, man tends to pursue his own headstrong purposes; by meddling and interfering with the processes of nature and countering the rhythm of Tao, he disarranges the cosmic order. It is thus, from the willfulness and waywardness of man, that all the ills of society are engendered. The solution lies, therefore, in resigning one's will to Tao and becoming the instrument of its eternal way. "Leave

TAOIST MYSTICISM is exemplified by its rituals. Here a priest burns incense before two minor deities of the Taoist pantheon. As it has evolved, the Taoist religion has little in common with the original doctrine of Lao Tzu.

SUBLIMITY OF NATURE is a theme that pervades Chinese religion and unites the elements in Taoist and Confucian thought. In former times the emperor made a tour every seven years to offer sacrifices to the principal rivers

all things to take their natural course and do not interfere. . . . What is contrary to the Tao soon perishes." Since Tao works in unobtrusive fashion, the wise man will not be self-assertive. "The Way of Heaven is not to contend and yet to be able to conquer."

If everyone were to live according to the precepts of Taoism, naturally and simply, free from ambition and aggression, the world would witness a spontaneous florescence of good fellowship and brotherly love. Applied to political problems, the law of Tao is patently *laissez faire;* the corridor to peace and freedom lies in noninterference by government in the lives and affairs of men. It also precludes war. "Soldiers are weapons of evil. They are not the weapons of gentlemen. . . . Even in victory, there is no beauty. And who calls it beautiful is one who delights in slaughter." Occasionally the *Tao Tê Ching* rises to heights surpassing all other teachings save those of Jesus Christ. "Repay evil with good. . . . For love is victorious in attack, and invulnerable in defense. Heaven arms with love those it would not see destroyed."

Although the *Tao Tê Ching* exerted little influence on Chinese thought for some time after its composition, which is supposed to have taken place in the Fourth Century B.C., its teaching was later elaborated by a succession of scholars and sages into the philosophy of life known as Taoism. As such it became one of the two great molding influences in Chinese thought. The other was the ethical system of Confucius and his disciples. Where Taoism preached the virtues of the simple life and communion with nature, the denial of selfishness and mystical union with

the Ultimate, Confucianism concerned itself with the immediate exigencies of mankind's existence and the problems of the social order.

For Confucius, as for Lao Tzu, the concept of Tao represented the great law of life. "If a man in the morning embrace the Tao," Confucius said, "then he may die the same evening without regret." And again, "As to the Tao, we must not be separated from it for a single moment." As opposed to Lao Tzu, however, Confucius was a pragmatic philosopher and a humanist, who never lost sight of the contemporary scene in rapt contemplation of a mystical ideal. The factor which most sharply distinguishes Confucius both from Lao Tzu and the philosophers of the Western world is that he dealt less in terms of general principles than of specific personal relationships. Where the Greek thinkers, the Platonists, the Scholastics, and their European successors juggled abstract concepts like "justice," "law," and "virtue," Confucius applied his thoughts to people. His great achievement was the establishment of a system of human relationships within the social order. From this system there emerged the principles of action and behavior that shaped the pattern of Chinese civilization for twenty-five centuries.

The essence of Confucius' ethics lies in his formulation of the Five Relationships: between ruler and subject, father and son, husband and wife, older brother and younger brother, older friend and younger friend. These five are the "great" relationships which Confucius recognized as fundamental to the social order. In accenting the necessity of their careful observance, Confucius uses an important word, li, which means,

and mountains of his realm—chief among them the Yellow River and the Yangtze, shown here threading the deep gorges of its upper reaches. "The virtuous," Confucius once said, "find delight in mountains; the wise in rivers."

CONFUCIAN FORMALISM is epitomized by the austere architecture of the Altar of Heaven in Peking. Here for centuries Chinese emperors officiated at solemn annual rites designed to invoke Heaven's favor for the coming year.

roughly, "propriety," "ideal standard of conduct." By universal devotion to li, human relationships can be so ordered that an ideal social structure will result and harmony reign throughout the land.

Although the Confucian emphasis dwells most weightily on reverence for elders—the ruler, the father, the older brother—social obligations are by no means one-sided. Confucius made this clear when a disciple asked him if there was one word which might serve as a cardinal precept of life. Confucius replied, "Never do to others what you would not like them to do to you." From this principle—analogous to the Golden Rule of Christianity—Confucius' disciples later evolved the ten attitudes by which the Five Relationships should be governed. They are: love in the father, filial piety in the son; gentility in the eldest brother, humility and respect in the younger; righteous behavior in the husband, obedience in the wife; humane consideration in elders, deference in juniors; benevolence in rulers, loyalty in subjects.

Confucius never claimed to be the originator of his ethical code. He drew many of his ideas from the classical writings of ancient China and constantly exhorted his pupils and disciples to revere the customs of the past. But by codifying traditional precepts, illuminating them with his own insights and contributing new principles of his own, he helped to create one of the world's most durable social edifices. Since Confucius' day, twenty-five hundred years ago, the whole of Chinese culture has rested on the solidarity of the family—an institution that has maintained the fabric of society through recurrent periods of chaos and disorder.

The Confucian concept of filial piety has permeated all Chinese thought; the empire itself became a kind of gigantic family in which the emperor was the benevolent father, the subjects his children.

Believing, like all Chinese, in the essential and original goodness of man, Confucius held that stern laws were unnecessary and that character was the root of civilization. "If the ruler is virtuous," he said, "the people will also be virtuous." Convinced that his teachings conformed to Tao and had the backing of Heaven, he had little to say about religious sanctions. While he acknowledged the existence of spirits and adhered to established rituals—especially those in honor of ancestors —he was indifferent to matters above and beyond the social order. "Absorption in the study of the supernatural is most harmful," he said. "To devote oneself earnestly to one's duty to humanity, and while respecting the spirits, to keep them at a distance may be called wisdom."

So together Confucius and Lao Tzu molded the Chinese temperament. And somehow the Chinese temperament has managed to reflect them both. Confucianism is rational, orderly, matter of fact, humanistic; Taoism is romantic, intuitive, mystical, vague. Yet each has deeply infiltrated and profoundly influenced Chinese culture, as the modern scholar and philosopher Dr. Lin Yutang points out in a special article at the conclusion of this section. Confucianism, he has observed, is a philosophy for times of peace and prosperity, and Taoism is a philosophy for times of trouble and disorder. "All Chinese," he says, "are Confucianists when they are successful, and Taoists when they are failures."

THE PHILOSOPHER LAO TZU, father of Taoism, is portrayed by an artist of the Sung Dynasty as a bald, benign old gentleman astride an ox, symbolizing spiritual strength. Red inscriptions are seals of picture's various owners.

CONFUCIUS' DESCENDANT, K'ung Te-cheng, is 77th in the line, has the world's oldest documented family tree. His great ancestor's portrait hangs on the wall.

THE TWO SAGES OF CHINA

In a feudal age Lao Tzu and Confucius shaped Chinese thought and character

It is one of history's spectacular coincidences that the two figures who most profoundly influenced Chinese culture are said to have lived in the fabulous Sixth Century B.C. which also produced Buddha, Pythagoras and perhaps Zoroaster. The first was Lao Tzu, a semilegendary philosopher whose personality has been elaborated by time and fancy. The other was Confucius, whose life has been well documented and whose family has flourished in an unbroken line down to the present day (*above*).

Although scholars disagree widely on Lao Tzu, tradition relates that he was born in 604 B.C. on a farm in Honan province. (The name Lao Tzu means literally "Old Boy" or "The Eldest," hence "Old Master.") Perhaps the one historic fact about him is that he held the post of curator of the imperial archives at the court of Chou, where he became renowned as a scholar and sage. Becoming disgusted with the disorder of the Chou Dynasty, Lao Tzu eventually resigned his post. Then, according to legend, he decided after a period of meditation to flee society and journey into the unknown west. Riding in a cart drawn by two black oxen, he came to a final outpost where the gatekeeper recognized him and begged him to stay long enough to write down the main tenets of his philosophy. Lao Tzu agreed and in a few days composed the *Tao Tê Ching*, the noble masterwork that has been called the bible of Taoism. He then vanished over the mountain pass, never to be seen again.

Confucius was born into a poor but aristocratic family in Shantung province in 551 B.C. His family name was K'ung—"Confucius" being a Latinization by Jesuit missionaries of K'ung Fu-tzu, *i.e.*, "Grand Master Kung." As a youth he became absorbed in the history, poetry and music of ancient China. Although he aspired to active statesmanship and for many years wandered from state to state offering his services, most of his life was spent as a teacher. Insisting that he was "a transmitter, not a creator," Confucius wrote little himself, although most scholars believe that he did write one of China's classics, *Annals of Spring and Autumn*. But from his utterances, lovingly recorded by his disciples, emerged the towering system of ethics by which China has subsequently lived. In the summer of 479 B.C. he fell ill and went to his bedchamber, muttering, "The great mountain must fall. The strong timber is broken. The wise man fades as does the plant." A week later he died.

THE TEACHER CONFUCIUS, depicted in a painting on silk, is shown here seated on a dais, lecturing his disciples. Traditionally he had 3,000 pupils. The painting, reproduced from an album among the Chinese national treasures now in Formosa, illustrates the first of the 18 chapters of the *Classic of Filial Piety*, the basic scripture of Confucian ethics, which states: "The duty of children to their parents is the fountain whence all other virtues spring."

CONFUCIAN VIRTUES are delineated in another painting from the *Classic*. The well-bred gentlemen in the foreground exemplify the quality of "respectful deference." The group under the tree demonstrates how people can live harmoniously if they have been educated in music and dance. The peasant walking away from sleeping figure (*right*) illustrates the virtue of "knowing what is wrong and forbidden"—in this case, apparently, napping in midday.

CONFUCIANISM From its ethics a cult evolved

Although Confucius never envisaged himself as the founder of a faith, the school of thought developed by his disciples in time acquired the aspects of a religious cult. Under successive dynasties state worship was accorded to Confucius—not as a god, but as a sage and as an ideal.

The first sign that he had become an object of veneration came in 195 B.C. when the Emperor Kao Tsu, founder of the Han Dynasty, visited his tomb and offered sacrifices. In 136 B.C. the Emperor Wu made Confucianism the basic discipline for the training of government officials. From that time onward emperor after emperor sought to outdo his predecessors in honoring Confucius' name. In 59 A.D. sacrifices were ordered for him in all urban schools. During the Seventh and Eighth Centuries temples were erected in every prefecture of the empire as shrines to him and his principal disciples. Twice a year the emperor would visit the great temple in Peking (*right, above*) and after kowtowing would apostrophize the sage: "Great art thou, O thou of perfect wisdom. Full is thy virtue, thy doctrine complete. Mortals have never known thy equal. All kings honor thee. Thine ordinances and laws have come down to us in glory. Filled with awe we clash our cymbals and strike our bells."

TEMPLE OF CONFUCIUS in Peking was begun in the 13th Century and augmented in later years. The arch opens into a unit called the Hall of Classics containing 300 stone tablets on which are inscribed the Confucian classics.

BIRTHDAY OF CONFUCIUS, his 2,505th, is celebrated at Sung Kyun Kwan Academy in Seoul, Korea. The elaborate ceremonies, held Aug. 27, 1954, included eulogies, offerings and dances by red-robed Korean students.

As the centuries passed, posthumous titles were heaped on Confucius. He was named progressively Duke, Prince, Venerable Sage of Former Times and Sacred Teacher of Antiquity. He was raised to the rank of the gods and awarded the same sacrifices as the sun and the moon. Finally, in 1906, the last Manchu emperor elevated him to a position beside Heaven and Earth, the highest objects of worship.

Although the cult of Confucianism languished after the Empire, the Nationalist government in 1934 proclaimed Confucius' birthday a holiday, still observed by free Chinese and others who venerate the sage.

TABLET OF CONFUCIUS reposes within the Hall of Great Perfection in the Peking temple. In accordance with tradition there are no statues or images of the sage in Confucian temples, only tablets inscribed with his name.

TAOISM

Its credo was lost
in myths and magic

Just as Confucianism evolved from a school of thought into a cult, so in time Taoism became overlaid with a farrago of occultism and magic. It developed a mythology of its own in which the hereafter sometimes became a kind of wonderland ruled by a fairy queen and peopled with happy immortals—as shown in the painting of the mountain heaven at right. The uneducated Chinese could find little solace in Lao Tzu's mystic philosophy. But there were two passages in the *Tao Tê Ching* that touched them deeply: "He who contains within himself the richness of Tao's virtue is like a babe. No poisonous insects sting him. Nor fierce beasts seize. Nor birds of prey strike him . . . . He who attains Tao is everlasting. Though his body may decay, he never perishes." The Chinese, more than any other people, have looked forward to old age—the time of ease envisaged by Confucianism—and sought ways of prolonging earthly existence. In time the hope of attaining Tao became the hope of attaining immortality on this earth.

Many Taoist teachers drifted away from Lao Tzu's original thought. Over and above their traditional functions, they began to claim supernatural powers: they could foretell the future, engender tempests, and prolong life through breathing exercises and diets of powdered dragon bones, moonbeams and mother of pearl. Driven by the desire for immortality, people left their homes and headed for lonely mountain retreats, there to spiritualize themselves through ascetic practices. Fields remained unplowed and business came to a halt because their owners were away on pilgrimages or engaged in spiritual disciplines.

During the First Century A.D. the popularity of Taoism was threatened by the official

importation from India of Buddhism, which swept across the country winning innumerable converts. In response to this challenge Taoism transformed itself into a formal religion. In the west a Taoist named Chang Ling (who supposedly had discovered the pill of immortality) founded a religious order which by the end of the Second Century had grown into a semiclerical state with organized worship, monasteries, fixed tributes and a priesthood.

In some matters, the new Taoism borrowed heavily from Buddhism; in others it developed its own ideas and practices. For example, although the concept of paradise was foreign to the Chinese, they quickly elaborated on it; where the Buddhists had thirty-three different kinds of heaven, the Taoists came up with eighty-one. Not only did they populate their heavens with many of the old gods of folk religion e.g., the God of Wealth, the Kitchen God, the City God, nature gods, but they also admitted some Mahayana Buddhist deities and created a great number of new ones. They dedicated gods to stars, metals, occupations, ancient heroes, epidemics, mythical animals and even such surprising activities as robbery and drunkenness. The supreme god of the Taoist pantheon, the fabled Jade Emperor, was allegedly invented in 1012 A.D. by the Emperor Chên Tsung who, for political reasons, needed a revelation from heaven.

As the centuries followed, Taoism slowly descended to gloomy levels of idolatry and superstition. Loaded down with an incubus of sorcery, fortune-telling, charm-selling and alchemy, it became more akin to voodooism than to the exalted philosophy of Lao Tzu. Worship became magic and its object the attainment of earthy blessings. Its priests were hired employes who performed rituals without any conception of spiritual leadership. Long before the end of the 19th Century, as a result of the spread of scientific awareness, Taoism was dying. The heritage of Lao Tzu was thus not Taoism, but his concept of Tao, whence come enlightenment and inner joy.

'RECEPTION OF THE IMMORTALS AT THE COURT OF HSI WANG MU'

In the cosmology of Taoism there evolved many different heavens where the spiritually minded journeyed after death and thereafter lived together in unending joy and happiness. Among the most important and enjoyable of these were the Three Isles of the Blessed, situated somewhere in the Eastern Sea; and Western Heaven, situated in the Kunlun Mountains of Turkestan and ruled by the Western Queen Mother, Hsi Wang Mu. The painting above shows the Western Queen Mother receiving various *hsien*, or immortals. She appears at the top of the picture, seated on her throne and about to receive a peach, symbol of immortality, from a monkey. Below her at left appear the best known and best loved characters in Taoist mythology: the so-called Eight Immortals, a varied group of personages, some of them historical, representing all types of humanity, who attained immortality through various acts of piety, charity or heroism. The five old men at lower right possibly symbolize the five elements, metal, wood, water, fire and earth. The blue animal at lower left is a lion-dog, a familiar figure borrowed from Buddhism. Directly to its left is a chi-lin, a gentle, one-horned beast, symbolizing happiness and good omens. Behind the chi-lin stands a deer, a symbol of official emolument. In the middle of the picture three female *hsien* talk together inside a cave, while to the left eight others disembark from a boat on the shore of Green Jade Lake.

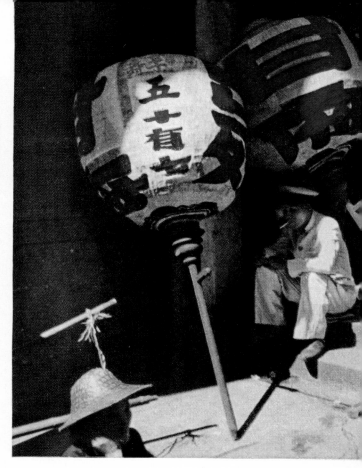

PAPER LANTERNS bearing the name of the deceased, his age, and perhaps some comment, are often borne at the head of funeral processions.

FUNERAL PROCESSION in Tainan, Formosa slowly escorts the deceased from his home to the graveyard. In the foreground Taoist priests ride in pedicabs. Behind them come floral wreaths, a Western innovation which has entered Chinese funerals. The coffin is carried by 32 pallbearers.

ANCESTORS To honor
them is heart of Chinese faith

Centuries before Confucius, in the dawn of Eastern culture, a reverence for the progenitors of the race formed the heart and core of Chinese religious life. Ancestral shrines existed as early as the Shang Dynasty (1776–1122 B.C.), and many of the rituals for mourning and burial that have become part of Confucian and Taoist tradition were prescribed in the ancient classics. The conviction that no person is an isolated entity but an indispensable link in an endless chain of humanity is the binding force underlying the solidarity of the Chinese family.

When the Chinese use the word family, they do not confine the term to those who live under a single roof, or even to all living kindred; they also include their forebears whom they regard as members of the living social group, present and proprietary, vitally concerned with the family heritage. No man's home or property, not even his body, is his exclusive possession, but belongs to his ancestors as well. The fortunes of the living and the dead, moreover, are inextricably intertwined. When an individual dies, he may become—and hopes to become—a good spirit, beneficent and helpful to his heirs; but it is also possible that he may join the army of demons. What fate befalls him is determined not only by his own past actions and consequent moral status, but by the solicitude with which his descendants honor his memory.

It is a practical mistake, therefore, as well as a sin, not to insure that all proprieties are observed—that the correct mourning cloth is worn (*left*), an adequate procession arranged (*above*) and food offerings regularly set forth (*right*). The more elaborate the funeral ceremonies and the more frequent the subsequent memorial rites, it is popularly believed, the better the prospect that the departed will become a happy and therefore a friendly spirit. "To serve those now dead as if they were living," Confucius said, "is the highest achievement of true filial piety."

BESIDE THE OPEN GRAVE two hooded wives (some Chinese still practice polygamy) and one child, all in coarse mourning cloth, pay final respects. The red objects they hold are dummy lanterns to light the spirit's way home.

FOOD AND MONEY for the spirits are offered by Chinese in a Malayan graveyard. They are observing the spring festival, which is a time for honoring ancestors by cleaning graves, repainting headstones and weeding plots.

TRADITIONAL PAPER DRAGON is exhibited by Chinese-American girls in Seattle. In Chinese mythology the dragon personifies the benign powers of nature, productive of rain and lush harvests, prosperity and peace. Dragon worship is associated with several festivals but chiefly with the Chinese New Year when, to the accompaniment of drums and firecrackers, its image is carried through streets. Where it passes, evil spirits and misfortune are expunged.

CONFUCIUS AND MARX

by LIN YUTANG

It is of the essence of life that living in the present, we must think of the present. Only through the vistas of history can man, by a foreshortening process of the mind, see patterns moving across the decades, even centuries. Back in 1928–29 Russian proletarian novels were popular reading among the youth of China. Twenty years later a Communist state came into being in the land of Confucius.

Long before the coming of the Communist regime, Confucianism underwent a period of decline capped by a wave of intellectual radicalism which started in 1919. A definite feeling was in the air that China must get on and change—and forget the past, or perish. The generation which grew up in the first years of the republic did not so much attack or oppose Confucianism as they ridiculed and ignored it. Confucius was also unfortunate in his allies—the warlords who were naturally supporters of old-fashioned morality. Sooner or later, there was bound to be a change and a better recognition of Confucian humanism and its appraisal of human nature and social values. As the years went by, the young radicals matured; the professors began to "see something" in Confucianism after all. Throughout the war years, a scholar at Tsing Hua University in Peking, Professor Fung Yu-lan, was laboring over a magnum opus, a new interpretation of Neo-Confucianism. Then his work was frustrated by political events under the new Communist regime. Professor Fung found it convenient to denounce the results of his lifetime of study, recant his beliefs, and publicly thank the "masses for opening [his] eyes." Whatever independent thinking there was came to a stop by the end of 1952. Both Confucian and Taoist ideas are now officially regarded as "poison," just as Christianity is regarded as dope for the poor. Confucian books are not so much *verboten* as ignored. All ancient books are supposed to contain "poison." History books are systematically rewritten. Communist workers are replacing village elders. An elder or anyone else respected by the village community is a potential leader of the opposition and as such is liquidated, no matter how innocent the partisans know him to be.

Westerners who have lived in China and come to know the Chinese people at first hand have found it hard to believe that a nation characterized by common sense, moderation and a homely geniality of living can be transformed into a band of zealots and fanatic followers of Marx. The question may be asked: how vital are Confucian ideas of humanism and Taoist ideas of *laissez faire* in modern Chinese society, and how will the Chinese philosophic temper reassert itself? The question should actually be divided into two: one, can there be a compromise between the ideology of Karl Marx and the precepts of Confucius? And two, how valid are Confucian and Taoist teachings today?

It is a truism to say that Confucianism, with its family system, its hard-boiled sense that charity must begin at home, its insistence on proper social relationships, has set the tone for Chinese society for 2,500 years. In every aspect of social life—filial piety, respect for scholars, respect for age, selection of talents for leadership—Chinese society bears the stamp of Confucius.

These positive aspects of Chinese life are offset by another important stream of negative characteristics—a certain nonchalant attitude of calm contentment and devil-may-care old roguery—in which we can recognize the influence of Taoism. The combination of the positive, responsible attitude when a Chinese gentleman bears the burden of the world on his shoulders, and the attitude of the old rogue on the open road, when the same person is willing to let the world take care of itself in a mood of poetic irresponsibility and truly religious trust in Tao —this peculiar mixture has produced the characteristic mores of the Chinese people. I personally think the second attitude is priceless.

However, every nation has its shortcomings, and if all the iniquities of the Chinese people are put upon Confucius' shoulders, the sins of Confucius are many. We tend to ascribe the character of a nation, necessarily complex, to one simple source. Anyway, Confucius, or the Chinese nation, forgot to develop something akin to habeas corpus, or anything remotely comparable to it. Personally I think that one writ of habeas corpus is worth more than the Confucian *Analects*.

It must be remembered, however, that Confucius was primarily a moral and social philosopher, and only secondarily a political theorist. In a time of chaos, he believed the solution was moral and social, rather than political. That idea is as good as gold. He aimed at political peace by first establishing a social order based on proper respect for human relationships. When men have been cultivated and reformed from within and live out their lives as good fathers, good brothers and good husbands, then political order will follow of its own accord. Somewhat idealistic, yes—but all great teachers are.

The first question about possible compromise between the Confucian temper and the Communist temper must be answered in the negative. Madame Sun Yat-sen expressed the Communist orthodox point of view best when she said, "Confucian teachings are feudalistic and autocratic from beginning to end. We must realize how deeply Confucian influences have been imbedded in our art, literature, social sciences and morals. We must make great efforts to uproot Confucian ideas from every nook and corner of our life and thoughts." Such great efforts are being made. Of the more than 15,000 books published by the Commercial Press in Chinese, only 1,224 titles remained on the selling list by the end of 1952. The rest were destroyed. Of the more than 12,000 titles published by Chung Hwa Book Company, some 1,500 remained.

In every country, society lives by a set of moral values. In Christian countries, these virtues—such as honesty, kindness, justice and the value of the individual—are represented by the Christian code. In China, they happen to be represented by Confucianism. Thus Communism has found it necessary to strike at the core of Confucian teachings by breaking up family loyalty. The denunciation of their parents by boys and girls of 13 and 14 has been systematically encouraged. And it is not difficult to teach the young to disobey parents.

The second question is: given normal freedom of thought, how valid are Confucian and Taoist teachings today? Generally, moral teachers outlast politicians. Mahatma Gandhi will outlast Jawaharlal Nehru; Confucius and Lao Tzu will outlast Mao Tse-tung. The Confucian golden rule must survive. As for the witticisms of Lao Tzu, his depth, his brilliance and his profound iconoclasm will always recommend themselves to the searching, questioning human mind. His teachings on gentleness and humility will always stand as the Sermon on the Mount will always stand, irrespective of political persecutions.

Can the Chinese people, as distinguished from their ideological rulers, accept the Communist negation of virtually all their traditional ways and beliefs? As I write, they have had to. Can they accept the more rigorous, severe totalitarian pattern of life geared to production for the state? The answer is again, they have had to.

But thoughts and ideas are somewhat like seeds. They have a way of lying dormant underground until a more favorable climate brings them again to life. As to when or how this will happen and when or how the Chinese people will return openly to Confucian ideals and the tolerance of Lao Tzu, that is a matter of international politics. But, as a Chinese, I hope that the triumph will come within my lifetime.

COMMUNIST PORTAL, the Gate of Heavenly Peace in Peking, was built during the Ming Dynasty of the 15th Century and was formerly used for the reading of Imperial decrees. The marble bridges (*foreground*) span a moat and beyond lies the Forbidden City. In bad repair for years, gate was renovated in 1952 by Mao Tse-tung, whose portrait hangs in the center between signs exalting the People's Republic. Mao uses the Gate to review May Day parades.

A PAPER HOUSE IS BURNED, along with other paper objects, to release a soul from purgatory. Centuries ago the Chinese gave up making actual sacrifices and substituted paper simulacra. The ceremony shown here, which took place in Singapore, is based on the idea that a spirit wanders in purgatory for two years after death and must be assisted before it can enter heaven. A son of the dead man watches the fire to make sure everything burns.

CHINESE PRECEPTS

Central to the teachings of Confucius is the doctrine that moral order is necessary to the achievement of political order, that until men can achieve moral harmony within themselves they can never obtain political or social harmony. The heart of Confucius' teachings is found in the Analects, *the Confucian bible, which is quoted on pages 91–95. The sacred texts of Taoism begin on page 96.*

The Analects *is a collection of short ethical maxims and proverbs attributed to or concerning Confucius. The work contains the essence of everything that Confucius did, said and taught. No one editor assembled the sayings; the Master's followers and disciples arranged them in a rather informal order in twenty books during the decades and centuries following his death in 479 B.C. As the various maxims throughout the* Analects *are not arranged in any sequence of ideas or subjects, the following selections have been regrouped for the reader's convenience without specific references to traditional arrangements.*

The Analects *includes a good deal of interesting and relevant information on Confucius' own life. He tried to practice what he preached on everything from omens to being a good sport. He fished with a line but not with a net, which he thought unfair to the fish; when fowling, he did not aim at a roosting bird. He hoped a dragon-horse would bring him the "river chart"—a magic arrangement of numbers—out of the Yellow River or that the sacred phoenix would come to him; when neither event happened, he decided Heaven did not intend him to become a Sage. But Confucius was comforted whenever he dreamed of the half-legendary Duke of Chou, an earlier Sage.*

THE LIFE OF CONFUCIUS

THE Master said, "I can claim that at Court I have duly served the Duke and his officers; at home, my father and elder brother. As regards matters of mourning, I am conscious of no neglect, nor have I ever been overcome with wine. Concerning these things, at any rate, my mind is quite at rest. As to being a Sage or even a Good Man, far be it from me to make any such claim. As for unwearying effort to learn and unflagging patience in teaching others, those are merits that I do not hesitate to claim. A Sage I cannot hope ever to meet; the most I can hope for is to meet a true gentleman. . . . A faultless man I cannot hope ever to meet; the most I can hope for is to meet a man of fixed principles. Yet where all around I see Nothing pretending to be Something and Emptiness pretending to be Fullness and Penury pretending to be Affluence, even a man of fixed principles will be hard to find."

The Master said, "At fifteen, I had set my heart upon learning. At thirty, I had formed my character. At forty, I no longer suffered from perplexities. At fifty, I knew what was the mandate of Heaven. At sixty, I heard it with docile ear. At seventy, I could follow the dictates of my own heart for what I desired no longer overstepped the boundaries of right." The Master said,

"Double joy" character denotes conjugal bliss

"Give me a few more years, so that I may have spent a whole fifty in study, and I believe that after all I should be fairly free from error."

The Grand Minister asked Tzu-kung, saying, "Is your Master a Sage? If so, how comes it that he has so many practical accomplishments?" Tzu-kung said, "Heaven certainly intended him to become a Sage; it is also true that he has many accomplishments." When the Master heard of it, he said, "The Grand Minister is quite right about me. When I was young, I was in humble circumstances; that is why I have many practical accomplishments in regard to simple, everyday matters."

The Duke of She asked Tzu-lu about Confucius. Tzu-lu did not reply. The Master said, "Why did you not say, 'This is the character of the man: he is so intent upon making efforts to learn that he forgets his hunger, and is so happy in doing so that he forgets the bitterness of his lot and does not realize that old age is at hand.' "

WHEN the Master went to see Nan-tzu [the wicked concubine of Duke Ling of Wei], Tzu-lu was not pleased. Whereupon the Master made a solemn declaration concerning his visit, saying, "Whatsoever I have done amiss, may Heaven avert it, may Heaven avert it!"

The Master said, "I have transmitted what was taught to me without making up anything of my own. I have been faithful to and loved the Ancients. . . . I have listened in silence and noted what was said; I have never grown tired of learning nor wearied of teaching others what I have learnt. These at least are merits which I can confidently claim."

The Master said, "Do I regard myself as a possessor of wisdom? Far from it. But if even a simple peasant comes in all sincerity and asks me a question, I am ready to thrash the matter out, with all its pros and cons, to the very end."

The Master said, "From the very poorest upwards—beginning even with the man who could bring no better present than a bundle of dried meat—none has ever come to me without receiving instruction. Only one who bursts with eagerness do I instruct; only one who bubbles with excitement do I enlighten. If I hold up one corner and a man cannot come back to me with the other three, I do not continue the lesson."

The Master took four subjects for his teaching: culture, conduct of affairs, loyalty to superiors and honesty or good faith. The Master's manner was affable yet firm, commanding but not harsh, polite but easy. There were four things that the Master eschewed: he took nothing for granted; he was never overpositive, never obstinate, never egotistic.

Ju Pei wanted to see the Master, who excused himself on ground of ill-health. But when the man who had brought the message was going out through the door, the Master took up his zither and began to sing, taking good care that the messenger should hear.

Tsai Yu used to sleep during the day. The Master said, "Rotten wood cannot be carved, nor a wall of dried dung be troweled. What use is there in my scolding him any more? There was a time when I merely listened attentively to what people said, and I took it for granted that they would carry out their words. Now I am obliged not only to give ear to what they say, but to keep an eye on what they do. It was my dealings with Tsai Yu that brought about the change."

Yuan Jang sat waiting for the Master in a sprawling position [he ought to have been standing and only sat down when specifically told to do so]. The Master said, "Those who, when young, show no respect to their elders, achieve nothing worth mentioning when they grow up. And merely to live on, getting older and older, is to be a useless pest." And he struck him across the shins with his stick.

Chi K'ang-tzu [a minister of state] was troubled by burglars. He asked what he should do. The Master replied, saying, "If only you were free from desire, they would not steal even if you paid them to."

The Master said, "There may well be those who can do without knowledge, but I for my part am certainly not one of them. To hear much, pick out what is good and follow it, to see much and take due note of it (as I do), is the lower of the two kinds of knowledge. I for my part am not one of those who have innate knowledge [which is the higher sort]. I am simply one of those who love the past and who is diligent in investigating it. Even when walking in a party of no more than three, I can always be certain of learning from those I am with. There will be good qualities that I can select for imitation and bad ones that will teach me what requires correction in myself."

The occasions upon which the Master used correct pronunciation [and not the Lu dialect he used in daily life] were when reciting the *Book of Songs* or the *Book of History* and when practicing ritual acts. At all such times he used the correct pronunciation. The rites to which the Master gave the greatest attention were those connected with purification before sacrifice, with war and with sickness.

The Master said, "Heaven begat the power that is in me. What have I to fear from such a one as Huan T'ui?" [A minister of war who attempted to have Confucius assassinated.]

The Master said, "I have never seen anyone whose desire to build up his moral power was as strong as his love of beauty."

When, in the Master's presence, anyone sang a song that he liked, he did not join in at once, but asked for it to be repeated and then joined in.

Yen Hui said with a deep sigh, "The more I strain my gaze up toward the Master's moral character, the higher it soars. The deeper I bore down into it, the harder it becomes. I see it in front, but suddenly it is behind. Step by step the Master skillfully lures one on. He has broadened me with culture, restrained me with ritual. Even if I wanted to stop, I could not. Just when I feel that I have exhausted every resource, something seems to rise up, standing out sharp and clear. Yet though I long to pursue it, I can find no way of getting to it at all."

TZU-CH'IN questioned Po Yu [Confucius' son], saying, "As his son, you must after all surely have heard something different from what the rest of us hear." Po Yu replied, saying, "No. Once when he was standing alone, and I was hurrying past him across the courtyard, he said, 'Have you studied the *Songs*?' I replied, saying, 'No.' He said, 'If you do not study the *Songs*, you will find yourself at a loss in conversation.' So I retired and studied the *Songs*. Another day he was again standing alone, and as I hurried across the courtyard, he said, 'Have you studied the rituals?' I replied, saying, 'No.' He said, 'If you do not study the rituals, you will find yourself at a loss how to take your stand [on public occasions].' So I retired and studied the rituals. These two things I heard from him." Tzu-ch'in came away delighted, saying, "I asked about one point, but got information about three. I learnt about the *Songs*, about the rituals, and also learnt that a gentleman keeps his son at a distance."

The Master said, "Little ones, why is it that none of you study the *Songs*? For the *Songs* will help you to incite people's

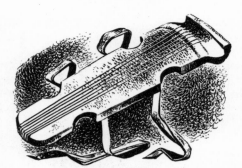

Long zither is like the one Confucius used to play

emotions, to observe their feelings, to keep company and to express your grievances. They may be used at home in the service of one's father; abroad, in the service of one's prince. Moreover, they will widen your acquaintance with the names of birds, beasts, plants and trees."

When the Master was very ill, Tzu-lu caused some of the disciples to get themselves up as official retainers [such as he would have been entitled to, had he held office]. Coming to himself for a short while, the Master said, "How like Tzu-lu to go in for this sort of imposture! In pretending to have retainers when I have none, whom do I deceive? Do I deceive Heaven? Not only would I far rather die in the arms of you disciples than in the arms of retainers, but also as regards my funeral—even if I am not accorded a State Burial, it is not as though I were dying by the roadside."

When the Master was very ill, Tzu-lu asked leave to perform the Rite of Expiation. The Master said, "Is there such a thing?" Tzu-lu answered, saying, "There is. In one of the Dirges it says, 'We performed rites of expiation for you, calling upon the sky-spirits above and the earth-spirits below!'" The Master said, "My expiation began long ago!"

In common with many early Chinese, Confucius seems to have attributed a potent influence to ritual. He did not pretend to know its full meaning; when asked for an explanation of the Ancestral Sacrifice, he said, "I do not know. Anyone who knew the explanation could deal with all things under Heaven as easily as I lay this here," and put his finger on the palm of his hand. But he considered ritual vitally important, insisting that if you try to keep the people of a country orderly by chastisements, they will flee; whereas if you "keep order among them by ritual, they will keep their self-respect and come to you of their own accord."

RITUAL AND SACRIFICE

THE Master said, "High office filled by men of narrow views, ritual performed without reverence, the forms of mourning observed without grief—these are things I cannot bear to see!" The Master said of the Wei grandee Ching, "He dwelt as a man should dwell in his house. When things began to prosper with him, he said, 'Now the household rites will begin to be a little more suitable.' When he was better off still, he said, 'Now they will be fairly complete.' When he was really rich, he said, 'Now I shall be able to make them quite beautiful.' "

The Master said, "In Yu [a sage ruler who quelled a flood that was devastating the country] I can find no semblance of a flaw. Abstemious in his own food and drink, he displayed the utmost devotion in his offerings to spirits and divinities. Content with the plainest clothes for common wear, he saw to it that his sacrificial apron and ceremonial headdress were of the utmost magnificence. His place of habitation was of the humblest, and all his energy went into draining and ditching. In him I can find no semblance of a flaw."

Lin Fang asked for some principles in connection with ritual. The Master said, "A very big question. In ritual at large, it is a safe rule always to be too sparing rather than too lavish; and in the particular case of mourning-rites, they should be dictated by grief rather than fear." Asked about the meaning of the saying, "Better pay court to the Stove than pay court to the Shrine," The Master said, "It is not true. He who has put himself in wrong with Heaven has no means of expiation left."

The Master said, "Courtesy not bounded by the prescriptions of ritual becomes tiresome. Caution not bounded by the prescriptions of ritual becomes timidity, daring becomes turbulence, inflexibility not bounded by ritual becomes harshness."

THE INDIVIDUAL PATH

TZU-KUNG asked, saying, "Is there any single saying that one can act upon all day and every day?" The Master said, "Yes, it is the saying about altruism—'Never do to others what you would not like them to do to you.' "

The Master said, "Who expects to be able to go out of a house except by the door? How is it, then, that no one follows this Way of ours? Set your heart upon the Way, support yourself by its power, lean upon Goodness, seek distraction in the arts. To prefer the Way is better than only to know it. To delight in it is better than merely to prefer it."

The Master said, "When the Way prevails in the land, be bold in speech and bold in action. When the Way does not prevail, be bold in action but conciliatory in speech."

The Master said, "Be of unwavering good faith, love learning; if attacked, be ready to die for the good Way. Do not enter a State that pursues dangerous courses, nor stay in one where the people have rebelled. When the Way prevails under Heaven, then show yourself; when it does not prevail, then hide. When The Way prevails in your own land, count it a disgrace to be needy and obscure; when the Way does not prevail in your land, then count it a disgrace to be rich and honored."

The Master said, "He who will not worry about what is far off will soon find something worse than worry close at hand. Learn as if you were following someone whom you could not catch up with, as though it were someone you were frightened of losing. One who will study for three years without thought of reward would be hard indeed to find."

The Master said, "If a man has gifts as wonderful as the Duke of Chou's, yet is arrogant and mean, the rest is of no account."

The Master said, "How can he be said truly to love, who exacts no effort from the objects of his love . . . [or] to be truly loyal, who refrains from admonishing the object of his loyalty?"

The Master said, "Just as lavishness leads easily to presumption, so does frugality to meanness. But meanness is a far less serious fault than presumption."

The Master said, "You may rob the Three Armies of their commander-in-chief, but you cannot deprive the humblest peasant of his opinion."

The Master said, "He that is really Good can never be unhappy. He that is really wise can never be perplexed. He that is really brave is never afraid."

Tzu-lu said, "Is courage to be prized by a gentleman?" The Master said, "A gentleman gives the first place to Right. If a gentleman has courage but neglects Right, he becomes turbulent. If a small man has courage but neglects Right, he becomes a thief."

The Master said, "The gentleman can influence those who are above him; the small man can only influence those who are below him. The common people can be made to follow the Way; they cannot be made to understand it. If you desire what is good, the people will at once be good. The essence of the gentleman is that of wind; the essence of small people is that of grass. And when a wind passes over the grass, it cannot choose but bend."

The Master said, "There are three things that a gentleman fears: he fears the will of Heaven, he fears great men, he fears the words of the Divine Sages. The small man does not know the will of Heaven and so does not fear it. He treats great men with contempt, and he scoffs at the words of the Divine Sages. A gentleman

The benevolent dragon is an omen of spring

in his dealings with the world has neither enmities nor affections, but wherever he sees Right, he ranges himself beside it. He does not mind not being in office; all he minds about is whether he has qualities that entitle him to office. He does not mind failing to get recognition; he is too busy doing the things that entitle him to recognition."

The Master said, "While a man's father is alive, you can only see his intentions; it is when his father dies that you discover whether or not he is capable of carrying them out. If, for the whole three years of mourning, he manages to carry on exactly as in his father's day, then he is a good son indeed."

GOODNESS

THE Master said, "It is Goodness that gives to a neighborhood its beauty. One who is free to choose, yet does not prefer to dwell among the Good—how can he be accorded the name of wise? Is Goodness indeed so far away? If we really wanted Goodness, we should find that it was at our very side. Imperturbable, resolute, tree-like, slow to speak—such a one is near to Goodness. Neither the scholar who has truly the heart of a scholar nor the man of good stock who has the qualities that belong to good stock, will ever seek life at the expense of Goodness, and it may be that he has to give his life in order to achieve Goodness. The Good man does not grieve that other people do not recognize his merits. His only anxiety is lest he should fail to recognize theirs.

"Wealth and rank are what every man desires, but if they can only be retained to the detriment of the Way he professes, he must relinquish them. Poverty and obscurity are what every man detests, but if they can only be avoided to the detriment of the Way he professes, he must accept them. The gentleman who ever parts company with Goodness does not fulfill that name. Never for a moment does a gentleman quit the way of Goodness. He is never so harried but that he cleaves to this; never so tottering but that he cleaves to this."

Yen Hui asked about Goodness. The Master said, "He who can himself submit to ritual is Good. If a ruler could for one day himself submit to ritual, everyone under Heaven would respond to his Goodness. For Goodness is something that must have its source in the ruler himself; it cannot be got from others." Yen Hui said, "I beg to ask for the more detailed items of this submission to ritual." The Master said, "To look at nothing in defiance of ritual, to listen to nothing in defiance of ritual, to speak of nothing in defiance of ritual, never to stir hand or foot in defiance of ritual." Yen Hui said, "I know that I am not clever, but this is a saying that, with your permission, I shall try to put into practice."

Chung-kung asked about Goodness. The Master said, "Behave when away from home as though you were in the presence of an important guest. Deal with the common people as if you were officiating at an important sacrifice. Never do to others what you would not like them to do to you. Then there will be no feelings of opposition to you, whether it is the affairs of a State you are handling, or the affairs of a family." Chung-kung said, "I know I am not clever, but this is a saying that, with your permission, I shall try to put into practice."

Ssu-ma Niu asked about Goodness. The Master said, "The Good man is chary of speech." Ssu-ma Niu said, "So that is what is meant by

Goodness—to be chary of speech?" The Master said, "Seeing that the doing of it is so difficult, how can one be otherwise than chary of talking about it?"

Tzu-kung said, "If a ruler not only conferred wide benefits upon the common people, but also compassed the salvation of the whole State, what would you say of him? Surely, you would call him Good?" The Master said, "It would no longer be a matter of 'Good.' He would without doubt be a Sage. Even Yao and Shun [both model rulers] could hardly attain it. As for Goodness—you yourself desire to establish your character; then help others to establish their character. You want to turn your own merits to account; then help others to turn theirs to account—in fact, the ability to take one's own feelings as a guide—that is the way to attain Goodness."

Numerous passages in the Analects *compare and contrast Confucius' various disciples. In one section the Master asks four of his followers what employment they would really like to have. Three indirectly ask for positions of influence and authority in kingdoms, one even doing so by a device of seeming humility: he merely seeks to be an assistant priest—but at a ceremony where even feudal princes would rank below him while he served in that capacity. The fourth disciple simply asks to take part in a quiet celebration of spring, and Confucius sides with him.*

INNER LONGINGS

ONCE, when Tzu-lu, Tseng Hsi, Jan Ch'iu and Kung-hsi Hua were seated in attendance upon the Master, he said, "You consider me as a somewhat older man than yourselves. Forget for a moment that I am so. At present you are out of office and feel that your merits are not recognized. Now supposing someone were to recognize your merits, what employment would you choose?" Tzu-lu promptly and confidently replied, "Give me a country of a thousand war chariots, hemmed in by powerful enemies, or even invaded by hostile armies, with drought and famine to boot; in the space of three years, I could endow the people with courage and teach them in what direction right conduct lies."

The Master smiled at him. "What about you, Ch'iu?" he said. Ch'iu replied, saying, "Give me a domain of sixty to seventy or, say, fifty to sixty leagues, and in the space of three years, I could bring it about that the common people should lack for nothing. But as to rites and music, I should have to leave them to a real gentleman."

"What about you, Ch'ih?" Kung-hsi answered him, saying, "I do not say that I could do this, but I should like at any rate to be trained for it. In ceremonies performed at the Ancestral Temple or at a conference or general gathering of the feudal princes I should like, clad in the Straight Gown and Emblematic Cap, to play the part of junior assistant."

"Tseng Hsi, what about you?" The notes of the zither Tseng was softly fingering died away; he put it down, rose and replied, saying, "I fear my words will not be so well chosen as those of the other three." The Master said, "What harm is there in that? All that matters is that each should name his desire."

Tseng Hsi said, "At the end of spring, when the making of the spring clothes has been completed, to go with five or six newly capped youths and six or seven uncapped boys, bathe in the river, take the air at the Rain Dance altars, and then go home singing." The Master heaved a deep sigh and said, "I am with Tseng."

When the three others went away, Tseng Hsi remained behind and said, "What about the sayings of those three people?" The

Master said, "After all, it was agreed that each should tell his wish and that is just what they did."

Tseng said, "Why did you smile at Tzu-lu?"

The Master said, "Because it is upon observance of ritual that the governance of a State depends, and his words were lacking in the virtue of ceding to others. That is why I smiled at him."

"I suppose you were contrasting him with Ch'iu who, by using the word 'domain,' did not mean kingdom?"

"Where have you ever seen 'a domain of sixty to seventy or fifty to sixty leagues' that was not a kingdom?"

"I suppose, then, you were contrasting him with Ch'ih, who was certainly not asking for a kingdom?"

"The business of the Ancestral Temple and such things as conferences and general gatherings can only be undertaken by feudal princes. But if Ch'ih were taking a minor part, what prince is there who is capable of playing a major one?"

One of the most fervently preached of Confucius' doctrines was government by example. He believed strongly in an intellectual upper class—but unless it was also a moral upper class, it would inevitably fail. He could be very rude about bad rulers; when asked about one ruling group of his day, Confucius snapped, "Oh, those are rice bags!" i.e., good only for filling themselves with rice. But a good ruler, constantly careful of his conduct, can have a tremendous influence over his country, just as lesser men can set a proper standard for their entire circle of colleagues.

GOVERNMENT

DUKE TING asked if there were any one phrase that sufficed to save a country. The Master replied, saying, "No phrase could ever be like that. But here is one that comes near to it. There is a saying among men: 'It is hard to be a prince and not easy to be a minister.' A ruler who really understood that it was 'hard to be a prince' would have come fairly near to saving his country by a single phrase."

Duke Ting said, "Is there any one phrase that could ruin a country?" The Master said, "No phrase could ruin a country." The Master said, "No phrase could ever be like that. But here is one that comes near to it. There is a saying among men: 'What pleasure is there in being a prince, unless one can say

Ceremonial burial vessel holds wine for deceased

whatever one chooses, and no one dares to disagree?' So long as what he says is good, it is of course good also that he should not be opposed. But if what he says is bad, will it not come very near to ruining his country by a single phrase?"

The Duke of She asked about government. The Master said, "When the near are happy and the distant approach."

When Tzu-hsia was Warden of Chu-fu, he sought advice about government. The Master said, "Do not try to hurry things. Ignore minor considerations. If you hurry things, your personality will not come into play. If you let yourself be distracted by minor considerations, nothing important will ever get finished."

Tzu-kung asked about government. The Master said, "Sufficient food, sufficient weapons, and the confidence of the common people." Tzu-kung said, "Suppose you had no choice but to dispense with one of these three, which would you forgo?" The Master said, "Weapons." Tzu-kung said, "Suppose you were forced to dispense with one of the two that were left, which would you forgo?" The Master said, "Food. For from of old, death has been the lot of all men, but a people that no longer trust its rulers is lost indeed."

Chi K'ang-tzu asked the Master about the art of ruling. The Master said, "Ruling is straightening. If you lead along a straight way, what man would dare go by a crooked one?"

One entire book of Confucius' sayings is devoted to the conduct of a gentleman, laying particular emphasis on matters of sacrifice and ritual. When one of his disciples wanted to stop presenting a sacrificial sheep to the Ancestors at the announcement of each new moon, Confucius said, "You grudge sheep but I grudge ritual." When he exorcised the evil spirits from his house at the start of each new year, Confucius took special pains in order to reassure his ancestral spirits who might otherwise have taken flight along with the noxious influences. He was careful to step over all thresholds, because he thought ghosts lived there. He believed that a mourner must lead a life apart for a long while, and that anyone brought into contact with a mourner must act in a propitiatory fashion and even follow part of his regimen. If, at a meal, Confucius found himself seated next to someone who was in mourning, he did not eat his fill; when he wailed at a funeral, during the rest of that day he did not engage in singing. Confucius believed that where the gentlemen are punctilious in all their ritual observances, other people in turn will be precise in their duties—and the country will consequently be easy to rule.

A GENTLEMAN'S CONDUCT

AT home in his native village his manner is both simple and unassuming, as if he did not trust himself to speak. But in the Ancestral Temple and at Court, he speaks readily, though always choosing his words with care. At Court, when conversing with the Under Ministers, his attitude is friendly and affable; when conversing with the Upper Ministers, it is restrained and formal. When the ruler is present, it is wary, but not cramped. When the ruler summons him to receive a guest, a look of confusion comes over his face and his legs seem to give beneath his weight. When saluting his colleagues, he passes his right hand to the left, letting his robe hang down in front and behind, and as he advances with quickened step, his attitude is one of majestic dignity. When the guest has gone, he reports the close of the visit, saying, "The guest is no longer looking back."

Upon entering the Palace Gate he appears to double up, as though there were not room. If he halts, it must never be in the middle of the gate, nor in going through does he ever tread on the threshold [which is unlucky]. As he passes the Stance [a ceremonial platform], a look of

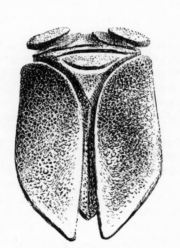

Cricket in mouth of dead helps bring resurrection

confusion comes over his face, his legs seem to give way under him and words seem to fail him. While, holding up the hem of his skirt, he ascends the Audience Hall, he seems to double up and keeps in his breath, so that you would think he were not breathing at all. On coming out, after descending the first step, his expression relaxes into one of satisfaction and relief. At the bottom of the steps he quickens his pace, advancing with an air of majestic dignity. On regaining his place, he resumes his attitude of wariness and hesitation.

When carrying the tablet of jade [symbolizing his office], he seems to double up, as though borne down by its weight. He holds it at the highest as though he were making a bow, at the lowest as though he were proffering a gift. His expression, too, changes to one of dread and his feet seem to recoil, as though he were avoiding something. When presenting ritual presents, his expression is placid. At the private audience his attitude is gay and animated.

A gentleman does not wear facings of purple or mauve, nor in undress does he use pink or roan. In hot weather he wears an unlined gown of fine thread loosely woven, but puts on an outside garment before going out-of-doors. With a black robe he wears black lambskin; with a robe of undyed silk, fawn. With a yellow robe, fox fur. On his undress robe the fur cuffs

are long, but the right is shorter than the left. His bedclothes must be half as long again as a man's height. The thicker kinds of fox and badger are for home wear. Except when in mourning, he wears all his girdle ornaments [which are lucky talismans]. Apart from his Court apron, all his skirts are wider at the bottom than at the waist. Lambskin dyed black and a hat of dark-dyed silk must not be worn when making visits of condolence. At the Announcement of the New Moon he must go to Court in full Court dress.

When preparing himself for sacrifice, he must wear the Spirit Robe [used during the period of purification], and it must be of linen. He must change his food and also the place where he commonly sits [during all periods when he prepares for sacrifice]. But there is no objection to his rice being of the finest quality.... Rice affected by the weather or turned he must not eat, nor fish that has become bad, nor meat that is tainted. He must not eat anything discolored or that smells bad. He must not eat what is overcooked nor what is undercooked, nor anything that is out of season. He must not eat what has been crookedly cut, nor any dish that lacks its proper seasoning. The meat that he eats must at the very most not be enough to make his breath smell of meat rather than of rice. As regards wine, no limit is laid down, but he must not be disorderly. He may not drink wine bought at a shop or eat dried meat from the market. He need not refrain from such articles of food as have ginger sprinkled over them, but he must not eat much of such dishes.

After a sacrifice in the ducal palace, the flesh must not be kept overnight. No sacrificial flesh may be kept beyond the third day. If it is kept beyond the third day, it may no longer be eaten. While it is being eaten, there must be no conversation, nor must any word be spoken while lying down after the repast. Any article of food, whether coarse rice, vegetables, broth or melon, that has been used as an offering, must be handled with due solemnity.... When the stables were burnt down, on returning from the Court, he said, "Was anyone hurt?" He did not ask about the horses. [This passage is a noted example of Confucius' humanism and his concern for people.]

When his prince sends him a present of food, he must straighten his mat and be the first to taste what has been sent. When what his prince sends is a present of uncooked meat, he must cook it and make a sacrificial offering. When his prince sends a live animal, he must rear it. When he is waiting upon his prince at mealtimes, while his prince is making the sacrificial offering, he tastes the dishes. If he is ill and his prince comes to see him, he has himself laid with his head to the East, his Court robes thrown over him and his sash drawn across the bed....

On entering the Ancestral Temple, he asks about every detail of the ritual. If a friend dies and there are no relatives to fall back on, he says, "The funeral is my affair." On receiving a present from a friend, even a carriage and horses, he does not prostrate himself. He does so only if sacrificial meat is sent.

In bed he avoids lying in the posture of a corpse [with his face to the North, where lies the land of the Dead]. When at home, he does not use ritual attitudes. When appearing before anyone in mourning, however well he knows him, he must put on an altered expression, and when appearing before anyone in sacrificial garb, or a blind man, even informally, he must be sure to adopt the appropriate attitude. On meeting anyone in deep mourning he must bow across the bar of his chariot; he also bows to people carrying planks. When confronted with a particularly choice dainty at a banquet, his countenance should change and he should rise to his feet. Upon hearing a sudden clap of thunder or a violent gust of wind, he must change countenance. When mounting a carriage, he must stand facing it and holding the mounting cord. When riding, he confines his gaze, does not speak rapidly or point with his hands....

—BOOK X

Many great teachers have said that their yoke was easy and their burden light—yet acknowledged that humanity would find it very hard to follow them. Lao Tzu taught the Tao —the Way—while maintaining from the start that it was impossible to give an exact name or description of the Tao. The writings traditionally attributed to Lao Tzu consist of eighty-one short chapters, often divided into two books, and from the very first of these chapters, a recurrent theme

appears: that the Tao cannot be named, told, or even discussed in any great detail. Lao Tzu argued further that the Tao should not be named, and that the only reason a name might be given it at all is that the simple necessities of human speech require it to be called something.

In the following stanzas—which in the past have been given many varied translations—the phrasing has been somewhat rearranged for greater clarity and simplicity.

THE MYSTERY OF THE TAO

The Tao that can be told of is not the Absolute Tao; the Names that can be given are not Absolute Names.
    The Nameless is the origin of Heaven and Earth; the Named is the Mother of All Things.
Therefore: oftentimes one strips one's self of passion in order to see the Secret of Life;
    Oftentimes, one regards life with passion in order to see its manifest forms.
These two (the Secret and its manifestations) are (in their nature) the same;
    They are given different names when they become manifest.
They may both be called the Cosmic Mystery:
    Reaching from the Mystery into the Deeper Mystery is the Gate to the Secret of All Life.

Before the Heaven and Earth existed there was something nebulous:
    Silent, isolated, standing alone, changing not, eternally revolving without fail,
Worthy to be the Mother of All Things. I do not know its name and address it as Tao.
    If forced to give it a name, I shall call it "Great." Being great implies reaching out in space,
Reaching out in space implies far-reaching, far-reaching implies reversion to the original point.
    Therefore: Tao is Great, the Heaven is great, the Earth is great, the King is also great.
These are the Great Four in the universe, and the King is one of them.
    Man models himself after the Earth; the Earth models itself after Heaven;
The Heaven models itself after Tao; Tao models itself after Nature.

My teachings are very easy to understand and very easy to practice,
    But no one can understand them and no one can practice them.
In my words there is a principle. In the affairs of men there is a system.
    Because they know not these, they also know me not.
Since there are few that know me, therefore I am distinguished.
    Therefore the Sage wears a coarse cloth on top and carries jade within his bosom.

—CHAPTERS 1, 25, 70

Lao Tzu enjoyed using paradoxes. Yet always, behind his seeming contradictions, there looms his theory of eternal cycles, in which everything eventually reverts to its opposite. Chuang Tzu (c. 300 B.C.), the most brilliant Taoist since Lao Tzu, had a similar fondness for paradoxes, but his writing was far more imaginative. In the next selection he tells how some trees, like some human beings, invite their own cutting down. Often it is useful to be useless.

A USELESS TREE

A CERTAIN carpenter Shih was traveling to the Ch'i State. On reaching Shady Circle, he saw a sacred li tree in the temple to the God of Earth. It was so large that its shade could cover a herd of several thousand cattle. It was a hundred spans in girth, towering up full eighty feet over the hilltop before it branched out. A dozen boats could be cut out of it. Crowds stood gazing at it, but the carpenter went on his way without casting a look behind. His apprentice, however, took a good look at it, and when he caught up with his master, said, "Ever since I have handled an adze, I have never seen such a splendid piece of timber. How was it that you, Master, did not look at it?"

"Forget about it. It is not even worth talking about," replied his master. "It is good for nothing. If it were made into a boat, it would sink; made into a coffin,

Taoist patriarch Lu Tung-pin wielded magic sword against evil

it would rot; into furniture, it would break easily; into a door, it would sweat; into a pillar, it would be worm-eaten. It is wood of no use. That is why it has attained its present age."

When the carpenter reached home, he dreamt that the spirit of the tree appeared to him in his sleep and spoke to him as follows: "What is it you intend to compare me with? Is it with fine-grained wood? Look at the cherry apple, the pear, the orange, the pumelo, and other fruit-bearers. As soon as their fruit ripens, they are stripped and treated with indignity. The great boughs are snapped off and the small boughs scattered abroad. Thus do these trees by their own value injure their own lives. They cannot fulfill their allotted span of years, but perish prematurely because they destroy themselves for the admiration of the world. Thus it is with all things. Moreover, I have tried for a long period to be useless. Many times I was in danger of being cut down, but at length I have succeeded, and so have become exceedingly useful to myself. Had I indeed been of use, I should not be able to grow to this height." . . . When the carpenter Shih awaked and told his dream, his apprentice said, "If the tree aimed at uselessness, how was it that it became a sacred tree?"

"Hush!" said his master. "It merely took refuge in the temple to escape from the abuse of those who do not appreciate it. Had it not become sacred, how many would have wanted to cut it down! Moreover, the means it adopts for safety are different from those of others, and to criticize it by ordinary standards would be far wide of the mark."

—CHUANG TZU I, 16

Lao Tzu wrote short, poetic, semimystical revelations that are often obscure and puzzling. His chief disciple, Chuang Tzu, was very similar in the substance but quite different in the style of his teaching. The next two passages, the first by Lao Tzu and the second one by Chuang Tzu—in which he reports a conversation of his master—agree in their fundamental outlook but are quite unlike each other in the way in which the two men have expressed themselves.

EMBRACING THE ONE

STRETCH a bow to the very full, and you will wish you had stopped in time. Temper a sword-edge to its very sharpest, and the edge will not last long. When gold and jade fill your hall, you will not be able to keep them safe. To be proud with wealth and honor is to sow the seeds of one's own downfall. Retire when your work is done; such is Heaven's way....

In embracing the One with your soul, can you never forsake the Tao? In controlling your force to achieve gentleness, can you become like the newborn child? In cleansing and purifying your Mystic vision, can you strive after perfection? In loving the people and governing the kingdom, can you rule without unnatural action? In opening and shutting the Gate of Heaven, can you play . . . the Female? In comprehending all knowledge, can you renounce the mind?

Water, in Chinese sign, is a life-giving source

To give birth, to take nourishment, to give birth without taking possession, to act without appropriation, to be chief among men without managing them—this is indeed the Mystic Virtue.

—CHAPTERS 9, 10

MENTAL HYGIENE

NAN-YUNG CH'U brought along his food and traveled for seven days and nights and arrived at Lao Tzu's place. "Do you come from Ch'u?" asked Lao Tzu.

"Yes," replied Nan-yung Ch'u.

"Why do you come with such a big crowd?" said Lao Tzu.

Nan-yung Ch'u's face changed and he looked behind him, and Lao Tzu said to him, "I suppose you don't understand what I mean."

Nan-yung Ch'u bent his head, embarrassed, and he lifted his head and said with a sigh, "I didn't know how to reply. . . ."

"What is on your mind?" said Lao Tzu.

"The trouble with me," said Nan-yung Ch'u, "is that if I do not learn knowledge, people call me a fool. And if I learn knowledge, it makes me so sad. If I do not learn kindness, I injure others, and if I learn kindness, I become worried for others. If I do not learn justice, I do harm to others, and if I learn justice, I cause sorrow to myself. How can I escape this dilemma? These three things worry me. That is why I have come to ask you."

"I saw something in your eyes a moment ago," said Lao Tzu, "and I knew your trouble already. Now you have told me exactly what I thought. You look as if you have lost your parents or like one who goes out to fathom the sea with a bamboo pole. Indeed, you are a lost soul! You wish to recover your original nature, but you are confused and do not know where to begin. I am so sorry for you."

Nan-yung Ch'u asked to withdraw, and he began to ponder over what he wanted and to try to dismiss his fears and worries. He sat in his room alone and sorrowful for ten days.

He came to see Lao Tzu again. "You have given yourself a bath," said Lao Tzu, "and the dirt seems to have come off with

the hot steam, but something still circulates inside. When you are disturbed by the external senses and worried and confused, you should rest your mind and seek tranquillity inside. When your mind is blocked and gets beyond your control, then you should shut out your external senses. Those who are disturbed by their senses and their minds cannot preserve their own character. How much less can they follow the Tao!"

"A man is sick," said Nan-yung Ch'u, "and his neighbor comes to visit him. The patient can tell his neighbor about his sickness, but the visitor who comes to see the sick man is not sick himself. What I have heard about the Tao is like taking medicine which increases my sickness. Can you tell me the principles of mental hygiene?"

"The principles of mental hygiene are as follows," said Lao Tzu. "Can you embrace the One? Can you never forsake the Tao? Can you divine fortune and misfortune without the help of soothsayers? Do you know where to stop? Can you let unimportant things go? Can you learn not to depend on others but to seek it in yourself? Can you come and go unfettered in spirit and can you purge your mind of knowledge? Can you be innocent like a newborn child? The baby cries all day and yet his voice never becomes hoarse; that is because he has not lost nature's harmony. The baby clenches his hands all day without holding anything; that is because he is following his original character. The baby looks at things all day without winking; that is because his eyes are not focused on any particular object. He goes without knowing where he is going, and stops without knowing what he is doing. He merges himself with the surroundings and moves along with it. These are the principles of mental hygiene."

—CHUANG TZU VI, 7

A significant aspect of the Tao is that, while it gives life to all things, it never seems to dominate.

THE GREAT TAO

THE Great Tao flows everywhere; like a flood it may go left or right. The myriad things derive their life from it, and it does not deny them. When its work is accomplished, Tao does not take possession. . . . Being the home of all things, yet claiming not, it may be considered great. Because to the end it does not claim greatness, its greatness is achieved.

—CHAPTER 34

Confucius actually lived; Lao Tzu is semilegendary and, even if he did exist, there is no evidence that he ever met Confucius. The two philosophies are very different in their teachings. Where Confucianism is pragmatic, Taoism tends to be mystical—which the first of the two selections below indicates. But the Taoists have long liked to fancy that Confucius came to sit at Lao Tzu's feet as a humble learner, as narrated in the imaginary conversation recorded in the second selection (next page).

THE CHARACTER OF TAO

TAO is a hollow vessel, and its use is inexhaustible! Fathomless! Like the fountainhead of all things. Its sharp edges rounded off, its tangles untied, its light tempered, its turmoil submerged. Yet, dark like deep water, it seems to remain. I do not know whose Son it is, an image of what existed before the Lord. . . . Great space has no corners; great talent takes long to mature; great music is faintly heard; great form has no contour; and Tao is hidden without a name. It is this Tao that is adept at lending its power and bringing fulfillment.

—CHAPTERS 4, 41

THE TAO IS A SEA

WE have a little time today," said Confucius to Lao Tzu. "May I ask what is the great Tao?" To this Lao Tzu replied, "Give a ceremonial bath to your mind! Cleanse your spirit! Throw away your sage wisdom! Tao is dark and elusive, difficult to describe. However, I will outline it for you.

"Light comes from the darkness, and the predicables come from the formless. Life energy comes from Tao, and bodily forms come from life energy, and thus all things of the creation evolve into different forms. Therefore the animals with nine external cavities reproduce by suckling their young, those with eight reproduce by hatching eggs. Life springs into existence without a visible source and disappears into infinity. It stands in the middle of a vast expanse, without visible exit, entrance or shelter. He who follows Tao is strong of body, clear of mind and sharp of sight and hearing. He does not clutter up his mind with worries and is flexible in his adjustment to external conditions. The heaven cannot help being high, the earth cannot help being wide, the sun and the moon cannot help going round, and all things of the creation cannot help but live and grow. Perhaps this is Tao. Moreover, the learned is not necessarily wise, and the good talker is not necessarily clever. The Sage eschews these things. But that which is added to and does not increase, is taken away from and does not decrease—that is what the Sage is anxious to preserve. Fathomless, it is like the sea. Awe-inspiring, the cycle begins again when it ends. In comparison with this, the teachings of the gentlemen deal with the superficialities. What gives life to all creation and is itself inexhaustible—that is Tao."

—CHUANG TZU VI, 2

Longevity, happiness are denoted by crane

If a Taoist accepts life as he accepts death, he does not really perish. This is based on the principle, advocated by both Lao Tzu and Chuang Tzu, that mind can conquer matter. But in the practices that have been carried out by some of Lao Tzu's followers, this doctrine has degenerated into various forms of witchcraft and spirit-worship. Lao Tzu's own preaching was far nobler, as were Chuang Tzu's writings on death and immortality.

THE SKULL

CHUANG TZU went to Ch'u and saw an empty skull with a sharp contour. He struck it with a horse whip and asked, "How did you come to this? Did you live an extravagant life and abuse your constitution? Were you a condemned criminal and killed by the executioner? Did you do something wrong which shamed your parents and your wife and children and commit suicide? Or did you die of hunger and starvation? Or did you live to an old age and die a natural death?" After saying this, he took the skull and used it as a pillow and lay down to sleep. At midnight, the skull appeared to him in a dream, and said to him, "You talked like a sophist. What you mentioned are the troubles of mortal life. When one dies, one does not have such troubles. Do you want to hear about life after death?"

"Yes," replied Chuang Tzu.

"In death," said the skull, "there are no kings and no subjects and no change of seasons. One is completely free, regarding heaven and earth as spring and autumn. Such happiness exceeds even that of a king."

Chuang Tzu would not believe him and he said, "If I asked the controller of life to restore your body, give you bones and flesh and skin, return you to your parents and family and let all your neighborhood know about it, would you like it?" The skull knitted its brows and deepened its eyes and said, "How can I exchange the happiness of a king for the manifold troubles encountered in the mortal world?"

—CHUANG TZU V, 2

Love, frugality and humility were high among the virtues that Lao Tzu preached. Among his last writings are found some of his finest thoughts on these qualities, including his assertion that the Sage can attain his true character only by being meek and disinterested. However all these virtues must be real and not feigned.

THE TREASURES

The great rivers and seas became the Lords of the Ravines by being good at keeping low.
    That was how they became the Lords of the Ravines.
Therefore in order to be the chief among the people, one must speak like their inferiors.
    In order to be foremost among the people, one must walk behind them.
Thus it is that the Sage stays above and the people do not feel his weight;
    Walks in front, and the people do not wish him harm.
Then the people of the world are glad to uphold him forever.
    Because he does not contend, no one in the world can contend against him. . . .
All the world says: my teaching greatly resembles folly. Because it is great, therefore it resembles folly.
    If it did not resemble folly, it would have long ago become petty indeed!
I have Three Treasures. Guard them and keep them safe. The first is Love.
    The second is, Never too much. The third is, Never be the first in the world.
Through Love, one will be courageous. Through not doing too much, one has amplitude of reserve power.
    Through not presuming to be the first in the world, one can develop one's talent and let it mature.
If one forsakes love and courage, forsakes restraint and reserve power,
    Forsakes following behind and rushes in front, he is doomed!
For love is victorious in attack and invulnerable in defense.
    Heaven arms with love those it would not see destroyed.

—CHAPTERS 66–67

THE WORLD
OF
ISLAM

THE WORLD OF ISLAM

ISLAM, the youngest of man's great universal religions, is also in many ways the simplest and most explicit. It venerates a single, all-powerful God. Its founder, Mohammed, was neither savior nor messiah, but one through whom God chose to speak. Its faith, unclouded by subtle dialectic, concerns itself as much with man's behavior in this world as with his fate in the hereafter. Unlike those religions which evolved slowly from obscure and legendary origins, Islam came into being in the full light of history and spread with hurricane speed. Within a few years of Mohammed's death in 632 A.D. it had overwhelmed the entire Middle East; within another century its dominions extended from Gibraltar to the Himalayas. Today its adherents, 300 million strong, encompass nearly one seventh of the total population of the earth.

The reasons for Islam's huge initial success lie entangled in the web of history—in the chaos of the Mediterranean world, and in the zeal and martial skill of the Arab armies. But its continued strength and durability derive from the nature of its appeal—simple, lucid and affirmative —which has preserved the unity of Islam through 1,300 years. For Islam is more than a formal religion; it is an all-pervasive way of life, guiding thought and action to a degree without parallel in the Western world. A key to its power lies in the word "Islam" which means "submission"—i.e., to the will of God. The word "Moslem" is derived from the same root, hence "one who submits." Each true Moslem, therefore, lives face to face with God at all times; wherever his prayer rug (*see page 99*) may lie is the house of Allah. To the believer, religion and life, faith and politics are inseparable. The conviction that God is omnipresent ruler and omniscient judge imparts to Moslems around the world a dignity and confidence that have rendered them impervious to both adversity and apostasy. In the broadest sense Islam is a brotherhood of men under God, transcending barriers of race and nation, united in an organized effort to execute God's will.

Another bulwark of Islam's strength is its assurance that the utterances of Mohammed, as preserved in the Koran and other less sacred writings, represent the final and absolute expression of the will of God. To the Moslems they supersede all previous revelations and confirm the truths of the Old and New Testaments. The God of Islam, Allah, is basically the God of Judaism and Christianity. But in Moslem eyes his word was incompletely expressed in the earlier scriptures and fulfilled only in the Koran. In the same way Islam reveres the biblical prophets from Abraham to Christ, contending only that Mohammed was the last and greatest, the Seal of the Prophets. Denying the divinity of Christ, Islam has also repudiated attempts to deify Mohammed who insisted that he was but a man chosen to be the spokesman of God.

At Mohammed's birth (traditionally 570 A.D.), Mecca was a prosperous transfer point on the ancient spice route between India and Syria. It was also a religious center to which the pagan Arab tribes made pilgrimages to worship at the city's numerous shrines. Of these the most revered was a rectangular edifice called the Kaaba (Cube), containing various idols and, in one corner, a black meteorite that had streaked out of the heavens one night in the forgotten past. Mohammed was born into a reputable family of the Koreish, the dominant tribe in Mecca. In youth he had ample opportunity to observe current religious practices, for the Koreish were custodians of the Kaaba and concessionaires to the pilgrims who came to visit the shrines. He early developed a distaste for the idolatry of the Bedouin and at the same time acquired a growing respect for Jewish and Christian monotheism.

Of sensitive and contemplative disposition, Mohammed often wandered into the hills to meditate, sometimes for days at a time. One night the archangel Gabriel appeared to him in a vision and cried, "Recite!" From this initial revelation Mohammed articulated the first units of the Koran. Overwhelmed at first with awe and terror, he became convinced, as other visions followed, that he was indeed the prophet of Allah, the true and only God. His wife Khadija, who was a rich and handsome widow when she married Mohammed, fifteen years her junior, was the first to believe in him and continually encouraged and supported him. For a decade or more the revelations continued. Sometimes even without his will, as he stood entranced in the city streets or beside the Kaaba, floods of rhythmic prose poured from his lips. Outraged by his denunciation of the idols that attracted the pilgrim trade, the Meccan merchants heckled him and threatened his life. At length, in 622, Mohammed fled Mecca to the friendlier city of Yathrib, 220 miles to the north. The year of the Hegira (flight) is the year One of the Moslem calendar.

At Yathrib, which was later renamed Madinat an-Nabi (City of the Prophet), Mohammed won quick success both as a religious leader and governor of the city. A series of armed encounters between his supporters and the Meccans led to an intercity war. It ended in 630 when Mohammed entered Mecca in triumph and destroyed the idols in the Kaaba, leaving only the Black Stone. In the next two years he so consolidated his position as prophet and ruler in Arabia that his death in 632 did not halt the impetus of the new faith which was ready now to erupt into the unsuspecting outside world.

Whether the Koran was set down in full during Mohammed's lifetime is unknown. It is certain that an authoritative version was prepared by one of Mohammed's secretaries soon after his death, approved by a committee of his followers and preserved thereafter as the accepted canonical text. The Koran contains many legends and traditions paralleling those of the Bible and pagan Arabia. Its teachings have been accepted by Moslems as the revealed word of God and have provided the basis of the law of Islam. Its primary doctrines are simple—pure monotheism and the Last Judgment. Although the existence of a supreme deity, Allah, had long been acknowledged by the Arabs, Mohammed emphasized Allah as the one and *only* God. (In Moslem eyes the Christian doctrine of the Trinity is faintly polytheistic.) Undergirding the principle of the Oneness of God as sole creator and sole judge is the doctrine of the Last Judgment. Far more than the Bible, the Koran is vivid and explicit (perhaps in metaphor) about the delights of Heaven and the terrors of Hell—the former featured by gardens, fountains, flowing wine and lovely virgins, "the Houris, with large dark eyes, like pearls hidden in their shells"; and the latter by "coverings of fire . . . pestilential winds and . . . scalding water."

Though he instituted neither an organized priesthood nor sacraments, Mohammed prescribed a number of ritualistic observances, known as the Five Pillars of Islam. They are: 1) Proclamation of the unity of God, and belief therein, as expressed in the creed, *la ilaha illa'llah; muhammad rasulu'llah*—"There is no God but Allah; Mohammed is the Messenger

MOSQUE OF THE SHAH at Isfahan, Iran, faces on lovely pool formerly used for ritual ablutions. Mosques, unlike churches, are unconsecrated shelters for prayer.

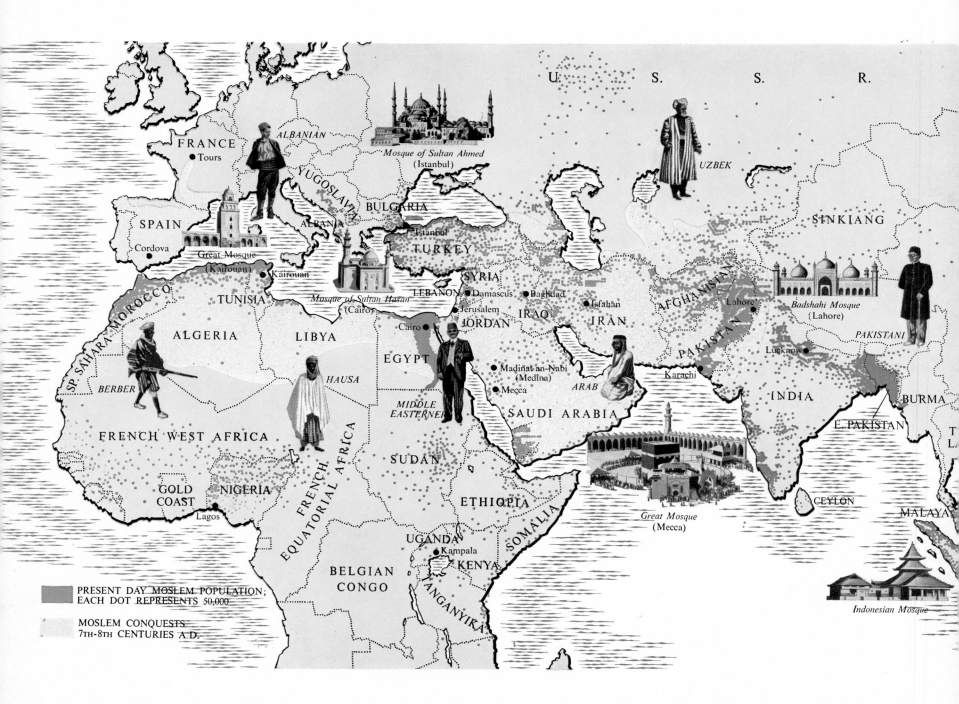

PRESENT DAY MOSLEM POPULATION;
EACH DOT REPRESENTS 50,000

MOSLEM CONQUESTS
7TH-8TH CENTURIES A.D.

of Allah"; 2) Prayer, performed five times daily, facing Mecca, wherever one might be; and on Fridays in the mosque; 3) Almsgiving, as an offering to Allah and an act of piety; 4) The fast of Ramadan; 5) Pilgrimage to Mecca. In addition to these major directives of religious duty, the Koran also contains certain moral and legal ordinance. It forbids believers to eat pork, gamble or practice usury. It lays down rules for marriage and divorce, and penalties for crimes. It forbids the making of images, an injunction that explains the absence of any picture or sculpture of Mohammed anywhere in orthodox Islam.

One year after Mohammed's death the forces of Islam burst out of the Arabian peninsula, into an astonished world that hitherto had scarcely known of their existence. Under the skilled generalship of the first three caliphs, Abu Bakr, Omar and Othman, it took less than two decades to invest the richest principalities of the Near East. Syria fell in 635, Iraq in 637, Palestine in 640, Egypt in 642, and in 650 the entire Persian Empire. So swiftly did Islam's onrushing armies advance that in the beginning they had time neither to convert nor govern their new domains. They contented themselves with exacting tribute, granting tolerance to all who paid it. Yet in ever-growing numbers, hordes of their conquered subjects embraced the new dynamic faith that had come upon them from the desert wastes.

As triumph piled on military triumph, the momentum of conquest carried the Arabs eastward to India, westward to the Atlantic, and across the Strait of Gibraltar into Spain, Portugal and France. At

THE KORAN is the revealed scripture of Islam, transmitted to Mohammed by Gabriel, as intermediary between Allah and His Messenger. Eighth Century copy shown here is in Cairo.

last in 732, in one of the decisive battles of history, they were halted by the Franks near Tours. Yet their energies were not yet spent. The Ninth, Tenth and Eleventh Centuries were the golden age of Islam. Awakened by exposure to the Greco-Roman, Byzantine and Persian heritage, Islam evolved a brilliant culture of its own. Art, philosophy and poetry flourished in Baghdad and other great cities of the Arab Empire; mathematics and medicine advanced; Moslem architects created masterworks like Cordova's mosque, shown as it looks today on the opposite page.

The message of Islam continued to spread, borne by merchants and wandering Sufis (mystics) across Asia to the Indonesian islands. Yet for all its vast successes, Islam was beset from the beginning by internal discord. The first differences had arisen over the question of Mohammed's successor, and out of these early conflicts rifts developed that persist to this day. In time, too, doctrinal differences gave rise to schismatic sects and to splinter groups. But a vast majority of Moslems is orthodox Sunni, and Islam stood outwardly intact. Today it looms, as it has through the ages, a religious monolith astride the middle latitudes of three continents. Though its once great empire has been dismembered by the surgery of modern nationalism and debilitated by economic adversity, Islam yet remains welded together by the binding force of the faith. From Morocco to the Malacca strait, Moslems profess the same beliefs, utter the same prayers, turn their eyes toward the same holy city. It is these things that make Islam, for its diverse millions, the kingdom of God on earth.

SPAN OF ISLAM constitutes one half of the globe from Morocco to Indonesia, which with its population of 70 million Moslems is largest of 32 predominantly Moslem nations. Dots on Chinese segment represent estimates.

ART OF ISLAM lives on at Cordova, Spain, within a shrine of Christianity. This old masterpiece of Moslem architecture was begun as a mosque in the Eighth Century, when city was Arab. It is now a famed cathedral.

THE GREAT MOSQUE OF MECCA is filled with the faithful during the days of the hadj. Here all pilgrims begin devotions by circling seven times around the Kaaba, holiest shrine in Islam, with its sacred Black Stone in the southeast corner. The Kaaba contains a single room which is empty save for hanging lamps and a ladder to the roof. The brocaded covering is renewed each year. The pavilion in center foreground houses the sacred well, Zamzam.

THE MOUNT OF MERCY, a low hill rising from the Plain of Arafat, is the focal point of the pilgrimage. Here, according to legend, Adam and Eve were reunited after their expulsion from Eden. Here too Mohammed preached his farewell sermon: "Know ye that every Moslem is a brother unto every other Moslem, and that ye are now one brotherhood." Pilgrims who climb its sun-baked slopes are forbidden to wear head coverings, but may carry umbrellas.

MECCA Every Moslem should visit the holy city once

More than any precept of Islam, the rule that each true believer should make a hadj, or pilgrimage, to Mecca at least once in his lifetime has proved the great binding force of Moslems around the world. No non-Moslems may make the pilgrimage or even enter Mecca. Pilgrims from every land approach the sacred city as members of the same family, wearing identical seamless white garments, practicing sexual continence, abstaining from shaving or having their hair cut, and doing no harm to any living thing, animal or vegetable. In their sense of common brother-hood, all barriers of race and class dissolve. It is not enough merely to visit Mecca: three main rituals are prescribed. The first of these, per-formed on arrival, is the sevenfold circumambulation of the Kaaba (opposite page). Starting at the Black Stone, the pilgrims run around the building three times quickly and four times slowly, pausing on each circuit to kiss the meteorite, or, if the throng is too great, to touch it with hand or stick. Next comes the Lesser Pilgrimage, in which the pilgrims must trot seven times across the valley between the low hills Safa and Marwa, in commemoration of Hagar's frantic search for water for her infant son Ishmael. Finally comes the Greater Pilgrimage to the Mount of Mercy in the Plain of Arafat (above and below), where from noon to sunset the pilgrims "stand before God." This is the climac-tic ceremony. He who misses it has missed the hadj. A jubilant exodus en masse from the plain, a night in the open, an animal sacrifice, then three days of feasting follow. With one final circumambulation of the Kaaba, the pilgrim's duty is fulfilled. For him, earth holds no greater joy.

THE PLAIN OF ARAFAT, 25 miles east of Mecca, teems with tents on the ninth day of the pilgrimage. For a few hours the barren expanse comes to life as the faithful wait from noon to sunset in the final ceremony of the hadj. Tradition holds that a constant 700,000 come to the plain each year, any deficit being made up by angels. (The actual average is about 70,000.) At sun-set the pilgrims start back to Mecca, accompanied by music, gunfire and din.

STONING THE DEVIL takes place at Mina on the way back to Mecca from Arafat. Emulating Ishmael, who, Moslems believe, thrice routed the Evil One there, pilgrims cast seven pebbles each at three pillars which represent Satan.

KISSING THE WALL surrounding the supposed grave of Ishmael is not a requirement but adds to the bliss of the pilgrims. The aged devotee in this photograph died on the pilgrimage; this is considered particularly felicitous.

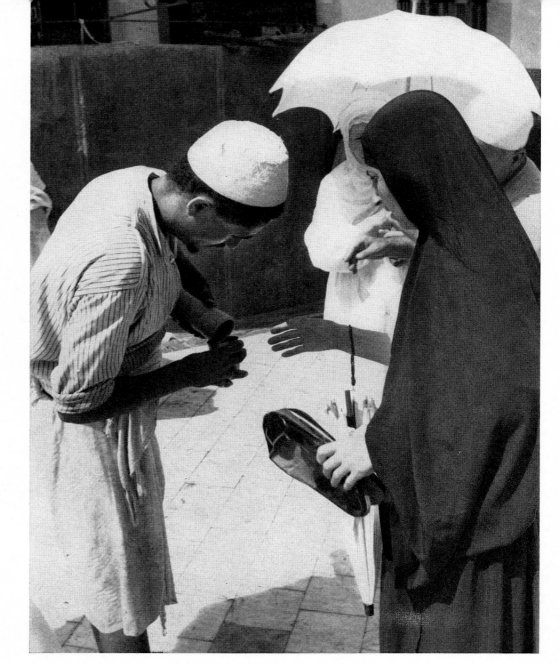

DRINKING FROM THE WELL of Zamzam is permitted to pilgrims after they have made their ritual circumambulation of the Kaaba. Many pilgrims bring their shrouds with them to dip in water from the sacred source, and others take some water home to give to the sick.

SAYING FRIDAY PRAYERS before the Kaaba is one of the supreme moments in a devout Moslem's life. In this closer view of the scene on page 104, pulpits used by the prayer leaders are seen in background. Wall at right of Kaaba surrounds what are said to be graves of Ishmael and Hagar.

MAKING OBEISANCE at Arafat, bearded pilgrims say their prayers at sunset, after meditations that began at noon. The vigil finished, they will hasten noisily to Muzdalifa, a quarter of the way back to Mecca, to spend the night in the open. The next day, at sunrise, they will proceed to Mina.

CHIEF MUEZZIN of the Dome summons the faithful to prayer. The vocal call to prayer was prescribed by Mohammed who disliked bells. The lofty minarets from which the muezzins cry were developed after Mohammed's time.

DOME OF THE ROCK looms above Jerusalem. In foreground of this picture, which was taken from the Mount of Olives, sprout the domes of the Russian Church of Mary Magdalene. At upper right is the square spire of the Lutheran Church of the Redeemer. Below wall around the Dome lies a Moslem graveyard and, hidden by Russian church, the Garden of Gethsemane.

108

JERUSALEM The city is revered for its sacred rock

Second only to Mecca and Madinat an-Nabi as a sacred spot to Islam is Jerusalem. There, beside the holy places of Judaism and Christianity, stands the Dome of the Rock, one of the oldest examples of Arabic architecture on earth today. Beneath the Dome, reared thirteen centuries ago, lies a hallowed rock long venerated by Moslems. In the interwoven fabric of Islamic, Jewish and Christian tradition, this ancient rock appears repeatedly as the scene of great events. According to the Moslems, angels visited it before the creation of Adam, and Noah's Ark sailed around it seven times. Here Abraham nearly sacrificed his son, and all the great prophets from Elijah to Mohammed came to pray. From the rock Mohammed ascended to heaven on his famous night journey and there on Judgment Day, the angel Israfil will sound the last trumpet.

The massive dome that houses the rock was completed in 691 A.D. Yet it was not the first, but the most recent of many shrines that stood on this holy ground from antiquity. Solomon built his splendid temple here in about 966 B.C. Destroyed by Nebuchadnezzar in 586 B.C., it was replaced after the Babylonian exile by a new temple built in 515 B.C. and by the temple of Herod the Great in 20 B.C. In 135 A.D. the Emperor Hadrian tore down Herod's edifice and erected a pagan temple in its place. Two centuries later Queen Helena, mother of Rome's first Christian emperor, Constantine, came to Jerusalem and ordered the destruction of all pagan shrines. Abandoned, the area of Hadrian's temple became a city dump. From then until the victory of the Caliph Omar in 638 all the refuse of Jerusalem was strewn on the holy site, a desecration which so shocked Omar that he himself helped clean away the filth.

Through the ages the Dome of the Rock has been revered by Moslems and cared for by rulers in each dynasty. During the Christian occupation by the Crusaders (1099–1187), a cross was mounted atop the dome and an altar reared upon the rock. For a time priests sold pieces of the rock (for their weight in gold) to pilgrims who carried them back to Europe as holy relics. Later the practice was stopped and the Crusader kings erected an iron grille that still protects the rock today.

When Saladin reconquered Jerusalem, he removed all Christian traces except the grille and redecorated the interior with new mosaics. In modern times the vicissitudes of history have taken a heavy toll. The urgent repairs begun by the British when they held Palestine by mandate were interrupted by World War II. Bombs falling during the 1948 fighting in Jerusalem caused heavy damage. Today, after 1,300 years of veneration, ravages of warfare, time and weather threaten the future of the Dome.

THE ROCK (*left*) lies stark within the splendor of the Dome. An outcropping of limestone, it measures 58 by 44 feet. The hole in foreground is a drain once used to bear away the blood of sacrifices. Small reliquary (*right rear*) contains two hairs of the Prophet. The picture above shows part of the grotto under the rock where the souls of unbelievers will convene on Judgment Day.

VEILED WOMEN glide by each other at a Karachi street corner. In strictest practice, the *burqa* covers the entire form, save eyes, hands and feet. The color is optional. The custom of veiling and rigidly secluding women, especially women of the middle and upper classes, goes back in what is now Pakistan to the 18th Century. Liberal Moslems like to point out that Mohammed's daughter Fatima once preached in a mosque and may never have been veiled.

GIRL BATHERS are members of Pakistan Women's National Guard, and although they wear *burqe* while cavorting in the surf, they unveil twice a week, don uniforms and carry rifles. But Western swimsuits are unthinkable.

WOMAN PHYSICIAN, Dr. Dilshad Begum, treats a patient in her private clinic, the Shad Nursing Home, in Karachi. Dr. Dilshad, wife of a Pakistani government official, is a leader in the movement to abolish custom of purdah.

PLAYFUL PICNICKERS, trying a kind of jackstraws with pebbles on the beach at Hawke's Bay, Karachi, are also in Women's National Guard. In public some of them would be veiled, but more and more the veils are left off.

CUSTOMS Social status of women is changing in Islam

As Islam spread around the globe, the customs of conquered or converted people became entwined in the social fabric with practices that had been ordained by the Koran. A notable instance is found in the attitudes toward women of the Moslem world. For many centuries and in many lands they were kept in seclusion and shrouded in heavy veils outside their homes. Today, however, many liberal Moslems recognize that the retardation of women is a prime reason for the long stagnancy of Islamic life, and the women themselves are rebelling against their fetters. In some countries, including Pakistan—which remains among the more conservative of Moslem nations in its attitude toward women —higher education is now open to them and a growing number may vote. The veil has disappeared almost entirely in Turkey, and in Egypt, Syria, Lebanon, Iran, Iraq and Palestine. But it still persists in parts of Arabia and North Africa and, notably, in Pakistan where perhaps half of the urban women—a small minority of the total population—are still in purdah (from the Persian for curtain or veil).

Though by Western standards some of the mores of Islam seem backward, Mohammed himself advanced the status of women; many of the rigorous restrictions on the sex derive not from the Koran but from later interpreters of Moslem law. Mohammed condemned the practice of burying alive unwanted baby daughters and taught that girls as well as boys were gifts of God. As against the unlimited polygamy of the Bedouin, he preached, "Of women who seem good in your eyes, marry but two, or three, or four; and if ye still fear ye shall not act equitably, then one only." For economic reasons the vast majority of Moslems now have only one wife; in some cases where prominent public figures have ventured to take a second, the clamor of protest from the women of Islam has been loud enough to be heard throughout the world.

LADY EDITOR, Zeb-un-Nissa Hamidullah, looks over an issue of *Mirror*, an illustrated magazine which she founded to escape assignment to women's pages. Poet and short-story writer, Miss Hamidullah is married and a mother.

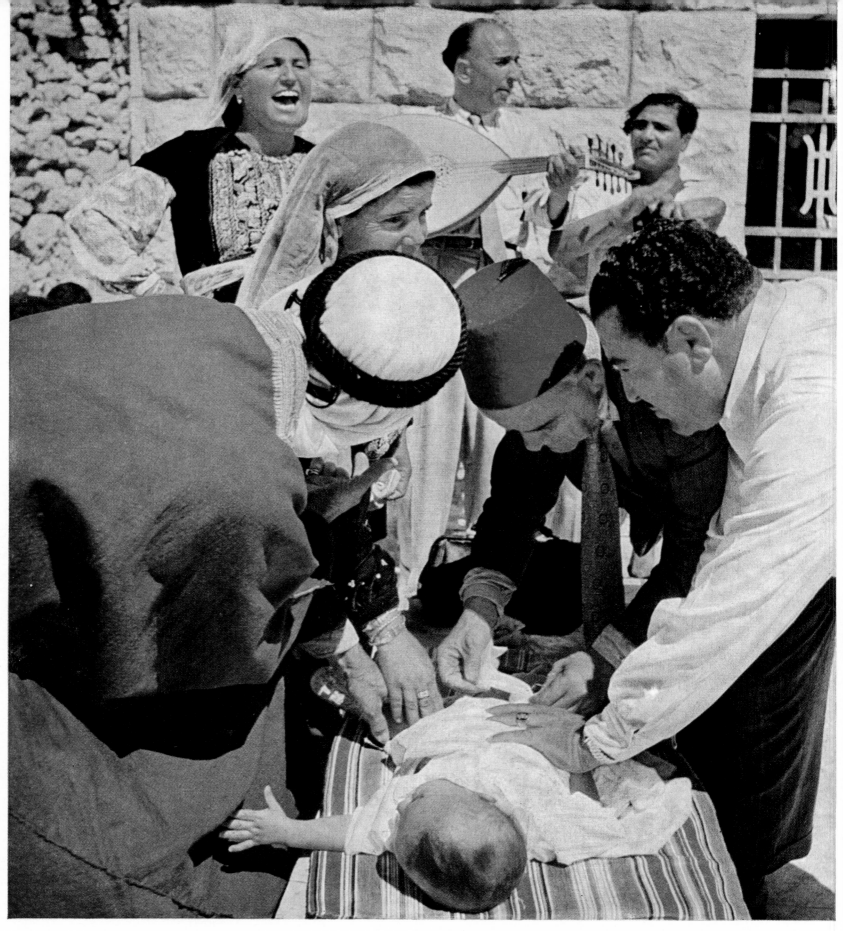

JOYFUL CEREMONIES accompany the circumcision of 7-month-old Salah Abu Riche outside his home in Bethany. As the local doctor (wearing red tarboosh) applies the bandage, he is watched anxiously by the child's parents (on either side) and by the local *mukhtar* or village chief (*left*). Below, exhilarated by the occasion, the father, Ibrahim, executes a joyous dance.

BIRTH Newborn Moslem

undergoes rite of circumcision

Like many other practices, circumcision was adopted by Moslems from the milieu in which Mohammed grew up. Since early times Egyptians, Phoenicians, Abyssinians, Arabs and Jews had believed in it, and it may have originated as a sacrifice to a fertility god. The Koran does not mention it, perhaps because mention seemed unnecessary. Today Moslems everywhere still practice it, though some consider it merely commendable while others regard it as imperative. Parades, feasting, dancing and song accompany the ceremony, which, in these pictures, centers on the son of Ibrahim Abu Riche, supervisor of a refugee colony in Jordan.

DEATH A Moslem funeral
prepares deceased for angels

FUNERAL RITES for Hadji Agus Salim, ex-foreign minister of Indonesia who died in November, 1954, conform to Moslem custom. The picture above shows the women of his household preparing tufts of cotton, perfumed with sandalwood, with which to plug the orifices of his body. Below, his son says farewell at their home in Djakarta, Java, prior to final ceremonies at the grave.

Details differ, but the Moslem funeral has a central core followed by most believers. At death, the body is washed, the hands arranged as for prayer and the corpse enshrouded. Before the head is covered, relatives say farewell (*below*). After graveside prayers, a catechism is often whispered to the dead: "Who is thy God? Allah. What is thy religion? Islam. Who is its prophet? Mohammed." This prepares him for interrogation by the angels Munkar and Nakir. Should he err, he may be tormented until the Last Judgment. The body is often buried coffinless so it may sit up for the angels. Mourning for notables may last 100 days.

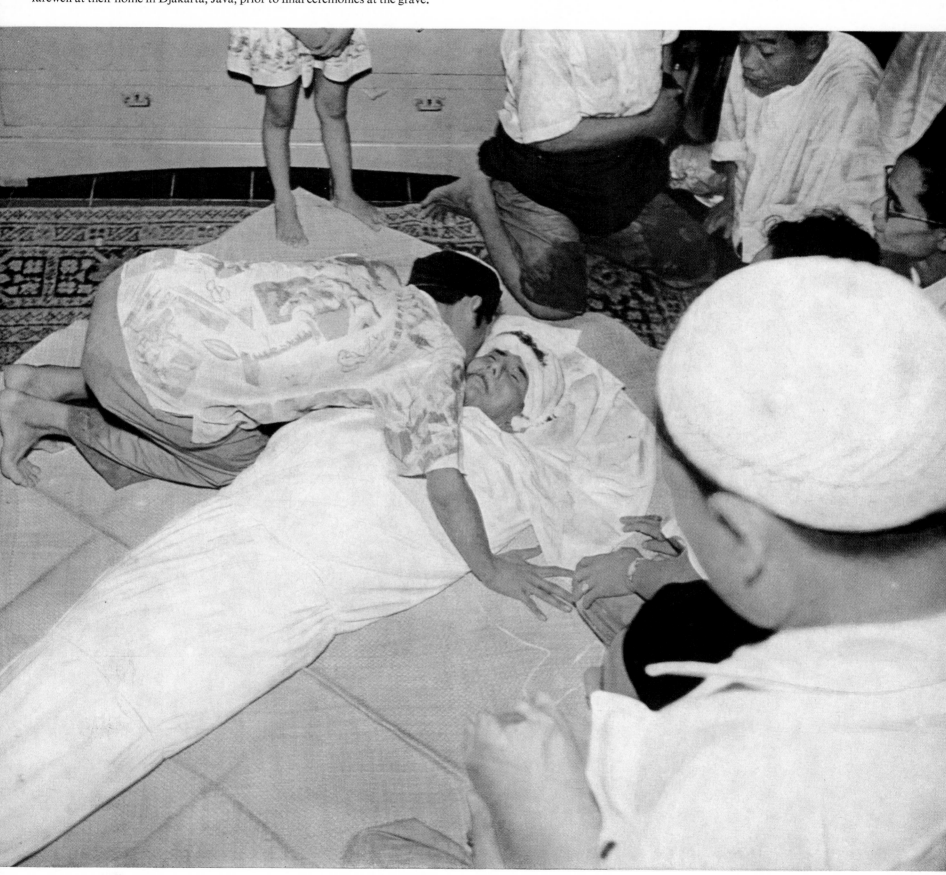

RAMADAN Month of fasting puts "devils in chains"

According to the Koran, Mohammed received the first of his revelations during Ramadan, the ninth month of the Moslem year. The Hadith or "Tradition" (of the Prophet) adds that this occurred on the Night of Power, which is considered to be the 27th of Ramadan, and that it is a time when "the gates of Paradise are open, the gates of Hell shut and the devils in chains." Subsequently Mohammed proclaimed all of Ramadan —which comes at a different time each year by the Western calendar— a time for fasting. The idea of fasting was familiar to Mohammed; it had long been an ascetic discipline practiced by Jews and Christians. As against the sunset-to-sunset fasts of the Jews, Mohammed ordained an entire month of fast days, but limited fasting to the daylight hours. "Eat and drink until so much of the dawn appears that a white thread may be distinguished from a black, then keep the fast completely until night."

By many Moslems, the fast of Ramadan is the most scrupulously observed of all religious duties. Excepting only the sick and aged, young children and pregnant women, all believers must refrain between dawn

WOMEN AT PRAYER sit tranquilly on bright carpets before the Abdine Palace, Cairo, in first dawn after Ramadan. Although Moslem women pray at home ordinarily, the end of the fast is an occasion for public rejoicing.

and dark from taking food or drink, and from any sexual act. A day's fast can be vitiated by a single lie or glance of passion. Although supposed to pass the daylight hours in meditation and prayer, in actual practice many simply sleep. Hence trade and public affairs slow down markedly during the day. But once the sunset cannon sounds (*right*), life begins anew. When Ramadan has passed, the Little Bairam begins—a festival somewhat analogous in spirit to Christmastime, marked by grateful prayers (*above, right*), expansive goodwill and the giving of presents.

SUNSET GUNS are fired before the Mohammed Ali Mosque in Cairo to announce the end of another day of fast. Throughout the month of Ramadan cannons proclaim the start of each day's fast at dawn, its termination at dusk.

116

A SUFI SAINT of the 16th Century, Shaikh Salim (in striped robe) was a member of the Chishti order and predicted the birth of a son to the Mogul Emperor Akbar. Here, beside a fakir, he is listening to a stringed sitar.

SERVANT OF EMPIRE, Shaikh Hasan, also of the Chishti order, tells his beads amid the splendor befitting his post as the adviser to a 17th Century Mogul ruler. Portrait was painted for a later Emperor, Shah Jahan.

MYSTICS Ascetic Sufis

seek direct experience of Allah

Just as in other faiths where an ascetic minority has felt a need for deeper religious experience, so in Islam there have been men who sought a closer union with God now rather than in the hereafter. These have been the Sufis, or "wool-wearers," so called from their coarse wool robes. Some early Sufis are shown in the miniature paintings reproduced here. The Sufi movement originated in the Seventh Century, when Syrian Moslems, influenced by Christian mystics, organized monastic houses. Despite vigorous opposition from traditionalists, Sufism introduced into Islam a saintly hierarchy, a strong asceticism and a lush poetry whose philosophical intent was clothed in the language of earthly passion.

Guided by the ideas of al-Ghazali, a legal and theological genius who was born in a Persian village in 1058 and is now revered as a saint, Sufism came to influence much of Islam. Today about 3 percent of Moslems are Sufis, who are divided into uncounted orders and fraternities. More than 70 of these orders are comprised of fakirs or dervishes, perhaps from the Persian *darwish* (mendicant), some of whom howl, bark or whirl to induce the ecstasy in which they believe they know God.

DANCE OF THE DERVISHES is shown in a 17th Century Indian painting. As the musicians bang drums and play pipes (*upper left*), the dervishes circle about with arms flailing. Two mystics at lower right have fallen from ecstasy.

SELF-INFLICTED WOUNDS dramatize Shiite mourning in Lucknow for the Prophet's grandson Husein, who was killed in battle. The gory rites, practiced by only a small minority of the sect, are illegal in Iran and elsewhere.

CAPARISONED HORSE and a replica of the tomb of Husein are paraded through Rawalpindi on the 10th of Muharram, anniversary of Husein's death. Animal represents Husein's steed, which sped from the battlefield to camp.

SECTS Shiites still mourn a leader and a lost leadership

Of Islam's scores of minority sects, the more than 20 million Shiites are the largest. Their most solemn holiday, observance of which is pictured on these two pages, mourns Husein, Mohammed's grandson, whose death brought about the sect's establishment. The Shiites, who share all the basic beliefs of orthodox Islam, derive from those who differed over choice of caliph ("successor"), the ruler of all Moslems. The orthodox Sunnis have always held that the post is elective, but restricted to members of the Koreish, the tribe of Mohammed. Shiites contend the post is God-given, though open only to descendants of Mohammed through his son-in-law Ali. Shiites credit Husein, through his dying in battle, with atoning for man's sins, an idea novel to Islam.

But like many other sects, Shiites, who live mainly in Iran, Iraq, Yemen and the Indian subcontinent, are themselves divided. Their largest subgroup, the Twelvers, recognizes as legitimate twelve Imams. The Seveners, or Ismailis, are loyal to the elder son of the sixth Imam. One of the Ismaili branches is headed by the Aga Khan, whose followers consider him to be the 48th Imam. One offshoot, the pacifist faith called Bahai, founded in Persia in the mid-Nineteenth Century, is now an independent religion intermittently persecuted in the land of its birth.

MINIATURE TOMB of Husein is admired by Shiites of Lucknow, India on the 9th of Muharram, eve of the holiday. Lucknow Shiites build hundreds of replicas and on the 9th go from house to house admiring each other's work.

ENTOMBMENT OF TOMBS ends the 10th of Muharram observance at Lucknow. In a special cemetery a devout Shiite pours water on a *tazia*, as the replicas are called. Then he will set it afire, bury it and light candles at the grave. Some scholars believe that use of the *tazia* was introduced into India by a Mogul emperor who found he would be unable to get to Karbala, site of Husein's tomb, in time for the holiday, and so ordered imitation tombs built.

MISSIONS New sects

strive to win converts to Islam

Until recently Islam had no organized missionary movement. For just as the orthodox Moslem abhorrence of mediation between man and God has obviated a priesthood, so individual faith makes every Moslem a missionary. Today, however, there are signs that Islam has begun to interest itself in the technique of Christian missions. Even Al Azhar University at Cairo, the intellectual center which has resisted Western influences, now trains a few students annually for missionary work in the field. And certain offshoot sects are exhibiting symptoms of religious energy. Of these, one of the most vocal is the Ahmadiyya movement, with headquarters in Pakistan and centers throughout Europe, Africa, America and the Far East. The pictures on these pages disclose some of the movement's efforts in Africa where Islam's doctrine of a true brotherhood of all mankind has appealed powerfully to Negroes.

For obvious reasons Islam is spreading wherever in the world the white man's prejudices about race and color seem to deny Christ's teachings. Like Christianity and Judaism, Islam began among the predominantly Semitic peoples at the southeastern corner of the Mediterranean basin. Today, most Moslems are from other ethnic groups. About three quarters of them live in Asia and most of the remainder in Africa where about 60 million, out of a total population of some 214 million, have already embraced Islam. In some areas where Christian and Moslem missionaries are in competition, Islam gains ten converts for every one who accepts the rival faith. In West Africa, especially in Nigeria (*right*), Islam has come to be regarded as the religion of the blacks as opposed to Christianity, the religion of the whites.

No less noteworthy is the fact that in India and Pakistan combined, where Islam enjoys its greatest numerical strength, most Moslems are converted Hindus or the descendants of converts who escaped from the ancient caste system into a faith which asserts the equality of all believers.

There are other signs that Islam may be emerging now from its long stagnation. In virtually every nation across the vast Islamic intercontinent, Moslems are reasserting their faith in various ways—politically, spiritually and culturally. In Turkey, where Islam was disestablished by decree of the Atatürk government, hundreds of mosques have been rebuilt; the state radio now broadcasts religious events; Turkish pilgrims to Mecca are annually numbered in the thousands. In Iran the enrollment of theological students increased 40% between 1951 and 1955. Similar portents are visible in North Africa.

Everywhere in Islam today there is a feeling of tension engendered by the growing impact of the West. The pressure of secular and nationalistic ideas and the inflow of vast wealth to certain areas such as Saudi Arabia and other oil countries have made Moslems aware of a deep conflict between the demands of Western civilization and their loyalty to Islamic tradition. In the past, for all its tolerance of diversity within itself, Islam has sometimes seemed to maintain an indifference, and even antipathy, to exterior influences. Today, however, Islam is adjusting to the forces of the modern world. Only its most reactionary spokesmen favor utter resistance to innovation and a return to lost ideals. Only the most radical favor utter abandonment of the past. Between these opposing views lies a middle ground whose exponents argue that Islam should make every effort to revise its society from within and meet the West on terms of equal and independent cooperation.

In the immense conflicts smoldering between East and West, Communism and democracy, Islam occupies a strategic position. For Islam is neither East nor West but partakes of both. It lies between Europe and Asia in one dimension, between Europe and Africa in another.

It would be an error for the Western world to regard Islam as an automatic barrier to Communism. For although its faith and that of the West stem from common ground, there are many ancient social differences to be harmonized. And in the present crisis of the Moslem spirit, Communism may yet offer Moslems the kind of absolute political dogma which democracy cannot provide. In this situation, the work of Islamic missions is of added importance. There is no question that the direction in which Islam turns will profoundly affect the future of the world. The direction will depend in the last analysis on how successfully Islam can reconcile its faith with the mutations of time and history. It is for this reason that many Moslems recognize that their spiritual problems are the truly crucial ones, as Mohammed discerned when, returning from battle, he told his followers, "You have come back from the lesser to the greater struggle." They asked, "What is the greater struggle, O Messenger of God?" And he replied, "The struggle within."

IN NIGERIA boys of the mosque school run by the Ahmadiyya mission at Lagos recite the Hadith or Tradition (of the Prophet). The Ahmadiyya sect was started in India in 1890 by Mirza Ghulam Ahmad, who compared himself

IN UGANDA a young Pakistani doctor, Mohammed Ibrahim (*seated right*), explains Islamic doctrine to a potential convert, an 18-year-old Negro boy named Vementura Mugasa (*just visible, second from left*). The others in the

to Christ and claimed to be not only the Messiah but the Mahdi, a Moslem version of the Messiah, and an incarnation of the Hindu Krishna. Ahmad foretold the deaths of some of his opponents so accurately that the government made him stop his prophesying. Despite Ahmad's bizarre aspects, his liberal, pacifist doctrines had wide appeal. The two branches of his movement, which split over his claims, enjoy considerable success in their missionary work today.

group are already converted Moslems. Dr. Ibrahim, 32, who was trained for African service at the Qadiani mission headquarters in Pakistan, is the only Ahmadiyya missionary in Uganda and bicycles more than 3,000 miles a year covering his sprawling territory. At the end of the discussion, Vementura signed papers, registering him as an Ahmadiyya, and changed his name to Ismail. Dr Ibrahim then congratulated him and rode off (*right*) on his bicycle.

A SHIITE SHRINE, this ornate mosque just outside Teheran immortalizes Shah Abdul Azim, Moslem saint who was a fourth generation descendant of Mohammed. Popularly revered for his virtue and supposed martyrdom at an early age, Abdul Azim lies buried under the golden dome, which was built by admiring kings after his burial in 861. Some 300,000 pilgrims come annually to pray at his tomb and touch the sacred golden fence which surrounds it.

MOSLEM TRUTHS

The Koran ("Reading") is the one sacred scripture of Islam. Moslems believe that all 114 of its chapters called suras came to Mohammed as revelations from God. All the words he received by revelation are held holy by Moslems, while his other remarks are preserved in the Hadith ("Tradition"), but not thought to be holy. Daily reading and recitation of the Koran in all Moslem schools and mosques make it one of the world's most widely known books.

It is not certain that Mohammed could read or write, but almost from the start his followers took down what he recited, using "scraps of parchment and leather, tablets of stone, ribs of palm branches, camels' shoulderblades and

ribs, pieces of board and the breasts of men." Soon after Mohammed died in 632, these fragments were collected and the Koran was assembled. Later explanatory additions by Moslem "readers" are shown here parenthetically.

No English translation of the Koran has ever fully conveyed the eloquence or flavor of the original Arabic. The following is a modern version by an English Moslem. The first sura is an invocation which has been called the Lord's Prayer of Islam and "the essence of the Koran." It is an essential part of all Moslem worship, both public and private, and no solemn contract or transaction is considered to be complete unless it is recited.

THE OPENING
Revealed at Mecca

In the name of Allah, the Beneficent, the Merciful!
Praise be to Allah, Lord of the Worlds, the Beneficent, the Merciful. Owner of the Day of Judgment,
Thee (alone) we worship; Thee (alone) we ask for help. Show us the straight path,
The path of those whom Thou hast favored; not (the path) of those who earn Thine anger nor of those who go astray.

The Koran is not arranged in chronological order but by the length of its suras, with the longer chapters coming first and the shorter ones last. All but one of the 114 suras begin with the sentence "In the name of Allah, the Beneficent, the Merciful!" a blessing which Moslems pronounce to invoke God's aid at the start of all their important actions. One of the earliest is Sura LXXXI, "The Overthrowing," in which Mohammed assured his followers that the Last Judgment would prove him a true prophet. In it he also denounced the ancient Arab custom of burying alive girl-children who were thought to be superfluous. Mohammed abolished this practice in Islam.

worthy to be stoned. Whither then go ye? This is naught else than a reminder unto creation, unto whosoever of you willeth to walk straight. And ye will not, unless that Allah willeth. . . .

Mohammed received nearly all his revelations in his native city of Mecca or in Madinat an-Nabi. But his first revelation came while he was sleeping in a cave near Mecca and the voice of the angel Gabriel recited the opening lines of Sura XCVI, known as "The Clot" and given in its entirety below. The Koran, like the Bible, is frequently divided into verses, but most selections given here are paragraphed.

THE OVERTHROWING
Revealed at Mecca

IN the name of Allah, the Beneficent, the Merciful! When the sun is overthrown, and when the stars fall, and when the hills are moved . . . and when souls are reunited, and when the girl-child that was buried alive is asked for what sin she was slain, and when the pages are laid open, and when the sky is torn away, and when hell is lighted, and when the garden is brought nigh, (then) every soul will know what it hath made ready.

Oh, but I call to witness the planets, the stars which rise and set, and the night when it closeth, and the morning when it breathes that this is in truth the word of an honored messenger, mighty, established in the presence of the Lord of the Throne, (One) to be obeyed, and trustworthy; and your comrade is not mad. Surely he beheld the angel Gabriel on the clear horizon. And he is not avid of the Unseen. Nor is this the utterance of a devil

Involved writing of Moslem creed is used for embellishing mosques

THE CLOT
Revealed at Mecca

IN the name of Allah, the Beneficent, the Merciful! Read: In the name of thy Lord who createth, createth man from a clot. Read: And thy Lord is the Most Bounteous, Who teacheth by the pen, teacheth man that which he knew not. Nay, but verily man is rebellious that he thinketh himself independent! Lo! unto thy Lord is the return.

Hast thou seen him who dissuadeth a slave when he prayeth? Hast thou seen if he (relieth) on the guidance (of Allah) or whether he enjoineth piety? Hast thou seen if he denieth (Allah's guidance) and is froward? Is he then unaware that Allah seeth?

Nay, but if he cease not. We will seize him by the forelock—the lying, sinful forelock— Then let this miserable wretch call upon his henchmen! We will call upon the guards of hell. Nay! Obey not thou him. But prostrate thyself, and do thou draw near (unto Allah).

DEFRAUDING
Revealed at Mecca

IN the name of Allah, the Beneficent, the Merciful! Woe unto the defrauders: Those who when they take the measure from mankind demand it full, but if they measure unto them or weigh for them, they cause them loss. Do such (men) not consider that they will be raised again unto an awful Day, the day when (all) mankind stand before the Lord of the Worlds? Nay, but the record of the vile is in *Sijjin*—Ah! what will convey unto thee what the *Sijjin* is!—a written record.

Woe unto the repudiators on that day! Those who deny the Day of Judgment which none denieth save each criminal transgressor, who, when thou readest unto him Our revelations, saith: (Mere) fables of the men of old. Nay, but that which they have earned is rust upon their hearts. Nay, but surely on that day they will be covered from (the mercy of) their Lord. Then lo! they verily will burn in hell, and it will be said (unto them): This is that which ye used to deny. Nay, but the record of the righteous is in *Illiyin*—Ah, what will convey unto thee what *Illiyin* is!—a written record, attested by those who are brought near (unto their Lord).

Lo! the righteous verily are in delight, on couches, gazing, thou wilt know in their faces the radiance of delight. They are given to drink of a pure wine, sealed, whose seal is musk—For this let (all) those strive who strive for bliss—And mixed with water of Tasnim, a spring whence those brought near to Allah drink. Lo! the guilty used to laugh at those who believed, and wink one to another when they passed them; and when they returned to their own folk, they returned jesting; and when they saw them, they said: Lo! these have gone astray. Yet they were not sent as guardians over them. This day it is those who believe who have the laugh of disbelievers, on high couches, gazing. Are not the disbelievers paid for what they used to do?

The Koran states that Allah is impartial toward all men. Reward and punishment do not depend on His whim but on whether men obey or reject His divine laws. This is trenchantly explained in Sura XIII, "The Thunder."

THE THUNDER
Revealed at Mecca

IN the name of Allah, the Beneficent, the Merciful! Allah it is who raised up the heavens without visible supports, then mounted the Throne, and compelled the sun and the moon to be of service; each runneth unto an appointed term; He ordereth the course; He detaileth the revelations, that haply ye may be certain of the meeting with your Lord. And He it is who spread out the earth and placed therein firm hills and flowing streams, and of all fruits he placed therein two spouses (male and female). He covereth the night with the day. Lo! herein verily are portents for people who take thought. And in the Earth are neighboring tracts, vineyards and plowed lands, and date palms, like and unlike, which are watered with one water. And We have made some of them to excel others in fruit. Lo! herein verily are portents for people who have sense. And if thou wonderest, then wondrous is their saying: When we are dust, are we then forsooth (to be raised) in a new creation? . . .

Those who disbelieve say: If only some portent were sent down upon him from his Lord! Thou art a warner only, and for every folk a guide. Allah knoweth that which every female beareth and that which the wombs absorb and that which they grow. And everything with Him is measured. He is the Knower of the invisible and the visible, the Great, the High Exalted. Alike of you is he who hideth the saying and he who noiseth it abroad, he who lurketh in the night and he who goeth freely in the daytime. For him are angels ranged before him and behind him, who guard him by Allah's command. Lo! Allah changeth not the condition of a folk until they (first) change that which is in their hearts; and if Allah willeth misfortune for a folk there is none that can repel it, nor have they a defender beside Him. He it is Who showeth you the lightning, a fear and a hope, and raiseth the heavy clouds.

The thunder hymneth His praise and (so do) the angels for awe of Him. He launcheth the thunderbolts and smiteth with them whom He will while they dispute (in doubt) concerning Allah, and He is mighty in wrath. Unto Him is the real prayer. Those unto whom they pray beside Allah respond to them not at all, save as (a response to) one who stretcheth forth his hands toward water (asking) that it may come unto his mouth, and it will never reach it. The prayer of disbelievers goeth (far) astray. And unto Allah falleth prostrate whosoever is in the heavens and the earth, willingly or unwillingly, as do their shadows in the morning and the evening hours. . . .

Ornately sculptured domes help glorify place of worship

Allah enlargeth livelihood for whom He will, and straiteneth (it for whom He will); and they rejoice in the life of the world, whereas the life of the world is but brief comfort as compared with the Hereafter. Those who disbelieve say: If only a portent were sent down upon him from his Lord! Say: Lo! Allah sendeth whom He will astray, and guideth unto Himself all who turn (unto Him), who have believed and whose hearts have rest in the remembrance of Allah. Verily in the remembrance of Allah do hearts find rest! Those who believe and do right: Joy is for them, and bliss (their) journey's end. . . . Allah effaceth what He will, and establisheth (what He will), and with Him is the source of ordinance. Whether We let thee see something of that which We have promised them, or make thee die (before its happening), thine is but conveyance (of the message), Ours the reckoning. See they not how We visit the land, reducing it of its outlying parts? (When) Allah doometh, there is none that can postpone His doom, and He is swift at reckoning. Those who were before them plotted; but all plotting is Allah's. He knoweth that which each soul earneth. . . . Say: Allah, and whosoever hath true knowledge of the Scripture, is sufficient witness between me and you.

The only passage in the entire Koran where Mohammed denounced an opponent by name is Sura CXI. Abu Lahab was a first cousin of Mohammed's grandfather and the one member of his clan who bitterly opposed him. It is said that he went out of his way to torment Mohammed, and that his wife enjoyed strewing thorn bushes in the sand where she knew Mohammed was sure to walk barefooted.

PALM FIBRE
Revealed at Mecca

IN the name of Allah, the Beneficent, the Merciful! The power of Abu Lahab will perish, and he will perish. His wealth and gains will not exempt him. He will be plunged in flaming fire, and his wife . . . will have upon her neck a halter of palm fibre.

THE MORNING HOURS
Revealed at Mecca

IN the name of Allah, the Beneficent, the Merciful! By the morning hours and by the night thy Lord hath not forsaken thee nor doth He hate thee, and verily the latter portion will be better for thee than the former, and verily thy Lord will give unto thee so that thou wilt be content. Did He not find thee an orphan and protect (thee)? Did He not find thee wandering and direct (thee)? Did He not find thee destitute and enrich (thee)? Therefore the orphan oppress not, therefore the beggar drive not away, therefore of the bounty of thy Lord be thy discourse.

By far the longest sura is the second, titled "The Cow," which has been called "the Koran in little," since it covers all the main points in Mohammed's revelation. It discusses the sacredness of Mecca as the qibla *(the place towards which the face is turned at prayer), hell and paradise, dietary regulations, the relationship of Islam to Judaism and Christianity, the need for fasting and pilgrimage, morals and ritual, women, marriage and divorce, the holy war and many other subjects. The title, as with many suras, is taken from some word or incident which surprised the listeners —in this case, the story of the yellow cow.*

THE COW
Revealed at Madinat an-Nabi

IN the name of Allah, the Beneficent, the Merciful! This is the Scripture whereof there is no doubt, a guidance unto those who ward off (evil). Who believe in the unseen, and establish worship, and spend of that We have bestowed upon them; and who believe in that which is revealed unto thee (Mohammed) and ... before thee, and are certain of the Hereafter. These depend on guidance from their Lord. These are the successful.

As for the disbelievers, whether thou warn them or thou warn them not, it is all one for them; they believe not. Allah hath sealed their hearing and their hearts, and on their eyes there is a covering. Theirs will be an awful doom. And of mankind are some who say: We believe in Allah and the Last Day, when they believe not. They think to beguile Allah and those who believe, and they beguile none save themselves; but they perceive not. In their hearts is a disease, and Allah doth increase the disease. A painful doom is theirs because they lie. And when it is said unto them: Make not mischief in the earth, they say: We are peacemakers only. Are not they indeed the makers of mischief? But they perceive not. And when it is said unto them: Believe as the people believe, they say: Shall we believe as the foolish believe? Are not they indeed the foolish? But they know not. And when they fall in with those who

Wooden stand holds the Koran for reader sitting cross-legged

believe, they say: We believe; but when they go apart to their devils they declare: Lo! we are with you; verily we did but mock. Allah (Himself) doth mock them, leaving them to wander blindly on in their contumacy.

These are they who purchase error at the price of guidance, so their commerce doth not prosper, neither are they guided. Their likeness is as the likeness of one who kindleth fire, and when it sheddeth its light around him, Allah taketh away their light and leaveth them in darkness, where they cannot see, deaf, dumb and blind; and they return not. Or like a rainstorm from the sky, wherein is darkness, thunder and the flash of lightning. They thrust their fingers in their ears by reason of the thunderclaps, for fear of death. Allah encompasseth the disbelievers (in His guidance). The lightning almost snatcheth away their sight from them. As often as it flasheth forth for them, they walk therein, and when it darkeneth against them, they stand still. If Allah willed, He could destroy their hearing and their sight. Lo! Allah is Able to do all things.

O mankind! Worship your Lord, Who hath created you and those before you, so that ye may ward off (evil). Who hath appointed the earth a resting place for you, and the sky a canopy; and causeth water to pour down from the sky, thereby producing fruits as food for you. And do not set up rivals to Allah when ye know (better). And if ye are in doubt concerning that which We reveal unto Our slave (Mohammed), then produce a sura of the like thereof, and call your witnesses beside Allah if ye are truthful. And if ye do it not—and ye can never do it—then guard yourselves against the fire prepared for disbelievers, whose fuel is of men and stones. And give glad tidings (O Mohammed) unto those who believe and do good works; that theirs are Gardens underneath which rivers flow; as often as they are regaled with food of the fruit thereof, they say: This is what was given us aforetime. ... There for them are pure companions; there forever they abide.

Lo! Allah disdaineth not to coin the similitude even of a gnat. Those who believe know that it is the truth from their Lord; but those who disbelieve say: What doth Allah wish (to teach) by such a similitude? He misleadeth many thereby, and He guideth many thereby; and He misleadeth thereby only miscreants; Those who break the covenant of Allah after ratifying it, and sever that which Allah ordered to be joined, and (who) make mischief in the earth: Those are they who are the losers. How disbelieve ye in Allah when ye were dead and He gave life to you! Then He will give you death, then life again, and then unto Him ye will return. He it is Who created for you all that is in the earth. Then turned He to the heaven and fashioned it as seven heavens. And He is Knower of all things. And when thy Lord said unto the angels: Lo! I am about to place a viceroy in the earth, they said: Wilt Thou place therein one who will do harm and will shed blood, while we hymn Thy praise and sanctify Thee? He said: Surely I know that which ye know not. ... Inform me of the names of these, if ye are truthful. They said: Be glorified! We have no knowledge saving that which Thou hast taught us. Lo! Thou, only Thou, art the Knower, the Wise.

He said: O Adam! Inform them of their names; and when he had informed them of their names, He said: Did I not tell you that I know the secret of the heavens and the earth? And I know that which ye disclose and which ye hide. And when We said unto the angels: Prostrate yourselves before Adam, they fell prostrate, all save Iblis. He demurred through pride, and so became a disbeliever. And We said: O Adam! Dwell thou and thy wife in the Garden, and eat ye freely (of the fruits) thereof where ye will; but come not nigh this tree lest ye become wrongdoers. But Satan has caused them to deflect therefrom and expelled them from the (happy) state in which they were; and We said: Fall down, one of you a foe unto the other! There shall be for you on earth a habitation and provision for a time. Then Adam received from his Lord words (of revelation), and then He relented toward him. Lo! He is the

Relenting, the Merciful. We said: Go down, all of you, from hence; but verily there cometh unto you from Me a guidance; and whoso followeth My guidance, there shall no fear come upon them, neither shall they grieve. But they who disbelieve, and deny Our revelations, such are rightful owners of the Fire. They will abide therein. . . .

O Children of Israel! Remember My favor wherewith I have favored you and how I preferred you to (all) creatures. And guard yourselves against a day when no soul will in aught avail another, nor will intercession be accepted from it, nor will compensation be received from it, nor will they be helped. And (remember) when We did deliver you from Pharaoh's folk, who were afflicting you with dreadful torment, slaying your sons and sparing your women: That was a tremendous trial from your Lord. And when We brought you through the sea and rescued you, and drowned the folk of Pharaoh in your sight. And when We did appoint for Moses forty nights (of solitude), and then ye chose the calf, when he had gone from you, and were wrongdoers. Then, even after that, We pardoned you in order that ye might give thanks. And when We gave unto Moses the Scripture and the Criterion (of right and wrong), that ye might be led aright. And when Moses said unto his people: O my people! Ye have wronged yourselves by your choosing of the calf (for worship), so turn in penitence to your Creator and kill (the guilty) yourselves. That will be best for you with your Creator, and He will relent toward you. Lo! He is the Relenting, the Merciful. And when ye said: O Moses! We will not believe in thee till we see Allah plainly; and even while ye gazed, the lightning seized you. Then We revived you after your extinction, that ye might give thanks. And We caused the white cloud to overshadow you and sent down on you the manna and the quails, (saying): Eat of the good things wherewith We have provided you—We wronged them not, but they did wrong themselves. . . .

LO! those who believe (in that which is revealed unto thee, Mohammed), and those who are Jews, and Christians, and Sabaeans—whoever believeth in Allah and the Last Day and doeth right—surely their reward is with their Lord, and there shall be no fear come upon them, neither shall they grieve. And (remember, O Children of Israel) when We made a covenant with you and caused the Mount to tower above you, (saying): Hold fast that which We have given you, and remember that which is therein, that ye may ward off (evil). Then, even thereafter, you turned away, and if it had not been for the grace of Allah and His mercy ye had been among the losers. And ye know of those of you who broke the Sabbath, how We said unto them: Be ye apes, despised and hated! And We made it an example to their own and to succeeding generations, and an admonition to the God-fearing. And when Moses said unto his people: Lo! Allah commandeth you that ye sacrifice a cow, they said: Dost thou make game of us? He answered: Allah forbid that I should be among the foolish! They said: Pray for us unto thy Lord that He make clear to us what (cow) she is. (Moses) answered: Lo! He saith, Verily she is a cow neither with calf nor immature; (she is) between the two conditions;

Assyrian archway is used as a symbol of the faith

so do that which ye are commanded. They said: Pray for us unto thy Lord that He make clear to us of what color she is. (Moses) answered: Lo! He saith: Verily she is a yellow cow. Bright is her color, gladdening beholders. They said: Pray for us unto thy Lord that He make clear to us what (cow) she is. Lo! cows are much alike to us; and lo! if Allah wills, we may be led aright. (Moses) answered: Lo! He saith: Verily she is a cow unyoked; she ploweth not the soil nor watereth the tilth: whole and without mark. They said: Now thou bringest the truth. So they sacrificed her, though almost they did not. . . .

Yet ye it is who slay each other and drive out a party of your people from their homes, supporting one another against them by sin and transgression—and if they came to you as captives, ye would ransom them, whereas their expulsion was itself unlawful for you—Believe ye in part of the Scripture and disbelieve ye in part thereof? And what is the reward of those who do so save ignominy in the life of the world, and on the Day of Resurrection they will be consigned to the most grievous doom. For Allah is not unaware of what ye do.

SUCH are those who buy the life of the world at the price of the Hereafter. Their punishment will not be lightened, neither will they have support. And verily We gave unto Moses the Scripture and We caused a train of messengers to follow after him, and We gave unto Jesus, son of Mary, clear proofs (of Allah's sovereignty), and We supported him with the holy Spirit. Is it ever so, that, when there cometh unto you a messenger (from Allah) with that which ye yourselves desire not, ye grow arrogant, and some ye disbelieve and some ye slay? And they say: Our hearts are hardened. Nay, but Allah hath cursed them for their unbelief. Little is that which they believe. And when there cometh unto them a Scripture from Allah, confirming that in their possession—though before that they were asking for a signal triumph over those who disbelieved —and when there cometh unto them that which they know (to be the Truth), they disbelieve therein. The curse of Allah is on disbelievers. . . .

Knowest thou not that Allah is Able to do all things? And knowest thou not that it is Allah unto Whom belongeth the sovereignty of the heavens and earth; and ye have not, beside Allah, any friend or helper? Or would ye question your messenger as Moses was questioned aforetime? He who chooseth disbelief instead of faith, verily he hath gone astray from a plain road. Many of the People of the Scripture long to make you disbelievers . . . through envy on their own account, after the truth hath become manifest unto them. Forgive and be indulgent until Allah give command. Lo! Allah is Able to do all things. Establish worship, and pay the poor-due; and whatever of good ye send before (you) for your soul, ye will find it with Allah. Lo! Allah is Seer of what ye do. And they say: None entereth Paradise unless he be a Jew or a Christian. These are their own desires. Say: Bring your proof (of what ye state), if ye are truthful. Nay, but whosoever surrendereth his purpose to Allah while doing good, his reward is with his Lord; and there shall be no fear come upon them, neither shall they grieve.

And the Jews say the Christians follow nothing (true), and the Christians say the Jews follow nothing (true); yet both are readers of the Scripture. Even thus speak those who know not. Allah will surely judge between them on the fearful Day of Resurrection concerning that wherein they differ. . . .

Lo! We have sent thee (O Mohammed) with the truth, a bringer of glad tidings and a warner. Thou wilt not be asked about the owners of hell-fire. And the Jews will not be pleased with thee, nor will the Christians, till thou follow in their creed. Say: Lo! the guidance of Allah (Himself) is Guidance. And if thou shouldst follow their desires after the knowledge which hath come unto thee, then wouldst thou have from Allah no protecting friend nor helper.

Those unto whom We have given the Scripture, who read it with the right reading, those believe in it. And whoso disbelieveth in it, those are they who are the losers. . . .

And (remember) when his Lord tried Abraham with (His) commands, and he fulfilled them, He said: Lo! I have appointed thee a leader for mankind. (Abraham) said: And of my offspring (will there be leaders)? He said: My covenant doth not include wrongdoers. And when We made the House (at Mecca) a resort for mankind and a sanctuary, (saying): Take as your place of worship the place where Abraham stood (to pray). And We imposed a duty upon Abraham and Ishmael, (saying): Purify My house for those who go around and those who meditate therein and those who bow down and prostrate themselves (in worship). And when Abraham prayed: My Lord! Make this a region of security and bestow upon its people fruits, such of them as believe in Allah and the Last Day, He answered: As for him who disbelieveth, I shall leave him in contentment for a while, then I shall compel him to the doom of fire—a hapless journey's end! And when Abraham and Ishmael were raising the foundations of the House, (Abraham prayed): Our Lord! Accept from us (this duty). Lo! Thou, only Thou, art the Hearer, the Knower. Our Lord! And make us submissive unto Thee and of our seed a nation submissive unto Thee, and show us our ways of worship, and relent toward us. Lo! Thou, only Thou, art the Relenting, the Merciful . . . the Mighty, Wise. Who forsaketh the religion of Abraham save him who befooleth himself? Verily We chose him in the world, and lo! in the Hereafter he is among the righteous.

When his Lord said unto him: Surrender! he said: I have surrendered myself to the Lord of the Worlds. The same did Abraham enjoin upon his sons, and also Jacob, (saying): O my sons! Lo! Allah hath chosen for you the (true) religion; therefore die not, save as men who have surrendered (unto Him). Or were ye present when death came to Jacob, when he said unto his sons: What will ye worship after me? They said: We shall worship thy God, the God of thy fathers, Abraham and Ishmael and Isaac, One God, and unto Him we have surrendered. Those are a people who have passed away. Theirs is that which they earned, and yours is that which ye earn. And ye will not be asked of what they used to do. And they say: Be Jews or Christians, then ye will be rightly guided. Say (unto them, O Mohammed): Nay, but (we follow) the religion of Abraham, the upright, and he was not of the idolaters. Say (O Moslems): We believe in Allah and that which is revealed unto us and that which was revealed unto Abraham, and Ishmael, and Isaac, and Jacob, and the tribes, and that which Moses and Jesus received, and that which the Prophets received from their Lord. We make no distinction between any of them, and unto Him we have surrendered. And if they believe in the like of that which ye believe, then are they rightly guided. But if they turn away, then are they in schism, and Allah will suffice thee (for defense) against them. He is the Hearer, the Knower. . . .

The foolish of the people will say: What hath turned them from the *qibla* which they formerly observed? Then say: Unto Allah belong the East and the West. He guideth whom He will unto a straight path. Thus We have appointed you a middle nation, that ye may be witnesses against mankind, and that the messenger may be a witness against you. And We appointed the *qibla* which ye formerly observed only that We might know him who followeth the messenger, from him who turneth on his heels. In truth it was a hard (test), save for those whom Allah guided. But it was not Allah's purpose that your faith should be in vain, for Allah is full of pity, Merciful toward mankind. We have seen the turning of thy face to heaven (for guidance, O Mohammed). And now verily We shall make thee turn (in prayer) toward a *qibla* which is dear to thee. So turn thy face toward the Inviolable Place of Worship, the Kaaba, and ye (O Moslems), wheresoever ye may be, turn your faces (when ye pray) toward it. Lo! those who have received the Scripture know that (this Revelation) is the Truth from their Lord. And Allah is not unaware of what they do. . . .

L O! those who disbelieve, and die while disbelievers; on them doth lie the curse of Allah and of angels and of men combined. They ever dwell therein. The doom will not be lightened for them, neither will they be reprieved. Your God is One God; there is no God save Him, the Beneficent, the Merciful. Lo! in the creation of the heavens and the earth, and the difference of night and day, and the ships which run upon the sea with that which is of use to men, and the water which

Mihrab, wall niche, points the way to Mecca

Allah sendeth down from the sky, thereby reviving the earth after its death, and dispersing all kinds of beasts therein, and (in) the ordinance of the winds, and the clouds obedient between heaven and earth: are signs (of Allah's sovereignty) for people who have sense. Yet of mankind are some who take unto themselves (objects of worship which they set as) rivals to Allah, loving them with a love like (that which is the due) of Allah (only)—Those who believe are stauncher in their love for Allah—Oh, that those who do evil had but known, (on the day) when they behold the doom, that power belongeth wholly to Allah, and that Allah is severe in punishment! . . . Thus will Allah show them their own deeds as anguish for them, and they will not emerge from the Fire.

O mankind! Eat of that which is lawful and wholesome in earth, and follow not the footsteps of the devil. Lo! he is an open enemy for you. He enjoineth upon you only the evil and the foul, and that ye should tell concerning Allah that which ye know not. And when it is said unto them: Follow that which Allah hath revealed, they say: We follow that wherein we found our fathers. What! Even though their fathers were wholly unintelligent and had no guidance? The likeness of those who disbelieve (in relation to the messenger) is as the likeness of one who calleth unto that which heareth naught except a shout and cry. Deaf, dumb, blind, therefore they have no sense. O ye who believe! Eat of the good things wherewith We have provided you, and render thanks to Allah, if it is (indeed) He whom ye worship. He hath forbidden you only carrion, and blood, and swineflesh, and that which hath been immolated to (the name of) any other than Allah. But he who is driven by necessity, neither craving nor transgressing, it is no sin for him. Allah is Forgiving, Merciful.

Lo! those who hide aught of the Scripture which Allah hath revealed, and purchase a small gain therewith, they eat into their bellies nothing else than fire. Allah will not speak to them on the Day of Resurrection, nor will He make them grow. Theirs will be a painful doom. Those are they who purchase error at the price of guidance, and torment at the price of pardon. How constant are they in their strife to reach the Fire! That is because Allah hath revealed the Scripture with the truth. Lo! those who find (a cause of) disagreement in the Scripture are in open schism. It is not righteousness that ye turn your faces to the East and the West; but righteous is he who believeth in Allah, and the Last Day, and the angels, and the Scripture, and the Prophets; and giveth his wealth, for love of Him, to kinsfolk, and to orphans, and the needy, and the wayfarer and to those who ask, and to set slaves free; and observeth proper worship and payeth the poor-due. And those who keep their treaty when they make one, and the patient in tribulation and adversity and time of stress. Such are they who are sincere. Such are the God-fearing.

O YE who believe! Retaliation is prescribed for you in the matter of the murdered; the freeman for the freeman, and the slave for the slave, and the female for the female. And for him who is forgiven somewhat by his (injured) brother, prosecution according to usage and payment unto him in kindness. This is an alleviation and a mercy from your Lord. He who transgresseth after this will have a painful doom. And there is life for you in retaliation, O men of understanding, that ye may ward off (evil). It is prescribed for you, when one of you approacheth death, if he leave wealth, that he bequeath unto parents and near relatives in kindness. (This is) a duty for all those who ward off (evil). And whoso changeth (the will) after he hath heard it—the sin thereof is only upon those who change it. Lo! Allah is Hearer, Knower. But he who feareth . . . some unjust clause, and maketh peace between the parties, (it shall be) no sin for him. Lo! Allah is Forgiving, Merciful.

O ye who believe! Fasting is prescribed for you, even as it was prescribed for those before you, that ye may ward off (evil); (Fast) a certain number of days; and (for) him who is sick among you, or on a journey, (the same) number of other days; and for those who can afford it, there is a ransom: the feeding of a man in need. But whoso doeth good of his own accord, it is better for him: and that ye fast is better for you if ye did but know. The month of Ramadan in which was revealed the Koran, a guidance for mankind, and clear proofs of the guidance, and the Criterion (of right and wrong). And whosoever of you is present, let him fast the month, and whosoever of you is sick or on a journey, (let him fast the same) number of other days. Allah desireth for you ease; He desireth not hardship for you; and (He desireth) that ye should complete the period, and that ye should magnify Allah for having guided you, and that peradventure ye may be thankful. And when My servants question thee concerning Me, then surely I am nigh. I answer the prayer of the suppliant when he crieth unto Me. So let them hear My call and trust in Me, that they may be led aright.

It is made lawful for you to go unto your wives on the night of the fast. They are raiment for you, and ye are raiment for them. Allah is aware that ye were deceiving yourselves in this respect, and He hath turned in mercy toward you and relieved you. So hold intercourse with them and seek that which Allah hath ordained for you, and eat and drink until so much of the dawn appears that a white thread may be distinguished from a black, then keep the fast completely until night and ... be at your devotions in the mosques. These are the limits imposed by Allah, so approach them not. Thus Allah expoundeth His revelations to mankind that they may ward off (evil). ...

FIGHT in the way of Allah against those who fight against you, but begin not hostilities. Lo! Allah loveth not aggressors. And slay them wherever ye find them, and drive them out of the places whence they drove you out, for persecution is worse than slaughter. And fight not with them at the Inviolable Place of Worship until they first attack you there, but if they attack you (there), then slay them. Such is the reward of disbelievers. But if they desist, then lo! Allah is Forgiving, Merciful. And fight them until persecution is no more, and religion is for Allah. But if they desist, then let there be no hostility except against wrongdoers. The forbidden month for the forbidden month, and forbidden things in retaliation. And one who attacketh you, attack him in like manner as he doeth unto you. Observe your duty to Allah, and know that Allah is with those who ward off (evil).

Ornamental chandelier
softly lights a mosque

Spend your wealth for the cause of Allah, and be not cast by your hands to ruin; and do good. Lo! Allah loveth the beneficent. Perform the pilgrimage and the visit (to Mecca) for Allah. And if ye are prevented, then send such gifts as can be obtained with ease, and shave not your heads until the gifts have reached their destination. And whoever among you is sick or hath an ailment of the head must pay a ransom of fasting or almsgiving or offering. And if ye are in safety, then whosoever doth content himself with the Visit for the Pilgrimage (shall give) gifts such as can be had with ease. And whosoever cannot find (such gifts), then a fast of three days while on the pilgrimage, and of seven when ye have returned; that is, ten in all. That is for him whose folk are not present at the Inviolable Place of Worship. Observe your duty to Allah, and know that Allah is severe in punishment. The pilgrimage is (in) the well-known months, and whoever is minded to perform the pilgrimage therein, (let him remember that) there is (to be) no lewdness nor abuse nor angry conversation on the pilgrimage. And whatsoever good ye do, Allah knoweth it. So make provision for yourselves (hereafter); for the best provision is to ward off evil. Therefore keep your duty unto Me, O men of understanding.

It is no sin for you that ye seek the bounty of your Lord (by trading). But, when ye press on in the multitude from Arafat, remember Allah by the sacred monument. Remember Him as He hath guided you, although before ye were of those astray. Then

hasten onward from the place whence the multitude hasteneth onward, and ask forgiveness of Allah. Lo! Allah is Forgiving, Merciful. And when ye have completed your devotions, then remember Allah as ye remember your fathers or with a more lively remembrance. But of mankind is he who saith: "Our Lord! Give unto us in the world," and he hath no portion in the Hereafter. And of them (also) is he who saith: "Our Lord! Give unto us in the world that which is good and in the Hereafter that which is good, and guard us from the doom of Fire." For them there is in store a goodly portion out of that which they have earned. Allah is swift at reckoning. ...

They ask thee (O Mohammed) what they shall spend. Say: That which ye spend for good (must go) to parents, and near kindred, and orphans, and the needy, and the wayfarer. And whatsoever good ye do, lo! Allah is Aware of it.

Warfare is ordained for you, though it is hateful unto you; but it may happen that ye hate a thing which is good for you, and it may happen that ye love a thing which is bad for you. Allah knoweth, ye know not. They question thee (O Mohammed) with regard to warfare in the sacred month. Say: Warfare therein is a great (transgression), but to turn (men) from the way of Allah, and to disbelieve in Him and in the Inviolable Place of Worship, and to expel his people thence, is a greater with Allah; for persecution is worse than killing. And they will not cease from fighting against you till they have made you renegades from your religion, if they can. And whoso becometh a renegade and dieth in his disbelief, such are they whose works have fallen both in the world and the Hereafter. Such are rightful owners of the Fire; they will abide therein. Lo! those who believe, and those who emigrate (to escape the persecution) and strive in the way of Allah, these have hope of Allah's mercy. ...

They question thee about strong drink and games of chance. Say: In both is great sin, and (some) utility for men; but the sin of them is greater than their usefulness. And they ask thee what they ought to spend. Say: That which is superfluous. Thus Allah maketh plain to you (His) revelations. ... And they question thee concerning orphans. Say: To improve their lot is best. And if ye mingle your affairs with theirs, then (they are) your brothers. Allah knoweth him who spoileth from him who improveth. Had Allah willed He could have overburdened you. Allah is Mighty, Wise.

Wed not idolatresses till they believe; for lo! a believing bondwoman is better than an idolatress, though she please you; and give not your daughters in marriage to idolaters till they believe, for lo! a believing slave is better than an idolater, though he please you. These invite unto the Fire, and Allah inviteth unto the Garden, and unto forgiveness by His grace, and expoundeth thus His revelations to mankind that haply they may remember. They question thee (O Mohammed) concerning menstruation. Say: It is an illness, so let women alone at such times and go not in unto them till they have cleansed. And when they have purified themselves, then go in unto them as Allah hath enjoined upon you. Truly Allah loveth those who turn unto Him, and loveth those who care for cleanness. Your women are a tilth for you (to cultivate), so go to your tilth as ye will, and send (good deeds) before you ... and fear Allah, and know that ye will (one day) meet Him. Give glad tidings to believers (O Mohammed). ...

THOSE who forswear their wives must wait four months; then, if they change their mind, lo! Allah is Forgiving, Merciful. And if they decide upon divorce, (let them remember that) Allah is Hearer, Knower. Women who are divorced shall wait, keeping themselves apart, three (monthly) courses. And it is not lawful for them that they should conceal that which Allah hath created in their wombs, if they are believers in Allah and the Last Day. And their husbands would do better to take them back in that case, if they desire a reconciliation. And they (women) have rights similar to those (of men) over them in kindness, and men are a degree above them. Allah is Mighty, Wise. Divorce must be pronounced twice, and then (a woman) must be retained in honor or released in kindness. And it is not lawful for you that ye take from women aught of that which ye have given them; except (in the case) when both fear that they may not be able to keep within the limits (imposed by) Allah. And if ye fear that they may not be able to keep the limits of Allah, in that case it is no sin for either of them if the woman ransom herself. These are the limits (imposed by) Allah. Transgress them not. For whoso transgresseth Allah's limits, such are wrongdoers. And if he hath divorced her (the third time), then she is not lawful unto him thereafter until she hath wedded another husband. Then if he (the other husband) divorce her, it is no sin for both of them that they come together again, if they consider that they are able to observe the limits of Allah. These are the limits of Allah. He manifesteth them for people who have knowledge.

WHEN ye have divorced women, and they have reached their term, then retain them in kindness or release them in kindness. Retain them not to their hurt so that ye transgress (the limits). He who doeth that hath wronged his soul. Make not the revelations of Allah a laughing-stock (by your behavior), but remember Allah's grace upon you and that which He hath revealed unto you of the Scripture and of wisdom, whereby He doth exhort you. Observe your duty to Allah and know that Allah is Aware of all things. And when ye have divorced women and they reach their term, place not difficulties in the way of their marrying their husbands, if it is agreed between them in kindness. This is an admonition of him among you who believeth in Allah and the Last Day. That is more virtuous for you, and cleaner. Allah knoweth: ye know not.

Mothers shall suckle their children for two whole years; (that is) for those who wish to complete the suckling. The duty of feeding and clothing nursing mothers in a seemly manner is upon the father of the child. No one should be charged beyond his capacity. A mother should not be made to suffer because of her child, nor should he to whom the child is born (be made to suffer) because of his child. And on the (father's) heir is incumbent the like of that (which was incumbent on the father). If they desire to wean the child by mutual consent and (after) consultation, it is no sin for them; and if ye wish to give your children out to nurse, it is no sin for you, provided that ye pay what is due from you in kindness. Observe your duty of Allah, and know that Allah is Seer of what ye do. Such of you as die and leave behind them wives, they (the wives) shall wait, keeping themselves apart, four months and ten days. And when they reach the term (prescribed for them), then there is no sin for you in aught that they may do with themselves in decency. Allah is Informed of what ye do.

There is no sin for you in that which ye proclaim or hide in your minds concerning your troth with women. Allah knoweth that ye will remember them. But plight not your troth with women except by uttering a recognized form of words. And do not consummate the marriage until (the term) prescribed is run. Know that Allah knoweth what is in your minds, so beware of Him; and know that Allah is Forgiving, Clement. It is no sin for you if ye divorce women while yet ye have not touched them, nor appointed them a portion. Provide for them, the rich according to his means, and the straitened according to his means, a fair provision. (This is) a bounden duty for those who do good. If ye divorce them before ye have touched them and ye have appointed unto them a portion, then (pay the) half of that which ye appointed, unless they (the women) agree to forgo it, or he agreeth to forgo it in whose hand is the marriage tie. To forgo is nearer to piety. And forget not kindness among yourselves. Allah is Seer of what ye do. . . .

These are the portents of Allah which We recite unto thee (Mohammed) with truth, and lo! thou art of the number of

Prayer call is given from a high minaret

(Our) messengers; of those messengers, some of whom We have caused to excel others, and of whom there are some unto whom Allah spake, while some of them He exalted (above others) in degree; and We gave Jesus, son of Mary, clear proofs (of Allah's sovereignty) and We supported him with the holy Spirit. And if Allah had so willed it, those who followed after them would not have fought one with another after the clear proofs had come unto them. But they differed, some of them believing and some disbelieving. And if Allah had so willed it, they would not have fought one with another; but Allah doeth what He will. . . . Allah! There is no God save Him, the Alive, the Eternal. Neither slumber nor sleep overtaketh Him. Unto Him belongeth whatsoever is in the heavens and whatsoever is in the earth. Who is he that intercedeth with Him save by His leave? He knoweth that which is in front of them and that which is behind them, while they encompass nothing of His knowledge save what He will. His throne includeth the heavens and the earth, and He is never weary of preserving them. He is the Sublime, the Tremendous.

There is no compulsion in religion. The right direction is henceforth distinct from error. And he who rejecteth false deities and believeth in Allah hath grasped a firm handhold which will never break. Allah is Hearer, Knower. Allah is the Protecting Friend of those who believe. He bringeth them out of darkness into light. As for those who disbelieve, their patrons are false deities. They bring them out of light into darkness. Such are rightful owners of the Fire. They will abide therein. . . .

The likeness of those who spend their wealth in Allah's way is as the likeness of a grain which groweth seven ears, in every ear a hundred grains. Allah giveth increase . . . to whom He will. Allah is All-Embracing, All-Knowing. Those who spend their wealth for the cause of Allah and afterward make not reproach and injury to follow that which they have spent; their reward is with their Lord, and there shall no fear come upon them, neither shall they grieve. A kind word with forgiveness is better than almsgiving followed by injury. Allah is Absolute, Clement. O ye who believe! Render not vain your almsgiving by reproach and injury, like him who spendeth his wealth only to be seen of men and believeth not in Allah and the Last Day. His likeness is as the likeness of a rock whereon is dust of earth; a rainstorm smiteth it, leaving it smooth and bare. They have no control of aught of that which they have gained. Allah guideth not the disbelieving folk. And the likeness of those who spend their wealth in search of Allah's pleasure, and for the strengthening of their souls, is as the likeness of a garden on a height. The rainstorm smiteth it and it bringeth forth its fruit twofold. And if the rainstorm smite it not, then the shower. Allah is Seer of what ye do.

Would any of you like to have a garden of palm trees and vines, with rivers flowing underneath it, with all kinds of fruit for him therein; and old age hath stricken him and he hath feeble offspring; and a fiery whirlwind striketh it and it is (all) consumed by fire. Thus Allah maketh plain His revelations unto you, in order that ye may give thought.

O YE who believe! Spend of the good things which ye have earned, and of that which we bring forth from the earth for you, and seek not the bad (with intent) to spend thereof (in charity) when ye would not take it for yourselves save with disdain; and know that Allah is Absolute, Owner of Praise. The devil promiseth you destitution and enjoineth on you lewdness. But Allah promiseth you forgiveness from Himself with bounty. Allah is All-Embracing, All-Knowing. He giveth wisdom unto whom He will, and he unto whom wisdom is given, he truly hath received abundant good. But none remember except men of understanding. Whatever alms ye spend or vow ye vow, lo! Allah knoweth it. Wrongdoers have no helpers. If ye publish your almsgiving, it is well, but if you hide it and give it to the poor, it will be better for you, and will atone for some of your ill-deeds. Allah is Informed of what ye do. . . .

Those who swallow usury cannot rise up save as he ariseth whom the devil hath prostrated by (his) touch. That is because they say: Trade is just like usury; whereas Allah permitteth trading and forbiddeth usury. He unto whom an admonition from his Lord cometh, and (he) refraineth (in obedience thereto), he shall keep (the profits of) that which is past, and his affair (henceforth) is with Allah. As for him who returneth (to usury), such are rightful owners of the Fire. They will abide therein. For Allah hath blighted usury and made almsgiving fruitful. And Allah loveth not the impious and guilty. Lo! those who believe and do good works and establish worship and pay the poor-due, their reward is with their Lord and there shall be no fear come upon them, neither shall they grieve. O ye who believe! Observe your duty to Allah, and give up what remaineth (due to you) from usury, if ye are (in truth) believers. And if ye do not, then be warned of war (against you) from Allah and His messenger. And if ye repent, then ye have your principal (without interest). Wrong not, and ye shall not be wronged. And if the debtor is in straitened circumstances, then (let there be) post-ponement to (the time of) ease; and that ye remit the debt as almsgiving would be better for you, if ye did but know. And guard yourselves against a day in which ye will be brought back to Allah. Then every soul will be paid in full that which it hath earned, and (verily) they will not be wronged.

O ye who believe! When ye contract a debt for a fixed term, record it in writing. Let a scribe record it in writing between you in (terms of) equity. No scribe should refuse to write as Allah hath taught him, so let him write, and let him who incurreth the debt dictate, and let him observe his duty to Allah his Lord, and diminish naught thereof. But if he who oweth the debt is of low understanding, or weak, or unable himself to dictate, then let the guardian of his interests dictate in (terms

Hanging oil lamps adorn mosque interiors

of equity). And call to witness, from among your men, two witnesses. And if two men be not (at hand), then a man and two women, of such as ye approve as witnesses, so that if the one erreth (through forgetfulness), the other will remember. And the witnesses must not refuse when they are summoned. Be not averse to writing down (the contract), whether it be small or great, with (record of) the term thereof. That is more equitable in the sight of Allah and more sure for testimony, and the best way of avoiding doubt between you, save only in the case when it is actually merchandise which ye transfer among yourselves from hand to hand. In that case it is no sin for you, if ye write it not. And have witnesses when ye sell one to another, and let no harm be done to scribe or witness. If ye do (harm to them), lo! it is a sin in you. Observe your duty to Allah. Allah is teaching you. And Allah is Knower of all things.

If ye be on a journey and cannot find a scribe, then a pledge in hand (shall suffice). And if one of you entrusteth to another, let him who is trusted deliver up that which is entrusted to him (according to the pact between them), and let him observe his duty to Allah. Hide not testimony. He who hideth it, verily his heart is sinful. Allah is Aware of what ye do. Unto Allah (belongeth) whatsoever is in the heavens and whatsoever is in the earth; and whether ye make known what is in your minds or hide it, Allah will bring you to account for it. He will forgive whom He will, and He will punish whom He will. . . . (Grant us) Thy forgiveness, our Lord. Unto Thee is the journeying. Allah tasketh not a soul beyond its scope. For it (is only) that which it hath earned, and against it (only) that which it hath deserved. Our Lord! Condemn us not if we forget, or miss the mark! Our Lord! Lay not on us such a burden as Thou didst lay on those before us! Our Lord! Impose not on us that which we have not the strength to bear! Pardon us, absolve us and have mercy on us, Thou, our Protector, and give us victory over the disbelieving folk.

The last three suras of the Koran (CXII-CXIV) are thought by some to be among the first that Mohammed received. Moslems hold the first of these in especial veneration, since the Prophet said "The Unity" was equal in value to a third part of the entire Koran. The other two are prayers for refuge and protection, the first against fears proceeding from the unknown, the second against the evil in a man's own heart and in the hearts of other men and genii.

THE UNITY
Revealed at Mecca

In the name of Allah, the Beneficent, the Merciful!
Say: He is Allah, the One! Allah, the eternally Besought of All!
He begetteth not nor was begotten. And there is none comparable unto Him.

THE DAYBREAK
Revealed at Mecca

In the name of Allah, the Beneficent, the Merciful!
Say: I seek refuge in the Lord of Daybreak from the evil of that which He created;
From the evil of the darkness when it is intense, and from the evil of malignant witchcraft,
And from the evil of the envier when he envieth.

MANKIND
Revealed at Mecca

In the name of Allah, the Beneficent, the Merciful!
Say: I seek refuge in the Lord of mankind, the King of mankind, the God of mankind,
From the evil of the sneaking whisperer, who whispereth in the hearts of mankind, of the jinn and of mankind.

THE LAW
OF
JUDAISM

READING THE TORAH, sacred Scroll of the Law, Avrim Fink points to and pronounces the Hebrew passages as father David (*right*) and grandfather Elias stand proudly by in Machzikeh Hadas synagogue in Scranton, Pa. To take part in the reading, central part of Sabbath service, is an honor in the congregation. The cap, or *yarmelke*, is worn in reverence to the Lord. Prayer shawl, or *tallit*, pulled over head signifies wish to commune with the Lord.

THE LAW OF JUDAISM

THE voice of Judaism can be heard in one sentence. Across the three millennia of history that slope away from Sinai, this sentence has echoed through civilization. It is faithfully repeated by every devout Jew every morning and every evening of his life. It is the first prayer he learns as a child, and the last he is commanded to say before he dies:

שְׁמַע יִשְׂרָאֵל יְהֹוָה אֱלֹהֵינוּ יְהֹוָה ׀ אֶחָד :

"*Shema Yisroel Adonoi Elohenu Adonoi Echod* (Hear, O Israel, the Lord our God, the Lord is One)."

These tremendous words, uttered to the Jewish people by Moses as the spokesman of God, mark a sharp dividing line in the world's religions. For they created a new concept of God. Not only Judaism, but Christianity and Islam rest on this concept—strict monotheism. That is what sets them apart from the world's other major concepts of divine and human order, *i.e.*, Oriental religions and Greek thought.

In Hinduism, the oldest Oriental religion, divinity assumes myriad personal shapes, but ultimate reality is a cosmic All-Soul, with which man hopes to merge after he has escaped the illusions of the world and the wearisome cycle of life. Greek thinkers could grasp the concept of a "first mover" at the beginning of the universe but they could not fully see his uniqueness and infinity. The God of the Jews, however, insists on His uniqueness: "I am that I am." All other beings depend utterly on Him, and all good flows from Him. He is a personal God, not in the sense that He has a body, but that He deals with man at will—through justice, anger and love. He is a God of hope: for the world, created by Him with a purpose, is not an illusion, and history is not an endless cycle. Rather, it is an ascent at the end of which is the promise—and the challenge—of the Kingdom of God. Life is not a burden to be escaped, but God's gift to be lived fully, according to His will. "Seek ye Me and live," He commanded in the words of the prophet Amos.

Judaism is a strongly earth-centered religion. It looks to an afterlife, but its practice is not so much to prepare man for the next world as to guide him in this. Its supreme preoccupation and guiding passion are ethics—the never-ending attempt to ascertain God's will in all things. That will is set down in the Torah, the heart of the Jewish religion. Torah, which means law and teaching, stands for the five books of Moses—Genesis, Exodus, Leviticus, Numbers and Deuteronomy. But Judaism also relies on the other books of Hebrew Scripture. Thus, in a larger sense, Torah stands for all Scripture and for all the Law based on it.

In Judaism, as God is one, so is life: every part of it must be sanctified. As life is one, so is man: there is no division between the evil represented by body and the good represented by soul, for both must serve God. Ideally, the table must be an altar, the home a house of God, the marketplace an expression of justice. That is why the religious Jew moves through life on a round of blessings. On page 131 a Jewish woman blesses the Sabbath lights. There are blessings also over food and drink, for new clothes, sighting the sea or seeing any beautiful object. That is also why the Torah ranges from minute instruction to sublime teaching. The Books of Moses set down the Ten Commandments. But they also set down the right way to prepare food, to give to charity, to pay for damage. Central to the concept of Judaism is the doctrine of *mitzvah*, a word that means commandment but, by implication, also "good deed."

In ancient times, rabbis listed 613 *mitzvot*. They range from visiting the sick, burying the dead and sparing another man's feelings to prayer and, above all, teaching and studying the Torah.

When a Jewish boy first starts Torah studies, a drop of honey is placed on the page to indicate that this duty is also a great joy. To fathom the meaning of the Torah, to interpret every word and every dot, has been the major intellectual preoccupation of Jews across the centuries. As a result, the scholar has always been a hero to Judaism.

Judaism sees man as a paradox: he is a handful of dust but he also carries the divine spark. He is fashioned in the image of God and this means, above all, that he has freedom. He lives in the perpetual crisis of free will, faced at every moment with the choice between good and evil. Judaism holds that man, being man, cannot escape sin. But in the main Adam's fall is not seen as a stain automatically transmitted—as in the orthodox Christian concept of original sin—but rather as a fault again and again repeated because of man's human weakness. Through loving God and striving to imitate Him man must also love his fellow human beings. Whether love goes beyond the Law, mercy beyond justice, is an ancient argument. The strict Jewish answer is that love and the Law must be one and the same.

Judaism sees the climax of history in the Messianic age, when all the nations "shall beat their swords into plowshares." Beyond the Messianic age, Judaism looks to the Kingdom of God, but there is no strict division between this world and the next. Most religious Jews believe in both resurrection and immortality of the soul, but in this as in many other matters Jews are free to make their own philosophical interpretation.

This is the faith of the Jews, a people which today numbers an estimated 11.8 million throughout the world—more than 5 million in the U.S., 1.5 million in Israel. Jews long have discussed the problem of defining Jewry. A race? There are Chinese Jews, black-skinned Ethiopian Jews, and Mexican Indian Jews. A religion? Jews who do not worship still consider themselves Jews. A nation? Though most Western Jews look sympathetically on the state of Israel, few consider it a homeland and Jews are loyal citizens of many countries. A leading Jewish spokesman, Dr. Mordecai M. Kaplan, defines Judaism as a civilization and the Jews as a people linked by a common history, a common language of prayer, a common and vast literature, and a sense of common destiny.

In Jewish law, a Jew does not cease being a Jew simply because he lapses from religious observance. It holds anyone born of a Jewish mother to be a Jew. Jewish ritual is relatively undramatic; its synagogues are without "graven images." Its real drama is its history, its greatest image an idea—the idea of the One Living God. When God elected them to be "The Chosen People," the Jews believe He gave them special responsibilities rather than privileges; He appointed Israel to be His suffering servant to bring His word to all peoples of the world. As the English novelist Israel Zangwill put it: "The people of Christ has been the Christ of peoples." Jewish as well as some Christian theologians believe that the Jews' mission till the end of history is to bear witness against idolatry, against manmade gods, which are fashioned not only of stone and bronze, but also of false ideas. The hope of this mission is that all men may one day learn and none forget that

The Lord our God, the Lord is One.

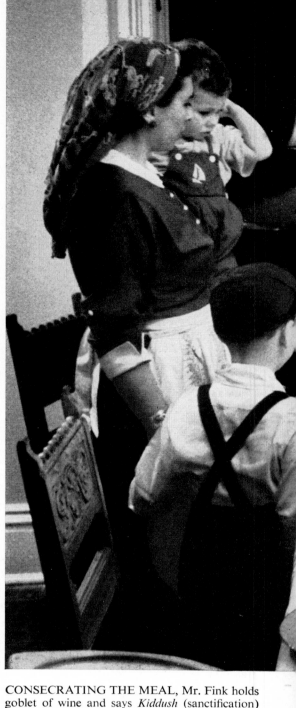

SABBATH CANDLESTICKS that will be used for festive Friday night dinner table in the home of David Fink of Scranton, Pa. are polished by the eldest son Avrim. Before sundown, when the Sabbath begins, Mrs. Tobi Fink will light the candles, then say an ancient blessing over them.

CONSECRATING THE MEAL, Mr. Fink holds goblet of wine and says *Kiddush* (sanctification) prayer: "Blessed art Thou, O Lord, King of the

FATHER TEACHES SON how to put on *t'fillin* (phylacteries), worn at weekday morning prayer. They are leather strips with boxes containing scriptural verses. One is placed around arm near the heart, other around the head.

FAMILY A home can be a fort of faith, a house of God

At the door of many a devout Jewish home hangs a small box called *mezuzah* (meaning doorpost) which holds 15 verses from Scripture. Often, as family members come or go, they kiss the *mezuzah*. It proclaims that the house is Jewish and also marks the fact that the home is the center of Jewish faith, equal with the synagogue as a house of God.

To raise a family is a sacred duty to Jews, and it is through family loyalty that they express loyalty to Judaism. In an Orthodox home, like the David Fink home in Scranton, Pa. which is pictured in these two pages, all daily life is touched by religion. Meals are prepared strictly according to dietary laws, which are derived from scriptural regulations about certain foods and practices which were declared unclean—prohibitions which also, incidentally, had a sound hygienic basis for the time and climate. Pork and shellfish, for instance, are forbidden foods; all meat must be from animals that were slaughtered quickly and neatly so as to prevent too much blood from staying in the flesh.

The height of the family ritual comes on the Sabbath. Rabbis have described it as the foretaste of the world to come. Orthodox Jews shun

Universe, who createst the fruit of the vine." From
left: Moshe, 5, Mrs. Fink, holding Shlomo, 2, Mr.
Fink, Avrim, 12, Jacob, 9, Joshua 7, Shirley, 11.

IN KOSHER KITCHEN (*below*) Mrs. Fink, 32,
and daughter Shirley stack dishes, making sure—
as dietary law requires—that none used for meat

touch any used for dairy foods. The dishpans are
marked for non-Jewish help employed by family. Finks own kosher chicken-packing business.

LEADING THE HANNUKKAH SINGING, Mrs. William G. Braude joins in with her rabbi husband and sons Joel, Danny and Benjamin in their Providence, R.I. home. Their favorite song is the Jewish hymn "Rock of Ages" (not the same as the Christian hymn of the same name) but their repertoire includes "Hannukkah, O Hannukkah" and "I Have a Little Dreidel." On the table is the *menorah*, one more candle of which is lit each night of the festival.

136

SIPPING THE WINE, Philip Green (*standing*) leads his family in the brief ritual which precedes the Sabbath meal in a Reform Jewish home. Mr. Green is a trustee, his wife and children members of Cleveland's Temple Emanu El.

work on the Sabbath and refuse to travel, use the phone, write, touch money or pose for photographs (the pictures here used to illustrate Sabbath customs were taken on other days). Many members of the Conservative movement relax these prohibitions somewhat and Reform Jews have generally abandoned them, but whatever the family's synagogue affiliation, the Sabbath will be honored. The photographs on these two pages show Reform Jewish families. For all devout Jews—Orthodox, Conservative, Reform—the Sabbath begins at dusk each Friday when the woman of the house, her husband and children grouped around her, lights the traditional candles with the following blessing: "Blessed art Thou, O Lord our God, King of the universe, Who hast sanctified us by Thy laws and commanded us to kindle the Sabbath light." Then the head of the house blesses the wine. In a Reform family, the blessing is: "Let us praise God with this symbol of joy and thank Him for the blessings of the past week, for life, health and strength, for home, love and friendship, for the discipline of our trials and temptations, for the happiness that has come to us out of our labors." . . .

The prayer concluded, everyone sips the wine and the father slices the Sabbath loaf. The Lord's day—a time for spiritual refreshment, for peace, rest and family reunion—has begun. Conservative and Reform families will go to synagogue after dinner and will follow worship with an hour of sociability in the temple's meeting hall. In an Orthodox family, the head of the house will have gone to synagogue before dinner.

The main Orthodox service is on Saturday morning; the Orthodox and most Conservatives attend still another service Saturday afternoon.

The Jews have an old saying: "More than Israel kept the Sabbath, the Sabbath kept Israel." Much the same thing might be said of the annual holy days. If each Jewish family is a brick in the structure of the Jewish faith, then the holy days are the mortar. Even families which have grown generally lax in their observances find themselves unable to ignore the important sacred festivals. The most solemn of these days, on

SPINNING THE DREIDEL, three young members of Temple Beth El play a traditional Hannukkah game on pavement mosaic, which tells the Hannukkah story, in front of the Providence, R.I. synagogue. The dreidel is a 4-sided top.

which many Jewish business and professional men shut their establishments and offices tight, are Rosh Hashanah (the Jewish New Year, in September or October) and Yom Kippur, the Day of Atonement. Together, they form a ten-day period of repentance, soul-searching and return to God. Yom Kippur requires a strict 24-hour fast, a thorough weighing of one's past deeds and synagogue prayer for God's mercy.

Next in importance among the holidays is Passover (March or April), the festival recalling the liberation from Egyptian bondage. Simchath Torah, or Rejoicing in the Law (September or October), marks the end of the yearly cycle of Torah reading.

But all Jewish families, whatever their branch, seize on most holidays as opportunities to acquaint the children with Jewish history and philosophy through games and gaiety. Thus Purim (March or April) is a time for masquerades (*left*) in which children re-enact Queen Esther's rescue of the Jews from the machinations of the tyrant Haman.

Shabuot, Feast of the First Fruits (May or June), commemorates the handing down of the Ten Commandments and among Reform families is the time for confirming boys and girls of 15 (*page 151*). Succoth, an eight-day autumn thanksgiving festival, marks not only the gathering of the harvest but the coming of the rains. It demands the building of leafy booths of boughs, which recall the flimsy shelters the Jews had after the flight from Egypt, and the children recruit all their neighborhood friends—Catholic, Protestant and Jewish—to aid in the project.

Hannukkah, the Feast of Lights (November or December), celebrates the victory of Judas Maccabaeus over the Syrians and the rekindling of the Temple light. It also demonstrates the remarkable adaptability of Judaism and the interrelationship of family and faith. Up to fifty years ago Hannukkah was a relatively unimportant festival. But it falls close to Christmas, and so Jewish families, especially in the Reform movement, have come to emphasize the time for the children's sake. Mothers lead their young ones in hymn-singing, cheer on the youthful top-spinners in a special Hannukkah game (in which the top, referring to the Temple light rekindling, bears Hebrew initials of the words, "A mighty miracle occurred there"), make a moving ceremony of the lighting of the Hannukkah *menorah*, or candelabra, and, in many families, provide gifts for the children on each of the festival's eight nights.

Beyond the holidays, family ritual follows the cycle of life. On the eighth day after a male child is born, he is circumcised to commemorate God's covenant with Abraham. At 13, a boy becomes *bar mitzvah* (a son of the commandment), *i.e.*, he assumes all adult religious duties.

But the family's triumphal day is a wedding. An Orthodox wedding, in the Fink family of Scranton, is pictured below and on the page opposite. The traditional service may include the usual formal questions and end with the breaking of a glass, to recall the destruction of Jerusalem. Marriage is considered sacred, though divorce is permitted. Jewish tradition makes the husband very much the master, but woman is held in the utmost esteem as mother and keeper of the home. "Love thy wife as thyself," says the Talmud, "and honor her more than thyself. Be careful not to cause woman to weep, for God counts her tears."

CELEBRATING PURIM, David Fink, in an Orthodox ceremonial smock, wears a paper crown and wields a tinfoil sceptre made by his children. For his son Shlomo he pretends to be the biblical King Ahasuerus (Esther 5:2).

OBSERVING THE SABBATH, Shirley Fink reads a prayer in Hebrew at the family dining table as her father listens carefully but proudly. They and the rest of the family also pray in unison during the quiet Friday evenings.

CONTRACTING A MARRIAGE, bridegroom Moishe Fink and members of his family examine the papers before the ceremony. At right is Elias Fink, father of Moishe and David. Contracts originally were designed to protect wife.

BLESSING THE BRIDAL PAIR, the rabbi offers them wine which they will sip to show they will share whatever fate may bring. The *chupah* or canopy symbolizes new home to which Moishe Fink will take his bride, Sonya Klein.

PASSOVER The ancient ritual's discipline reminds Jews

CHILD: "Why is this night different from all other nights?"
ELDER: "We were slaves unto Pharaoh in Egypt and the Eternal our God led us from there with a mighty hand." . . .

With this formal exchange between the head of the family and the carefully drilled youngest son, the services of Passover start—four questions and the answer which, repeated through the generations of Jewry, explain the holiday's triumphant significance. Passover joyously recalls the greatest drama in Jewish tradition—the Israelites' deliverance from Egyptian bondage and the great Exodus which led to the covenant of Mount Sinai. It symbolizes the Jewish view of the special grace as well as the special burden of service the Lord gave Israel. But Passover is never free of an element of sadness. Passover prayers remind the Jews that, after Egypt, there were other times of exile and bondage.

The name Passover derives from the last of the 10 plagues, for the Lord promised to "smite all the first-born in the land of Egypt," but "passed over the houses of the Children of Israel." When the Pharaoh let them leave, he did not even give them time to finish baking their bread, which they carried along on their shoulders, unleavened. As a reminder "throughout your generations," God commanded Moses to set aside a seven-day festival, during which no Jew may eat leaven.

To whet enjoyment of holidays by anticipation—an implied but basic tenet of Jewish religious practice—Jewish law prescribes detailed preparations. In an Orthodox household no festival receives more painstaking and loving care than Passover. At least a week before the holiday begins, the housewife who follows tradition to the letter embarks on a thorough housecleaning ostensibly designed to root out the forbidden leaven. She attacks with whiskbroom or vacuum every crevice in the upholstery, shakes out every book in the family library, lest a crumb remain. She puts aside the dishes and utensils used through the year, and brings out the special Passover sets. If the family is not prosperous enough to own the extra equipment, she scrubs, scours and boils the year-round plates and pots. After sundown the evening before Passover,

# of their deliverance from Egypt

the whole family makes the final search for leaven, beginning with a blessing. Then, in silence and by candlelight, both parents and children together seek out possible contraband. The youngsters always find some, for an adult has hidden a crumb or two to keep them on their toes.

At Passover the ceremonial evening meal called Seder is presided over by the family head. Prayers and food rites are noted in a book called Haggadah "Narration". The dishes have special meanings, *e.g.*, the thin, unleavened *matzot* stand for the "bread of affliction," the *haroset*, a paste of apples and nuts, for the mortar used by Jews as they labored for Pharaoh. Participants sit leaning to the left, the attitude of free men in the ancient world. The Seder is specially intended to instruct children in the glad meaning of Passover, and in this spirit the last *matzah* to be eaten is usually hidden and later searched for by a child amid much merriment. Since some Jews believe that Elijah will announce the coming of the Messiah on a Passover, they put out an additional glass of wine for the prophet and leave the door open for him to enter freely.

BURNING BREAD soaked in kerosene, Orthodox Jews in Jerusalem obey Mosaic Law against leavened food in the house at Passover. Burning generally takes place outdoors to prevent contamination of house by unburnt leaven.

BAKING MATZOT in Jerusalem, workers from a theological school groove dough with rollers and thrust it into the oven with a pole. To ensure that dough will not rise, *matzot* are made rapidly, process taking eight minutes.

REVIVED RITUAL of offering God the first spring grain at Passover is observed by the members of collective farm near Herzelia, in Israel. The farm is nonreligious, and celebrates the ancient festival simply as a historic holiday.

141

HERITAGE
OF SINAI

The Law and the prophets sustained Jews
in centuries of dispersion and persecution

"Look from heaven and see how we have become a scorn and a derision among the nations; we are accounted as sheep brought to the slaughter, to be slain and destroyed or to be smitten and reproached.

"Yet, despite all this, we have not forgotten Thy Name: we beseech Thee, forget us not." . . .

This is the special prayer inserted in the Orthodox Jewish morning service, originally designed to be said "in time of martyrdom and defamation of Israel." There have been few mornings in Jewish history when the prayer was not appropriate. In Judaism, religion and history are inseparable, and the whole can be regarded as a continuing re-enactment of the drama of Exodus: bondage, liberation by God's grace, service to God as a result. Countless times, from Egypt to the Spanish Inquisition, from Babylon to Germany, the Jews were in bondage and on the point of being wiped out. Yet each time, what the prophet Isaiah called a saving remnant survived, while dynasties of pharaohs with their armies and empires were drowned in the sea of history. That is the miracle of Judaism. In the figurative sense, survival is the Jewish sacrament.

The masters of the world in which Judaism was born—proud Egypt, brazen Tyre—must have accounted early Israelite tribes of no importance: they were not different from countless, nameless other tribes who pitched their tents and worshiped their idols in the desert. The patriarchs Abraham, Isaac and Jacob in the scriptural account knew God and served Him. But the real transformation of the wandering tribes into a nation of rocklike endurance—into a "kingdom of priests" —is summed up by a single name: Moses, to whom God issued the commandment, "Thou shalt have no other gods before Me." Not many men before his time had glimpsed the idea of monotheism. Their concept fell far short of the Mosaic vision which overwhelmed the Jewish people with the revelation of One Living God and His Law.

It was not an easy revelation to live by. In the three centuries between Moses, who led his people from Egypt probably around 1400 B.C., and the founding of the Israelite monarchy by Saul in the Eleventh Century B.C., the Jews fought not only with foreign invaders but with their soul. The memories of older, less morally demanding gods kept rising up to challenge the new authority of Jehovah. There was continuous rebellion also against human authority. The reigns of David and his son Solomon ended in despotism and division, the realm splitting into the kingdom of Israel in the north, the kingdom of Judah in the south. Yet out of these struggles emerged an unforgettable group of men who renewed Moses' vision—the prophets.

The prophets stood behind the throne, casting a warning shadow over pomp and power. They stood in the Temple courtyard, hurling faith against mere forms of worship. They stood outside the rich man's house, bringing the protest of the poor to the opulent table. They were imprisoned, stoned, reviled. But they could not be silenced, for they were the people's living conscience. They were God's revolutionaries.

The great age of prophecy came in the Eighth and Seventh Centuries B.C. The Scriptures tell how Amos appeared in Bethel, a wild-looking figure in a shepherd's cloak. It was a holiday, filled with elaborate ritual. "Hear ye this word," his message went, "I hate, I despise your feast days . . . take thou away from me the noise of thy songs. . . . But let judgment run down as waters and righteousness as a mighty stream." Amos denounced the idle rich: "I saw the Lord standing upon the altar: and He said, 'Smite the lintel of the door, that the posts may shake: and cut them in the head, all of them. . . .'" But there is more

REPAIRING THE TORAH, a scribe in Jerusalem mends a scroll of the Law. Behind him are some 80,000 Torah fragments saved from European synagogues ruined by Nazis. A new Torah must be handwritten according to strict rules, and always on parchment. A worn Torah is repaired or put aside, never destroyed. Nothing on which the name of God is written may be destroyed.

WRATHFUL MOSES breaks the tablets of the Law at Mount Sinai when he finds that the Children of Israel, abandoning Jehovah, have taken to worshiping the golden calf: "He saw the calf, and the dancing; and Moses' anger waxed hot, and he cast the tables out of his hands, and brake them beneath the mount." This etching and that below are part of a series by Marc Chagall.

MOURNFUL PROPHET (Isaiah II) prays during the Babylonian captivity when the Jews were conquered and taken from Judah: "We grope for the wall like the blind, and we grope as if we had no eyes; we stumble at noon day as in the night; we are in desolate places as dead men. We roar all like bears, and mourn sore like doves. We look . . . for salvation but it is far off from us."

in the voice of the prophets than God's wrath; there is, above all, His mercy. The early Mosaic faith, as it is recorded in Exodus, still contained a strong admixture of stern justice of the desert tribes. It was the prophets who transformed that harsh, austere faith into a religion of mercy, who showed most clearly that Jehovah was not only an angry but a loving God. Hosea, through the famous story of the erring wife whom he forgave, taught the divine quality of forgiveness. Isaiah echoed the same message, in which the Jews hear the heralding of the Messiah: "For unto us a child is born, unto us a son is given. . . . The mighty God, The Everlasting Father, The Prince of Peace."

Despite the warnings of the prophets, the Jews became entangled in the wars of their bigger neighbors. In 722 B.C. the kingdom of Israel was destroyed by the Assyrians and its people vanished, ever after haunting history as "the 10 lost tribes." In Judah, Jeremiah, the relentlessly pacifist prophet, cried out his curses on war, on those who were "saying, 'Peace, peace'; when there is no peace. . . . 'I will surely consume them,' saith the Lord." But Judah ignored Jeremiah and by 586 the Babylonians under Nebuchadnezzar conquered the kingdom. Solomon's great Temple was razed, the leading Jewish families were carried into Babylonian captivity. The exile raised the overwhelming question of how to face the God of the Covenant when He brings disaster to His chosen people. From this dilemma arises rebellion against God, the desperate daring of Job when he cries out against God's cruelty. Yet such rebellion must always end, as it does with Job, in atonement. To this Isaiah adds the insight that the suffering of the prophet may redeem the whole people, or the suffering of the whole people may redeem the world.

Many of the homeless, homesick Jews were tempted to accept the gods and the magic of their captors. This threat of assimilation was met by Ezekiel, who heard God's command: "Son of man, I have made thee a watchman unto the house of Israel." Where earlier prophets had thundered against empty ritual, Ezekiel insisted on ritual as the essential means to keep his people's identity, to set the Jews apart. From then on, Judaism can be seen as a continuing dialogue between observance and faith, between letter and spirit, between the Law and the prophets.

The Babylonian exile ended with the destruction of yet another pharaoh: Belshazzar's Babylon was conquered by the Persians, the Jewish state was re-established and the Temple was rebuilt by 515 B.C. But now the Jewish nation faced the inroads of Greek thought.

The Greeks, as a famous epigram has it, worshiped the holiness of beauty, while the Jews worshiped the beauty of holiness. The Greek spirit stood for reason and human self-sufficiency. It also led some to a mystically abstract view of God. Philo of Alexandria (20 B.C.–40 A.D.) sought to fuse Greek reason and Judaism, partly by treating Scripture as allegory. But in the main the dominant Jewish tradition remained impervious to Greek culture. This remarkable resistance was due to the spirit of Ezekiel—a dogged devotion to the Law of the Torah perpetuated by the *soferim* (scribes) and later by the Pharisees.

While the Jews resisted the culture of Hellenism, they were unable to resist its armies. Judah was swept by successive conquests: in 332 B.C. Alexander the Great came, in 198 B.C. the Syrians. Then in 63 B.C. Palestine became a Roman province, ruled by the Roman puppet kings, the Herods (37 B.C.–44 A.D.). As the Jews continued to break out rebelliously, Roman armies under Titus took Jerusalem in 70 A.D. and

THE LORD SAVES HIS PEOPLE, parting the Red Sea to bring the fleeing Children of Israel to the other shore. Then, when the Egyptians kept up pursuit, "The Lord said unto Moses, 'Stretch out thine hand over the sea, that the

destroyed the Second Temple. Later, Jews were forbidden access to Jerusalem except once a year, on the anniversary of the Temple's fall, when they were allowed, at a fee, to enter the city and mourn.

There was no longer a Jewish king who must be recalled to righteousness, no longer a Jewish caste of Temple priests who must be reminded of the living faith. The place of the prophets was taken by the Law—the Torah and its teachers, the rabbis.

For centuries the commandments of the Mosaic books had been interpreted, expanded and adapted. Where the Bible spoke of "an eye for an eye," the rabbis decided that the Law's intention had been merely some form of compensation, not literally the taking of an eye. Every biblical commandment, in fact every word, went through such elaboration. Talmudic arguments and definitions may sometimes appear futile to the modern lay mind which is willing to spend such tireless attention only on science. But this was the expression of a passionate conviction that God's will can and must be determined in all things. The result was a body of oral law (Mishna) which was preserved, generation after generation, only in memory. It was feared that, if committed to writing, it would become too rigid and might rival the sacred Torah. Incredibly detailed, the Mishna concerned itself with such questions as how to pray while laboring on top of a wall or while on horseback (riding a horse was considered a proud action not easily compatible with the humility needed for prayer). It listed all charitable duties and, since traditionally the gleanings of the harvest were turned over to the poor, the Mishna discussed who was to get grain that had fallen into ant holes. It ruled on what objects might be worn on the Sabbath (ornaments and amulets were forbidden, but false teeth and wooden legs were allowed).

About this code of oral law there developed in turn a vast body of commentary (Gemara). Every argument of the rabbis, every minority opinion and every majority ruling, was preserved in the academies. Probably late in the Sixth Century A.D., both the Mishna and the Gemara were finally committed to paper. The result is known as the Talmud.

Along with Halakha (law) it also contained Haggadah (narration). These are comprised of fables, history, folklore, medicine, astronomy. The rabbinical arguments are infinitely detailed. A discussion of the duty to return lost property, as, for example, a bundle of promissory notes, would lead to a scrupulous examination of what constituted a bundle, as distinguished from a roll. Much of the Talmud was given over to ethical precepts, as, for instance, the beautiful "Sayings of the Fathers," whose tenor may be sensed from a brief passage: "Who is wise? He who learns from all men. . . . Who is mighty? He who controls

THE TOMBS OF THE SANHEDRIN, where members of the highest council in Jewish state were buried, were hewn out of rock near Jerusalem. Sanhedrin became merely a religious body, regulating ritual and interpreting the Law.

waters may come again upon the Egyptians, upon their chariots, and . . . horsemen.' . . . And the sea returned to his strength. . . . And the Lord overthrew the Egyptians in the midst of the sea." This engraving is by John Martin.

his passions. . . . Who is rich? He who rejoices in his portion. . . . Who is honored? He who honors others. . . . Despise not any man, and carp not at any thing; for there is not a man that has not his hour, and there is not a thing that has not its place. . . ."

To the Talmud, God is so close that at times He almost seems to be a member of the family. Yet all through it runs a strong strain of skepticism. It is told, for example, that Rabbi Eliezer could not convince the majority of his fellows on some point of law and, in order to sway them, caused a tree to move 100 yards and a stream to flow backward. The rabbis were still unimpressed. Finally a heavenly voice was heard upholding Eliezer's point. Whereupon the leader of the opposition rose calmly and said, "The Torah declares concerning itself 'it is not up in heaven.' Once the Torah was given to us on Mount Sinai, we pay no heed to heavenly voices but follow the opinion of the majority."

The Talmud became for Jews the only homeland. After the Roman conquest of Jerusalem, they were scattered throughout the Near East countries and Europe. They fared best in Spain during the five centuries of Moslem rule. In Christian Europe they too often lived as despised strangers, and persecution kept welling up from below. "Whenever the pagan within the Christian soul rises in revolt against the yoke of the cross, he vents his fury on the Jews," an eminent Jewish theologian, Franz Rosenzweig, has written.

The world came to personalize the Talmud which again and again was put on trial by the Church, excommunicated and burned. It was believed that there was some magic in it that ensured Jewish survival. In a sense there was. The Talmud was a world in which Jews could escape from the reality of the ghetto, a world in whose regulations the Temple still stood and the fields of Israel were still under the plow.

The brilliant 12th Century Jewish philosopher Moses Maimonides, who was strongly influenced by Aristotle, codified the mass of traditional teaching. Maimonides also set down what he considered to be the 13 basic dogmas of Judaism, including belief in God's existence, unity, incorporeality, timelessness, justice, as well as belief in resurrection and human immortality. But after Maimonides, the great dialogue of Jewish history took another turn—an old strain of mysticism came to the fore.

In all ages, the mystic tries to find—in addition to truths of the Law and philosophy—direct experience of God. Out of such yearning arose the vast, much misunderstood movement called the Cabala (literally, tradition). Its starting point was the problem of creation: how God, an infinite, spiritual being, could create the finite, material world. To fill that apparent gap, Cabalists constructed a whole new metaphysical universe of "intermediary substances," ranging in complex constellations from divine will to angels, from the Eternal Light to Sammael, the archfiend. The Cabala was deeply ethical and pious in its aims. But in time, some of its practitioners became mere verbal alchemists, juggling letters of the alphabet (which were thought to represent divine emanations) and searching the Scriptures for secret magical formulas.

The Jews now lived not only in a physical but a spiritual ghetto. Too often Talmud study became only an exercise in *pilpul* (hairsplitting). Jewish annals in those centuries are a succession of persecutions, expulsions and stretches of uneasy peace. History was the morning prayer and the evening prayer. There are no dynasties and no epics: only an accumulation of that wry humor with which the Jews sometimes managed to laugh at their misfortunes, and which is epitomized by the Polish rabbi who prayed in the midst of a pogrom, "God, if it is not yet time to redeem the Jews, please, at least redeem the Gentiles."

The Renaissance bypassed the mass of Jews. For them, the Middle Ages did not end until after the French Revolution, when they gradually won equal rights. In the 19th Century they burst out of the ghetto in a great sweep of intellectual and artistic achievement. Centuries in which they had been barred from owning land and from many occupations had turned them inward, had developed the skills of the mind.

The ghetto, often voluntarily created by the Jews, had not been all black. It had at least given them a warm, closely knit community in which the old faith survived, unquestioned and intact. Now, three developments shook that faith deeply.

First, as Jews moved into the outside world, ancient customs became archaic burdens. Jews sought to adjust their traditions to modern times. The attempt has, in the U.S., divided the Jews into three kinds of congregations: Orthodox, Conservative, Reform.

Second, as the Jews became full citizens of the nations in which they lived, they imitated those nations by reasserting Jewish nationalism in a new, fervently hopeful form—Zionism. Few Jews anywhere failed to be moved by the historic adventure which is the state of Israel. Yet many were troubled by the emergence of a new type of Jew: unreligious, Jewish only by virtue of nationality.

Third, just 300 years ago the Jews reached America, a land which never knew a ghetto. They were free to live and work where they pleased, and yet maintain their faith and customs intact. On the other hand, they were also freer than ever to abandon their faith. Medieval Europe gave them only one alternative to being Jews: conversion to Christianity. But in a secular society, they were in effect able to abandon Judaism without actually having to join another religion. Some Jewish thinkers feared that this "crisis of freedom" might do more to undermine Judaism than centuries of persecution. But the outstanding fact about recent Jewish history is that, given a relatively free choice, the majority of Jews have chosen to remain Jews, not only in a general sense of loyalty to their history but in a specific sense of religious practice.

The ancient dialogue between the Law and the prophets continues. There can be no question of victory or defeat: the dialogue itself is the basis of Judaism, and its gift to the world. Jews believe that they need both the Law and the prophets, a union of practice and spirit, if they are to fulfill the injunction placed upon them by Moses: "Love the Lord thy God with all thine heart, and with all thy soul, and with all thy might."

THE PILLAGE OF THE TEMPLE in Jerusalem in 70 A.D. is depicted on triumphal arch of conqueror Titus, which still stands in Rome. Relief shows a *menorah* and other objects of Judaism being carried off by Roman soldiers.

GREAT TALMUDIST, Professor Saul Lieberman, dean of the seminary's rabbinical school, leads a class in session on Jewish divorce laws. Dr. Lieberman teaches in English, but his lectures are salted with classic Hebrew phrases.

PONDERING A POINT, Professor Abraham Joshua Heschel holds tutorial session in mysticism—one of his specialties—with Marshall Meyer, rabbinical student. Meyer, a Dartmouth graduate, won own family back to Judaism.

VOICE OF CONSERVATISM, Dr. Louis Finkelstein is chancellor and professor of theology at Jewish Theological Seminary. Author of *The Beliefs and Practices of Judaism*, he is a leading spokesman of the Conservative movement.

PREPARING FOR PRAYER before beginning daily studies, a seminary student adjusts the phylacteries, which are worn during weekly devotions at home or in synagogue by those who adhere literally to traditional Jewish practices.

STUDY The Conservatives
honor old traditions, new ideas

In their determination to know the will of God to the full, throughout the centuries Jews have devoted countless lifetimes to studying His Law. Knowledge of Talmud and Torah was the path to direct communion with God. Judaism still emphasizes learning. But many Jewish thinkers agree with Dr. Simon Greenberg, a leader of the Conservative movement which takes a middle way between Orthodox and Reform and attempts to reconcile tradition with modernity. Said Dr. Greenberg, "Since the rise of the modern scientific method and the modern study of history, knowing our tradition as our fathers knew it is not enough."

At New York's Jewish Theological Seminary, which was founded in 1887 and has become the focal point of Conservatism, the 153 rabbinical students delve into the world's largest Jewish library for original sources in original tongues. They get instruction not only in modern and historic Jewish literary, legal and philosophical thought, but in such practical matters as synagogue administration, tact and the delivery of a provocative sermon; there is also a school for cantors. The seminary's extracurricular activities include an annual graduate school in which Catholic and Protestant theologians also participate. But the seminary never permits its students to forget the precept enunciated by its chancellor, Dr. Louis Finkelstein, that it is the fundamental "business of the Conservative rabbi, as of all good men, to win people back to the disciplined life."

CHANTING THE LITURGY, Max Wohlberg (*right*) of the seminary's Cantors Institute instructs Robert Zalkin, now a graduate cantor too. Sonorous voices of the cantors add a solemn beauty to severely simple Jewish services.

CHANGE 3 groups differ on the sanctity of Jewish tradition

While the fundamental precepts of Judaism have not changed for thousands of years, Jews since the Age of Reason and the Industrial Revolution have held differing views on the value of ritual and tradition. In the U.S. they have disagreed principally on when—and how—the old traditions should yield to modern times. Among the approximately four million U.S. synagogue members (out of a total U.S. Jewish population of 5.2 million), some 40 percent are Orthodox, 30 percent Conservative and 30 percent Reform. The three branches agree on most matters of theology, but disagree profoundly on practice. As Rabbi Meir taught 18 centuries ago, even a non-Jew who lives by the Torah is as good as a Hebrew high priest. The idea is basic to Judaism: the philosophy transcends dogma and ritual. Within the bounds of God's laws, a Jew is free to choose what he believes and to believe what he chooses.

The earliest Jewish settlers in America—the first arrived in 1654—were simple men of action little interested in philosophic dissent from Orthodoxy. Two centuries later, in the 1840s and 1850s, the idea of modernizing the old ritual was brought to America by liberal, economically advanced German Jews who had started the Reform movement in Europe in the 1820s. Orthodox congregations in turn were enormously strengthened when Jews from Russia and Poland began arriving in the 1880s. But many of these newcomers were also partially attracted to Reform. This led during the next two decades to the establishment of Conservatism, designed as a bridge for those who wanted some concessions to modern ways but were wary of the Reform movement itself as too far from the traditions they considered integral to Judaism.

To the Reform movement, with 550 congregations and more than a million members, only the spiritual and ethical values of Judaism cannot be changed. "Judaism," says a Reform spokesman, "contains principles and practices. The practices are secondary; they are designed to dramatize the principles and the ideals. Hence, customs which no longer have an impact on the worshiper may be abandoned; new ones may be fashioned; and . . . older ones may be restored or reintroduced in modified form." Reform Jews treasure the Torah as a repository of ideals, but do not necessarily accept it as divine revelation. They generally look upon the biblical miracles as inspiring allegories.

In a Reform temple such as Beth El, of Providence, R.I., which is pictured on these two pages, most of the 776 member families do not observe the dietary laws, which they consider outmoded by present-day sanitation, or the Sabbath restrictions, which they consider impractical. They reject skull caps, phylacteries or prayer shawls, regarding them as archaic incrustations without religious validity.

Like other temples belonging to the central Reform organization, the Union of American Hebrew Congregations, Beth El has adopted innovations in worship. Recognizing modern habits of work and play, Beth El holds Sabbath services after dinner Friday evening. The rabbi reads the Torah in English as well as Hebrew, and the prayerbooks used by the congregation have the two languages in parallel columns. Music, once frowned upon by the devout, is provided by an organ and a choir. Women, once kept apart from the men as a distraction at prayer, participate in the services and in the temple's leadership. Some Reform congregations have gone further; one of the largest in America has elected a woman president, and another has employed a woman cantor. Many innovations, Reform spokesmen argue, have been adopted now by traditionalists who opposed them at first.

Orthodoxy, indeed, does not rule out adaptations of the Law to modern times, but insists that they must not follow merely a desire for human convenience. The leading Orthodox groups (Union of Orthodox Jewish Congregations of America, National Council of Young Israel, Yeshiva University Synagogue Council) insist that their nearly two million members in some 2,000 congregations adhere strictly to the dietary and Sabbath laws, that men and women be segregated at prayer, that Hebrew predominate at worship. If such restrictions make life difficult in a modern society, Orthodox Jews answer that to modify the Law except "in fear and trembling [as] part of a religious agony" is to destroy it. In the Orthodox concept, not only was every word of the Torah directly revealed to Moses, but even the Talmud's later interpretations of the Mosaic books were divinely guided.

The Conservatives (United Synagogue of America) attempt to make Orthodoxy compatible with modern life. In the 600 Conservative congregations with approximately one million members, services resemble the Orthodox except that men and women usually sit together and

AT CHILDREN'S SERVICE on Saturday morning Beth El's Rabbi William G. Braude reads the Torah, assisted by Howard Rabinowitz. On table are Torah cover, bell-hung crown. Over Ark, letters spell Shaddai (the Almighty).

MERRY FOLK DANCE, one that is popular in Israel, is performed by Beth El pupils after their Hebrew lesson as instructor, Seymour Krieger (background), looks on. Dancing is included in the program to attract the young.

TEACHING HEBREW by modern methods, an instructress at Beth El uses movable letters which the students make into words. Unlike most Orthodox Hebrew schools, which teach mainly biblical Hebrew, Beth El teaches Hebrew both in ancient and modern form. Pupils like Marcia Kaufman (*left*) and Sheila Nelson go to class three times each week and start by learning the more familiar words. Letters at the upper right spell Purim, the name of a major holiday.

EVENING BLESSING is delivered in Hebrew and English by Rabbi Alan S. Green of Temple Emanu El, Cleveland, Ohio, as a Sabbath service ends. Reform Jews do not oppose the use of Hebrew at worship. On the contrary, they would prefer to employ the sacred tongue more. But they believe that the saying of prayers simply by rote without comprehension is worthless, and so they permit only as much Hebrew as every worshiper is able to understand.

an organ and choir are permitted. Some leaders accept modifications of the Law, asserting that a Conservative Jew may ride to the synagogue on the Sabbath but may not ride for pleasure or business. In the Conservative view, Talmudic interpretation of the Torah was a product of its age, subject to revision by a later age.

In addition to these three large groups, there is a small but influential movement called Reconstructionism that sees in Judaism principally a certain culture and a certain set of ethics.

But whatever the differences within its ranks, Judaism is finding new strength in the American Jewish community, which—now the world's largest and richest—is giving essential support to the little state of Israel (approximately $701 million from 1945 through 1955). American Jewry has achieved a leading position in Jewish learning, having gathered in the new world all the traditions of Judaism's many old worlds. Enjoying unprecedented freedom in the U.S., Judaism has also enjoyed unprecedented success. The three movements all have more members and are building more synagogues than ever; in part this may be because many hitherto unaffiliated Jews are rediscovering the fact that while Judaism indeed includes the concepts of a nation, a culture and a set of ethics, all these things together are insufficient unless they rest on Mount Sinai.

CHORAL GROUP at Temple Beth El in Providence represents the active role women play today in a Reform congregation's life. The women sing at various gatherings, but at the actual services a paid choir provides the music.

CONFIRMATION (*opposite*) for boys (in blue) and girls (in white) at 15 is innovation of which the Reform movement is very proud. Here Rabbi E. E. Klein of New York's Stephen Wise Free Synagogue blesses the youngsters.

SCHOLARLY TRADITION is carried on by teacher, Dov Arie Cohen, an immigrant to Israel from Hungary, shown here reading the Talmud at Safad, settlement which for centuries has been a center of study for Jewish mystics.

ISRAEL Elders seek haven
for the ancient law of the Torah

"If I forget thee, O Jerusalem, let my right hand forget its cunning," sang Jewish captives in Babylonian exile. The Jews never forgot, never ceased dreaming of the Return. After World War II, from 65 nations, from North African hovels, Nazi death camps and even from some New York apartments, thousands converged on the new Jewish state.

Yet the Orthodox found in the Promised Land a government of socialist and secularist bent, which felt that Orthodox customs were anachronistic leftovers from the ghetto. Orthodox political parties forced the government to uphold many religious observances. But small fanatical Orthodox factions advocate strictest following of biblical laws. They stone cars that move on Saturday, fight state education and conscription of women, refuse to recognize the Israeli state because it was not set up by the Messiah. But most of the Orthodox work with the government, hoping to build a new home for Judaism on the ancient rock of the Torah.

FESTIVE SABBATH gets early start (*left*) on religious collective farm. On Friday afternoon family goes to dining hall, father carrying sacred wine for the meal. From sundown Friday to sundown Saturday no work is done on farm.

ISRAEL'S DIVERSITY is seen even in a synagogue for non-European Jews. Here, from left, are Meir Abrahamoff of Bukhara, in U.S.S.R., Zadok Harari of Yemen, Rabbi Shalom Azulei of Morocco, Ephraim Gol of Afghanistan, Menache Cohen Johaninoff of Israel. No service is being held now but the elders, who have read the Talmud many times, are "learning"—reading it again, for to Orthodox Jews the Talmud is an eternal source of instruction.

TEACHING THE TORAH to children 3 and 4 years of age is considered essential by the small group called *Hassidim* (pious ones). The movement originated with an 18th Century Polish village teacher who, in revolt against superorthodoxy, preached that salvation was to be found in joyous communion with God rather than in the Torah alone. But the *Hassidim* themselves became superorthodox, now cleave to beards, side curls and archaic garb.

JEWISH WISDOM

The sacred books of Judaism are the Bible, divided into three parts—the Law (Torah), the Prophets (Nebi'im) and the Writings (Ketubim)—and the rabbinic works which include the Talmud and the Midrash. The most revered are the five books of the Pentateuch, known as the Torah: Genesis, Exodus, Leviticus, Numbers and Deuteronomy. Most of the following selections are taken from these, which Rabbi Philip S. Bernstein calls "the acknowledged foundation of Judaism, containing the principles of the faith, the Ten Commandments, the Golden Rule, the laws of holiness." The Pentateuch is both the biography of Moses, greatest Jew of all time, and the history of the Jewish nation's start.

The translation used here of Judaism's scriptures—which are the Old Testament of Christianity—is the standard one issued by the Jewish Publication Society of America, printed in paragraphs for easier reading.

The magnificent passage on the creation (below) opens the book of Genesis and sets the theme of the entire Bible: that God created the cosmos, that man is the apex of His creation and that through man God's aims will be fulfilled.

CREATION

IN the beginning God created the heaven and the earth. Now the earth was unformed and void, and darkness was upon the face of the deep; and the spirit of God hovered over the face of the waters. And God said: "Let there be light." And there was light. And God saw the light, that it was good; and God divided the light from the darkness. And God called the light Day, and the darkness He called Night. And there was evening and there was morning, one day.

And God said: "Let there be a firmament in the midst of the waters, and let it divide the waters from the waters." And God made the firmament from the waters which were above the firmament; and it was so. And God called the firmament Heaven. And there was evening and there was morning, a second day.

And God said: "Let the waters under the heaven be gathered together into one place, and let the dry land appear." And it was so. And God called the dry land Earth, and the . . . waters called He Seas; and God saw that it was good. And God said: "Let the earth put forth grass, herb yielding seed, and fruit tree bearing fruit after its kind." . . . And God saw that it was good. And there was evening and there was morning, a third day.

And God said: "Let there be lights in the firmament of the heaven to divide the day from the night; and let them be for signs, and for seasons, and for days and years." . . . And God made the two great lights, the greater light to rule the day, and the lesser light to rule the night; and the stars. . . . And God saw that it was good. And there was evening and there was morning, a fourth day.

And God said: "Let the waters swarm with swarms of living creatures, and let fowl fly above the earth in the open firmament of heaven." And God created great sea monsters, and every living creature that creepeth, wherewith the waters swarmed,

Tablets with the Ten Commandments recall God's covenant with Israel

after its kind, and every winged fowl after its kind; and God saw that it was good. And God blessed them, saying: "Be fruitful, and multiply, and fill the waters in the seas, and let fowl multiply in the earth." And there was evening and there was morning, a fifth day.

And God said: "Let the earth bring forth the living creature after its kind, cattle, creeping thing, and beast of the earth after its kind." . . . And God created man in His own image, in the image of God created He him; male and female created He them. And God blessed them; and God said unto them: "Be fruitful, and multiply, and replenish the earth, and subdue it; and have dominion over . . . every living thing." . . . And God saw every thing that He had made, and, behold, it was good. And there was evening and there was morning, the sixth day.

And the heaven and the earth were finished, and all the host of them. And on the seventh day God finished His work which He had made; and He rested on the seventh day from all His work which He had made. And God blessed the seventh day and hallowed it; because in it He rested from all His work. . . .

—GENESIS 1, 2

All five books of the Torah are traditionally attributed to Moses. But modern scholars think that they combine source materials from many centuries and were probably first written down between 800 and 600 B.C. The different original sources seem to have been woven together with a minimum of rewriting, causing some repetitions and inconsistencies. Thus, the first account of creation (above) is followed by the story of Adam and Eve where, instead of man and woman being created at the same time, Adam is created first "of the dust of the ground" and Eve from Adam's rib.

Many parts of the world have traditions involving a flood (Cf. Hinduism's legend of Manu, pages 32-33). But the Hebrew story of Noah shows how early Judaism emphasized the spiritual doctrines taught through a merciful God.

NOAH AND THE FLOOD

THE Lord saw that the wickedness of man was great in the earth, and that every imagination of the thoughts of his heart was evil continually. And it repented the Lord that He had made man on the earth, and it grieved Him at His heart. And the Lord said: "I will blot out man whom I have created from the face of the earth; both man and beast, and creeping thing, and fowl of the air; for it repenteth Me that I have made them." But Noah found grace in the eyes of the Lord. . . . Noah was in his generations a man righteous and wholehearted; Noah walked with God. And Noah begot three sons, Shem, Ham and Japheth. . . .

And God said unto Noah: "The end of all flesh is come before Me; for the earth is filled with violence through them; and, behold, I will destroy them with the earth. Make thee an ark. . . . And I, behold, I do bring the flood of waters upon the earth . . . every thing that is in the earth shall perish. But I will establish My covenant with thee; and thou shalt come into the ark, thou, and thy sons, and thy wife, and thy sons' wives with thee. And of every living thing of all flesh, two of every sort shalt thou bring into the ark, to keep them alive with thee; they shall be male and female. Of the fowl after their kind, and of the cattle after their kind, of every creeping thing of the ground after its kind, two of every sort shall come unto thee, to keep them alive. And take thou unto thee of all food that is eaten, and gather it to thee; and it shall be for food for thee, and for them." . . . And Noah did according unto all that the Lord commanded him. . . .

On the same day were all the fountains of the great deep broken up, and the windows of heaven were opened. . . . And the waters prevailed, and increased greatly upon the earth; and the ark went upon the face of the waters. . . . And all the high mountains that were under the whole heaven were covered. . . . And all flesh perished . . . and Noah only was left, and they that were with him in the ark. And the waters prevailed upon the earth a hundred and fifty days. . . .

And the ark rested in the seventh month, on the seventeenth day of the month, upon the mountains of Ararat. . . . And it came to pass at the end of forty days, that Noah . . . sent forth a dove from him, to see if the waters were abated from off the face of the ground. But the dove found no rest for the sole of her foot, and she returned unto him to the ark, for the waters were on the face of the whole earth; and he put forth his hand, and took her, and brought her in unto him into the ark. And he stayed yet other seven days; and again he sent forth the dove out of the ark. And the dove came in to him at eventide; and lo, in her mouth an olive leaf freshly plucked; so Noah knew the waters were abated from off the earth. . . .

And God spoke unto Noah, saying: "Go forth from the ark, thou, and thy wife, and thy sons, and thy sons' wives with thee. Bring forth with thee every living thing that is with thee." . . . And God blessed Noah and his sons, and said unto them: "Be fruitful, and multiply, and replenish the earth. And the fear of you and the dread of you shall be upon every beast of the earth, and upon every fowl of the air, and upon all wherewith the ground teemeth, and upon all the fishes of the sea; into your hand are they delivered. Every moving thing that liveth shall be for food for you; as the green herb have I given you all." . . .

And God spoke upon Noah, and to his sons with him, saying: ". . . I will establish My covenant with you; neither . . . shall there any more be a flood to destroy the earth." And God said: "This is the token of the covenant which I make between Me and you and every living creature that is with you, for perpetual generations: I have set My bow in the cloud, and it shall be for a token of a covenant between Me and the earth. And it shall come to pass, when I bring clouds over the earth, and the bow is seen in the cloud, that I will remember . . . the everlasting covenant between God and every living creature of all flesh upon the earth." . . . And the sons of Noah, that went forth from the ark, were Shem, and Ham and Japheth; and Ham is the father of Canaan. These were the sons of Noah, and of these was the whole earth overspread. . . .

—GENESIS 6–9

Shofar, ancient battle horn, signals the Jewish New Year

The stories of the patriarchs Abraham, Isaac, Jacob and Joseph fill about four-fifths of Genesis. With them, the Jewish scriptures move into recorded history. These ancestors of the Hebrew people were seminomads who, around 2000 B.C., roved on the edges of the already settled civilizations of Egypt, Syria and Mesopotamia. Haran, Terah and Nahor—names which are all listed at the beginning of the selection below—were Semitic settlements in the upper Euphrates area, and the proper names of Abram and Jacob

have been found in the contemporary records of the region. Many of the customs recorded in Genesis still exist among the Arabs, who trace their ancestry through Abraham's son Ishmael, just as the Jews trace theirs through Abraham's son Isaac. (Moslems believe that Abraham and Ishmael built the Kaaba, their holiest shrine.)

Abraham received God's earliest covenant with the Jews. Noah's rainbow covenant had been for all mankind; now the Jews were singled out especially, with circumcision decreed as a mark of their divine covenant. God called and tested Abraham: first, in ordering him to migrate to Canaan (Palestine), and later, in many other ways, including a demand that he sacrifice his son Isaac. Abraham's unswerving faithfulness allowed him to sire a dedicated people through whom God could bless all men everywhere.

Yet Abraham and his descendants also had their weaknesses. The narrative is as candid in castigating their faults as in praising their virtues, thus emphasizing that any man or woman—however weak—can rise to great heights of spiritual achievement, like the human beings in the Bible. The resulting picture of God's spirit working on sinful man is so strikingly fresh and dynamic in its wealth of deep meaning and vivid detail that the scriptural narrative has gripped the attention of its readers ever since.

ABRAHAM

NOW these are the generations of Terah. Terah begot Abram, Nahor and Haran. . . . And . . . Abram's wife was Sarai. . . . And Sarai was barren; she had no child. . . . Now the Lord said unto Abram: "Get thee out of thy country, and . . . I will make of thee a great nation, and I will bless thee . . . and in thee shall all the families of the earth be blessed." So Abram went, as the Lord had spoken unto him . . . into the land of Canaan. . . . And the Lord appeared unto Abram, and said: "Unto thy seed will I give this land. . . . I am thy shield.". . . And Abram said: "O Lord God, what wilt Thou give me, seeing I go hence childless?" . . . And He brought him forth abroad, and said: "Look now toward heaven, and count the stars. . . . So shall thy seed be." . . .

Now Sarai, Abram's wife, bore him no children; and she had a handmaid, an Egyptian, whose name was Hagar. And Sarai said unto Abram: "Behold, the Lord hath restrained me from bearing; go in, I pray thee, unto my handmaid; it may be that I shall be builded up through her." And Abram . . . went in unto Hagar, and she conceived. . . . And Sarai said unto Abram: "My wrong be upon thee: I gave my handmaid unto thy bosom; and when she saw that she had conceived, I was despised in her eyes: the Lord judge between me and thee." . . . And Sarai dealt harshly with [Hagar], and she fled from her face. . . . And Hagar bore Abram a son . . . Ishmael. . . . And when Abram was ninety years old and nine, the Lord appeared to Abram, and said unto him: "I am God Almighty; walk before Me, and be thou wholehearted. . . . Neither shall thy name any more be called Abram, but thy name shall be Abraham; for the father of a multitude of nations have I made thee. . . . This is My covenant, which ye shall keep, between Me and you and thy seed after thee: every male among you shall be circumcised. And ye shall be circumcised in the flesh of your foreskin; and it shall be a token of a covenant betwixt Me and you. And he that is eight days old shall be circumcised among you. . . . And the uncircumcised male . . . shall be cut off from his people; he hath broken My covenant."

And God said unto Abraham: "As for Sarai thy wife, thou shalt not call her name Sarai, but Sarah shall her name be. And I will bless her, and moreover I will give thee a son of her; yea,

I will bless her, and she shall be a mother of nations; kings of people shall be of her." Then Abraham . . . laughed, and said in his heart: "Shall a child be born unto him that is a hundred years old? and shall Sarah, that is ninety years old, bear?"

And Abraham said unto God: "Oh, that Ishmael might live before Thee!" And God said: "Nay, but Sarah thy wife shall bear thee a son; and thou shalt call his name Isaac; and I will establish My covenant with him for an everlasting covenant for his seed after him. And as for Ishmael, I have heard thee; behold, I have blessed him, and will make him fruitful, and will multiply him exceedingly; twelve princes shall he beget, and I will make him a great nation. But My covenant will I establish with Isaac." . . .

And Abraham took Ishmael his son, and all . . . among the men of Abraham's house, and circumcised the flesh of their foreskin in the selfsame day, as God had said unto him. . . .

And the Lord did unto Sarah as He had spoken. And Sarah . . . bore Abraham a son . . . Isaac. . . . And Sarah said: "God hath made laughter for me; every one that heareth will laugh on account of me." And she said: "Who would have said unto Abraham that Sarah should give children suck? for I have borne him a son in his old age." . . . And Sarah saw the son of Hagar the Egyptian, whom she had borne unto Abraham, making sport. Wherefore she said unto Abraham: "Cast out this bondwoman and her son; for the son of this bondwoman shall not be heir with my son, even with Isaac." . . . And God said unto Abraham: "Let it not be grievous in thy sight because of the lad, and because of thy bondwoman; in all that Sarah saith unto thee, hearken unto her voice; for in Isaac shall seed be called to thee. And also of the son of the bond-woman will I make a nation, because he is thy seed." . . .

Rainbow was God's assurance to Noah that a second flood would not occur

And it came to pass after these things, that God did prove Abraham, and said: ". . . Take now thy son, thine only son, whom thou lovest, even Isaac, and get thee into the land of Moriah; and offer him there for a burnt offering upon one of the mountains which I will tell thee of." . . . And Isaac spoke unto Abraham his father, and said: ". . . Behold the fire and the wood; but where is the lamb for a burnt offering?" And Abraham said: "God will provide Himself the lamb for a burnt offering, my son." So they went both of them together. And they came to the place which God had told him of; and Abraham built the altar there, and . . . took the knife to slay his son. And the angel of the Lord called unto him out of heaven, and said: " '. . . Lay not thy hand upon the lad, neither do thou any thing unto him; for now I know that thou art a God-fearing man, seeing thou hast not withheld thy son, thine only son, from Me.' " And Abraham lifted up his eyes, and looked, and behold, behind him a ram caught in the thicket by his horns. And Abraham went and took the ram, and offered him up for a burnt offering in the stead of his son. . . . And the angel of the Lord called unto Abraham a second time out of heaven, and said: " 'By Myself have I sworn,' saith the Lord, 'because thou hast done this thing, and hast not withheld thy son, thine only son, that in blessing I will bless thee, and in multiplying I will multiply thy seed as the stars of the heaven, and as the sand which is upon the seashore; and thy seed shall possess the gate of his enemies; and in thy seed shall all the nations of the earth be blessed; because thou hast hearkened to My voice.' " . . . And Abraham expired, and died in a good old age, an old man, and full of years; and was gathered to his people. And Isaac and Ishmael his sons buried him. . . .

—GENESIS 11–25

Isaac was followed by Jacob, one of whose sons—Joseph —went to Egypt about 1700 B.C., became a trusted coun-selor at Pharaoh's court, and persuaded his clan to join him. Later Egyptians enslaved the Jews. About 1300 B.C.

came Moses, the mightiest man in Hebrew history. Guided by God through crisis after crisis, Moses set his people free and led them back toward the Promised Land.

By tireless, forceful leadership Moses brought all the Jews to belief in one God, the supreme Ruler of the universe. He established their moral and legal codes, which have been a major force in Judaism and all Western civilization to this day, though later Jews have adapted and developed the message of Moses, just as Moses did to that of Abraham.

MOSES AND EXODUS

NOW there arose a new king over Egypt, who knew not Joseph. And he said unto his people: "Behold, the people of the Children of Israel are too many and too mighty for us." . . . Therefore they did set over them taskmasters to afflict them with their burdens. . . . And the king of Egypt spoke to the Hebrew midwives . . . saying: "Every son that is born ye shall cast into the river, and every daughter ye shall save alive." And there went a man of the house of Levi, and took to wife, a daughter of Levi. And the woman con-ceived, and bore a son; and . . . when she could not longer hide him, she took for him an ark of bulrushes, and daubed it with slime and with pitch; and she put the child therein, and laid it in the flags by the river's brink. And his sister stood afar off, to know what would be done to him. And the daughter of Pharaoh came down to bathe in the river; and her maidens walked along by the riverside; and she saw the ark among the flags, and . . . a boy that wept. And she had compassion on him, and said: "This is one of the Hebrews' children." Then said his sister to Pharaoh's daughter: "Shall I go and call thee a nurse of the Hebrew women . . . for thee?" And Phar-aoh's daughter said to her: "Go." And the maiden went and called the child's mother. And Pharaoh's daughter said unto her: "Take this child away, and nurse it for me, and I will give thee thy wages." And the woman took the child, and nursed it. And the child grew, and she brought him unto Pharaoh's daughter, and he became her son. And she called his name Moses, and said: "Because I drew him out of the water."

And it came to pass in those days, when Moses was grown up . . . he saw an Egyptian smiting a Hebrew, one of his brethren. And he . . . smote the Egyptian. . . . Now when Pharaoh heard this thing, he sought to slay Moses. But Moses fled from the face of Pharaoh, and dwelt in the land of Midian. . . .

Now Moses was keeping the flock of Jethro. . . . And the angel of the Lord appeared unto him in a flame of fire out of . . . a bush; and he looked, and, behold, the bush burned with fire, and the bush was not consumed. And Moses said: "I will turn aside now, and see this great sight, why the bush is not burnt." And . . . God called unto him out of the midst of the bush, and said: "Moses, Moses." And he said: "Here am I." And He said: "Draw not nigh hither; put off thy shoes . . . for the place whereon thou standest is holy ground." . . .

And the Lord said: "I have surely seen the affliction of My people that are in Egypt, and have heard their cry by reason of their taskmasters; for I know their pains; and I am come down to deliver them out of the hand of the Egyptians, and to bring them up out of that land unto a good land and a large, unto a land flowing with milk and honey; unto the place of the Canaanite." . . .

And Moses said unto God: "Who am I, that I should go unto Pharaoh, and that I should bring forth the Children of Israel out of Egypt?" And He said: "Certainly I will be with thee. . . ." And Moses said unto God: "Behold, when I come unto the Children of Israel, and shall say unto them: 'The God of your fathers hath sent me unto you'; and they shall say to me:

'What is His name?' what shall I say unto them?" And God said: "I AM THAT I AM"; and He said: "Thus shalt thou say unto the Children of Israel: 'I AM hath sent me unto you.' " . . .

And Moses . . . returned to the land of Egypt. . . . And the people believed; and when they heard that the Lord had remembered the Children of Israel, and that He had seen their affliction, then they bowed their heads and worshiped. . . .

Then the Lord said unto Moses: "Go in unto Pharaoh, and tell him: Thus saith the Lord, the God of the Hebrews: 'Let My people go, that they may serve Me.' " . . . And the heart of Pharaoh was hardened, and he did not let the Children of Israel go. . . . And the Lord said unto Moses: "Yet one plague more [the tenth] will I bring upon Pharaoh, and upon Egypt; afterwards he will let you go hence." . . .

And the Lord spoke unto Moses and Aaron [Moses' brother] in the land of Egypt, saying: ". . . All the congregation of Israel . . . shall take to them every man a lamb . . . and . . . shall kill it at dusk. And they shall take of the blood, and put it on the two side posts and on the lintel, upon the houses wherein they shall eat it. And they shall eat the flesh in that night, roast with fire, and unleavened bread; with bitter herbs they shall eat it. . . . And thus shall ye eat it: with your loins girded, your shoes on your feet, and your staff in your hand; and ye shall eat it in haste—it is the Lord's passover.

"For I will go through the land of Egypt in that night, and will smite all the first-born in the land of Egypt, both man and beast. . . . And the blood shall be to you for a token upon the houses where ye are; and when I see the blood, I will pass over you, and there shall no plague be upon you. . . . And this day shall be unto you for a memorial, and ye shall keep it a feast to the Lord; throughout your generations ye shall keep it a feast by an ordinance for ever." . . .

And it came to pass at midnight, that the Lord smote all the first-born in the land of Egypt. . . . And Pharaoh rose up in the night, he, and all his servants, and all the Egyptians; and there was a great cry in Egypt; for there was not a house where there was not one dead. And he called for Moses and Aaron by night and said: "Rise up, get you forth. . . ." And the Egyptians were urgent upon the people, to send them out of the land in haste; for they said: "We are all dead men." . . . And the Children of Israel . . . asked of the Egyptians jewels of silver, and jewels of gold, and raiment. And the Lord gave the people favor in the sight of the Egyptians, so that they let them have what they asked. And they despoiled the Egyptians. . . .

God led the people about, by way of the wilderness by the Red Sea; and the Children of Israel went up armed out of the land of Egypt. . . . And the Lord went before them by day in a pillar of cloud, to lead them the way; and by night in a pillar of fire, to give them light. . . .

And the Egyptians pursued after them, all the horses and chariots of Pharaoh. . . . And when Pharaoh drew nigh, the Children of Israel lifted up their eyes, and . . . were sore afraid; and . . . cried out unto the Lord. . . .

And Moses stretched out his hand over the sea; and the Lord caused the sea to go back. . . . And the Children of Israel went into the midst of the sea upon the dry ground; and the waters were a wall unto them on their right hand, and on their left. And the Egyptians pursued . . . them into the midst of the sea. . . . And Moses stretched forth his hand over the sea, and . . . the waters returned, and covered . . . all the host of Pharaoh. . . .

And Moses led Israel onward from the Red Sea, and they went out into the wilderness. . . . And the whole congregation of the Children of Israel murmured against Moses. . . . "Would that we had died by the hand of the Lord in the land of Egypt, when we sat by the fleshpots, when we did eat bread to the full; for ye have brought us forth into this wilderness, to kill this whole assembly with hunger." Then said the Lord unto Moses: "Behold, I will cause to rain bread from heaven for you;

and the people shall go out and gather a day's portion every day, that I may prove them, whether they will walk in My law, or not." . . . And it came to pass at even, that the quails came up, and covered the camp; and in the morning there was a layer of dew round about the camp. And when the layer of dew was gone up, behold, upon the face of the wilderness a fine, scale-like thing, fine as the hoarfrost on the ground. And when the Children of Israel saw it, they said one to another: "What is it?"—for they knew not what it was. And Moses said unto them: "It is the bread which the Lord hath given you to eat." . . . And the house of Israel called the name thereof manna; and it was like coriander seed, white; and the taste of it was like wafers made with honey. . . . And the Children of Israel did eat the manna forty years, until they came . . . unto the borders of the land of Canaan. . . .

In the third month after the Children of Israel were gone forth out of . . . Egypt . . . came they into the wilderness of Sinai . . . and there Israel encamped before the mount. And Moses went up unto God, and the Lord called unto him out of the mountain, saying: "Thus shalt thou . . . tell the Children of Israel: 'Ye have seen what I did unto the Egyptians, and how I bore you on eagles' wings, and brought you unto Myself. Now therefore, if ye will hearken unto My voice indeed, and keep My covenant, then ye shall be Mine own treasure from among all peoples . . . and a holy nation.' " . . .

And it came to pass on the third day, when it was morning, that there were thunders and lightnings and a thick cloud upon the mount, and . . . all the people that were in the camp trembled. And Moses brought forth the people out of the camp to meet God; and they stood at the nether part of the mount. Now mount Sinai was altogether on smoke, because the Lord descended upon it in fire; and the smoke thereof ascended as the smoke of a furnace, and the whole mount quaked greatly. . . . And the Lord came down upon mount Sinai . . . and . . . called Moses to the top of the mount. . . .

And God spoke all these words, saying:

"I am the Lord thy God, Who brought thee out of the land of Egypt, out of the house of bondage.

"Thou shalt have no other gods before Me.

"Thou shalt not make unto thee a graven image, nor any manner of likeness, of any thing that is in the heaven above, or that is in the earth beneath, or that is in the water under the earth; thou shalt not bow down unto them, nor serve them; for I the Lord thy God am a jealous God, visiting the iniquity of the fathers upon the children unto the third and fourth generation of them that hate Me; and showing mercy unto the thousandth generation of them that love Me and keep My commandments.

"Thou shalt not take the name of the Lord thy God in vain; for [He] will not hold him guiltless that taketh His name in vain.

"Remember the sabbath day, to keep it holy. Six days shalt thou labor . . . but the seventh day is a sabbath unto the Lord thy God; in it thou shalt not do any manner of work, thou, nor thy son, nor thy daughter, nor thy manservant . . . nor thy cattle, nor the stranger that is within thy gates; for in six days the Lord made heaven and earth, the sea, and all that in them is, and rested on the seventh day; wherefore the Lord blessed the sabbath day, and hallowed it.

"Honor thy father and thy mother, that thy days may be long upon the land which the Lord thy God giveth thee.

"Thou shalt not murder.

"Thou shalt not commit adultery.

"Thou shalt not steal.

"Thou shalt not bear false witness against thy neighbor.

"Thou shalt not covet thy neighbor's house; thou shalt not covet thy neighbor's wife, nor his manservant, nor his maidservant, nor his ox, nor his ass, nor anything that is thy neighbor's." . . . And the Lord said unto Moses: ". . . Now these are the ordinances which thou shalt set before them. . . . If men strive together, and . . . any harm follow, then thou shalt

Dove, with an olive branch, is biblical symbol of peace

give life for life, eye for eye, tooth for tooth, hand for hand, foot for foot, burning for burning, wound for wound, stripe for stripe. And if a man smite the eye of his bondman, or the eye of his bondwoman, and destroy it, he shall let him go free for his eye's sake. . . .

"Thou shall not suffer a sorceress to live.

"Whosoever lieth with a beast shall surely be put to death.

"He that sacrificeth unto the gods, save unto the Lord only, shall be utterly destroyed." . . .

And Moses came and told the people all the words of the Lord, and all the ordinances; and all the people answered with one voice, and said: "All the words which the Lord hath spoken will we do." . . .

And the Lord said unto Moses: "Come up to Me into the mount, and be there; and I will give thee the tables of stone, and the law and the commandment, which I have written, that thou mayest teach them." . . . And Moses entered into the midst of the cloud, and went up into the mount; and Moses was in the mount forty days and forty nights. . . .

When the people saw that Moses delayed to come down from the mount, the people gathered themselves together unto Aaron, and said unto him: "Up, make us a god who shall go before us; for as for this Moses, the man that brought us up out of the land of Egypt, we know not what is become of him." And Aaron said unto them: "Break off the golden rings, which are in the ears of your wives, of your sons, and of your daughters, and bring them unto me." . . . And he . . . made . . . a molten calf; and they said: "This is thy god, O Israel, which brought thee up out of the land of Egypt." And when Aaron saw this, he built an altar before it; and Aaron made proclamation, and said: "Tomorrow shall be a feast to the Lord." And they rose up early on the morrow and offered burnt offerings. . . .

And the Lord spoke unto Moses: "Go, get thee down; for thy people . . . have turned aside quickly out of the way which I commanded." . . . And Moses turned, and went down from the mount, with the two tables of the testimony in his hand. . . . And . . . he saw the calf and the dancing; and Moses' anger waxed hot, and he cast the tables out of his hands, and broke them. . . . And he took the calf . . . and burnt it with fire. . . .

And the Lord said unto Moses: "Hew thee two tables of stone like unto the first; and I will write upon the tables the words that were on the first tables, which thou didst break." . . . And Moses . . . went up unto mount Sinai. . . . And the Lord passed by before him, and proclaimed: "The Lord, God, merciful and gracious, long-suffering and abundant in goodness and truth; keeping mercy unto the thousandth generation, forgiving iniquity and transgression and sin; and that will by no means clear the guilty." . . . And Moses made haste, and bowed his head toward the earth, and worshiped. And he said: "If now I have found grace in Thy sight, O Lord . . . I pray Thee, go in the midst of us; for it is a stiffnecked people; and pardon our . . . sin, and take us for Thine inheritance." . . .

And the Lord spoke unto Moses, saying: "On the first day of the first month shalt thou rear up the tabernacle of the tent of meeting." . . . And Moses reared up the tabernacle. . . . Then the cloud covered the tent of meeting, and the glory of the Lord filled the tabernacle. And Moses was not able to enter into the tent of meeting, because the cloud abode thereon, and the glory of the Lord filled the tabernacle. And whenever the cloud was taken up from the tabernacle, the Children of Israel went onward, throughout all their journeys. . . .

—EXODUS

Judaism traversed an evolutionary process in its gradual discovery of the greatness and graciousness of God. The book of Leviticus records some of the noblest of all ethical

injunctions, including the Golden Rule. It also explores the inner significance of sacrifice, which is that man must share his possessions with people in need and institutions that advance human welfare. Chapters 17–26, known as the Holiness Code, assume that God has chosen the Hebrew nation for righteous living, and that through its efforts toward holiness the will of God may be realized.

BE RIGHTEOUS

AND the Lord spoke unto Moses, saying: "Speak unto all the congregation of the Children of Israel, and say unto them: 'Ye shall be holy; for I the Lord your God am holy. . . . When ye reap the harvest of your land, thou shalt not . . . gather the gleaning of thy harvest. . . . Thou shalt leave [it] for the poor and the stranger. . . . Ye shall do no unrighteousness in judgment; thou shalt not . . . favor the person of the mighty. . . . Thou shalt not take vengeance, nor bear any grudge against the children of thy people, but thou shalt love thy neighbor as thyself. . . .

Grapes and leaves, fruit of the vine, signify God-given earthly abundance

" 'Ye shall not . . . practice divination nor soothsaying. Ye shall not round the corners of your heads, neither shalt thou mar the corners of thy beard. . . . Turn ye not unto the ghosts, nor unto familiar spirits; seek them not out, to be defiled by them. . . . If a stranger sojourn with thee in your land, ye shall not do him wrong. The stranger that sojourneth with you shall be unto you as the homeborn among you, and thou shalt love him as thyself; for ye were strangers in the land of Egypt.' "

—LEVITICUS 19

The book of Numbers contains a benediction used daily by Jews and also widely loved by Christians.

BLESSING

AND the Lord spoke unto Moses, saying: "Speak unto Aaron and unto his sons, saying: 'On this wise ye shall bless the Children of Israel; ye shall say unto them:

" 'The Lord bless thee, and keep thee;

" 'The Lord make His face to shine upon thee, and be gracious unto thee;

" 'The Lord lift up His countenance upon thee, and give thee peace.' " . . .

—NUMBERS 6

The book of Deuteronomy, while ascribed to Moses, is believed by scholars to date long after Moses, probably from the Seventh Century B.C. In helping to record the upward march of man from primitivism, it adapts the earlier codes of a primarily agricultural people to an urban civilization around Jerusalem. It thus regulates the interest on loans, permits sanctuary for escaped bondmen, and says a man has the right to privacy in his own home.

Deuteronomy has been called "Israel's testament of faith in which the redemptive love of God and the whole duty of man in God's service is nobly and convincingly proclaimed." Jesus said that the passage on loving God given below is the greatest commandment, adding that the next most important is "love thy neighbor," given in Leviticus above. Known as the Shema ("Hear"), the entire passage is one which devout Jews repeat in their daily prayers, teach their children and often post on their doorways.

'LOVE THE LORD'

THESE are the words which Moses spoke unto all Israel beyond the Jordan, in the wilderness: ". . . Now this is the commandment, the statutes, and the ordinances, which the Lord your God commanded to teach you. . . .

"HEAR, O ISRAEL: THE LORD OUR GOD, THE LORD IS ONE. And thou shalt love the Lord thy God with all thy heart, and with all thy soul, and with all thy might. And these words, which I command thee this day, shall be upon thy heart; and thou shalt teach them diligently unto thy children, and shalt talk of them when thou sittest in thy house, and when thou walkest by the way, and when thou liest down, and when thou risest up. And thou shalt bind them for a sign upon thy hand, and they shall be for frontlets between thine eyes. And thou shalt write them upon the doorposts of thy house, and upon thy gates.

"And it shall be, when the Lord thy God shall bring thee into the land which He swore unto thy fathers . . . to give thee—great and goodly cities, which thou didst not build, and houses full of all good things, which thou didst not fill, and cisterns hewn out, which thou didst not hew, vineyards and olive trees, which thou didst not plant, and thou shalt eat and be satisfied—then beware lest thou forget the Lord. . . .

"And thou shalt remember all the way which the Lord thy God hath led thee these forty years in the wilderness, that He might afflict thee, to prove thee, to know what was in thy heart, whether thou wouldest keep His commandments, or no. And He afflicted thee, and suffered thee to hunger, and fed thee with manna, which thou knewest not, neither did thy fathers know; that He might make thee know that man doth not live by bread only, but by every thing that proceedeth out of the mouth of the Lord doth man live." . . .

—Deuteronomy 1, 6, 8

For centuries the Hebrews were ruled by kings. The spiritual episodes of this long period include Solomon asking for wisdom and building the Temple.

SOLOMON

IN Gibeon the LORD appeared to Solomon in a dream by night; and God said: "Ask what I shall give thee." And Solomon said: ". . . Thy servant is in the midst of thy people which Thou hast chosen. . . . Give Thy servant therefore an understanding heart to judge Thy people, that I may discern between good and evil." . . . And God said unto him: "Because thou hast asked this thing . . . lo, I have given thee a wise and an understanding heart; so that there hath been none like thee before thee, neither after thee shall any arise like unto thee. And I have also given thee that which thou hast not asked, both riches and honour—so that there hath not been any among the kings like unto thee—all thy days." . . .

And the house which king Solomon built for the LORD, the length thereof was threescore cubits. . . . And Solomon stood before the altar . . . and he said: "O LORD . . . the heaven of heavens cannot contain Thee; how much less this house that I have builded! Yet have Thou respect unto the prayer of Thy servant. . . . And of Thy people Israel, when they shall pray toward this place; yea, hear . . . and when Thou hearest, forgive. . . . Moreover concerning the stranger that is not of Thy people Israel, when he shall . . . pray toward this house; hear Thou . . . and do according to all that the stranger calleth to Thee for; that all the peoples of the earth may know Thy name." . . .

—I Kings 3, 6, 8

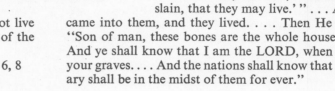

Solomon's Temple served as God's house on earth

Prophets in Jewish scriptures were men of moral courage and pioneers in the realm of the spirit (see pages 143–144). Among them were Isaiah (c. 710 B.C.) and Ezekiel (c. 590 B.C.). The following selections are Ezekiel's vision of a valley of bones coming to life and Isaiah's prophecy of peace.

THE DRY BONES

THE hand of the LORD was upon me, and the LORD carried me out in a spirit, and set me down in the midst of the valley, and it was full of bones; and He caused me to pass by them round about, and, behold, there were very many . . . and . . . they were very dry. And He said unto me: "Son of man, can these bones live?" And I answered: "O Lord GOD, Thou knowest." Then He said unto me: ". . . Say unto them: 'O ye dry bones, hear the word of the LORD: Thus saith the Lord GOD unto these bones: Behold, I will cause breath to enter into you, and ye shall live. And I will lay sinews upon you . . . and cover you with skin, and . . . ye shall know that I am the LORD.' "

So I prophesied as I was commanded; and . . . there was a noise, and behold a commotion, and the bones came together, bone to its bone. And I beheld, and, lo, there were sinews upon them, and flesh came up, and skin covered them above; but there was no breath in them. Then said He unto me: "Prophesy unto the breath, prophesy, son of man, and say to the breath: 'Thus saith the Lord GOD: Come from the four winds, O breath, and breathe upon these slain, that they may live.' " . . . And the breath came into them, and they lived. . . . Then He said unto me: "Son of man, these bones are the whole house of Israel. . . . And ye shall know that I am the LORD, when I have opened your graves. . . . And the nations shall know that . . . My sanctuary shall be in the midst of them for ever."

—Ezekiel 37

PROPHECY OF PEACE

AND it shall come to pass in the end of days, that the mountain of the LORD'S house shall be established as the top of the mountains, and shall be exalted above the hills; and all nations shall flow unto it. And many peoples shall go and say: "Come ye, and let us go up to the mountain of the LORD, to the house of the God of Jacob; and He will teach us of His ways, and we will walk in His paths." For out of Zion shall go forth the law, and the word of the LORD from Jerusalem. And He shall judge between the nations, and shall decide for many peoples; and they shall beat their swords into plowshares, and their spears into pruninghooks; nation shall not lift up sword against nation, neither shall they learn war any more.

—Isaiah 2

The Psalms, which are traditionally attributed to King David, have been called "the immortal song book of the human heart." Two of the best loved follow.

PSALM 1

HAPPY is the man that hath not walked in the counsel of the wicked, nor stood in the way of sinners, nor sat in the seat of the scornful. But his delight is in the law of the LORD; and in His law doth he meditate day and night. And he shall be like a tree planted by streams of water, that bringeth forth its fruit in its season, and whose leaf doth not wither; and in whatsoever he doeth he shall prosper. Not so the wicked. . . . For the LORD regardeth the way of the righteous; but the way of the wicked shall perish.

PSALM 23

THE LORD is my shepherd; I shall not want. He maketh me to lie down in green pastures; He leadeth me beside the still waters. He restoreth my soul; He guideth me in straight paths for His name's sake. Yea, though I walk through the valley of the shadow of death, I will fear no evil, for Thou art with me; Thy rod and Thy staff, they comfort me. Thou preparest a table before me in the presence of mine enemies; Thou hast anointed my head with oil; my cup runneth over. Surely goodness and mercy shall follow me all the days of my life; and I shall dwell in the house of the LORD for ever.

Who Ecclesiastes was, or when he lived, is not certain. But "the Preacher," as he is also known—the term is koheleth *in Hebrew,* ekklesiastes *in Greek—produced a classic pronouncement on disillusionment and on how to attain some happiness amid life's seeming futilities.*

ECCLESIASTES

VANITY of vanities, saith Koheleth; vanity of vanities, all is vanity. What profit hath man of all his labour wherein he laboureth under the sun? One generation passeth away, and another generation cometh; and the earth abideth for ever. . . . All the rivers run into the sea, yet the sea is not full. . . . And there is nothing new under the sun. . . .

To every thing there is a season, and a time to every purpose under the heaven: a time to be born, and a time to die; a time to plant, and a time to pluck up that which is planted; a time to kill, and a time to heal; a time to break down, and a time to build up; a time to weep, and a time to laugh; a time to mourn, and a time to dance; a time to cast away stones, and a time to gather stones together; a time to embrace, and a time to refrain from embracing; a time to seek, and a time to lose; a time to keep, and a time to cast away; a time to rend, and a time to sew; a time to keep silence, and a time to speak; a time to love, and a time to hate; a time for war, and a time for peace. . . .

Remember then thy Creator in the days of thy youth, before the evil days come . . . before the silver cord is snapped asunder, and the golden bowl is shattered, and the pitcher is broken at the fountain, and the wheel falleth shattered, into the cistern; and the dust returneth to the earth as it was, and the spirit returneth unto God who gave it. Vanity of vanities, saith Koheleth; all is vanity.
—ECCLESIASTES 1, 3, 12

The seven-branched menorah *is familiar sign for Judaism*

About the Fifth Century B.C., when the Torah became established as Jewish law, sages began devoting themselves to interpreting its precepts. Such elaboration became vital, since the conditions in which the Jews lived kept changing, and modifications were needed. These sages were first known as "Men of the Great Synagogue," later as the "Fathers," and by the First Century A.D. were being addressed as "rabbi" (the Hebrew term meaning "my master"). These rabbis first taught a body of oral law known as the Mishna

("Repetition"). The Mishna in turn was greatly expanded in a still longer work called the Gemara ("Learning") about 500 A.D. The two together became known as the Talmud ("Teaching"). "The Talmud," wrote Will Durant, "is not only an encyclopedia of Jewish history, theology, ritual, medicine, and folklore; it is also a treatise on agriculture, gardens, industry, the professions, commerce, finance, taxation, property, slavery, inheritance, theft, legal procedure and penal law." The Talmud is also, above all, a subtle and elaborate code of ethics. One of the earliest rabbinical writings which shows this ethical tone is the Pirke Aboth, *quotations from which appear below.*

THE FATHERS' SAYINGS

MOSES received the Law on Mount Sinai and handed it down to Joshua, who handed it down to the Judges, who handed it down to the Prophets, who handed it down to the Men of the Great Synagogue. These used to say three things: Be deliberate in passing judgment, and raise up many disciples, and build a hedge around the Law."

Simeon the Just [died around 270 B.C.] was one of the last members of the Great Synagogue. His favorite saying was: "The world is established on three things—on Law, on Worship, and on Generosity." . . .

Hillel [about 70 B.C.] used to say: "Be among the disciples of Aaron, loving peace, cherishing mankind, and bringing [people] ever closer to the Law." [Also] he would say: "He who advertises his name, loses it; he who does not increase [knowledge], diminishes it; he who refuses to learn, merits extinction; and he who puts his talent to selfish use, wastes away." [Also] he would say: "If I am not for myself, who will be, but if I am only for myself, what am I?" And if [the time for action is] not now, when [is it]?" . . .

Hillel . . . used to observe: "More flesh, more worms; more wealth, more worry; more women, more witchcraft; more concubines, more lechery; more slaves, more thievery. [But] more law, more life; more study, more wisdom; more counsel, more clarity; more righteousness, more peace. . . .

Rabban Gamaliel used to say: "Get yourself a teacher, and keep away from doubtful matters, and never tithe by guesswork." . . .

Rabbi Eliezer said: "Let your comrade's honor be as dear to you as your own; and do not be quick to get angry; also repent before it is too late. Warm yourself at the fire of the learned, but beware of their glowing coals, lest you get scorched. The bite of the learned is like the bite of a fox, their sting is like a scorpion's, their hiss like a serpent's, and all their words are like coals of fire." . . .

Rabbi Elazar said: "Be avid to learn Torah, and know how to refute a disbeliever."

Akabya ben Mahalalel said: "Keep three things in mind, and you will escape the toils of wickedness—know whence you have come, whither you are going, and before whom you will have to give a strict account of yourself. Whence did you come?—from a fetid drop [of sperm]. Whither are you going? —to a place of dust, worms, and maggots. Before whom will you have to give a strict account of yourself?—before the King of Kings, the Holy One, blessed be He." . . .

Rabbi Nehorai said: "Move to a place where there is learning, because you cannot expect learning to move to you."

Rabbi Jannai said: "It is beyond our power to explain . . . the prosperity of the wicked or the afflictions of the righteous."

Rabbi Mattithiah ben Harash said: "Be first in greeting all men, and be rather a tail to lions than a head to foxes."

Rabbi Jacob used to say: "This world is no more than the vestibule of the world to come, so get ready in the vestibule to enter the banquet hall. [However] one hour of repentance and good deeds in this world is better than a lifetime in the World to Come, and one hour of bliss in the World to Come is better than a lifetime in this world." . . . Jehudah ben Tama used to say: "At the age of five one is ready to study the Bible, at ten to study the Mishna, at thirteen to observe the Commandments, at fifteen to study the Talmud, at eighteen to get married, at twenty to start earning a livelihood, at thirty to enter into one's full strength, at forty to show discernment, at fifty to give counsel, at sixty to start feeling old, at seventy to turn white, at eighty for travail and trouble, at ninety for senility; and at one hundred . . . for death." . . . Ben Bag-Bag said: "Study [the Torah] over and over again, for everything is in it."

—PIRKE ABOTH

For more than a thousand years after the fall of Jerusalem in 70 A.D., the Jews, scattered through the Near East and Europe, were often persecuted. Among the rabbinical writings which reflect the faith of those difficult times are the Midrashic compilations. Rich in folklore and ethical teaching, they largely consist of moral comment, narrative and exposition. In them, the pride of kings and emperors is often humbled, and instructive fables are told of such familiar figures as Hadrian and Solomon.

THE MIDRASH

THE emperor Hadrian, having returned from conquering the world, called his courtiers and said to them, "Now I demand that you consider me God." Hearing this, one of them said, "Be pleased then, Sire, to aid me in this hour of need." "In what way?" asked the emperor. "I have a ship becalmed three miles out at sea, and it contains all I possess." "Very well," Hadrian said, "I will send a fleet to rescue it." "Why bother to do that?" asked the courtier. "Send merely a little puff of wind." "But whence am I to get the wind?" "If you do not know," the courtier retorted, "then how can you be God who created the wind?" Hadrian went home highly displeased [at this challenge]. . . .

King Solomon received from the Lord a wondrous gift, namely, a silken carpet which flew through the air. The king and his associates would take breakfast in Damascus and supper in Media, carried to and fro on the magic carpet. Once the king passed an ant-hill. Since he understood the speech of all living creatures, he overheard the queen-ant order the subject-ants to hide from Solomon. "Why hast thou said this?" the king called down.

"Because I was afraid they might look up to thee, and learn from thee pride in place of humility, diligence and praise for their Maker."

"Let me ask a question of thee," Solomon said. "Take me up to thee, then," answered the queen-ant. When he took the little creature in his palm, the king asked: "Is there anyone in the world greater than I?" "Yes," answered the ant, "I am greater, since God has sent thee to carry me." . . .

—TANHUMA BERESHIT 7:10; MIDRASH VAAYOSHA, end

Scales, for justice, denote fall equinox and atonement

Among Jews there are many concepts about life after death, from the literal to the symbolic. For many the approach of death is a time for solemn confession to God. The Mourner's Kaddish *(or prayer honoring the dead) is second only to the* Shema *in its deep hold upon Jews; it does not mention death but glorifies God. Rabbi Joseph Hertz says of the Kaddish: "The Prayer in its entirety we find neither in the Bible, nor in the Mishna, nor in the vast Talmudic and Midrashic literatures. It seems to be a gradual growth, continued from generation to generation, from age to age."*

THE MOURNER'S KADDISH

MOURNER.—Magnified and sanctified be his great Name in the world which he hath created according to his will. May he establish his kingdom during your life and during your days, and during the life of all the house of Israel, even speedily and at a near time; and say ye, Amen.

Congregation and Mourner.—Let his great Name be blessed for ever and to all eternity.

Mourner.—Blessed, praised and glorified, exalted, extolled and honoured, magnified and lauded be the Name of the Holy One, blessed be he; though he be high above all the blessings and hymns, praises and consolations, which are uttered in the world; and say ye, Amen. May there be abundant peace from heaven and life for us and for all Israel; and say ye, Amen. He who maketh peace in his high places, may he make peace for us and for all Israel; and say ye, Amen.

One Jewish creed has been widely recognized. This is the Thirteen Principles of the Faith, drawn up by Moses Maimonides, the greatest Jewish thinker of medieval times, who died in Cairo in 1204. While not all Jews believe it in its entirety, this creed of Maimonides has been incorporated in the Jewish liturgy in the hymn "Yigdal" and is the best known creedal formulation of Orthodox Jewish concepts.

CREED OF MAIMONIDES

I BELIEVE with perfect faith that the Creator, blessed be his Name, is the Author and Guide of everything that has been created, and that he alone has made, does make, and will make all things. 2. I believe with perfect faith that the Creator, blessed be his Name, is a Unity, and that there is no unity in any manner like unto his, and that he alone is our God, who was, is and will be. 3. I believe with perfect faith that the Creator, blessed be his Name, is not a body, and that he is free from all the properties of matter, and that he has not any form whatsoever.

4. I believe with perfect faith that the Creator, blessed be his Name, is the first and the last. 5. I believe with perfect faith that to the Creator, blessed be his Name, and to him alone, it is right to pray, and that it is not right to pray to any being besides him. 6. I believe with perfect faith that all the words of the prophets are true.

7. I believe with perfect faith that the prophecy of Moses our teacher, peace be unto him, was true, and that he was the chief of the prophets, both of those that preceded and of those that followed. 8. I believe with perfect faith that the whole Torah, now in our possession, is the same that was given to Moses our teacher, peace be unto him. 9. I believe with perfect faith that this Torah will not be changed, and that there will never be any other Law from the Creator, blessed be his Name.

10. I believe with perfect faith that the Creator, blessed be his Name, knows every deed of the children of men, and all their thoughts, as it is said, It is he that fashioneth the hearts of them all, that giveth heed to all their works. 11. I believe with perfect faith that the Creator, blessed be his Name, rewards those that keep his commandments, and punishes those that transgress them. 12. I believe with perfect faith in the coming of the Messiah; and, though he tarry, I will wait daily for his coming. 13. I believe with perfect faith that there will be a revival of the dead at the time when it shall please the Creator, blessed be his Name, and exalted be his fame for ever and ever.

For thy salvation I hope, O Lord!

—MAIMONIDES, THIRTEEN PRINCIPLES OF THE FAITH

THE FAITH
OF
CHRISTIANITY

IN SOLEMN PROCESSION behind cross and candles the 48-voice male choir of the Episcopalian National Cathedral in Washington, D.C. marches from the great altar. For nearly 2,000 years Christians, lifting their voices to praise the Lord, have found in music a path to the heart of their faith. The superbly trained Washington choir is notable for the range of religious music it sings, from hymns and Gregorian chants to works of Palestrina and Bach.

THE FAITH OF CHRISTIANITY

"O UR Father," begins the prayer which Jesus taught in the Sermon on the Mount (*see pages 268–69*). No other religion, not even Judaism, has ever placed such emphasis on the fatherhood of God, or such significance on the fact that *every* human being is more than God's servant—he is God's own child. The spiritual force that radiates from this stupendous concept has gone far toward making Christianity the most active of all faiths on earth and the Lord's Prayer by far the most widely used prayer in the history of man.

How can Christianity be defined? In the broadest sense, Christianity welcomes all who will acknowledge Christ and try to follow His example. In following its way of life, human souls respond to a divine faith and love which make everything else shrink into insignificance. In the doctrinal sense, millions of Christians find the central convictions of their faith expressed in the 110 words illuminated below. This is the Apostles' Creed, used by Roman Catholics, Anglicans, Presbyterians, Lutherans, Methodists and many other Christians with only slight variations (*e.g.*, "Creator" for "Maker," "Spirit" for "Ghost," "living" for "quick"). Eastern Orthodox Christians hold the same beliefs but recite them and other key doctrines in the longer Nicene Creed. Groups totaling about five percent of the world's Christians, the largest being Baptists and Congregationalists, accept no binding creed. For the individual Christian, saying the creed is now—as it always has been—a personal avowal, in historic words, of the faith that man is saved through God's grace and Christ's life and death.

Christianity is firmly based on actual events. Christ's death provides its chief symbol, the Cross (the magnificent crucifix on page 163 is an 11th Century bronze that now hangs in Essen, Germany). But Christians also believe that the risen Lord "ever liveth to make intercession" for mankind. The Swiss theologian Emil Brunner writes, "Faith in Jesus Christ is not an interpretation of the world, but it is participation in an event: in something which has happened, which is happening, and which is going to happen." Christianity also places far more consistent emphasis than any of the other great faiths on having its Lord ever personally present in the *here* and *now*. Brahman, supreme Hindu god, is at once impersonal and personal. Buddhists believe that their founder passed into Nirvana about 483 B.C. Neither Confucianism nor Taoism preaches a personal God. Jews consider their Messiah has not yet come. Mohammed insisted he was only a prophet, and he died in 632 A.D.

The "holy catholic Church" of the creed represents a universality which spans the earth and all its ages, including all races and peoples. But though it claims universality, Christianity is—in hard, sad fact—fragmented as it faces the present era. It does offer some indications of a desire to bring together all its followers: Roman Catholicism through a common allegiance to one head of the church on earth, the other churches largely through a common membership in the World Council of Churches or their global coordination of missionary activities. Yet in a divided world few divisions seem more implacable than those between the Christian communions. And too often the churches, while talking in universals, act as though they are little more than pawns of political circumstance, as in South Africa and Communist China today.

But the number of baptized Christians is now at an all-time high. Roman Catholicism, despite its losses in Europe when the map was redrawn after both World Wars, is more influential than at any previous time in the modern era. The Eastern Orthodox churches have undergone some purification and found some renewal of spirituality under the Communist scourge and other recent pressures. The "younger churches" of Asia, Africa and Oceania are growing, though amid difficulties. In Europe, Protestantism is more vigorous intellectually than at any time in the last 200 years, though it has yet to win back the working masses and in many areas still seems to be catching its breath after the two wars. For its future, a vigorous youth movement holds out promise.

The United States is witnessing an undeniable, indeed unprecedented, rush to the churches. A century ago, in what is often recalled as a more religious age, less than one American in five held church membership. Today more than three out of five do so. But membership increases, however gratifying, do not mean that the Kingdom of God is about to arrive on earth, and not all U.S. Christians lead dedicated lives. The National Council of Churches has voiced its concern that "the average church member is not conspicuously different from the average nonmember." Theologians share the same concern. Paul Tillich has served notice that "if Christianity ever dies in America, it will die in the suburban church . . . not under attacks from without, but of its own respectability." Joseph Sittler adds, "We make God say amen to what we believe instead of saying amen to God."

Because of its activist character, Christianity is deeply involved in the world around it. This has its risks, but Christians must take them or their religion may lose its living dynamism and become static. The Christian is infinitely responsible: both for his own soul, and for his neighbor's. His reward is also infinite: God's justice, mercy and love.

I BELIEVE IN GOD THE FATHER ALMIGHTY Maker of heaven and earth:

And in Jesus Christ His only Son our Lord: Who was conceived by the Holy Ghost, born of the Virgin Mary: suffered under Pontius Pilate, was crucified, dead, and buried: He descended into hell; the third day He rose again from the dead: He ascended into heaven, and sitteth on the right hand of God the Father Almighty: from thence He shall come to judge the quick and the dead.

I BELIEVE in the Holy Ghost: the holy catholic Church; the communion of saints: the forgiveness of sins: the resurrection of the body: and the life everlasting. *Amen*

THE LIFE OF CHRIST

The story and the spirit of Jesus are illumined in art masterpieces spanning fourteen centuries

Ever since its birth almost 2,000 years ago, Christianity has anchored its beliefs on two forceful convictions: that Jesus Christ is the Son of God, and that God sent Christ to earth to live as humans live, suffer as humans suffer, die for mankind's redemption and gloriously rise again.

"For God so loved the world, that he gave his only begotten Son, that whosoever believeth in him should not perish, but have everlasting life." So it is written in John 3:16. And Paul promises in Romans 5:19, "For as by one man's disobedience many were made sinners, so by the obedience of one shall many be made righteous."

These two interlocked ideas separate Christianity from all other religions. To Christians Jesus is not just the founder of Christianity, but the essence of it. Adam and Eve, by disobeying God, sinned. In His wrath, God expelled them from Paradise and thus they and all posterity came to know death, which is not a condition of nature, but the result of sin. At the same time, God foretold the coming of a Redeemer; He warned the serpent who had led Adam and Eve into sin that "I will put enmity between thee and the woman, and between thy seed and her seed."

This Redeemer and Savior was Jesus, sent to bring salvation, to atone for the sins of all mankind, and thus to open to all mankind the door to eternal life. He was, as the Son of God, divine. But He was also truly human, though He had been conceived by the Holy Ghost and born to the Virgin Mary, and Himself was free of the stain of original sin.

What Christ said and did on earth has been and is a hope and a guide for millions of men. His life has inspired some of man's greatest creations—masterworks of poetry and music, of architecture, paintings and sculpture. To emphasize the greatness of the treasury of Christian art, the National Council of the Churches of Christ in the U.S.A. in 1955 asked a special panel from its Commission on Art to select some of the most beautiful and moving portrayals of Christ and His life. On these and the following 14 pages the panel's selections, encompassing the work of 16 artists and spanning 14 centuries, are reproduced to tell the story of that life on earth.

The early years, which began in the stable at Bethlehem (*right*) were, in the main, uneventful. Then, when He was about 30, the carpenter of Nazareth emerged and began to unfold His message. In this climactic period of His earthly life, which may have lasted no more than three years, Christ revealed Himself as a man of simple speech but profound wisdom, as a storyteller who could enthrall multitudes and as a being of all-embracing compassion and love.

It was His lot as Redeemer that He should suffer. He was born poor. He toiled. He was tempted by the devil. He knew hunger. He thirsted. He shrank from pain, and in the Garden of Gethsemane He asked: "O my Father, if it be possible, let this cup pass from me: nevertheless not as I will, but as thou wilt." As He suffered on the Cross, He cried: "My God, my God, why hast thou forsaken me?" He died in agony.

Not until after His death and Resurrection did Christ's life reveal its true purpose. Then His words, "because I live, ye shall live also," took on their full significance. Ever since, through changing times and succeeding generations, the impact of His life and words has lifted men to unexpected heights and illumined their lives and works with beauty.

THE ADORATION

In the rude setting of a stable in Bethlehem the Infant Christ was born. Mary and Joseph had come to be registered for taxation and because the little town was crowded, they found no room at an inn. But Christ's lowly birth was attended with joy and reverence and

OF THE HOLY CHILD BY THE SHEPHERDS IN THE STABLE

this the Flemish painter Hugo van der Goes portrayed around 1475 in an altarpiece, of which the center panel is shown above. While graced with worshipful angels—"Glory to God in the highest," they chorused—the painting conveys an earthy actuality through the presence of the awed and animated shepherds. Like most other painters of his time, van der Goes depicted the miracle as coming to pass in a landscape that was medieval European, rather than pre-Gospel Palestinian. To his contemporaries the effect was of realism.

THE TEMPTATION IN THE WILDERNESS

The years of Jesus Christ's preparation for His God-appointed mission came to their end in the wilderness where He had been led by the Holy Spirit to undergo physical and worldly temptation. After He had fasted for 40 days and nights, Satan appeared before Him and attempted, with all the argument his guile could muster, to make Him yield to earthly enticements. Around 1575 the Venetian Tintoretto visualized the dramatic encounter (*shown in detail above*) in which the Prince of Darkness tempts Christ to turn stones into bread. Jesus' restrained gesture conveys to the full His answer: "Man shall not live by bread alone."

THE BAPTISM IN THE JORDAN

At the outset of His active ministry, Christ had John the Baptist perform for Him the ritual of baptism. In a painting (*left*) by the 15th Century Italian Piero della Francesca, John is shown completing the ceremony with water from the Jordan. As Jesus came "up out of the water," the Holy Spirit "like a dove" descended to mark Him as God's Son.

THE DIVINE TEACHER

As Christ began to teach of a kingdom "not of this world" and of God as Father, "there followed him great multitudes of people from Galilee, and from Decapolis, and from Jerusalem, and from Judaea, and from beyond Jordan. . . ." The love that drew men to Him is reflected in the face of this 13th Century French sculpture at Chartres.

169

CALLING HIS DISCIPLES

From the beginning Jesus moved among humble folk, gathering a band of disciples to follow Him and spread His teachings. First to be chosen were the fishermen Peter and Andrew, encountered by Jesus as He walked by the Sea of Galilee. "Follow me," He said, "and I will make you fishers of men." The Gospels relate: "And they straightway left their nets, and followed him." The calling of the two brothers was depicted around 1308 by the Sienese Duccio who, in a design of rhythmic simplicity, managed to convey the wonderment of the simple fishermen at being chosen by the Teacher.

THE TRIBUTE MONEY

Jesus several times counseled His disciples to fulfill their duty to temporal rulers as well as to God. On one occasion, which is portrayed with power and gravity in this detail from a fresco (c. 1427) by the Florentine Masaccio, Christ told Peter to pay tribute money to a collector. After miraculously finding money in a fish, Peter paid the agent (right), carrying out the obligation which Christ expressed in answering a taunting question asked of Him by Pharisees and Herodians: "Render therefore unto Caesar the things which are Caesar's; unto God the things that are God's."

170

THE STORM ON GALILEE

Christ tried to instill in His disciples an abiding faith, but during a tempest on the Sea of Galilee they were overwhelmed by fear. Jesus was asleep in the stern of the boat; they awakened Him and demanded: "Master, carest thou not that we perish?" The Bible relates, "He arose and rebuked the wind, and said unto the sea, Peace, be still. And the wind ceased, and there was great calm." Turning to the disciples, Jesus asked, "How is it that ye have no faith?" The incident was dramatized around 1853 by the Frenchman Delacroix, who showed Jesus as tranquil amid the turbulence.

171

PERFORMING A MIRACLE

Many times Christ was called upon to heal the sick and the blind. He often emphasized that faith played an important part in the miracles: when a woman who had been in pain for a dozen years was cured by touching His garments, He said: "Daughter . . . thy faith hath made thee whole." The small ivory relief above, possibly carved in Constantinople about 500 A.D., shows Jesus restoring a man's sight by a mere touch. In its directness and simplicity it suggests the larger significance of Christ's miracle—His opening the eyes of mankind to God.

THE TRANSFIGURATION

A crucial point in Jesus' life came with His Transfiguration, when the fact of His divinity was revealed to Peter, James and John. They had gone together up a high mountain. Suddenly Jesus' countenance "was altered" and "his raiment became shining, exceeding white as snow." Then the prophets Moses and Elijah appeared, to tell of His coming sacrifice, and a voice from a cloud said: "This is my beloved Son in whom I am well pleased." The episode was depicted (*left*) about 1480 by the Venetian Bellini, who caught the spell of the moment.

173

THE LAST SUPPER: CHRIST

The evening before His Crucifixion Christ shared His final meal, a Passover seder, with His disciples in the upper room of a house in Jerusalem. Troubled in spirit, He told them: "Verily I say unto you, that one of you shall betray me." He asked them to remember His coming sacrifice through the act of eating the bread which "is my body" and drinking the wine which "is my blood." In Venice around 1593 Tintoretto re-created the

FORETELLS HIS BETRAYAL

scene with a strikingly dramatic blend of worldliness and mysticism. On a huge canvas he depicted eleven of the disciples gathered along one side of the table, with the betrayer Judas Iscariot sitting alone, facing Jesus.

As Christ offers the bread to a disciple, a luminous tumult of angels swirls down from the dark recesses of the chamber, unnoticed either by the intent apostles or by the servants who are hurrying about their duties.

175

THE CROWN OF THORNS

After Jesus had been sentenced by Pontius Pilate to be crucified, the Roman soldiery beat Him, mocked Him as the "King of the Jews" and crowned Him with a wreath of thorns. In the agonized image (*left*) by the French modern Rouault, the face of Christ holds the suffering of all victims of human cruelty everywhere.

THE CRUCIFIXION

On Calvary, Christ was nailed to the Cross. Such a death was then ignominious; the skulls scattered about were those of common criminals. But the Cross soon became the symbol of Christianity, and the Crucifixion, pictured in this 1477 painting by the Sicilian Antonello da Messina, assumed the beauty of eternal sacrifice.

THE AGONY IN GETHSEMANE

Praying in Gethsemane before His betrayal, Jesus revealed His human dread of the Crucifixion. But as the German Wolf Huber shows in his 1530 work, Christ's spiritual strength sustained Him, in contrast to the sad fleshly weakness of the disciples, who sleep (*left*) as the soldiers approach (*right*) to take away the Master.

THE DESCENT FROM THE CROSS

At a dark hour after the Crucifixion, some of Christ's followers came to remove His body and bear it off to a tomb. Their mournful task was depicted by the Italian Pietro Lorenzetti in a fresco painted about 1325 and shown here in detail. As the disciples tenderly lift the body of Jesus from the Cross, it assumes an angular line which heightens the scene's pervading mood of deep anguish.

THE ENTOMBMENT

The Gospels say that "a rich man of Arimathea, named Joseph . . . went unto Pilate, and begged the body of Jesus. Then Pilate commanded the body to be delivered." Joseph bought fine linen, wrapped Jesus in it, "and laid him in a sepulchre . . . hewn out of a rock, and rolled a stone unto the door of the sepulchre." In this 1559 work by Titian, the women are Mary and Mary Magdalene.

THE RESURRECTION

Three days after His death, Christ arose triumphant from the tomb. About 1463 Piero della Francesca pictured Him towering over the futile guards set to watch His grave. The painting conveys with stark majesty the wonder of His Resurrection and the hope it holds for all men of victory over death.

178

CHRIST RISEN Jesus' words
attest to His presence in the world today

"Christian faith," the Protestant theologian Reinhold Niebuhr says, "stands or falls on the proposition that a character named Jesus, in a particular place at a particular time in history, is more than a man in history, but is a revelation of the mystery of self and of the ultimate mystery of existence."

Or, as Paul wrote to the Corinthians: "And if Christ be not risen, then is our preaching vain, and your faith is also vain."

To a vast host of Christians, Christ not only is risen, manifesting Himself as in the painting reproduced below, but is actually present in the world today as Christus Pantocrator, the Savior, Teacher, Supreme Judge and All-Ruler (*portrayed in the mosaic at the right*) Who proclaims, "I am the light of the world."

Doctrinal beliefs differ in some details, but the Roman Catholic, Orthodox and Anglican churches, along with most Protestant groups, hold that Christ is inseparable from the triune God—the Father, the Son and the Holy Spirit —and that God, in His unity and His trinity, is and always has been present and active in the world; He makes Himself felt in the lives of human beings through the influence of the Third Person of the Trinity, the Holy Spirit.

The Catholic communions believe also that the Savior is really present in Holy Communion; the faithful actually partake of the Body and Blood of Christ when they accept the bread and wine and are thereby influenced to good. Most Protestants consider the bread and wine symbolic, but share the conviction of Christ's presence and His active participation in mundane affairs. The great majority of Christians rejects the Deist premise that God observes but remains aloof, and the opposite position that God's intervention is manifested only in the occurrence of miracles.

Most theologians are in agreement that for men of faith no miracles are needed. Jesus' own words to His eleven apostles before His Ascension suffice: "All power is given unto me in heaven and in earth. Go ye therefore, and teach all nations, baptizing them in the name of the Father, and of the Son, and of the Holy Ghost: teaching them . . . all things whatsoever I have commanded you: and, lo, I am with you alway, even unto the end of the world."

THE LOUVRE, PARIS

THE SUPPER AT EMMAUS

After His Resurrection Christ revealed Himself often, but never more movingly than at Emmaus when the disciples' "eyes were opened, and they knew him." Rembrandt painted the scene in 1648.

CHRISTUS PANTOCRATOR

In this enormous mosaic above the altar of the cathedral at Monreale, Sicily, the All-Ruler holds His right hand in the gesture of blessing. Directly below Him is the Virgin holding Christ on her lap.

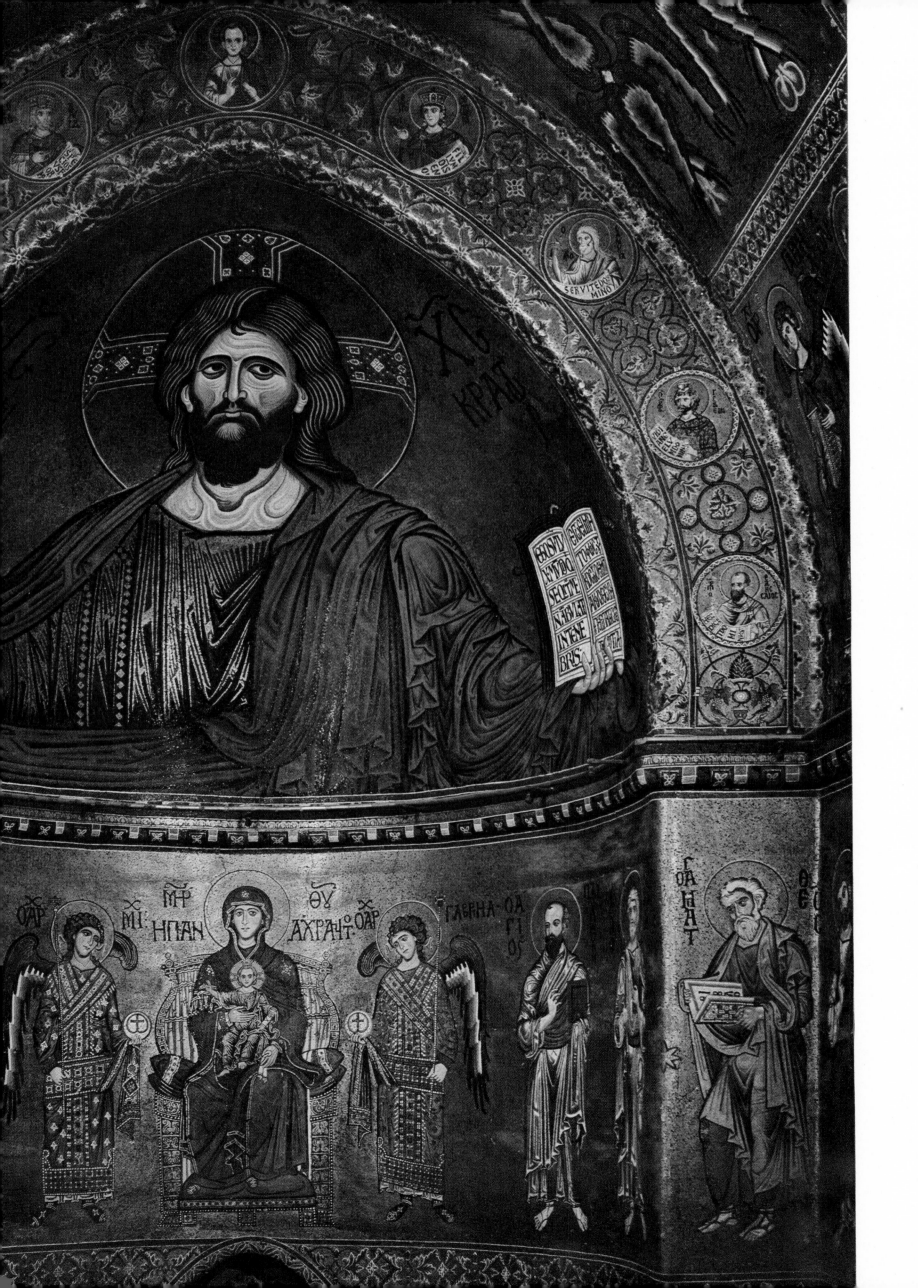

SEA OF GALILEE, where Jesus calmed the waves and walked on the water, is 13 miles long, eight wide and 696 feet below sea level. Near it are Nazareth, Capernaum and Cana, where in His first miracle Jesus turned water to wine.

VALLEY OF ELAH, in background of picture below, is the scene of David's encounter with Goliath around 1000 B.C. The Philistines, after whom Palestine is named, used the valley to go inland from coastal plain below Joppa.

BETHLEHEM, whose Church of the Nativity (*center*) rises above the grotto which tradition asserts is Christ's birthplace, also contains Greek (*left*) and Armenian (*right*) monasteries. To this town the widowed Ruth came with her mother-in-law Naomi after having pledged, "whither thou goest, I will go." Here Herod the Great, who built Caesarea (*map, page 185*), ordered the slaughter of the innocents for whom Rachel wept, as Jeremiah had prophesied.

THE COUNTRY OF GOD

The spiritual impact of little Palestine has powerfully influenced Western civilization

The classic boundaries of the Holy Land or Palestine (*see map, pages 184–86*) are from Dan to Beer-sheba (150 miles) and from Gaza to the Dead Sea (54 miles). This is barely 6,000 square miles. Even including the territory east of the River Jordan, the Holy Land is smaller in area than Maryland or Albania. Modern Israel's borders are roughly similar.

It is a land hemmed in on the south and east by wilderness and desert. To the north rise steep mountains. To the west is the Mediterranean, breaking against a coast that offers little hospitality to ships. Never the seat of great material cultures such as those of neighboring Egypt and Babylonia, Palestine nevertheless has been a focal point of history for 4,000 years. The great trade routes of the Ancient World traversed it, and through them the world first learned of Palestine's unique possession, the Judaeo-Christian heritage which since has powerfully shaped Western civilization. Naaman the Leper, "captain of the host of the King of Syria," summed up that heritage after Elisha had cured him: "Behold, now I know that there is no God in all the earth, but in Israel."

BIBLE LAND Its soil has felt weight of great events

As Biblical times have receded farther and farther into the past, modern man has learned more and more about them. Since 1920 archaeologists have made unprecedented progress in the Holy Land, and discovery of the Dead Sea Scrolls (*see pages 260–64*) has quickened the pace.

Although the details shown on this map, including costumes and architecture, are based on the best research, much remains unknown. The locations of Sodom, Gomorrah and Tirzah, one of Israel's ancient capitals, can be only approximated. The first two probably stood in the area now engulfed by the Dead Sea, which has grown since Lot fled. The exact sites of Job's lamentations, of Abraham's sacrifice (*pages 156–57*), and Christ's baptism may always remain debatable.

But many other sites named in the Bible can be identified. After he had married Rebekah, Isaac dug three wells at Beer-sheba and today Arab girls still draw water there in dress that has changed little from Rebekah's time. The wilderness into which Isaac's half-brother Ishmael was cast with his mother Hagar is still desolate today, as it was when Moses led his people through it during 40 years of wandering.

At Jericho, to the north, Moses' successor Joshua won a decisive victory in his conquest of the land of Canaan. Farther north, near Tirzah, Gideon (one of the early Judges) chose 300 from his army of 32,000, and then triumphed over the Midianites. Next to Jericho lies Gilgal, where Samuel and the Israelites acclaimed Saul king to lead them against the Philistines. Samuel derived his authority from having heard the voice of God in the temple at Shiloh. After Samuel died Saul enlisted the Witch of En-dor to raise up the prophet to counsel him, but Saul died defeated at Mt. Gilboa near Jezreel. Saul was succeeded by Samuel's protégé David, who still outranks all other Hebrew heroes from Joshua to Judas Maccabaeus as a warrior, ruler and organizer. Founder of a dynasty, David had many wives. One of them, Abigail, is pictured with the servant who bore David's marriage proposal. David's son Solomon built the Temple in Jerusalem with "timber of cedar, and . . . timber of fir" which King Hiram of Tyre harvested in Lebanon and shipped by sea to Joppa. Among the prophets who worshiped in the Temple was Isaiah who, for forty years and under four kings of David's line, served his people as statesman, teacher and spokesman for righteousness.

Most other scenes and place names on the map are discussed on adjacent pages or elsewhere in the book. Arrows indicate locations off map.

Cedars of Lebanon

River Abana

Damascus

Paul's Conversion on Road to Damascus

MT. HERMON

MOUNTAINS OF LEBANON

Noah's Ark

ARARAT

Nomad Camp

Caesarea Philippi

• Dan

Sidon •

Naaman the Leper on Way to Elisha

Sermon on the Mount

Bethsaida Julias

Hazor •

Hiram King of Tyre

Peter and Andrew

Capernaum •

Sea of Galilee

Magdala •

Tiberias •

Tyre •

Jesus' First Miracle

Cana •

Jesus as a Boy

Accho, Ptolemais •

MT. CARMEL

Phoenician Cargo Ships with Cedar for Solomon's Temple

Adam and Eve

GARDEN OF EDEN →

Daniel in
the Lions' Den →

BABYLONIA

Rabbath-ammon,
Philadelphia

Reunion of Jacob and Esau

Jabbok

Penuel

River

Moses Sees
the Promised Land

MT. NEBO

Destruction of
Jericho's Walls

Baptism of Jesus
by John the Baptist

Arnon

River

Ruth's Loyalty

Jordan

River

Saul and the
Witch of En-dor

Gideon's Test
for Warriors

Gilgal

Jericho

En-dor

Tirzah?

Jacob's Ladder
Dream at Bethel

Dead Sea
Scrolls Site

Jezreel

MT. GILBOA

Samaria

Shiloh

Dead Sea
(Salt Sea)

ESDRAELON

Megiddo

MT.
GERIZIM

Shechem

Bethel

Jerusalem

Bethlehem

at Armageddon

Dothan

Joseph and Brothers

Samuel Hears God

The
Beth-horons

Birth of Jesus

Herod the Great

Abraham's Sacrifice
of Isaac

Judas Maccabaeus

Rachel Weeping
for Massacred Children

Hebron

Caesarea

PLAIN OF SHARON

VALLEY
OF ELAH

Prophet Isaiah

Mediterranean

Paul's Travels

Joppa

David and Goliath

Gath

Lachish

Sea

Jonah and the Whale

Ashkelon, Ascalon

Gaza

structure just beyond Dome of the Rock is the Church of the Holy Sepulcher. Beyond the blue and white Mosque el-Aksa in left center is the Wailing Wall of the Jews. In extreme left background are the supposed sites of King David's tomb and the Last Supper. This picture was made near the Mount of Olives (*see map opposite*). Most of the terrain shown is now held by the Arab Kingdom of Jordan. Jewish Jerusalem begins just this side of the distant ridgetop.

THE CITY OF JERUSALEM perches on a rock plateau 2,550 feet above and 33 miles to the east of the Mediterranean, looking down on valleys of Kidron (*foreground*) and Hinnom, from which comes the name Gehenna for hell.

The wall in the center encloses the area in which stood Solomon's Temple. The site of Solomon's throne is near the blue Moslem Dome of the Rock (*at right, in the middle distance, and shown in detail on pages 108–9*). The two-domed

Babylonian Fort and Warrior

Lamentations of Job

N

A. Petruccelli

Lot's Escape from Sodom

Zered

Brook

Gomorrah?

Sodom?

Moses with Ten Commandments

MT. SINAI →

Samson in the Temple

Beer-sheba

David's Betrothal of Abigail

WILDERNESS

Pillar of Fire for Children of Israel

Manna Sent by God to Israelites

Jeremiah's Flight to Egypt

Rebekah at the Well

Holy Family's Flight to Egypt

Hagar and Ishmael

Queen of Sheba's Visit to Solomon

Red Sea →

◄ EGYPT

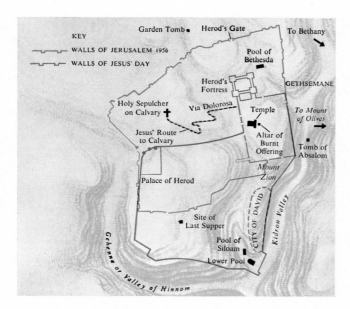

SACRED PLACES in Jerusalem, often disputed, are located on map according to the best evidence. Mt. Zion, often thought to be in city's southwest, is probably south of the Temple.

HOLY CITY It thrived
in spot that promised obscurity

An Egyptian outpost before David took it about 1000 B.C., Jerusalem had the prerequisites of obscurity: it lacked a harbor and dominated no main roads. But the hill-fort was near Beer-sheba, Hebron, Bethlehem, Bethel and Shiloh, where altars had been raised to God; its central location made it a convenient political capital; and the Temple that Solomon built provided a platform for prophets. In Old Testament times its streets were swept, its markets inspected. When the sunrise lit its enfolding mists, it looked indeed "the city which the Lord did choose out of all the tribes of Israel, to put his name there" (I Kings 14:21). But 4,000-year-old Jerusalem ("City of Peace") has seen little peace. For Jews and Christians the most sacred of places, for Moslems surpassed only by Mecca and Madinat an-Nabi (Medina), it remains divided by war.

RIVER JORDAN, in which Jesus was baptized, rarely exceeds 10 feet in depth or 100 feet in width, but its water is vital to the Holy Land. Rising in north, it enters Dead Sea at 1,292 feet below sea level. Its name means "descender."

MOUNT OF THE BEATITUDES by the Sea of Galilee may be the site of the Sermon on the Mount in which Jesus, proclaiming "Blessed are the peacemakers . . ." enunciated many of the basic principles of the Christian ethic.

The discourse included the Golden Rule and the Lord's Prayer and "when Jesus had ended these sayings, the people were astonished at his doctrine: for he taught them as one having authority. . . ." Hilltop building is a hospice.

IN GROTTO OF NATIVITY in Bethlehem, traditional site of Christ's birth is marked by silver star with hole to permit pilgrims to kiss original rock floor. Lamps were hung by Greek Orthodox, Roman Catholic, Armenian groups.

AT ALTAR OF THE MANGER, close to star of the Nativity in top picture, the Franciscan custodian of the grotto stands (*in back*) with fellow-worshiper on Christmas Eve in silent adoration before a tiny figure of the Infant Jesus.

AT JESUS' TOMB COPTS HOLD HOLY SATURDAY RITES

ON THE WAY OF THE CROSS in Jerusalem on Good Friday, pilgrims carry a huge crucifix step by step from scene of Christ's condemnation to Calvary and sacred tomb. At each of the 14 Stations of the Cross they pause to pray.

PILGRIMS Each year
they retrace footsteps of Christ

On Christmas at the place of Christ's birth in Bethlehem (*far left*), the air hums with softly chanted prayers at midnight Masses and services. On Good Friday great sorrowing processions follow the Via Dolorosa along which He suffered and was crucified. On Easter joyous throngs sing of His Resurrection. These people pray and worship in vast dogmatical diversity. Roman Catholic, Orthodox and other Eastern rites use the Church of the Holy Sepulcher, and Protestants appear both there and at a separate sepulcher (*next page*) which many believe to be the real tomb of the Lord. But binding all the worshipers together—as it binds the whole Christian world together—is the one faith kindled in the Holy Land 20 centuries ago by the life and the agony of Jesus.

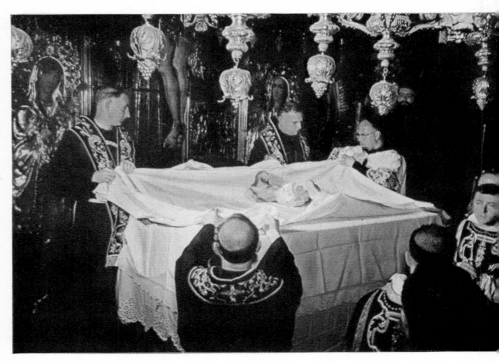

AT THE 12TH STATION on the Way of the Cross, where Christ died, Roman Catholic priests hold Good Friday services at a Greek Orthodox altar. After prayer a small image of Jesus is taken from cross, borne to Holy Sepulcher.

191

AT STONE OF UNCTION, under the hanging lights in right foreground, a Roman Catholic procession pauses in prayer. Here the mourners, many believe, enshrouded Jesus' body in linen with "a mixture of myrrh and aloes."

AT GARDEN TOMB outside Jerusalem, Protestants from U.S. and England hold services on Easter morning. Some Bible students contend that this spot, rather than Church of the Holy Sepulcher, actually represents Christ's tomb.

TWO THOUSAND YEARS AFTER THE BEGINNINGS OF CHRISTIANITY, 25,000 PEOPLE GATHER ON EASTER MORNING IN HOLLYWOOD BOWL TO CELEBRATE

THE ONWARD MARCH

Through the centuries great men have taught the gospel of Jesus,

AMONG all the religions by which men seek to worship, Christianity is the most widely spread, has the most adherents and makes the most stupendous claims for the divinity of its Founder and the finality of its teaching. Of the two and a half billion human beings on earth, about 850 million—one out of every three—are listed as Christians.

The churches in which Christians worship have, during their nearly 2,000 years since Christ lived and died, developed such an astonishing diversity of belief and ritual that it is sometimes difficult to recognize that they all acknowledge the same Lord. The glittering spectacle of an Easter Mass in St. Peter's, the stillness within the bare walls of a Quaker meetinghouse, the squatting circle of Congo tribesmen around the white-haired medical missionary, the chanting monks cut off from the world on the forbidden peak of Mount Athos, a hundred thousand Mar Thoma devotees gathered in a dry river bed to join their prayers under the blazing sun of South India, thousands pressing forward in Wembley Stadium at the appeal of an evangelist, wraithlike figures kneeling in perpetual adoration before the altar in a Quebec convent, a sea of dark faces swaying while the tide of the spiritual rolls across them: "It's me,

O, Lord, standin' in the need of prayer"—how can these, and hundreds of other differing manifestations, all be accounted parts of the whole to which we give the name of Christianity?

Some will deny that they are. But there is justification for the habit of including all such diversities in the reckoning. For all, under whatever form, acknowledge one God; all declare their loyalty to one Lord; all find in one Cross the symbol of their faith. The differences they present to the world are endless, confusing even to themselves, often enfeebling. It is not true, as one of their most sung hymns affirms, that "We are not divided/All one body we/One in hope and doctrine/One in charity." But in their ultimate allegiance, they are one. They are Christians.

Inevitably the questions rise: Where did this Christian religion come from? How did it spread? Why has it taken so many forms? The answers make up one of the most dramatic and, in some parts, romantic stories known to history. From the days of St. Luke, who wrote his account of the Acts of the Apostles some time in the first Christian century, down to the present, thousands of scholars have labored to tell this story. Within the limits of such a sketch as this, one can name only a few of

194

THE RESURRECTION OF THEIR SAVIOR, AS THE WHITE-VESTMENTED CHOIR, STANDING IN THE FORM OF A CROSS, SINGS A HYMN TO THE RISEN LORD

OF CHRISTIAN FAITH

building the world's most widespread religion   by PAUL HUTCHINSON

the men and women who bore leading parts in making Christianity what it is today, trying to catch them in characteristic moments which suggest their importance to the record.

A recent cartoon showed a matron asking at a bookstore for "an impartial history of the Civil War written from the Southern point of view." Accounts of the way in which Christianity has developed are usually impartial in much the same sense. No matter who writes them —Protestant, Catholic, Marxist or agnostic—the author's background shows through. So it will be here, in a sketch written by a Protestant who believes that his Protestant heritage preserves vital spiritual values while at the same time it respects the values embodied in other traditions.

I

CHRISTIANITY is the religion which springs historically from Jesus of Nazareth. The first followers of Jesus believed that He traveled about Palestine as a preacher and teacher; that He healed and worked wonders; that He ran afoul of the conservative religious and political

forces in that land, was crucified and rose from the dead. They declared that, in a resurrected and glorified form, He appeared to many of them. They *must* have believed it, for within 40 days after Jesus had been executed, what had been a despairing and disintegrating band of disillusioned dreamers was transformed into a company of zealots ready to dare any fate to proclaim that this resurrected Jesus was in fact God's promised Messiah, or, in Greek, the Christ. The Christian religion is founded on the fact that their Master rose from the dead.

In the company of Jesus' 12 specially chosen disciples—reduced to 11 by the treachery of Judas Iscariot—the one who stands out is Simon, better known as Peter, a name derived from the Greek *petros* meaning "rock." In Matt. 16:18, 19, Jesus is reported to pun on the name and its meaning: "Thou art Peter, and upon this rock I will build my church. . . . And I will give unto thee the keys of the kingdom of heaven. . . ."

The other apostles, as this band of Jesus' intimates came to be known, are shadowy figures. But Peter, headstrong, blundering, violently temperamental, easily influenced by his surroundings or by the words of others, yet always ardent and—after one terrible experience while Jesus

195

was on trial—always courageous, Peter is unforgettable. It is Peter to whom the Gospels accord the honor of first openly saluting Jesus as the Messiah. And when, 50 days after the Resurrection, the followers of the new faith made their first attempt to win a public hearing, it was Peter who preached the sermon on that first Pentecost. In his subsequent career he preached and taught in many places, finally reaching, in some unknown fashion, Rome, where he is generally believed to have suffered martyrdom under Nero about 65 A.D.

Besides Peter, the outstanding figure in Christianity's formative first century was the man who has been credited—though with some scholarly dissent—with having written most of the Epistles which form such an important part of the New Testament, St. Paul. In his fine study on early Christianity, Dr. J. W. C. Wand has explained its rapid expansion from a Jewish sect into a world-wide religion by the fact that "the Christian society was born at the place where two worlds met, the East and the West, the Semitic and the Graeco-Roman, the Jew and the Gentile." This mingling of cultures was very nearly incarnated in this one man, St. Paul.

Born in Tarsus (a city now in south Turkey), a Pharisaic Jew acquainted with the Greek Stoic teaching which was popular in his native city, Saul—as he was known before his conversion—went to Jerusalem as a youth to complete his Talmudic education under the famous Rabbi Gamaliel. Soon he was going all-out to suppress the new teaching, even having a part in the stoning of St. Stephen, the first Christian martyr. In 35 A.D., as he was riding to Damascus, bent on destroying a company of Christians there, he underwent the shattering experience so vividly described in Acts and reported in the apostle's own letters. From there, having adopted the name Paul (meaning "little"), he went on to become the great missionary to the Gentiles, journeying from one major

ST. PAUL'S TRAVELS to spread the gospel took him through Asia Minor, Greece, the Mediterranean islands and to Rome. He sought out cities where no Christian had ever preached before, often plying his trade of tentmaker.

city in the Roman Empire to another until he had covered almost all Asia Minor, Greece and various Mediterranean islands. After preaching his way possibly as far west as Spain, tradition says he was finally beheaded in Rome in about 65 A.D.

In Peter and Paul the Christian religion can be seen beginning to develop along both the great avenues which give it permanent importance. It develops as an institution (the church) and as a teaching, a theology, a faith. The institution is named first because the theology came out of it, not the institution out of the theology. The New Testament—Gospels, Epistles, Apocalypse—is a product of the church. Little of it was written until there was a flourishing church all over the Roman world. It was not gathered in its finally agreed-on form until 692.

With Peter the rudimentary original nature of the Christian institution and the Christian teaching stands out. The early chapters of Acts show Peter rushing about to set up emergency forms of organization in the first Christian community in Jerusalem. They were improvisations, and some did not work out well. Peter's teaching, as shown in the long report of his sermon on the first Pentecost and in I Peter, was just as rudimentary. Jesus was the Messiah, sent by God, rejected by His nation but certified by His Resurrection, Who was soon to return to lift into a glorious and eternal state of bliss all who acknowledged Him as Lord and were baptized in His name. The tremendous questions regarding the nature of Christ and His relation to God and to humanity, which were to rend later generations and still torment men's minds, seem scarcely to have occurred to Peter.

Paul was of a different stripe. He was no Galilean fisherman being carried to immortality by the intensity of his devotion to a Master with Whom he had lived on terms of personal intimacy. Paul was a sophisticated Roman citizen and a product of the Greek-Hebrew culture. He was an indefatigable founder of churches, and in these churches he had to deal with all sorts of competing interpretations of what Christian teaching was. So he wrote letter after letter to straighten out the thinking —and at times behavior—in these churches. Many of these letters have not survived, but those that have are the real beginning of the attempt to formalize, rationalize, put down in logical argument the Christian faith. So much so that it has been charged that Paul, not Jesus, is the

true author of what we know today as Christianity—that differences and divisions among Christians have resulted from the obscuring of the simple moral precepts of the Galilean by the sophisticated metaphysical speculations of this man from Tarsus.

One trouble with this interpretation is the increasing realization that what Jesus taught was by no means confined to simple moral precepts. Along with the Beatitudes and the rest of the Sermon on the Mount, along with His assurances of God's fatherly love and care, must be set His prediction of impending catastrophe, of coming judgment and punishment—and only after these the coming of a new age. When Paul, writing 20 to 30 years later, tried to give a satisfying interpretation of these teachings to the Gentile converts in his churches, naturally the first question he had to answer was: Who was this Jesus Christ? By what authority did He make His tremendous declarations about the relationship of God to the world and man, and about what was to be the ultimate outcome of their relationship? When Paul attempted to answer those inescapable questions—inescapable if Christianity was to survive—the theology which was to take hard-and-fast form in the later creeds was born.

II

FOR 250 years after the martyrdoms of Peter and Paul the Christian church continued to spread steadily over the Mediterranean world. By 287 A.D., it was the state religion of Armenia, and its expansion was generally unaffected by eras of official repression and persecution. During the same period, whether Christians were enjoying a respite from state interference or being driven underground, there emerged gradually a formulation of Christian teachings (although never complete agreement) and of ways in which the congregations should be governed. Concerning this latter phase of Christian development legions of scholars have battled for centuries, and are still battling. As someone has said, the history of Christianity between the time when the first Christian congregation fled from Jerusalem, just before Titus' triumph in 70 A.D., and a century later, is like a plunge into a tunnel. We know it came out at this end with a fully articulated institution— churches, the equivalent of dioceses, bishops, minor clergy, sacraments and all the rest—together with a proliferating and subtle theology. But we really do not know a great deal about what went on in the tunnel. Not as much as it is sometimes claimed we know.

The Second and Third Centuries witnessed an accelerating decline of the Roman Empire. A rough-handed old soldier, Diocletian, who became emperor in 284, stopped the retreat for a time and even reconquered most of Britain and Persia. But for reasons not entirely clear, Diocletian's reign also brought the most terrible of all the persecutions of Christians. For two ghastly years the old emperor did his best to drown Christianity in blood. One legend says that when the emperor's order to destroy churches was affixed to the palace gate at Nicomedia, a high-ranking officer tore it down and was immediately executed—to become St. George, patron saint of England. If he ever fought a dragon, it must have been imperial Caesar.

In 305 Diocletian gave up his effort to destroy the young religion and abdicated. A struggle for the imperial power between two "Caesars" and two "Augusti" began at once, but it was speedily decided in favor of Constantine, who led his troops from York, in England, first to victory in Italy, and later to control of the eastern portion of the empire as well. It is said that Constantine, before a decisive battle at the Milvian Bridge outside Rome, saw a vision of a lighted Cross in the afternoon sky and the words "In hoc signo vinces." After that his legions bore standards with Chi Rho, the first Greek letters of Christ's name, above a Cross.

Constantine was not then an avowed Christian; indeed, he was not baptized until on his death bed. But his political sagacity told him that he required some strong cultural cement to hold together his sprawling, multicultured empire, and he believed that he could find that binding element in Christianity. He began, in the so-called Edict of Milan of 313, by extending complete toleration to Christians. As emperor in his new capital of Constantinople, he became the great patron of the church. Theodosius I, who became emperor only 42 years after the death of Constantine, made Christianity the only official religion of the empire.

But Constantine must have begun to wonder whether Christianity was the unifying force he had believed. From all quarters came reports of the bitterness with which Christians were disputing over theological issues, excommunicating and denouncing each other. These disputes came to a focus in Alexandria, where the elderly and popular presbyter of a fashionable church, Arius, had challenged the teaching of his bishop, Alexander, on the Trinity. The issue was whether Christ was of the *same* substance as God the Father, or, as Arius held, of *like* substance. Because the two Greek words involved, *homoousion* and *homoiousion*, were so similar, Gibbon later passed on a sneer that in the struggle which followed for more than a century, Christians fought each other over a diphthong. But that diphthong carried an immense meaning. This battle raged and spread until finally the emperor, who was not capable of understanding the theological subtleties involved but was determined to have internal peace, summoned all Christian bishops to a council at Nicaea in 325. The first great Christian historian, Eusebius, who participated in that historic meeting, tells how some 300 bishops—all but 10 from the eastern section of the empire—rushed with their attendants to Nicaea in a frenzy of excitement, many scarred by what they had undergone in Diocletian's persecutions, with eyeless sockets, disfigured faces, twisted limbs, paralyzed hands. Constantine himself presided, and out of an assembly which partook more of the characteristics of a political convention than a religious convocation there came finally that Nicene Creed which declares Christ was of the *same* substance as God.

Despite Nicaea it looked for a while as though Arius, with his teaching of *like* substance, would win. The great theologian Athanasius was now Arius' chief opponent. When the issue went to a series of other church councils, the champions of the Arian formula had political connections which seemed to make their triumph certain. Athanasius, in a dark moment during one of the five exiles he endured, appeared to himself to be almost alone in defending the full deity of Christ. He stood, he said, Athanasius *contra mundum*—against the world. But the Nicene Creed won out and still remains a standard of orthodoxy for Roman, Eastern Orthodox, Anglican and some other churches.

III

FROM Constantine on, the Christian record undergoes a fundamental change. Many will contend that it was not a change for the better. "After Constantine," said the late Dean William Inge, "there is not much that is not humiliating." This is, of course, too sweeping. But certainly life in a church which had vanquished its rivals, in which membership was soon by imperial decree to include all loyal subjects, was bound to differ from that in a church where membership was by individual choice and might bring martyrdom.

In such a changed situation the Eastern Church instinctively sought to protect its spirituality by withdrawal from worldly contacts. The deserts near Antioch and in Egypt filled with anchorites who, despairing of the fate of society and living alone in caves, huts or in small companies, followed extremely ascetic practices for the subjugation of the flesh and the cultivation of poverty. From the solitary hermits, this movement toward asceticism developed into the establishment of monasteries. St. Jerome, the scholar who translated into Latin both Old and New Testaments from their Hebrew and Greek originals, was one of the notable champions of early monasticism. His version, the Vulgate, is the Bible of the Roman Catholic Church of this day.

The coming of the Papacy

THESE were the decades, likewise, during which the firm grip of the emperors, far away in Constantinople, was loosening on their Italian, North African and western European possessions; when successive Germanic tides began to flow southward and even to cross the Strait of Gibraltar; when the bishops of Rome, beginning to exercise civil as well as ecclesiastical authority—often because there was no one else to do so—found their position developing steadily toward that eminence which was presently to be accorded the Papacy (*see page 207*).

There were some great church names in that period—St. Ambrose of Milan, Innocent I, Leo I, St. Benedict—but the greatest shines out from the forgotten little seaport of Hippo in North Africa, the more luminous because it blazes against the black political night which was rolling down: St. Augustine. As a young man, he had lived a sensual life and had a son by a concubine with whom he lived for years, at the same time studying the classical philosophers and for a brief time allying himself with the heretical Manichaean sect. Then he reached a psychological crisis. Walking in his garden, he seemed to hear a voice: "Take and read!" He picked up the copy of the Epistles which lay at hand and his eyes fell on Romans 13:13-14: "... Not in rioting and drunkenness, not

DELIVERANCE OF ST. PETER from prison was achieved, according to the Bible, by an angel. He had been imprisoned during a period of Christian persecution but escaped to found churches all over the Holy Land and Asia Minor.

SHIPWRECK OF ST. PAUL occurred during his voyage to Rome. He was being carried under guard, but when a storm arose, he promised that all would survive. Doré's engraving shows them safely reaching the island of Malta.

in chambering and wantonness, not in strife and envying: but put ye on the Lord Jesus Christ, and make not provision for the flesh, to fulfil the lusts thereof." At that moment Augustine found his spiritual haven.

Augustine's mark can be seen on every later theologian, Protestant as well as Roman Catholic. Two of his books, his *Confessions*, an account of his spiritual pilgrimage, and *The City of God*, a philosophy of history which sought, in that hour of civilization's disintegration, to justify the ways of God to man by contrasting the Earthly and Heavenly cities, are among the world's classics. He died in 430. Within 25 years the Vandals sacked Rome. In another two centuries Hippo and the other Christian bishoprics of North Africa had been swept under by an Islamic tide.

IV

FOR a thousand years after Rome's fall, Europe was one vast welter of fighting and political anarchy. Emperors in Constantinople from time to time tried to assert their shadowy claim to monarchy over the West, but like the grin of Alice's Cheshire cat, their authority faded and faded until nothing was left. On Christmas Day, 800, the Bishop of Rome crowned in St. Peter's the German chieftain Charlemagne, who had conquered Germany, France, northern Spain and most of Italy, bestowing on him the title of Roman Emperor. Charlemagne, who admired St. Augustine, tried to rule by Christian principles.

Yet while the massive political institution which had been history's longest-lived empire was falling into chaos, the Christian Church was steadily widening its boundaries. Many of the Goths and Huns who captured Rome and broke up the western empire had been baptized. To be sure, most of them were Arian Christians and therefore considered heretics by the Roman Church because they still held the beliefs that had been rejected by the Nicene Council. They were converts of the great missionary Ulfilas or his successors. Ulfilas, who left Constantinople to preach among the Visigoths, illustrates how Christianity helped keep learning alive through what are called the Dark Ages, for he reduced the Gothic languages to writing and translated the Bible into them. (He would not, however, translate the Old Testament books of Kings, saying that the tribesmen already knew too much about fighting.)

G. A. Studdert-Kennedy once remarked that no miracle in the Bible begins to equal in incredibility the miracle that Europe's warlike tribes should have chosen Jesus of Nazareth for their God. Yet they did, sometimes because tribal kings were converted by daring missionaries and then ordered their subjects to accept baptism, and sometimes as a consequence of more gradual and deep-going social transformations brought about by missionary labors. As an illustration of the sort of thing that happened, recall the young Patrick born in a Christian family in Britain late in the Fourth Century. Raiders carried him off to six years of slavery in Ireland. From there he seems to have escaped to a monastic life in France. Eighteen years later he responded to voices which he said sounded constantly in his ears: "We beseech thee, holy youth, to come and walk again amongst us as before." He was consecrated a bishop and started back to convert the people among whom he had suffered as a slave. He not only converted Ireland, but covered it with churches for worship and missions in which many pupils were taught. It is notable that St. Patrick, unlike many church leaders of later centuries, gave women an important part in the work of evangelizing Ireland. So thoroughly was Ireland evangelized that the impulse carried Irish priests to the conversion of Scotland, parts of England and even as far as Switzerland. Wherever they went, they carried Irish learning.

While the territorial extension of Christianity thus continued, the institutional authority of the Western Church came steadily to center in the bishops of Rome. By the middle of the Fifth Century, these bishops were asserting that, as successors of St. Peter in that office, they outranked other patriarchs. When the see of Constantinople refused to acknowledge that claim, as well as to concur in some of Rome's doctrinal decisions, there began the schism between Western and Eastern Churches (*pages 245–46*), a great Christian tragedy which directly led to the crusaders' sacking of Christian Constantinople (*next page*).

When Charlemagne conquered most of western Europe, he gave the harried common people almost the only extended period of order they experienced from the fall of Rome to the end of the Napoleonic wars. Feudalism—the social system in which every person from serf upward was expected to render service in some form to an owner or superior— grew amid the constant guerrilla warfare of the period, and gradually the Dark Ages merged into the Middle Ages. As feudalism grew, Popes struggled with monarchs over the question whether, because of the ghostly powers of the pontiffs, kings were vassals of the heads of the church. This contest reached its dramatic climax when Gregory VII, one of those short men who stand tall in history, forced Henry IV, the German ruler, to stand for three successive days in the snow, barefoot and clad in penitent's garb, at the castle of Canossa in Tuscany, while he besought the Pope to lift his excommunication. Henry later captured

TURNING POINT FOR CHRISTIANITY, up to then outlawed by Rome, came at Battle of Milvian Bridge (312 A.D.) where Constantine (*center, wearing crown*) fought under the sign of the Cross. Before the battle, Constantine

Rome and Gregory VII died in exile. But history has never forgotten that picture of the barefoot king waiting in the courtyard in Canossa.

By the end of the 12th Century, a Pope such as Innocent III could dictate the imperial succession in Germany, by interdict force a French king to take back a wife he had divorced, make a king of Leon in Spain give up his wife and a neighboring king of Aragon acknowledge his vassalage, and by interdict and excommunication compel King John of England to sue for absolution, hand over his kingdom as a fief of the Papacy and agree to pay an annual fee to the Pope as recognition of his ultimate power over the Plantagenet kingdom.

The issue on which Gregory VII and Innocent III carried the Papacy to its greatest secular power continues to this day and crops up in many forms. It is the issue of church and state relations, the effort to draw a dividing line between the powers of ecclesiastical and secular authorities. Specific issues change with the centuries, and modern totalitarianism has added its special complications. But every branch of the Christian Church has, at one time or another, been troubled by that issue. The attempts made by Popes and Protestant reformers to settle it by appeal to the words attributed to Christ, "Render therefore unto Caesar the things which be Caesar's, and unto God the things which be God's," have settled nothing, for this leaves unanswered who is to say what is Caesar's and what God's. Modern Popes, patriarchs and theologians have advanced many theoretical answers, but in actuality the relations of church and state are being fixed in our time, whether in the United States, Spain or the Soviet Union, on a basis of pragmatic workability.

While the medieval Church in the West was building up its power, that in the East, under the immediate shadow of the corrupt Byzantine court, was passing through a sad period when servility to the throne, incessant intrigues against the Church—the golden-tongued Chrysostom of Constantinople, twice exiled from his bishopric, died on his way to a final exile in the far Caucasus—and too frequent scandalous conduct by clergy and laity were undermining its spirituality. Yet this Church also had its missionaries, who converted the Bulgarians, the Moravians in what is today Czechoslovakia, and finally the Russians.

Typical of some of the "conversions" of the time is that of Vladimir, the Grand Duke of Kiev, an early ruler in what is now Russia. After capturing the Byzantine town of Kherson in the Crimea, he was given the Princess Anne, sister of the Byzantine emperor Basil II, for his wife in the year 989. In due course Vladimir became Christian, and thereupon ordered the baptism of all his subjects. When Russia was overrun by the Mongols, the Orthodox Church was not disturbed. By the end of the

had seen a vision of a fiery cross in the afternoon sky with the words "*In hoc signo vinces*" ("By this sign thou shalt conquer") and had quickly arranged to have crosses added above the eagles on his standards. The next year, in the Edict of Milan, he extended complete toleration to Christians throughout the Roman Empire and encouraged their activities. Later Caesars made Christianity the state religion. This fresco, designed by Raphael, is in the Vatican.

16th Century, with the country again free and unified, Moscow was declared a patriarchate. When Peter the Great ascended the throne, one of his first moves to "modernize" Russia was to place the Church under control of the czar. So it remained until the Communist revolution of 1917. Today it lives, no longer "established" but not actively suppressed, under a Communist government officially atheist, to which it renders as obsequious political obedience as in former days it did to the Romanov czars. Even so, the Orthodox Church in both of its major groupings, Greek and Russian, is significant. Its many patriarchates are, in effect, all part of one large, loosely knit ecclesiastical federation (*see page 246*), of which the senior partner is the Ecumenical Patriarch in Constantinople. They include 18 self-governing churches with a total of 150 million communicants, about 2.4 million of them in the U.S.

The rise of Islam

BUT to get back to feudal Europe. Early in the Seventh Century there came out of Arabia another religion, Islam (meaning "submission"). This passionately monotheistic faith, which numbers Jesus among the true prophets but exalts its founder Mohammed as the greatest of all Allah's interpreters to man, quickly overran Syria, Persia, Egypt, Palestine and North Africa. Then it crossed the Mediterranean, conquered Spain and was pressing northward when, in 732, near Tours in France, an army under Charles Martel drove it back in one of history's decisive battles. The Moors stayed in Spain until their last stronghold fell into the hands of the Christian monarchs Ferdinand and Isabella in 1492, just before Columbus sailed for the New World. Moslem and Christian fought bitterly in Europe and around the Mediterranean for a thousand years. The Turks besieged Vienna as late as 1683, holding Greece and much of the Balkans into the 19th Century (*see page 242*).

After capturing Palestine, Islam halted medieval Christians' pious habit of making pilgrimages to the shrines there. For some 200 years Christian crusaders fought bloodily—and sometimes successfully—to win back the holy places. The First Crusade recaptured Jerusalem in 1099, and after a hideous massacre of its inhabitants, a French knight was proclaimed "Defender and Baron of the Holy Sepulchre." A whole Kingdom of Jerusalem was established, with vassal principalities and a religious allegiance to Rome. It lasted for nearly a century. But the First Crusade succeeded largely because internal dissensions were then weakening the Moslems. When Islam put its full strength in the field, however, it soon obliterated the Christian principalities in Asia Minor.

One Crusade after another was launched to push back the Moslem counterattack, but in vain. The crusaders' motives kept deteriorating. Their campaigns became mere marauding forays, and once they did not even fight the Moslems, but instead sacked their fellow-Christian city of Constantinople which never fully recovered from this pillage and in turn fell to the Turks in 1453. Christians and Jews alike along the crusaders' line of march learned to dread their approach. By the end of the 13th Century, the crusading impulse in western Europe was exhausted. If it left any religious legacy, that might be the firm resistance since then of Moslems to Christian efforts at conversion.

It must not be thought, however, that the struggle to establish the authority of the Popes over the brawling nobles and monarchs, or to suppress the Moslem rivalry by force, was all there was to Western church life in medieval Europe. There was, to be sure, rising popular criticism of the life lived by some clerics. Any reader of Dante or Boccaccio or the *Canterbury Tales* will find that reflected there. But there was another side. Chaucer showed that when, over against his ecclesiastical "lord ful fat and in good poynt" who loved "a fat swan," he also drew a sympathetic portrait of his "poore Persoun of a Toun . . . riche . . . of hooly thoght and werk," who "Cristes loore . . . he taughte, but first he folwed it hymselves."

The medieval period, especially as it flowered in the early 13th Century, has been held by many the apogee of the Church's glory. It was "the age of faith," an age when the authority of the Church was accepted almost without question. The claims of the Papacy to a universal sovereignty, though rejected in the East, were seldom denied in theory in the West and came nearer to realization in practice than ever before or since. Marvelous monuments to the religious devotion of that time are in the cathedrals (*see page 252*), which can still enthrall even such an agnostic mind of our time as Henry Adams.

The saint who 'had everything'

THAT was also the age which could produce world-renouncing piety that reached its highest attainment in St. Francis of Assisi. In his figure, as appealing to our own as to his world, medieval Europe saw the embodiment of its religious ideals. Francis, one might say, "had everything." His was a life of wealth voluntarily renounced for extreme poverty, of humble identification with the poor, the sorrowing and the loathsomely afflicted, of consecration to the service and discipline of the church, of founding a large monastic order, of readiness to court death in missionary ventures, especially to the infidel, and of a sweetness and exhilaration of spirit which found expression in companionship with all living creatures and all the facets of nature.

Another aspect of medieval religion that commands respect was the intellectual subtlety of monkish schoolmen which reached its highest expression in St. Thomas Aquinas. Born into the nobility in 1225, Thomas, who early entered the Dominican Order, was enraptured by the new learning sweeping across western Europe with the rediscovery of Aristotle. He had a brief life, largely spent in the new university centers of France, Germany and Italy. A humble, introspective man, Thomas had one of the most logical, integrating minds in the history of philosophy. His *Summa Theologica* remains the greatest compendium of Roman Catholic theology. It deserves, and receives, respectful study not only from contemporary Thomists, but from all thinkers who find in the universe a realm of revelation as well as of reason and see the fundamental human problem as that of delimiting and integrating the two.

Aquinas is the master for all time of the syllogism: his premises granted, he moves to his conclusions with the inexorability of the mathematician. Today the Aristotelian science on which he relied is mainly of antiquarian interest, but Aquinas remains a living influence in Western thought, as well as a reminder that the "age of faith" could produce discriminating, rigorous minds dedicated to the service of God.

Out of the medieval era were emerging the modern kingdoms of Europe. As the kings slowly established their rule over their great vassals, they found galling the claims of Popes that they were themselves vassals to whoever might be on the throne of St. Peter. In the 14th Century, Philip the Fair of France determined to elect a Pope he could control. A French archbishop was elevated and moved the papal court to Avignon in southern France, where he and his successors lived for 70 years as French puppets. Two remarkable women, St. Catherine of Siena and St. Bridget of Sweden, played important roles in stirring up popular demand which finally brought the Popes back to Rome from what has been called their "Babylonian captivity" in Avignon. But this return served only to expose the Papacy to other secular ambitions.

If France could control the head of the Church for almost three generations, why not the fiercely rival dukedoms of Italy or the "Holy Roman" emperor of Germany? The consequence was the most melancholy 40 years in papal history, with rival Popes hurling anathemas at each other and, in the end, three Popes, each claiming to be the legitimate successor of Peter, while the nations divided their allegiance among them according to what seemed their political interest. "The miserable truth has to be faced," says the Catholic historian Philip Hughes, "that no pope, on either side, was at all worthy of his office. They were, all of them, little better than partisan leaders of rival factions."

Not until 1417 did the Council of Constance straighten out this scandalous state of affairs and a single Pope reign again. However, two legacies had been left by this century of division which were to have profoundly disturbing effects. On one hand, the Popes were determined to surround themselves with such power and pomp in Rome that there could never be another "captivity." And on the other hand, the decisive part of the Council of Constance in cleaning up the mess spread widely the idea that the ultimate seat of decision in Church affairs was not the Pope but the general councils of the Church.

As the Papacy sank in public esteem, movements for Church reform multiplied in many countries. There were men like Peter Waldo, who founded still existing "Protestant" churches in Italy almost four centuries before the term Protestant was coined. Others, such as the Oxford scholar, John Wycliffe, were apparently blotted out, only to revive in the preaching career which gave Bohemia its martyr hero, John Hus. Still another type of protest, against the secularism and downright immorality which had penetrated even the papal court by the time of the Renaissance Popes, found expression in the puritanism preached by the Dominican Savonarola in Florence. Savonarola, who at first swept all before him, lost his moral authority in the ambiguities of Italian politics, and died at the stake. Yet, fleeting as seemed the influence of such men, they were the forerunners of the most violent struggle in the annals of the Church. It is time for the curtain to go up on the Reformation, and the modern history of Christianity.

V

WHEN Martin Luther, an Augustinian monk serving as professor of theology at the University of Wittenberg in Saxony, posted his historic 95 theses on the door of the castle church on October 31, 1517, he had no inkling of the dimensions of the Church schism which was to follow. But his study of the Pauline Epistles, as interpreted by St. Augustine, had already caused him to reject the conception of salvation as being earned partly by human works of righteous living, penance and appropriation of the merits of the sacraments and the saints. Salvation, he believed, was the unmerited gift of God to sinful man, gained by faith in the divine promise that Christ by His atoning death had paid the penalty for sin. When man experienced the inner transformation achieved through God's mercy, he then had access to God and assurance of salvation without the need of any intermediary—church or sacrament, priest or saint. Pushed to its logical conclusion, as the theologians who met Luther in debate quickly forced him to push it, Luther's declaration of salvation by faith alone and of the priesthood of all believers led to denial of the Pope's infallibility as a source of doctrine, thence to denial of the inerrancy of general church councils, and finally to affirmation that the Bible is the sole and sufficient source of the Christian's spiritual guidance. (*For more details on the Reformation, see pages 230–37*)

How could a monk guilty of such defiance of churchly authority not only escape the extreme penalties pronounced against him, but carry a large part of Germany into revolt with him? History contains few more dramatic scenes than that at the Diet of Worms, with Luther facing Charles V, the Holy Roman emperor, and the papal legate, his life hanging in the balance as he was bidden to repudiate his books: "I cannot revoke anything, nor do I wish to, since to go against one's conscience is neither safe nor right. Here I stand. I cannot do otherwise. God help me. Amen." Why did this not lead to the same end that befell John Hus? It was not because Luther came to Worms under safe conduct. Hus had gone to Constance under safe conduct, where he was burned at the stake.

Very largely the answer lay in the political situation of that time. The shift from feudalism to territorial monarchies, with paid armies (and soon navies) instead of feudal levies, required heavy taxes and forced the monarchs to build up their treasuries. At the same time, the Papacy, building St. Peter's and maintaining the most extravagant court in Europe, found it increasingly difficult to draw large revenues from the strong new monarchies of Spain, France and England; it looked much easier to levy on divided Germany. But many of the German princes were fed up with the sight of revenues from their states going south over

THE CRUSADES, symbolized in Gustave Doré's engraving, were massive armed pilgrimages to recover the Holy Land from the Moslems. The fervor which inspired them produced 10 expeditions, some of which lost the spiritual

the Alps. They were thus in a mood for political rebellion, and when the monk from Wittenberg raised a doctrinal and ecclesiastical rebellion which sparked an immense popular response, some of these German princes stepped forward to champion the Lutheran revolution. To see how inextricably these political strands run through the Reformation, one need only note the peace finally made at Augsburg in 1555, after the fighting which swept over Germany in the wake of Luther's defiance. It was a peace of princes which established the rule that the religion of a territory would be that of its prince, thus fastening the system of state churches as firmly on Protestant as on Catholic Europe.

A genial but furious reformer

MARTIN LUTHER was a great bull of a man, bursting with animal spirits, whose sermons and tracts seemed to erupt from him in an undammable flood. His voice could summon to spiritual battle with a power that still reaches across the years as one reads his greatest writings. In his home, sitting at his table drinking "good Wittenberg beer" while he regaled his innumerable guests with the *Table Talk* that still makes good reading, playing his flute in the orchestra he formed with his children, visiting like a good pastor the sick and the poor—this is a Luther of infinite fascination. But there was another Luther, also a full-fledged German—a Luther who could flame into towering rages, who could vilify his opponents with disgraceful abuse dredged from the gutter, who could command the princes who had protected him to crush with unbridled ferocity the social uprising of what he called "the Murderous and Thieving Rabble of the Peasants." It is strange to see how this ambivalence between the *gemütlich* and the furious Luther persists in the German soul to this day.

The other "father of the Reformation" was about as different from Luther as a mortal could be. John Calvin was a wispy French intellectual

ardor so evident in the warriors and priests in this picture. The Fourth Crusade even turned aside to sack Christian Constantinople and was condemned by the Pope. Except for brief periods, most of Palestine has since belonged to Islam.

with an introspective, syllogistic mind. Forced to flee from France for his heretical views, he settled in Geneva. There he set up a theocratic city-state with such relentless care for the morals and beliefs of its citizens that on one occasion they drove him into a three-year banishment.

Calvin's great contribution was to reduce the Protestant revolt to theological coherence. This he did in his *Institutes of the Christian Religion*, which he first published, at 26, to persuade the king that the Protestant faith should not be persecuted. This first edition consisted of only six chapters, but Calvin kept adding and expanding as long as he lived. At his death the *Institutes* contained 104 chapters, organized in four great books. To this day, this presentation of Christian doctrine, based on the absolute sovereignty of God and the omnipotence of His inscrutable will, remains the greatest of all Protestant theological volumes. It is as remorselessly logical as Aquinas' *Summa*, pursuing the Pauline-Augustinian doctrine of predestination to the conclusion that those whom God has chosen for salvation cannot resist nor fall from that choice, but that those who are chosen for damnation are doomed to everlasting hell, even though they be infants who die before they are capable of conscious acts.

The Presbyterian and Reformed churches, which regard themselves as the spiritual heirs of Calvinism, today handle with extreme reticence John Calvin's views on predestination. Yet the *Institutes* remain the basis for the theological training of their ministry, and the Westminster Confession (a later revision of Calvinistic doctrines) is the standard of orthodoxy to which agreement is required at the ordination of their elders. But the figure of Calvin himself remains cool, remote, as repellent of familiarity as was the living man when, accosted on a Geneva street by an enthusiastic refugee as "Brother Calvin," he frostily answered that he was to be correctly addressed as "Monsieur."

The Counter Reformation

SHOCKED by the revolt in Germany, which spread rapidly to other parts of Europe, the Roman Catholic Church wasted no time in embarking on that period of internal correction and external opposition to the Protestant advance that is usually called the Counter Reformation. The Council of Trent, which met intermittently for 18 years, ended many abuses and laid down a body of Catholic doctrine that is still definitive. Its recognition of the legitimacy of tradition as well as of the Scriptures as a source of truth has had an immense influence on later dogmatic declarations, especially those defining papal infallibility and the Immaculate Conception and Assumption of the Virgin. At the same time, the Inquisition was revived to suppress heresy wherever the civil authorities favored its operations (*see page 240*).

A main glory of the Counter Reformation, from the Catholic point of view, was the organization and spread of the Society of Jesus—the Jesuit order which stopped Protestantism in its tracks in Hungary and Poland, won back to papal allegiance much of Germany and most of France, all but wiped out the feeble beginnings of Protestantism in Italy, spread excellent schools over Europe and thrust Catholic missions into India, Japan, China and the New World.

Ignatius Loyola, the founder of the Society of Jesus, is a figure as fascinating as any of the Protestant reformers, though utterly different. A Spanish grandee whose military career had been ended by wounds, he became a student at the University of Paris where he gathered half a dozen devoted companions—one of them Francis Xavier, later to become the missionary saint to India and the East. One August day in 1534, in the church of St. Mary on Montmartre in Paris, this little group formed the oath-bound band—later formally named the Society of Jesus—which Ignatius proposed. As a former soldier who had dedicated his armor to the Virgin, he established a military company with discipline as strict and obedience as unquestioning as in any army. He was the "general" until he died, by which time his order had grown into a great company, every recruit sworn in only after long mental and spiritual preparation. The *Spiritual Exercises* of Ignatius remain the world's most famous manual of discipline for the individual will.

VI

FROM the years of the Reformation down to the present, the history of Christianity becomes inextricably interwoven with the history of national states. It was partly nationalism—manifesting itself in a determination to be sole ruler of his realm—that led King Henry VIII to denounce the Pope's authority and proclaim himself the "head of the church" in England. Thus the Church of England, with its Anglican affiliates throughout the world including the Protestant Episcopal Church in the U.S., still claims a succession of bishops from the apostles and considers that doctrinally it is Catholic as well as Protestant.

In France, Cardinal de Richelieu was as ready as Henry VIII to subordinate the interests of the Church to those of the French throne, never hesitating to put the power of French arms in alliance with Protestant princes in the Thirty Years' War, when he saw a chance to build the French monarchy into Europe's dominant reigning house. One of the Cardinal's contemporaries was Oliver Cromwell, a country gentleman whose military genius raised him out of England's Civil War to the eminence of Lord Protector of the Realm. He was a Puritan, but one who believed in tolerance for all forms of worship except Roman Catholic. He was horribly ruthless in his suppression of revolt in Ireland. Everywhere in Europe—as much in Protestant England and Scandinavia as in Catholic Spain—religion became an ally, and often an agent, of statecraft. Dissent from the claims of the established churches, whether Catholic or Protestant, was often sternly put down, not so much for doctrinal reasons as because dissent was regarded as disloyal.

Discovery of the New World brought a race between the three most robust monarchies, as they were suddenly faced with the dazzling prospect of expanding their small European

ST. AUGUSTINE, a Roman aristocrat, was 32 before he found his faith in Christianity. From then until he died at 76, he wrote 96 pious works.

kingdoms into world empires. Political and economic motives dominated in the building of the French, Spanish and British empires—in Asia as well as in the Americas—but the religious motive was a not inconsiderable factor. Settlers in New England felt its influence more directly than those in the southern colonies, but from Florida to the St. Lawrence the scattered settlements along the Atlantic seaboard, as W. E. Garrison has written, "were not allowed to forget that they were holding a Protestant 'rampart' (the word was often used) against an otherwise solidly Roman Catholic New World."

At the start the American colonies accepted the European pattern of church establishment almost without question. The founders of Massachusetts were dissenters from the established church in old England, but after they had set up their own commonwealth in New England, they took it for granted that dissenters from *their* Puritan Congregational establishment would be suppressed or deprived of civil rights. Only in Rhode Island (purchased from the Indians by that congenital dissenter, Roger Williams), in Pennsylvania (a private preserve for the Quaker William Penn, who welcomed dissenters from anywhere) and in Maryland (where the Catholic proprietor had to assure toleration to satisfy a Protestant king and Parliament) was the conception of a state church at first challenged. Nine of the 13 colonies had state churches.

By 1776, however, there was a fast-growing conviction that a church establishment was a prolific source of political and religious evils. The revolution, during which the ministers of the Anglican establishments largely supported the crown, produced swift changes in the legal picture. Virginia's "Declaration of Rights," adopted a few weeks before the Declaration of Independence, asserted that "all men are equally entitled to the free exercise of religion." A decade later its "Act for Establishing Religious Freedom"—one of the three achievements Thomas Jefferson chose to be recorded on his tomb—denied the right of the state to levy taxes for the support of a church or to require church membership as a test of eligibility for public office. Finally, the adoption by the young republic of the First Amendment to its Federal Constitution, providing "Congress shall make no law respecting an establishment of religion," completed the federal process of giving legal status to the principle of separation of church and state.

Establishment of this principle has been the most important contribution of American churches to the development of Christianity. It has not meant that there has been no contact between the American churches and the American state. On the contrary, the churches time and again have exerted great moral influence on decisions of the state, while the state has repeatedly acknowledged its indebtedness to religion: "In God We Trust." But there has been no "establishment of religion," no state church with tax support, no interlocking of the official machinery of the church with the official machinery of the government. The churches have been on their own, growing by their own efforts—which largely accounts for

MARTIN LUTHER, leader of the Reformation, ran the risk of execution for criticizing the Church but German princes, angry at Rome, saved him.

that interest in revivalism and "activism" (*see pages 279–85*) that has exposed them to criticism from European churches under no need to support themselves.

This had not been heard of in organized Christianity since the edict of Theodosius I in 380 A.D. made political loyalty and membership in the Christian Church virtually synonymous. For 1,400 years after that, membership in the church and in the state was regarded as two aspects of the same thing—which was one reason for brutal treatment of the Jews. This was as true in the Protestant countries which emerged from the Reformation as in the Catholic monarchies. But the United States, from its infancy as a nation, turned back to the concept of the Christian Church as it was held before Constantine, when men joined of their own free will and supported it of their own voluntary desires, and the Church in consequence was a free institution. Judged by what has followed, the American adoption of the principle of church and state separation has been a godsend for the churches, Protestant, Roman Catholic and of every sort. The voluntary principle has gained, in the friendly American climate, an impressive pragmatic sanction.

VII

HERE, then, is organized Christianity as it now appears after almost 2,000 years. Missionary labors have planted churches in almost every nation (*for a new development in India, see pages 286–91*). The 850 million Christians fall into four great branches—the Roman Catholic, Eastern Orthodox, Anglican and Protestant—with the last designation including an amazing array of denominations and sects (*chart, pages 204–5*). In the U.S. alone 255 Protestant sects are recognized. But most American Protestants are in a half-dozen denominational families; 173 of the Protestant churches reporting membership figures contain less than two percent of the 59 million Protestant total. To an outside observer, the most striking fact about Christianity in the U.S. today is likely to be its numerical force—nearly 100 million adherents in a population of 168 million—and its divisions. Why these divisions?

Usually it is answered that these represent differences in doctrine. But this is true to a limited extent only. As Christianity has spread around the globe in recent centuries, differences in local customs have also notably affected it. Roman Catholicism in the U.S. has been rather more puritanical than in the Latin countries, while Protestantism in the U.S. has been rather more concerned with social questions—such as slavery, liquor, the eight-hour day—than has its European counterpart. In the field of doctrine a few churches eschew all creedal affirmations, but most of them recite that ancient formulation of Christian belief known as the Apostles' Creed (*page 165*). As for the divisions among American Protestants, Professor H. Richard Niebuhr of Yale has conclusively shown that they more frequently represent differing national origins in Europe or differing social groupings in the U.S. than differing theologies. Of course there is theological and dogmatic division between Protestant and Protestant, as well as between Protestant and Roman Catholic and Eastern Orthodox. But there are other divisions which the ordinary American churchman encounters far more frequently.

What are these intimately, emotionally experienced divisions? One concerns the nature of the Church. What is the Church? Until recently, Protestants have tended to ignore that question. Today, as they strive to end some of their debilitating divisions by cooperating in bodies like the World Council of Churches or America's National Council of Churches, they find the question lying right across the line of advance. Moreover, this is a question which has a direct bearing on the attitudes of individual Christians, as truly as on the deliberations of great Church councils.

To a Roman Catholic, Orthodox, or high-church Anglican, the Church is a body divinely instituted and with a priesthood which is primarily ordained to re-enact at the altar the miracle of the Mass, by which in a symbolic manner, through the consecration of the two elements of bread and wine into the veritable Body and Blood of the Lord Jesus Christ, the Son of God made man is really present, offering Himself as the "food of souls." The Catholic, therefore, also the Orthodox or Anglican, when he enters a church of his persuasion, enters a place of mystery. His devotion focuses on the altar, where the miracle of his redemption is re-enacted, with Christ Himself mysteriously present. But if a Protestant finds himself in this sanctuary, he is bewildered by this mystery and repelled by the notion of a sinful man, even though he be an ordained priest, having the power to change bread and wine into the true flesh and blood of Christ.

When, however, the Protestant enters his church, while there may be quite an elaborate ritual centering on the service of Holy Communion, most typically he is waiting for that moment in the service which was the highest of moments to Luther, Calvin, Knox and all the other great Reformers—the moment when the minister enters the pulpit for the preaching of the Word in the form of the sermon. The sermon is the climax of Protestant worship, though often the feeble capacities of the preacher make it the anticlimax. The congregation is there to hear, not to see. But if a Roman Catholic, risking rebuke from his confessor, finds himself in this service, the chances are that he will be repelled by its verbalism, by its refusal to point him to the very spot where he may meet God.

From this it follows that a second great line of division between the churches is drawn by their antagonistic conceptions of the sacraments (*see page 292*). The difficulty is not only that the Catholics, Orthodox and many Anglicans say there are seven sacraments and the Protestants only two (with the Quakers, Unitarians and Universalists recognizing none as such), but that the sacrament itself, for whatever end administered, is differently conceived. The familiar definition of a sacrament is that it is "an outward and visible sign of an inward and spiritual grace." But there is a wide gulf between Protestant and Catholic use of the word "sign." The latter holds that the sign itself accomplishes what it stands for; the former that the effects follow only from the faith of the believer. The gulf here is as wide, for example, as that between those who consider baptism a saving rite and those who reject that belief.

And yet again, these worshipers who profess "one Lord, one faith, one baptism" find themselves sundered by their differing conceptions of the nature of religious authority. Most Protestants will say that the final authority to which they appeal is that of the Word of God—not simply the text of the Bible, but that text as interpreted either by the Church through its ordained ministry or by the spirit of the individual Christian. Protestants, Anglicans and Orthodox differ widely among themselves, however, as to how this access to the Word is to be sought and, when found, safeguarded. Some of their churches look for authority to a historical succession of episcopally ordained bishops, priests and deacons; some to ministers chosen by vote of the congregations; some to rule by elders.

The Roman Catholic position is clear-cut. Spiritual authority is centered in a priesthood hierarchically organized in a great pyramid, at the apex of which stands the Pope, direct successor of St. Peter as Bishop of Rome and head of the visible Church, endowed by virtue of his exalted office to guide his Church infallibly in all matters of faith and morals. From him the power of the keys descends to bishops, and from the bishops to the humblest priest. The priest, accordingly, is clothed with the authority of his Church to bind and free from sin. The role of the laity in doctrine and sacraments is to receive the spiritual gifts that come through the priest all the way from the Pope.

IN so brief an account of a religion which, for almost 20 centuries, has been attempting to put its mark on all societies and to draw its worshipers from all nations, it has manifestly been impossible to tell of all those who have borne great parts in the story or of all the institutional forms the Christian enterprise

ST. IGNATIUS LOYOLA founded the Jesuit order. Brought up as a soldier, he turned to the religious life while recovering from bullet wound.

has taken. What, it may be asked, of Origen, Chrysostom, Ximenes, Knox, Fox, Edwards, Wesley, Livingstone, Newman, Booth, Leo XIII, Soderblom, Azariah, Schweitzer? What of a hundred, a thousand, others? Space does not permit, and libraries abound. What of the Nestorians, the Montanists, the Albigenses, the Brethren of the Common Life, the Anabaptists, or of all the contemporary denominations and organizations—*e.g.*, the Y.M.C.A. and the Bible societies—unmentioned here? Their histories, also, can be found in a good library. Here it has only been possible to try to glimpse the Christian record in the large, pausing now and again to note certain turning points and certain figures.

Christ's birth, which happened so inconspicuously so long ago, marked the greatest watershed in history. The religion which was born out of that event developed mankind's most enduring and world-encompassing institution, the Christian Church. The Church has taken many forms; its divisions go back to the very beginning of the record in the Acts of the Apostles, and they appear more implacable as the centuries pass. At present an "ecumenical" (*i.e.*, all-embracing, universal) sentiment calls for bridging some of the chasms, but it is hardly attempting to close the great divisions between East and West, between Catholic and Protestant (*pages 278–79*). Yet despite the fragmentation of institutionalized Christianity into innumerable churches, there is a fact—the Christian Church—which men everywhere must take into their reckonings, and do. The whole is greater than the sum of its parts.

Insight and prophetic ardor

TODAY the churches of the West are well into the most productive intellectual period they have known since the 16th Century. From the proclamation of *Rerum novarum* (1891) to the present, they have spoken with more insight and prophetic ardor on the ills of a social order in the revolutionary flux than since the collapse of feudalism. The defensive note, so strong in Christian preaching during the half-century before the outbreak of the world wars, has nearly died away. The churches have a renewed confidence in the relevance and adequacy of their gospel. The confidence is assuredly not unrelated to the renewed seriousness and respect with which our storm-tossed generation regards the religious approach to life's problems and the Christian explanation of its meaning (*see pages 248–51*).

What, then, is the outlook for Christianity and its churches? It is not one to sustain a boundless optimism, but it is by no means hopeless. Thoughtful Christians see the weaknesses of the churches. If Christianity is responsible for the character of civilization, then its task is hardly more than begun. Nevertheless, the prevalent sense of unsatisfied spiritual needs among men, and of the insufficiency of other answers to their problems, makes this an hour of opportunity for religion. Freud and the neo-orthodox theologians are one in locating man's ills far below the outer layers. Can the Christian churches now help man to realize that the grace of God can penetrate deeper, and with more saving power, than any analyst's probing?

Never has the figure of Christ risen higher or in more compelling majesty over the debris of human failure.

Never has the Cross stood out more clearly as the symbol of man's ultimate hope.

Never has the prayer for the Church used in ecumenical conferences seemed more timely or pertinent:

"O Gracious Father, we humbly beseech Thee for Thy holy Catholic Church, that Thou wouldest be pleased to fill it with all truth, in all peace. Where it is corrupt, purify it; where it is in error, direct it; where in any thing it is amiss, reform it. Where it is right, establish it; where it is in want, provide for it; where it is divided, reunite it; for the sake of Him Who died and rose again, and ever liveth to make intercession for us, Jesus Christ, Thy Son, our Lord. *Amen.*"

JOHN CALVIN, who next to Luther was the Reformation's leading figure, lived in Geneva, where he rewrote his *Institutes* and ran the city.

MEMBERSHIP, ASSETS	Basis of Authority, Government of Church	Fundamental Theology: Some Basic Beliefs
ROMAN CATHOLICS Members in world, 484 million children and adults; in the U.S., 33.4 million children and adults. Total U.S. assets, over $2 billion.	Faith means assent to truths revealed to apostles by Christ, contained both in tradition and the Bible; the Church officially teaches and interprets these. As head of Church, the Pope is infallible when defining faith and morals ex cathedra (Latin, from the chair—of Peter). Church is visible society of the faithful.	Acknowledge Trinity (God is three persons, one nature); original sin (the fall of Adam, which has affected all men); Incarnation (God's Son made man); redemption (Christ's sacrificial death on the Cross). Specially venerate Virgin Mary whose Immaculate Conception preserved her from original sin.
EASTERN ORTHODOX Members in world, 150 million children and adults, Russian Orthodox probably largest group; in U.S. over 2 million. Greek Archdiocese largest of about a dozen groups in U.S. Total U.S. assets, $251 million.	Bible is word of God interpreted by Church guided by Holy Ghost, third person of the Trinity, who lives and works in men to make them true sons of God, true brothers of Christ. Also binding: traditions of church fathers and decisions of bishops in council, who spiritually descend from Christ's apostles.	The Trinity is one God in three persons. Where Roman Catholics believe Holy Ghost proceeds from God the Father and Christ the Son, Orthodox believe the Holy Ghost proceeds directly from God the Father—a historic disagreement. Virgin Mary is revered but without accepting her Immaculate Conception.
LUTHERANS Members in world, 70 million children and adults; in U.S., 7 million children and adults. There are 19 groups in U.S., the largest being The United Lutheran Church in America. Total U.S. assets, over $1 billion.	The Bible is inspired by God and is the only guide to religious truth. Believe in priesthood of all believers in the sense that every man can approach God directly with no one coming between. U.S. Lutheran congregations have some autonomy; their local synods and national conferences decide policy.	Accept the Trinity, Christ as both God and man. Also officially accept Virgin Birth. Luther's doctrine of justification by faith (salvation by belief alone without trust in good works as such) has caused Lutherans to stress theology more than many groups.
PRESBYTERIANS Members in world, 41 million adults, including members of Reformed churches; in U.S., 3.9 million. Of 11 Presbyterian churches in U.S., largest is Presbyterian Church in the U.S.A. U.S. assets, over $1 billion.	Bible, the word of God, is the source of authority for faith, conduct. Church is governed by representatives elected by people, organized in sessions, presbyteries, synods, annual General Assembly. Headed by a moderator and a stated clerk (executive officer).	Emphasize sovereignty of one God in three persons, supremely revealed in Jesus Christ His Son, and in the power of the Holy Spirit. Have considerable freedom of religious thought and interpretation.
ANGLICANS Members in world, 40 million children and adults; in U.S., 2.8 million children and adults, members of The Protestant Episcopal Church which is part of Anglicanism. Total U.S. assets, $750 million.	Share with Catholics belief that church's bishops trace their spiritual authority to Christ and the apostles; share with Protestants belief in the Bible as the inspired final standard of faith and life. Presiding bishop heads church governed by two-house General Convention: Deputies (clerical and lay), Bishops.	Members differ somewhat in beliefs but accept the Trinity of one God in three persons, the doctrines of Incarnation, Virgin Birth. Clergy are sworn to uphold the Apostles' and Nicene Creeds. Its famous Book of Common Prayer is widely used by other churches.
BAPTISTS Members in world, 22 million adults; in U.S., 18.8 million adults. Largest of at least 27 bodies in the U.S. is the Southern Baptist Convention with 8.5 million members. Total U.S. assets, $1.5 billion.	Bible, the guide inspired by God, is first authority for faith; many Baptists accept it literally. Every person is himself competent to approach God directly; church is the community of forgiven sinners headed by Christ. Each congregation is self-governing, associates with others for common action.	Have no formal creed but an informal unity of belief with freedom of interpretation for the individual. Generally accept the Trinity and the Virgin Birth of Christ; emphasize that Christ heads the church.
METHODISTS Members in world, 16 million adults; in U.S., 11.8 million adults. There are now 22 groups in U.S. Largest is The Methodist Church; next, African Methodist Episcopal Church. Total U.S. assets, $2.7 billion.	Bible is the authority by which Christians live. Inspired by God, it contains everything men need for their salvation. U.S. church government is through executive Council of Bishops, legislative General Conference and the Judicial Council.	Personal religious experience and love of God are more important to Methodists than is doctrine, but they accept Trinity as formula for understanding God and Christ. Most believe in the Virgin Birth.
CONGREGATIONALISTS Members in world, 2.5 million adults; in U.S., 1.3 million. Congregational Christian Churches are uniting in 1957 with Evangelical and Reformed Church. Total U.S. assets of Congregationalists, $500 million.	Basis of faith is the Bible, which is God's revelation and the final religious authority, though individuals are free and responsible and have the right of personal judgment. Churches are self-governing but associate for common action in state conferences.	Individual is free to interpret God's word within the Christian revelation, so beliefs vary. But all Congregationalists acknowledge one God, supremely revealed in Jesus Christ His Son. Most believe in the Trinity; many accept the Virgin Birth.
DISCIPLES OF CHRIST Disciples: members in world, 2 million adults; in U.S., 1.9 million. Historically related Churches of Christ: world and U.S., 1.6 million. Total U.S. assets: Disciples, $291 million; Churches of Christ, $147 million.	Accept Bible as divinely inspired, the only rule of life and faith, and Christ (as presented in New Testament) as the basis of religious authority. Disciples' churches are self-governing, join for common action. Church of Christ congregations autonomous; unlike Disciples, do not cooperate with other churches.	Disciples, doctrinally close to Baptists, "have no creed but Christ," but stress one God and the Trinity. Many accept the Virgin Birth. Church of Christ members are more literal believers in Bible.
LATTER-DAY SAINTS Members in world, 1.5 million children and adults; in U.S., 1.4 million. Six groups; much the largest is The Church of Jesus Christ of Latter-day Saints (Mormons). Total U.S. assets, $160 million.	Bible, "Book of Mormon," "Pearl of Great Price" and "Doctrine and Covenants" are scripture for Mormons. God reveals Himself and His will with regard to the church continuously through His apostles and prophets who guide it. The Mormon church is organized along biblical lines with high priests, patriarch, etc.	Mormons generally accept the Trinity as three distinct personages. Christ is mediator between God and man. They acknowledge the Virgin Birth.

CHRISTIANS, THEIR PRACTICES

This capsule examination of 10 large and six smaller Christian groups covers some areas of general agreement, though beliefs and practices vary widely within some of the churches. All figures are estimates; those for assets are for 1952. Some churches number only adults as members while others include children. The Coptic Church, with about 10 million members mostly in Ethiopia and Egypt, is the largest Christian group not described. It calls itself Orthodox and Catholic and doctrinally is Monophysite, holding Christ human and divine in one nature, not two.

Baptism, Communion, Other Sacraments	Concepts of Salvation and Afterlife	History and Special Characteristics
Sacraments, conferring grace (life in Christ) on those rightly disposed, are: baptism (by flow of water, for infants, adults), confirmation, penance (confession, absolution, expiation), Eucharist (Communion, sacrifice of Christ's Body and Blood in the Mass), extreme unction (near death), holy orders, matrimony.	Salvation is by God's grace; man helps gain it by faith, obedience to divine law. Damnation is man's fault, by rejection of grace. Man's final state after death will be heaven (for which purgatory purifies soul), or hell (eternal torment). At man's bodily resurrection and the Second Coming, Christ will judge all men.	In Catholic belief, Christ founded the Church. This is the world's largest Christian body. The first parish in what is now U.S. started 1565 in St. Augustine, Fla. In U.S. it now has 48,349 priests in 90 different religious orders, and 159,545 nuns in 324 orders.
Practice seven sacraments called mysteries: baptism (by immersion for infants, adults), confirmation (called Holy Chrism), penance, Eucharist (Communion in Liturgy), unction of sick, matrimony, orders (of ministry).	Salvation, either from original sin or breaking of God's law, comes only through the Church, faith in Christ (Whose atonement removes sin) and good works. At death souls go to heaven, hell or intermediate state, which are real places and states of mind. Last Judgment will be at Christ's Second Coming.	Christ founded church, in Orthodox belief. In 1054 Orthodoxy and Roman Catholicism broke apart. Orthodoxy came to Alaska in 1792. Different national groups agree on basic doctrines and practices. Orthodox revere saints and their icons, believe in saints' intercession for us with God.
Practice sacraments of baptism (by sprinkling, for children and adults) and Communion, in which Christ is a real presence, not simply there in spirit. Confirmation is a rite, not a sacrament.	Men sin in disobeying God; salvation is from God's grace through repentance and faith in Christ, specifically through the sacraments. Christ will come to judge all souls. The good will live with Him eternally, the unregenerate will be punished.	Much the largest Protestant denomination in the world today, they began in Germany in 1517, first settled in America in 1623. The fact that they are divided into many groups is largely accounted for by the growth of national churches in northern European countries.
Practice sacraments of baptism (generally by sprinkling, for children and adults) and Communion, in which Christ is present in spirit.	Salvation is the free gift of God, gained through man's repentance and faith in Christ. Predestination (God's determining of a man's destiny) was once a basis of faith but is no longer emphasized. Heaven and hell are real but not necessarily material places.	Historically grew from the 16th Century Reformation, specifically from Calvin. It arrived in American colonies in 1611. Presbyterianism came to the U.S. chiefly from Scotland, is virtually identical with faith of the Reformed churches of Switzerland, Holland, France, Germany, Hungary with which it is allied.
Chief sacraments are baptism (by pouring or immersion, for children or adults) and Communion (Christ is a real presence). Confirmation, penance (in which Christ absolves sin), ordination (of priests), unction (healing) and matrimony are also considered sacramental. Formality of services varies greatly.	Salvation comes through man's repentance and faith in Christ. After death men will be close to or alienated from God. Heaven and hell increasingly interpreted in symbolic terms though church officially accepts bodily resurrection and the Last Judgment.	The Protestant Episcopal Church, autonomous U.S. branch of world-wide Anglicanism, reached America in 1607. Services range from the informal to a Mass like that of Roman Catholics. There are 12 Episcopal religious orders for men in U.S., 14 for women.
Unlike many other Christian groups, which permit the baptism of infants and baptize by sprinkling or pouring, Baptists restrict baptism to those old enough to understand its meaning. Practice total immersion. Take Communion as a remembrance of Christ's death.	Sin is not living up to God's law; salvation is by God's grace and one's personal faith in Christ. Some Baptists accept literal heaven, hell, others interpret them symbolically. Many accept physical resurrection, the Second Coming of Christ and Last Judgment.	Historically Baptists stem from Reformation in northern Europe, came to U.S. about 1640, are nearly a third of U.S. Protestants. They have over 3 million adherents in Russia. Fight vigorously for religious freedom and separation of church from state.
Practice sacraments of baptism (usually by sprinkling, for children, adults) and Communion. Communion symbolizes redemption through Christ's death and the love of Christians for one another; Christ is considered to be present in spirit, not body.	Salvation is through repentance and faith. Stress is placed on the individual experience of God's grace and power and a life of "social holiness" including the Christianizing of men's life and conduct. Most Methodists accept a divine judgment after death with rewards and punishments of some kind.	Offshoot of Anglicanism, Methodism was founded in England in the 18th Century by John Wesley. It soon spread to U.S. Many Methodists have taken emphatic stands on national issues like slavery, prohibition, war.
Practice the two sacraments of baptism (generally by sprinkling, for children and adults) and Communion in which Christ is a real presence.	Salvation is through repentance in faith, in striving to know God's will and live by it. After death man will live on, either with God or away from Him, but every individual interprets what this means.	Congregationalism began as a 17th Century Puritan movement within Anglicanism. It was brought by the Pilgrims and Puritans to America, where it became the state religion in some colonies.
Baptism (by immersion, for adults) and weekly Communion (in memory of Christ) are practiced by both groups as divine ordinances, not sacraments.	Disciples believe that salvation is through confession of faith in Christ, Who saves men from the sin that alienates every soul from God. Salvation also requires repentance and obedience to the gospel. After death men will be with God or away from Him.	Disciples started in U.S. in early 19th Century as an effort to rid churches of sectarian divisions. Churches of Christ finally split off in 1906, in arguments chiefly over missionary societies and use of organs in church. Disciples are largest native American denomination.
Mormon baptism (by immersion, for those over 8) includes a unique form of vicarious baptism for the dead. Mormons call Communion the sacrament in memory of Christ. Have a special form of marriage ceremony (sealing) for eternity.	Through the atonement of Christ and by obedience to the laws and ordinances of the gospel, in Mormon belief, mankind may be saved. Life after death is a state of spiritual progress, first in the spirit world and later in the resurrected state, when men are judged.	Founded in upper New York by Joseph Smith in 1830. Mormons stress missions, have a broad program of welfare, education, employment for members. Believe some members of lost tribes of Israel were ancestors of American Indians and were visited here by Christ.

Theologically some of the most interesting among the other Christian groups in the U.S. are:

ADVENTISTS have 300,000 U.S. members (one million in world); largest are Seventh-day Adventists. Stress imminent end of world and Second Coming of Christ, Who will destroy evil, reign on a purified earth.

CHURCH OF CHRIST, SCIENTIST has some 3,100 branches in the world. It was founded by an American,

Mrs. Mary Baker Eddy. Doctrinally it holds that God is "all that really is," and it puts considerable emphasis on spiritual healing. Evil, disease, and death are errors of belief to be overcome by spiritual understanding.

JEHOVAH'S WITNESSES have 187,000 U.S. workers (642,000 in world). Persistent missionaries, they stress one God (Jehovah), believe His kingdom is here now and will replace earthly governments which should not be obeyed against the law of God.

UNITARIANS and UNIVERSALISTS are considering merger which would have total U.S. membership of 160,000 (500,000 in world). Stress freedom of belief; most hold God is one, not Trinity; Christ was human; salvation comes by man's efforts, not God's grace.

FRIENDS (Quakers) have 121,000 U.S. members (in world, 186,000). They emphasize direct experience of God's guiding spirit (Inner Light) and service to others. They are known for pacifism, work as mediators.

CHRISTENDOM

It is the earthly embodiment of the profound, manifold inspiration of Jesus Christ

IN ST. PETER'S BASILICA Pope Pius XII officiates from the throne of Peter's successors over a consistory in which 24 archbishops are elevated to the college of cardinals. The old and new cardinals, robed in white ermine, are seated on long benches facing each other. Illumining the scene are almost 100 chandeliers and many spotlights. The Cross (*center foreground*) is the 95-ft.-high top of Bernini's baldachino over the High Altar and Peter's tomb.

SISTINE CHAPEL

Michelangelo's incomparable frescoes depict the Creation, Flood and Last Judgment

Within the encompassing walls of the Vatican and almost in the shadow of St. Peter's stands the Sistine Chapel (*above*). First built in 1473 for the Renaissance Pope Sixtus IV, after whom it is named, and used for a while as a fort, it became the Popes' private chapel. Outwardly it is a homely stone box. But as Goethe wrote, "he who has not seen the Sistine Chapel can form no comprehensive idea of what man is capable." For this austere structure—132 feet long, 45 feet wide and 68 feet high —houses Michelangelo's ceiling frescoes of the Creation, the Fall of Man and the Flood, and on the altar wall, his Last Judgment. The greatest religious art ever produced, the paintings contain—in the words of Ludwig Goldscheider—"everything that, without assuming visible shape, has filled the minds of all the thinkers of all times—the beginning and end of the world." They are reproduced on the following 19 pages.

But Michelagniolo di Lodovico di Lionardo di Buonarroto Simoni of Florence, who was born in 1475, just two years after the chapel was built, created much of the work reluctantly, in anguish of body and soul. The Sistine Chapel's walls already bore the masterpieces of Botticelli, Perugino, Signorelli and the Ghirlandaios when Pope Julius II decided that Michelangelo must decorate the ceiling. Michelangelo, who usually appended "sculptor" to his signature, did not consider himself a painter. He had quarreled bitterly with the Pope over designs and fees for earlier commissions. Once he had stormily abandoned a papal assignment, returning to Florence and leaving only a snippy note for the Pope.

In anger and fear, Michelangelo for two years rebuffed Julius' invitations and defied his commands, yielding only when the government of Florence warned: "We do not want to go to war with Pope Julius because of you. . . ." A contract was concluded May 10, 1508. The artist was to receive 3,000 ducats (about $70,000 today), pay expenses and paint what he wished. Soon after work began Michelangelo testily

dismissed the assistants he had brought from Florence. He locked the chapel and, lying on his back almost seventy feet above the floor, painted furiously with either hand. Falling plaster blinded him. His neck stiffened and he could read only what was held above his head. He rarely ate. When he did at last—after weeks—take off his shoes, the skin of his feet went with them. He was bothered by the Pope, who climbed the scaffold to hurry him and once hit him with a stick. He was overcome by self-doubts, "this not being my trade." He was disturbed by the contradictions of the times: a protégé of the gay Lorenzo the Magnificent when he was 15, he had been troubled by Savonarola's streetcorner tirades. As devout a Catholic as he was a great artist, he was tormented by the problem: Should life be the cultivation of perfect beauty in the visible world, or the search for perfect sanctity in the invisible world?

When the first Mass was celebrated on October 31, 1512 under the 10,000 square feet of ceiling paintings—a total of 343 figures, some of them twelve feet in height—it was clear that Michelangelo had found at least a partial answer. In his own words, "Good painting is nothing else but a copy of the perfections of God and a reminder of His painting."

Twenty-four years later, Michelangelo returned to the Sistine Chapel to paint the Last Judgment. When it was finished, Pope Paul III—who had had two mistresses and four illegitimate sons before he became a priest at 51—fell on his knees and prayed, "Lord, charge me not with my sins when Thou shalt come on the Day of Judgment."

For four centuries, the work that Michelangelo accomplished in his 89 years has affected most of Christendom as it did Paul. He was, says Francis Henry Taylor, long director of the Metropolitan Museum of Art, "the incarnation of the intellectual, moral and religious crisis of the Renaissance" and "the precursor of a rational approach to religious experience"—which led inevitably to the Reformation (*page 230*).

GOD'S SEPARATION of light and dark (*opposite*) is the first of the five great Creation scenes on the Sistine ceiling. God appears here as a relatively indistinct shape.

A MIGHTY GESTURE OF GOD
SUMMONS A SUN AND MOON

With His work of Creation in full progress, God (*right and below*) has become a clearly visible figure in Whom Michelangelo personified the awesome forces of the universe. Terrible in His wrath, gentle in His love of man, Michelangelo's God is a super-being Who, like a stern and magnificently bearded judge, commands the love and the fear of ordinary mortals. At right God is surrounded by frightened young spirits as He proceeds with the tremendous task of creating the sun, which is symbolized here by the sphere at the top, and the moon (*right*), with a single mighty gesture. Then, whirling through space (*left, rearview*) under the blinding light of the new sun, He brings into being the first plant life (*lower left*). In the panel below, God looks down upon the beginnings of the earth and, stretching out His massive arms, creates the sky and the water.

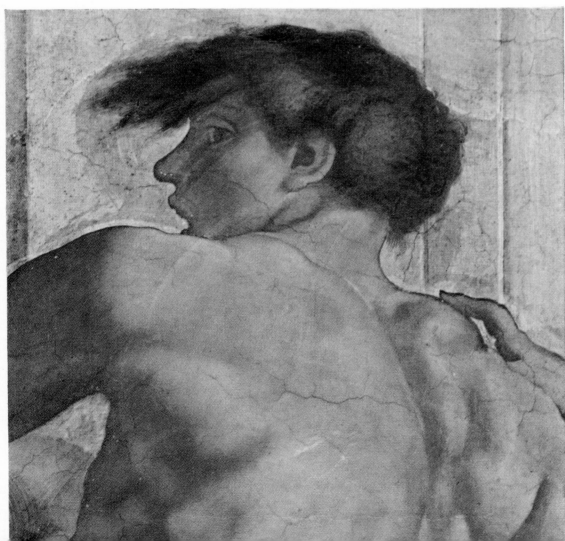

YOUTH'S HEAD is a detail from one of 140 figures that Michelangelo painted to decorate the edges of his huge composition. Despite their number, the artist is said never to have duplicated an expression or posture, in either the ceiling frescoes or the great Last Judgment.

GOD TOUCHES ADAM'S HAND AND HE BEGINS TO BREATHE

In the Bible God breathed life into Adam's nostrils. But to achieve a more powerful composition, Michelangelo, in his Creation of Adam (*above*), has God stretching out His right arm to touch Adam's still limp hand. The hands (*close-up*, *opposite*) tell the story. Under God's left arm is a girl, identified as the yet uncreated Eve. Other figures are genii, symbols of God's omnipotence, and the head at left, from the border around the Creation panels, suggests mortal awe at the miracles. Adam was painted on wet plaster in three days and needed no correction. "This superb giant is more beautifully articulated and immeasurably more vital than anything the Greeks ever did," writes the critic Thomas Craven, "and it is not rash to say that the figure of Adam is superior to all other nudes not only in size, power and physical perfection but also in those qualities which are the opposite of the material."

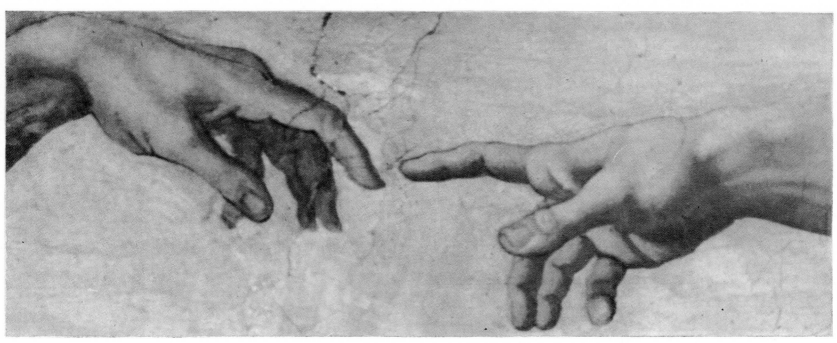

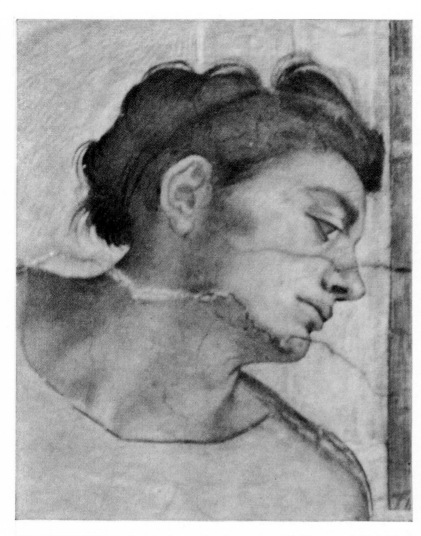

HELLENIC HEAD, from a decorative figure near the Eve panel (*right*) has a dreamy, almost feminine expression even though, as in many of Michelangelo's paintings, it is set on a torso that is big and aggressively masculine.

REFLECTIVE GAZE of another decorative figure conveys a feeling of deep insight into the mysteries of the universe. This head repeats the feminine and essentially Greek cast of features of the head shown at the top of page.

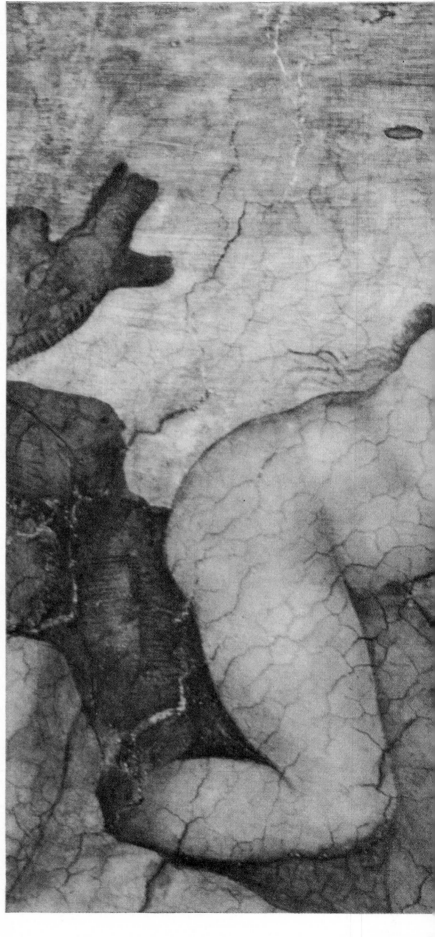

EVE RISES UP

A man of noble soul and generous manner, Michelangelo was also a man of many moods, a fact reflected in the scene above from the Creation of Eve. Here God has lost His formidably heroic appearance and has become instead a philosophical patriarch who looks more like mortal man than He does in any other place on the Sistine ceiling. Eve, moreover, appears as a plain, buxom peasant with long, stringy hair. Only the act of the Creation, quietly going on in a lonely setting of infinite sea and sky, gives the impression of being entirely divine. Had Michelangelo's mysterious inner feelings permitted, the

FROM ADAM'S BODY AS GOD BECKONS TO HER

artist might have spared himself the tremendous labors which these paintings represent. When Pope Julius II—who for all his faults was a great statesman, a great warrior and the greatest patron of the arts that the Papacy has known—finally induced Michelangelo to undertake the Sistine ceiling, he suggested that the artist put the figures of the twelve apostles in the lunettes, and fill the remaining space with handsome but conventional work. "It seemed to me a wretched project and I told the Pope that I thought the apostles would make a poor impression," Michelangelo has written. "When the Pope asked

why, I answered: 'Because they themselves were poor.'" It was then that Michelangelo countered with his awesome scheme to depict, as Giovanni Papini puts it, "the divine and human history of mankind, a proem to the coming of Christ: the creation of the universe; the creation and fall of man; the sin and chastisement of man; all the events that made the Redemption both possible and necessary. As if this were not enough, he proposed to paint . . . all those who were the direct precursors of the Redeemer; all the ancestors of Christ in the flesh, all the prophets and sibyls who announced His coming."

GRINNING HEAD (*above*) and the nude (*right*) are two details from figures bordering sacrifice scene below. Though unrelated to it, they add a pagan touch that Michelangelo often showed.

NOAH'S SACRIFICE, which occurred after the Deluge, shows the hero of the ark (*top center*) with his wife (*right*) presiding over a sacrifice of his animals to demonstrate obedience to God. His sons and their wives (*foreground*) are preparing for the ceremony. One son, kneeling in the center, is busy kindling a fire on the altar. Another, astride the slaughtered ram, passes along an offering of entrails while one son's wife (*right*) brings in an armful of firewood.

ANGEL OF THE LORD DRIVES

In illustrating the two decisive episodes in the Garden of Eden—the taking of the forbidden fruit (*left*) and the abrupt expulsion (*right*)—Michelangelo gave his own interpretation to the famous biblical stories. Once again humanizing his subject, he stressed the basic qualities he saw in the daily relationships between the sexes: the aggressiveness of man and the passiveness of woman. He depicted Adam as a huge, muscular primitive, reaching out aggressively to pick the forbidden fruit. Eve, on the other hand, is a voluptuous girl who passively accepts the fruit from the serpent. In the expulsion scene Michelangelo developed this theme still further. Beaten across the back with a sword by an angel, Adam groans with remorse. But Eve is already seeking the protection of Adam. Condemned by the judgment of God, the two suddenly find themselves

219

THE CEILING IN FULL VIEW REFLECTS THE OLD TESTAMENT'S GRANDEUR

light from darkness. The next four show Him creating successively the sun and moon (*pictured on pages 212–213*), the sky and water, Adam (*pages 214–215*) and then Eve (*pages 216–217*); the last four illustrate the first sin in Eden (*pages 219–220*), Noah's sacrifice of the rams (*page 218*), the Flood (*pages 224–225*) and finally Noah's drunkenness. In the triangular sections around the border, called spandrels, the artist placed the ancestors of Christ. In the corner ones are scenes of the saving of Israel—David and Goliath (*upper right*). Between the spandrels he enthroned prophets, including Jonah

222

Only when the ceiling is viewed directly from the floor 68 feet below can the overwhelming power of Michelangelo's conception and accomplishment be fully realized. In the central rectangular section, the first panel at left is the one which appears on page 211, depicting God separating

ADAM AND EVE OUT OF EDEN

alone in a flat dreary wasteland where, dependent only on each other, they must till the soil for their livelihood until the end of their days.

Michelangelo acquired his knowledge of human anatomy, which the Sistine paintings reveal so dramatically, with the help of the church; the Augustinian monastery of Santo Spirito supplied him with cadavers from the monks' charity hospital. His human interpretation of Adam and Eve reveals Michelangelo's intense awareness and perceptive analysis of life. By filling his works with meaning that stemmed from both his intellect and emotions, he lifted his art far above the mastery of execution. Bernard Berenson, the great critic of Renaissance art, has written of Michelangelo: "At last appeared a man who was pupil of nobody, the heir of everybody . . . who saw and expressed the meaning of it all."

(*extreme left, center*), Jeremiah (*top, far left*) and the Delphic Sibyl (*bottom, far right*). In painting, Michelangelo began with the Deluge. His first figures were comparatively small in scale, but as he progressed, his style loosened up and by the time he had finished the ceiling, he had created a race of giants.

223

AS THE RAINS FLOOD THE EARTH

In painting the Flood Michelangelo shattered the traditional concept of his time, in which the ark usually appeared tossing on a raging sea, and depicted the effects of the Deluge on the people caught in it. At left doomed couples, their children clinging to them, desperately scramble onto a last outcropping of dry land. Some have salvaged a few possessions. A woman (*center*) carries her kitchen stool on her head, while a young man next to her clutches a bundle of clothes and a frying pan. Above them is a foundering skiff crowded

MAN FLEES TO THE ARK OF NOAH

with men clubbing and punching each other in their frantic efforts to save themselves. At the right a second tribe has sought refuge on a rock. While a father raises his dead son's body from the waters and wife and patriarch stretch out compassionate hands, a despairing youth finds no solace in the wine keg on which he rests. At the top, Noah's ark dominates the composition. Formerly a tree was visible behind the lefthand corner of the tent (*right*), but it was almost entirely effaced by an accidental explosion in 1797.

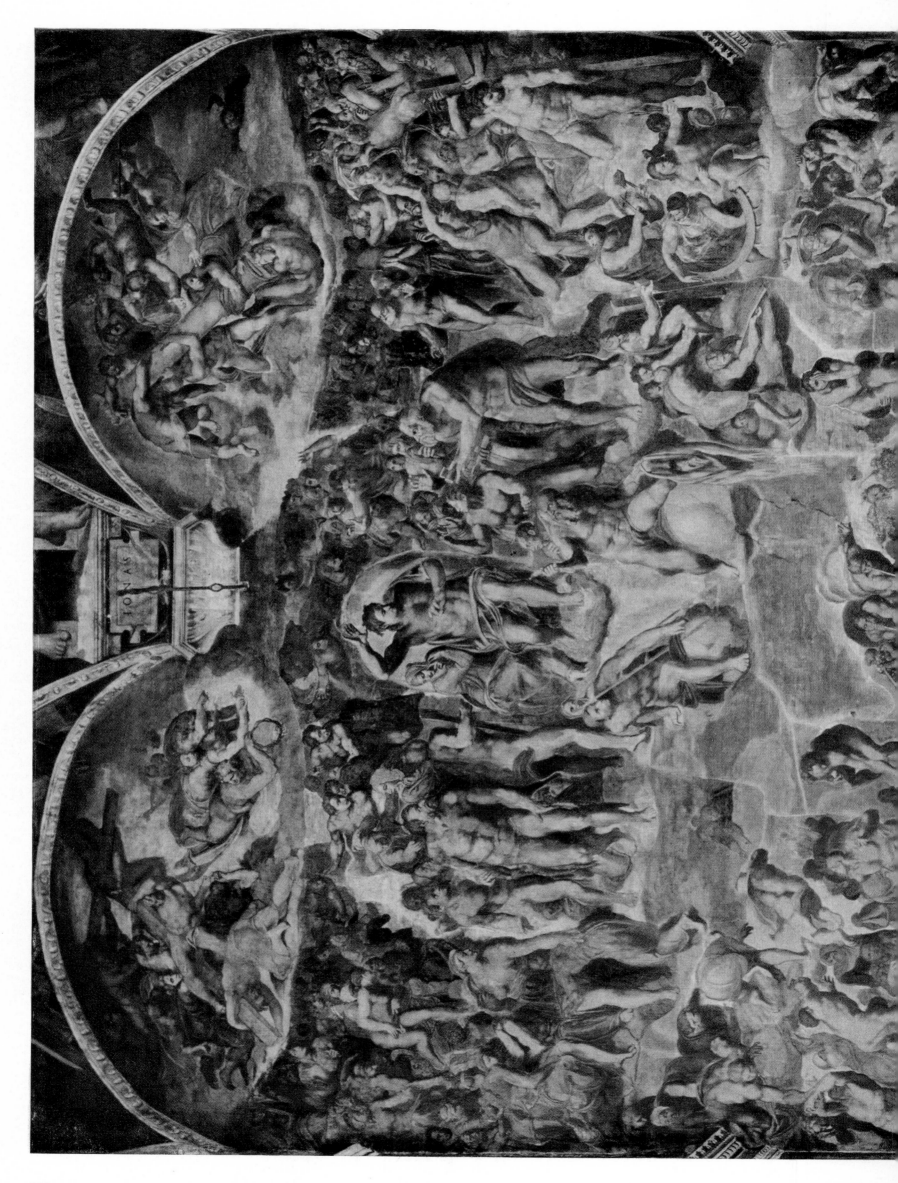

CHRIST THE JUDGE CONDEMNS SINNERS TO HELL

Twenty-four years and four Popes after Michelangelo had finished the Sistine ceiling, Pope Paul III summoned him back to the chapel to decorate the wall behind the altar. Michelangelo was in his sixties and failing physically, but the resulting 40-ft.-wide, 45-ft.-high Last Judgment is vigorous and passionate. Under the arches at top, Michelangelo symbolized man's sins by painting demonic angels pulling down the Cross (*left*) and the post (*right*) where Christ was whipped. Below, Christ rises from His throne, His face turned toward the damned, and with a mighty gesture speaks His terrifying verdict. This is no gentle Jesus, but an angry deity out of Dante and Savonarola. Beside Him, the Virgin Mary flinches from His anger; flanking Him are the saints sharing Christ's rage. One, St. Bartholomew, sits below and to the right of Christ. In one hand he holds the knife with which he was flayed, in the other his

mortal skin. To the right of him are St. Catherine, with part of the spiked wheel on which she was tortured, and St. Sebastian, gripping the arrows that caused his death. Below the saints, cherubim summon the dead (*bottom left*) to judgment. Opposite, fiends herd the damned before Minos (*extreme lower right*), the Judge of Hell. Some of the details are shown in larger scale on the next two pages. Michelangelo put many identifiable figures into the work. His own face appears on St. Bartholomew's mortal skin. Bartholomew's face was borrowed from the bawdy Pietro Aretino, whose complaints about the painting's nudes were followed by an ecclesiastical order to put pants on them. Minos is Biagio de Cesena, Pope Paul's Master of Ceremonies, who asked the Pope to order the face changed. Paul, in the full spirit of the painting, replied firmly that not even a Pope could rescue the damned from Hell.

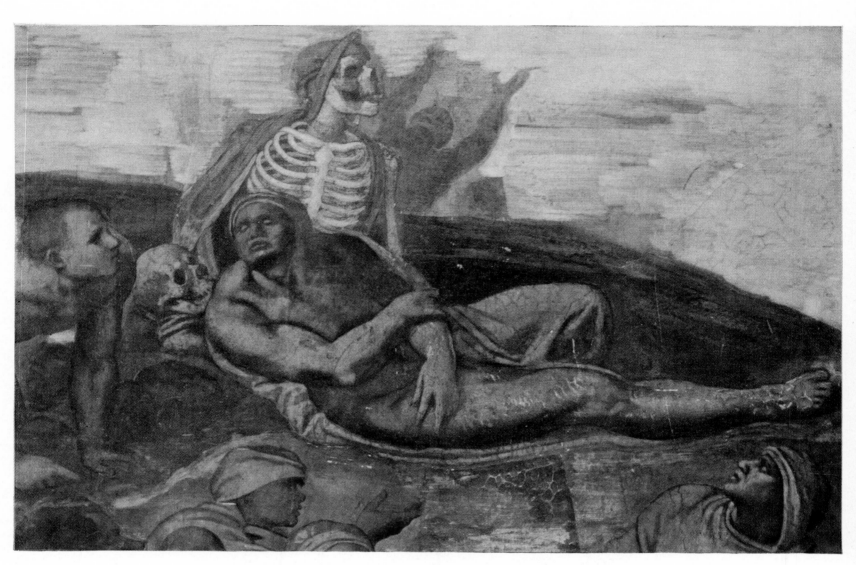

THE DEAD (*above*), responding to the chorus of cherubim's trumpets, emerge from the soil in varying degrees of decay, still draped in their shrouds. This detail is from the lower left corner of Michelangelo's Last Judgment.

CONDEMNED SINNER, also from the Last Judgment, clutches his face in horror as he realizes he has been committed to Hell. Here Michelangelo caught the full implication of the man's fate, an eternity totally without hope.

THE FERRYMAN of Hell, Charon (*opposite*), beats the damned with an oar, driving them toward Minos. Michelangelo drew from Dante's *Inferno*, in which Charon is described as a "demoniac form with eyes of burning coal."

WALDO'S HEIRS, Waldensian women in ancestral costumes sing psalms after church in the isolated Pellice Valley in northern Italy. The Waldensians, Protestantism's oldest denomination, were persecuted for several centuries before allying themselves with the Reformation in 1532. In 1655 they were almost wiped out, but survivors returned to the valleys in 1689. Religious liberty was finally granted in 1848. Today there are 100,000 Waldensians in Italy.

THE SPARKS
OF REVOLT

Plain scenes recall the Reformation's fervor

At the Renaissance height of its ecclesiastical pomp and power, Roman Catholicism was challenged by a widespread, urgent call for a return to early Christian simplicity. The Protestant Reformation, which resulted, now has more than 200 million followers—one-fourth of the world's Christians. It was led by bold but devout men who were ready to die for their beliefs. The shrines and events that represent the start of the key Protestant groups are presented on these and the next six pages.

The first rumblings directed against abuses within Roman Catholicism came in three chief medieval sectarian movements, by the Waldensians, Wycliffites and Hussites. The Waldensians (*opposite*), who believe any Christian can be his own priest, still live in the Alpine valleys where they retreated after Peter Waldo's excommunication in 1184. The Englishman John Wycliffe, preaching in a quiet country church (*right*) and at

WYCLIFFE'S CHURCH, St. Mary's in Ludgershall near Oxford, was the scene of his influential preaching from 1368 to 1374. While here, Wycliffe first became deeply aware of how much religion could mean to ordinary people.

LUTHER'S HERITAGE, the University of Marburg, founded in 1527 by a local count, Philip the Generous, became the first Protestant university. The city was for many years a refuge for Protestants like Britain's Bible translator

William Tyndale. Nearby is Marburg Castle, where in 1529 Luther engaged in a crucial debate with the reformer Huldreich Zwingli of Switzerland on transubstantiation. Their lack of accord kept German and Swiss Protestants apart.

CHAIR FOR PREACHING was used by Calvin in Geneva's Cathedral of St. Pierre, from which he ruled the city religiously and politically. Calvin did not bring Reformation to Switzerland, but organized it and assumed its leadership.

SANCTUARY FOR REFORMERS, St. Andrew's Castle on Scotland's coast (*below*), was refuge for Knox and other Protestants after Fifeshire Protestants murdered Catholic cardinal, David Beaton, and hung him over castle walls.

Oxford, laid the theological foundation for rebellion. Attacking such Church practices as pilgrimages and the sale of indulgences, Wycliffe also disputed the doctrine of transubstantiation. Denying that consecration by a priest during communion actually changes the substance of the bread and wine into Christ's Body and Blood, he began a controversy that still smolders in Christendom. Wycliffe also made the first English translation of the Bible (". . . And sche bare hir first borun sone, and wlappide hym in clothis, and leide hym in a cratche. . . ."). He died peacefully in bed in 1384, but 44 years later the Pope, belatedly recognizing the explosiveness of the Englishman's views, had Wycliffe's body disinterred, burned and flung into the Swift River, a tributary of the Avon. "The Avon to the Severn runs/And Severn to the sea;/ And Wycliffe's dust shall spread abroad/ Wide as the waters be." Wycliffe inspired John Hus, in distant Bohemia, and after Hus was martyred in 1415 his unintimidated followers founded the Moravian Church.

The full-scale Reformation began in 1517, when the German monk Martin Luther posted his 95 theses attacking papal authority (*page 200*). Luther felt the essence of Christianity lay not in an elaborate hierarchy headed by the Pope, but in each believer's humble, direct communion with God, seeking "that righteousness by which through grace and sheer mercy God justifies us through faith." Within 20 years Luther saw a strong German Lutheran Church established, the first Protestant university (*page 231*) chartered and a host of other reformers flourishing —some of them far too radical for Luther's own tastes.

Among these were the Anabaptists, who believed that only those old enough for a heartfelt experience of grace—*i.e.*, adults—should be baptized. The first Anabaptist church was in the Swiss village of Zollikon (*opposite, top*), where converts were even baptizing each other out of the public fountain. The Anabaptists are direct forerunners of the Mennonites and Hutterites and collateral ancestors of today's Baptists.

More influential in Switzerland and elsewhere was John Calvin. From his chair in Geneva's cathedral (*above*), Calvin held sway over a kind of Protestant city-state. He called his church "the most perfect school of

SEEDBED FOR ANABAPTISTS, the Swiss town of Zollikon near Zurich, was first center of movement led by Conrad Grebel, who urged abolition of infant baptism and the Mass and who held "last supper" meetings in Zollikon houses. One Sunday in 1525 one of Grebel's followers, George Blauroch, entered the church (*above*), ordered the minister from the pulpit and began to preach vociferously until forces of the law were summoned to arrest him.

WHERE BUNYAN RANG BELLS, Elstow Church, still has old bell tower which was probably model for the Castle of Beelzebub in *Pilgrim's Progress*. Even after giving up bellringing as sinful, Bunyan came to watch others ring.

Christ that ever was on earth since the days of the apostles." It became a model for Reformed and Presbyterian churches in most of Europe— and later throughout the world.

After a sojourn in Calvin's Geneva, John Knox became Scotland's most dramatic Reformation figure. "Others snipped at the branches of the Papistry," said a listener, "but he strikes at the root." Knox had condoned the murder of a Catholic cardinal at St. Andrew's Castle (*page 232*). His thunderous sermons now helped to overthrow Mary, Queen of Scots. In a day when too many allowed their opinions to be determined by their rulers, Knox "neither feared nor flattered any flesh." Unswerving, incorruptible and utterly unafraid, he had no tact—and thereby was quite incapable of those politic compromises by which immediate situations are saved and ultimate causes lost. His religious defiance of secular powers has affected the world ever since.

The Church of England broke with the Papacy under Henry VIII, declaring: "The Bishop of Rome hath not by Scripture any greater authority in England than any other foreign bishop." Its doctrines have remained Catholic as well as Protestant. Henry's daughter Mary tried to force the church back to Rome and burned many Anglican leaders at the stake. The Martyrs' Memorial (*left*) honors three of these. One

WHERE ENGLISH PRELATES BURNED, Martyrs' Memorial in Oxford, marks place where Cranmer, Latimer and Ridley died. Latimer is said to have "received the flame as if embracing it. . . . He soon died with very little pain."

QUAKER'S VISION came to Fox as he stood atop Pendle Hill in 1652. He was "moved to sound the day of the Lord; and the Lord let me see . . . in what places he had a great people to be gathered." View is from where Fox stood.

PILGRIMS' PORT in Delfshaven, a small town now a part of Rotterdam in Holland, is marked by a church overlooking the Voorhaven Canal where the Pilgrims worshiped before setting out in 1620 by way of England for America.

of them, Latimer, spoke prophetic words there: "We shall this day light such a candle, by God's grace, in England as shall never be put out."

Because Anglicanism did not have the plainness that so many Protestants desired, the Reformation raged on in England after settling down elsewhere. One of its notable figures was John Bunyan, a forerunner of the present Baptists and Disciples of Christ, who as a youth loved to ring bells in the Anglican church at Elstow (*page 235*). After his conversion in 1650 he went to prison repeatedly for his beliefs. In jail Bunyan wrote *Pilgrim's Progress*, one of the great works of the Reformation.

Equally defiant of authority was George Fox, whose vision from Pendle Hill (*above*) in 1652 led him to found the Society of Friends, also known as Quakers because a derisive judge thought Fox quaked before the Lord. Fox and his followers were persecuted in England. In New England (*page 240*) they were harassed by the Separatists, who had only recently escaped from Anglican tyranny and are ancestors of today's Congregationalists, Unitarians and Universalists. The original Pilgrim Fathers had banded together in England and emigrated to Holland in 1608, whence from Delfshaven (*left*) they sailed for America in 1620.

The inspiration for the last large church that emerged from the Reformation came from an Anglican clergyman, John Wesley, who never intended a break at all. In 1738, attending a meeting of Moravians, he suddenly felt his heart "strangely warmed," whereupon he embarked on a preaching campaign throughout England that lasted until his death. Wesley remained an Anglican but his followers began a church, called Methodist for its methodical organization, that stressed the personal approach to religion. "A Methodist," wrote Wesley, "is one who has the love of God shed abroad in his heart by the Holy Ghost given unto him. . . . God is the joy of his heart and the desire of his soul, which is constantly crying out, '. . . My God and my all! Thou art the strength of my heart, and my portion forever!'" Simple fervor—like that of Luther, Knox and Protestantism's other leaders—spelled a quickening of faith which has been the Reformation's most lasting result.

METHODISM'S SHRINE is chapel built by John Wesley in 1777 in London where he often preached. At cornerstone laying he described Methodism as "Not a new religion, but the old religion of the Bible . . . of the Primitive Church . . . of the Church of England. . . . No other than the love of God and all mankind." During his first sermon from the pulpit he spoke for 15 minutes to women present on "the absurdity of the enormous dressing of their heads."

DEFYING THE POPE, Martin Luther (*center*) burns the papal bull in which Leo X in 1520 condemned his views as heretical. At the same time Luther burned copy of the Canon Law which, he said, sanctioned ecclesiastical abuses.

DYING AT THE STAKE, Anglican bishops Hugh Latimer and Nicholas Ridley are burned at Oxford in 1555 on order of "Bloody Mary" Tudor. Archbishop Cranmer, who had been Henry VIII's adviser, was also burned here.

MASSACRE OF ST. BARTHOLOMEW is shown as it was launched in Paris on August 24, 1572 with the murder of Huguenot leaders by troops of the Duke of Guise. At upper right is Admiral Coligny's house, with the Huguenot

VIOLENT

The Wars of Religion from 1550 to 1650

The simple Christianity of the early church, which the Reformation's leaders so deeply desired, could not be attained simply or even peacefully. Protestant desire to affirm fundamental points of Christian faith and doctrine—by force, if need be—resulted in the Wars of Religion, which are among the bloodiest conflicts in history. The record on both the Roman Catholic and Protestant sides is stained with ferocity.

Wars of religion neither began nor ended with the Reformation, and Christian Europe lived for more than a thousand years under the threat of Islamic invasion (*page 242*). But the century from 1550 to 1650 saw sharper conflicts than any before or since, for the age of the Reformation, while a time of profound piety, was also a time of deep hatreds and abiding bitterness. Ambitious leaders of the new national states used the

chief already hanging dead from a window. Coligny appears again before the house, his head cut off. Guise is one of the armed men standing over him. Other atrocities occur nearby. In one night many hundreds were slain. Then the massacre spread and in six weeks at least 10,000 Huguenots were killed. Philip II of Spain laughed at the news, but most of Europe was shocked and England's Queen Elizabeth dressed in black to receive the French ambassador.

CENTURY

brought Reformation to a bloody climax

conflict to further their own interests, their cynicism aptly summed up by Henry IV of France who agreed to become a Catholic for political reasons with the remark, "Paris is worth a Mass." Yet both Catholics and Protestants retained noble Christian aspirations in the heat of the fight. John Calvin expressed the spiritual significance of the struggle when he wrote five young Frenchmen facing death in Lyons for their Protestantism: "If [Jesus] pleases to make use of you even to death in His battle, He will uphold you by His mighty hand to fight firmly, and will not suffer a single drop of your blood to remain useless."

The first few decades of the Reformation, when Protestantism made almost all the gains within Europe it would ever make, were relatively peaceful. From 1517, when Luther proclaimed his 95 theses, to the

MASSACRE OF HAARLEM followed the successful siege of the Dutch city in 1572–73 by troops of Catholic Spain. The 1,200 remaining Dutch troops were killed in the massacre together with about 1,100 residents of the town.

239

HANGING CATHOLIC MONKS, a band of Huguenots show ruthlessness of the French religious strife of the late 16th Century. The Huguenots were strongest in southwest France, their unofficial capital the city of La Rochelle.

EJECTING CATHOLIC OFFICIALS, Protestants throw two representatives of Catholic Habsburg Empire from a Prague window in 1618. Victims landed on a dung heap and lived, but the incident touched off the Thirty Years' War.

GOING TO EXECUTION, three Quakers—Marmaduke Stevenson, Mary Dyer and William Robinson—go to gallows in Boston in 1659 during Puritans' drive against dissenters. Mrs. Dyer was pardoned, but in 1660 she was hanged.

early 1550s there were few outbreaks of religiously inspired violence. In Germany, where Luther had publicly burned the papal bull of 1520 that condemned his intransigeance (*page 238, top*), a "peasants' revolt" broke out in 1524, caused partly by a desire for religious freedom. Luther first applauded the revolt but later denounced it. The 1546-47 Schmalkaldic War did little more than make official the division of Germany into rival Catholic and Protestant camps.

The century's second half, however, saw the Counter Reformation under way in earnest, and nowhere so brutally as in France (*above, left*). There the Protestants, Calvinists who came to be known as Huguenots, grew rapidly to become a powerful political party, led by the strong-willed Admiral Gaspard de Coligny. The Catholics were led by the equally resourceful Dukes of Guise, Francis and later his son Henry. For years, writes one historian, "the whole sweet and pleasant land of France . . . was widowed and desolated, her pride humbled by her own sons and her Golden Lilies trampled in the bloody mire." Atrocities were committed by both sides, culminating in 1572 in the six-week-long Massacre of St. Bartholomew, from which French Protestantism never fully recovered. With the crowning of Henry IV, a Protestant turned Catholic, France at the century's end won a respite from religious strife.

Similarly England, spared in the first half of the century, had its share of violence with the accession of Mary Tudor ("Bloody Mary") in 1553. Queen Elizabeth, who succeeded Mary, brought an era of moderation, but when she found a number of English Catholics plotting to dethrone her, she unhesitatingly executed them all. In 1587, with another plot confronting her, she permitted the execution of her cousin, Mary of Scotland. The following century, when Catholic Ireland rose up against Oliver Cromwell, the Lord Protector crushed the insurrection with a brusque vigor that the Irish have never forgotten or forgiven. In the English colonies the Puritans were equally intolerant (*left*).

The Low Countries, under Spain, erupted in 1566. Denied religious tolerance by the Spaniards, Calvinists there rioted and burned 400 Catholic churches. Spain's Duke of Alva inaugurated a reign of terror ending in the "Spanish Fury" of 1576, when thousands of Antwerp citizens were killed. But Alva could not stop the Calvinists. The Pacification of Ghent in 1576 gave the Protestants religious freedom, and in 1581 the Dutch Republic was born. Within her own borders Spain remained staunchly Catholic, thanks partly to the work of the Inquisition (*right*), an effective and often destructive instrument against all forms of "heresy." It has ever since remained a symbol of bigotry and

JUDGING A HERETIC, St. Dominic (founder of the Dominican Order) is shown at a 13th Century auto-da-fé, Inquisition ceremony in which judgments are given. As other victims await their fate, St. Dominic pardons man at left.

persecution. Spain's leadership in the Counter Reformation was bolstered by the formation of Ignatius Loyola's Society of Jesus in 1540.

The last of the great religious upheavals was the Thirty Years' War, a confused and desperate struggle which turned large areas of central Europe into wilderness and shrank the German population from 18 to four million. Touched off by an unlikely event in 1618 in Bohemia, the Defenestration of Prague (*page 240*), the war began as a minor affair between the Catholic Habsburgs and the independent German Protestant princes. Before long, however, France, Denmark and Sweden were in it, and the fighting spread to Italy and the Lowlands. By far the most compelling personality of the war was Sweden's soldier king, Gustavus Adolphus, the Protestant "Lion of the North," whose soldiers sang Luther's hymn *Ein'feste Burg* in battle. But in one of the fiercest battles of the war, Lützen (*below*) in 1632, Gustavus Adolphus was slain. The war ended indecisively in 1648, both Catholic and Protestant camps too exhausted to continue. Never again did Christians as such fight each other on such a tremendous and destructive scale.

For many Christians another foe remained. During all the years in which the Christian world had been divided, soldiers of another faith menaced it from the east. Moslem warriors had stood on European soil since they took the Spanish peninsula in the 8th Century. To the east, after the Great Schism of 1054 had sundered the Christian Church into Eastern and Western branches, the Moslem Turks soon conquered most of Asia Minor and advanced into the Balkans. In 1453 Constantinople fell after a long siege, erasing the last vestige of the old Eastern Empire.

Against this force Christendom enjoyed its earliest successes in Spain. Christians from Spain's north, taking advantage of struggles between Moslem sects, finally captured Cordova (1236) and Seville (1248) and reduced Moslem holdings to a ring around Granada. That bastion held out for 200 years. In the 15th Century, after a series of campaigns before the city (*opposite*) Ferdinand of Aragon subdued the city of Granada and occupied the Alhambra in January, 1492—the same year Ferdinand and Isabella dispatched Columbus to the New World.

In central Europe, however, the Moslem threat was far more pressing. A powerful ruler ascended the throne of the Ottoman Empire in 1520. Suleiman the Magnificent and his crack troops, the Janissaries, soon became the scourge of the Balkans. After conquering Hungary in 1526, Suleiman in 1529 marched to Vienna, to which he laid siege. Four hundred Turkish vessels sailed up the Danube to join the attack. The small Austrian and Spanish garrison fought magnificently and Suleiman's siege guns failed to arrive. After three weeks the Turks retreated. Mortified by his failure, Suleiman appeared again in 1532, but a large force under Habsburg Emperor Charles V persuaded him to withdraw.

The Turks made one last try. In 1571 their navy had been badly beaten by Venice and its allies at Lepanto, but they were still a power on land. Under the Grand Vizier Kara Mustapha, in 1683, they again assaulted Vienna and Emperor Leopold fled. Mustapha could very likely have taken the city by storm if he had not preferred to wait for a peaceful capitulation. But after nearly two months King Sobieski of Poland and Duke Charles of Lorraine arrived, struck Mustapha's forces from the rear and shattered them. Mustapha was routed, Vienna was saved and Europe's thousand-year dread of Islamic conquest dissolved. Only in the Balkans did the Ottomans remain 200 years longer, casting a cloud over the Eastern Orthodox churches there and elsewhere that still exists.

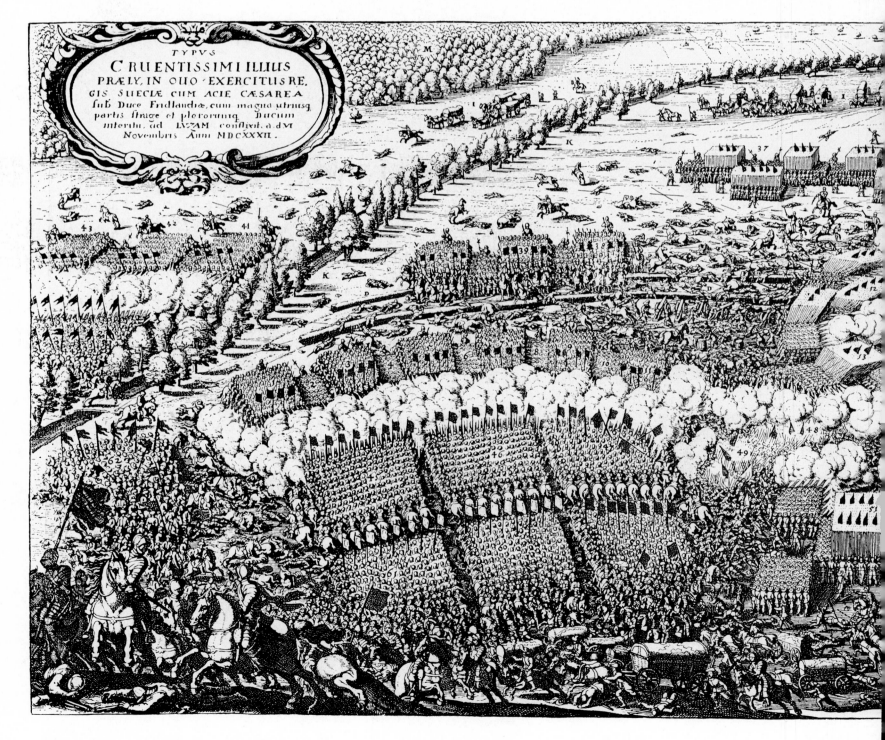

BEFORE GRANADA at the Battle of La Higuera in 1431, Christian forces at left engage Moors (*upper right*). The Moors managed to save Granada, held it until 1492.

NEAR LÜTZEN, Swedish troops (*background*) in 1632 battle attack across Leipzig road (*center*) toward Habsburg force (*in foreground*). Smokepuffs show battle line.

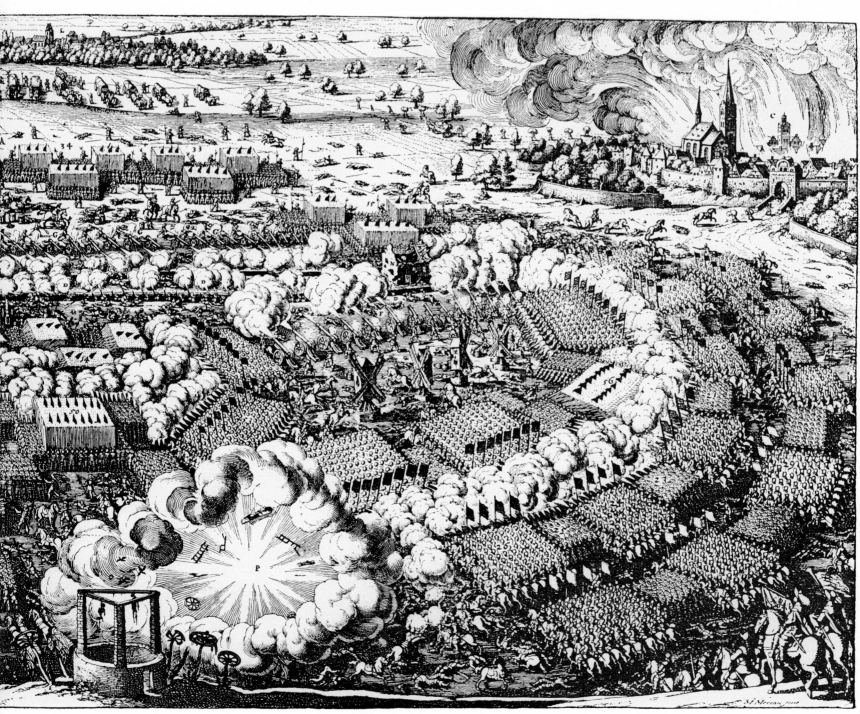

GREAT ORTHODOX EMPERORS Justinian (*left*) and Constantine (*right*) pay homage to the Virgin and Child in one of the finest mosaics in the Church of Haghia Sophia (Greek for "Holy Wisdom"). It was Constantine who laid Haghia Sophia's original foundations and Justinian who, after the edifice twice had burned, rebuilt it for the ages. When the Turks took Constantinople, they plastered over the mosaics, which have been brought to light again only

in recent years. Greek inscription at top is a monogram for "Mother of God" and those at sides praise the two emperors. Orthodoxy has canonized Constantine for serving Christianity, though he was baptized only on his deathbed.

SYMBOL OF ORTHODOXY, Haghia Sophia has watched over the city of Constantinople, now called Istanbul, ever since its consecration in 537 A.D. The Turks turned it into a mosque and added four minarets. It is now a museum.

THE EASTERN ORTHODOX

Oldest established church in Christendom faces difficult politico-religious problems

No part of Christendom is so little known or so badly misunderstood by Western Christians as the Eastern Orthodox Church. Yet it is the world's second largest Christian communion. It spiritually dominates Eastern Europe and its 150 million followers also extend from the Belgian Congo to the Aleutians to Australia. They pray in Avar, Eskimo, Kipchak, Kirghiz and other tongues as well as in Greek, Russian and English.

The Orthodox churches began in the Holy Land before there were any Christians in Rome. The New Testament was first written in Greek (the original language of Orthodoxy) and most of the early church councils were Orthodox in character. Like Roman Catholicism, Orthodoxy (from the Greek *orthos* and *doxa*, "true belief") considers that it was founded directly by Jesus. For Christianity's first thousand years the two together comprised the One, Holy, Catholic and Apostolic Church. But politico-religious cracks in the unity appeared early. For a time the tides ran eastward. After Constantine shifted the Roman Empire's throne to Constantinople in 330 A.D., the two great centers of Christianity—Rome headed by its Pope and Constantinople headed by its Patriarch—were competing for converts, dioceses and power.

Rome never surrendered its claims to primacy and after Islam conquered much Orthodox territory, the Papacy felt strong enough to try to enforce these claims. The climactic effort came in 1054 after the Patriarch of Constantinople had warned South Italy's bishops, over whom he claimed jurisdiction, against what he considered Roman errors in doctrine and discipline, including clerical celibacy and the use of unleavened bread for Communion. Most of all, he objected to Rome's adding the words "and the Son" to the phrase in the Nicene Creed: "in the Holy Ghost . . . who proceedeth from the Father." Pope Leo IX replied that Rome must remain supreme "over the Churches of God throughout the world," and sent legates to Constantinople who, on July 16, 1054, slapped on the altar of Haghia Sophia Church (*above*) a bull excommunicating the Patriarch and all his adherents. The Patriarch in turn

245

CHURCH INSIDE KREMLIN, the Cathedral of the Annunciation, is one of several in the fortress and epitomizes the close relationship which always has existed between the Russian Orthodox Church and the Russian state. Long the favorite church of the wives and daughters of the czars, it was built between 1482 and 1490. Paul of Aleppo said, "The value of the icons in this church would fill several treasuries." Now a museum, it is a favorite stop for sightseers.

excommunicated the Pope. Thus began the Great Schism between two Catholic churches. The shameful sack of Christian Constantinople by the Crusaders in 1204 made reconciliation unthinkable. Today Orthodoxy considers Rome heretical; Rome considers Orthodoxy schismatic.

The Orthodox Church historically has been a tool of government. During the centuries after the fall of Constantinople in 1453 when the Ottoman Empire ruled most of Orthodoxy's area, the Turks dealt with their Christian subjects through Orthodox prelates, who, combining temporal and spiritual leadership, had to mix politics with religion. In Russia, which got its alphabet along with its religion from Orthodox missions, the czars long dominated Orthodoxy. Peter the Great even abolished the Moscow patriarchate to make the czar head of the church.

After the Russian empire ended, the Communists persecuted the Russian church. Because of its continued hold on the masses, the Kremlin allowed a new Moscow Patriarch to be chosen in 1943. Since World War II the Russian church has again been an arm of the Soviet state, which permits the clergy to flourish on fees and even to print Bibles in Russian, some of them for export. The Russian Orthodox Church claims 50 million adherents, served by 35,000 priests in 20,000 parishes.

Eastern Orthodoxy is now a loose federation including the four historic patriarchates—Constantinople, Jerusalem, Antioch, Alexandria —and the self-governing Orthodox churches of Russia, Yugoslavia, Romania, Greece, Bulgaria, Poland, Georgia, Albania, Cyprus, Sinai, Finland, Estonia, Latvia and Czechoslovakia. The U.S. branches of most of these are also self-governing, but observe the tradition that the Patriarch of Constantinople (the city's old name is still used) has primacy; they look to him for spiritual guidance. Both church doctrine and practice are nearly identical everywhere (*for beliefs, see pages 204–5*), though the ritual's language may vary with the church's national origin.

Three of the patriarchates—Jerusalem, Antioch and Alexandria—are now little more than relics. Moscow has been trying to subordinate Constantinople, and a conflict now rages within Orthodoxy between those who oppose and those who accept Communist control of their church. When Archbishop Athenagoras, who headed Greek Orthodoxy in the U.S., was elected Patriarch of Constantinople in 1948, President Truman considered it politic to send him to Turkey in his official plane and to have him bear a special message to the president of Turkey. The position of Athenagoras as a friend of the West is a difficult one. He has to live in Turkey, but most of his followers are Greek. Both Turkey and Greece are allies of the West. Their interests, however, conflict sharply on the British-controlled island of Cyprus. The Greek majority of the population wants union with Greece. Turkey and the Turkish minority on Cyprus oppose it. And to complicate the situation, the Cypriot archbishop, Makarios, is the Greek Cypriots' political leader.

Meanwhile, Patriarch Alexei of Moscow has led a Communist-backed drive to capture control of Orthodoxy away from Constantinople. He courts the Orthodox churches of the Near East and has forced Orthodoxy in the satellite lands to look to Moscow instead of Constantinople.

The Orthodox in the U.S., who total some 2.4 million, with 1,700 ordained priests and 1,385 parishes, have inevitably been drawn into this struggle. Here the Russian Orthodox Greek Catholic Church of North America, which claims 750,000 members in 350 churches, considers the jurisdiction of the Moscow patriarchate "in suspension" until the patriarchate is free of Communist rule. Only one tiny Russian Orthodox group in the U.S. is in full communion with Moscow, but other Eastern Orthodox jurisdictions in the U.S., especially those whose mother churches are in the Soviet orbit, are sharply divided. The Greeks, whose million members are the largest Orthodox group in the U.S., remain loyal to the Patriarch of Constantinople.

Some younger Orthodox Christians in the U.S. would like a single church cutting across lines of national origin. Many of these are active in tackling social problems their church has traditionally neglected, helping recruit men for the priesthood and doing parish work. They also want their great stream of Christian tradition to merge itself into American life. They rejoice when a Greek Orthodox Sunday-school teacher in Oregon becomes Mrs. America, and a member of the Ukrainian Orthodox Church in Pittsburgh wins the national spelling bee. But in the U.S., as elsewhere, Orthodoxy's divisions are likely to continue for a long time.

246

CONSECRATING A U.S. BISHOP, Metropolitan Leonty of the Russian Orthodox Greek Catholic Church of North America holds up candelabra as he blesses the congregation in San Francisco's Holy Trinity Cathedral. In this ceremony Archimandrite Ambrosius, who is behind screen at rear, was raised to the bishopric of Sitka and All Alaska. The czars reportedly gave more to Russian churches in America than the $7.2 million the U.S. paid for Alaska.

THE SWORD OF

How the religion of Christ stands in relation to mankind and to history's broad stream

WHERE History and Eternity meet, the faith of Christianity stands —both to proclaim the meeting and to declare its meaning. This is the unique mark of Christianity. For it is a religion of events—of things which happened in History, whose essence transcends History and whose meaning explains History. Thus does the fall of man announce the beginning of the pilgrimage of History and the reason for its tragedies. Thus, in the Old Testament, does the call of Abraham, father of the faithful, echo the great promise of Providence: You will be my people, and I shall be your God. And thus, in the New Testament, do the most awesome affirmations of the Christian faith speak of events in History. At the crossroads of the world, where East met West and Jew met Gentile, God became man: He was born of Mary in Bethlehem, He suffered under Pontius Pilate, and the Cross upon which He found death became, for all who followed Him, the way to eternal life. And thereby were defined, by the word and the life of Christ upon earth, both the end of History and the reason for its hopes.

Going forth to teach all nations, the men who heard this Word were, and remain, bound by a unique commission: to be in this world, yet not of this world. Like Him, they are to be in History, but belong to eternity. Hence the sacraments of Christianity. Hence all the devices and institutions of this world through which the Church would speak in His name. Hence, through the ages, the authentic spiritual experiences of the saints—testifying to the Word, yet always belonging to History as surely as the poetry of a Shakespeare or the music of a Beethoven. Hence the everlasting and unchanging truth so purely perceived in the awesome sentence of St. Augustine, "We are in Christ—and also in this age."

By this commission there were conferred upon the Church two clear charges. Christianity must teach History—and it must act History. By the first charge, Christianity must define the nature of man and his true destiny. By the second, it must bring moral force to bear upon the decisions of men and of nations, so that these may respect that nature and further that destiny. Both are matters which deeply concern the distinguished theologians portrayed on these pages.

And so, in this age as in all others, the Christian weighs two questions. Where stands his faith at this moment as a force in History? And what instruction does it bring to this moment?

THE SCENE seems dark. Europe—once, it seemed, a land specially chosen by Christianity, as Israel was by Christ—honors many and strange gods. Asia and Africa, righteous in their wrath against the West, seem in no temper to receive the religion that has found its historic home in the West. A single generation has witnessed the forging of the most aggressive power in the world by Nazi Germany and Soviet Russia, both dedicated to denying the Word. Upon all the earth, some 850 million souls call themselves Christian—but their number is less than those who are soldiers, or prisoners, of Communism. Finally has come the ghastly revelation: humanity has gained the power to destroy itself.

These are apparent facts. But they are not all the facts. For there are three striking marks of the Christian present. And, together, they define such a moment as has never come before.

For the first time since men sought to spread the Word of Christ, Christendom can signify nothing less than the world itself: not one continent, nor one culture, nor one civilization. Once, Europe might seem enough; later, the West. It can no longer be so.

Not the power of Christianity, but the course of the world, has decreed this, surely and swiftly. One may measure the speed of this in terms of the life-span of one man, Pope Pius XII. Two years after he was born in 1876, the Congress of Berlin met to weigh the problems of nations in a spirit ruled by a few prevailing beliefs: progress was sure, peace was the will of all men, nationality was sacred. Not much of that creed has survived the wars that have since scarred the world or the science that has shrunk it, the corruption of nationalism or the death agony of colonialism. Pius XII, heeding the times, has given to the Far East its first cardinals, and to China, no longer a missionary area, its own hierarchy.

Today, therefore, as never before in History, Christianity is called to testify to the literal truth of another famous avowal of Augustine, "The Church recruits her citizens from all nations and in every language assembles her community of pilgrims upon earth."

The seeming advent of an age of plenty raises issues that History has never before known, nor Christianity confronted. Such an age, glittering with the marvels of science, may suggest to the Christian only dark

tragedy. It could indeed be so. Even falling short of the deadly ultimate achievement—making this planet uninhabitable for man—the worldly wonders of the 20th Century after Christ may bloat the vanity of man beyond the most fatuous pretenses of all past pagan ages.

But something else is no less possible: a change in the very conditions of human society. Such a change may already be in the making in the United States and, ultimately, it must affect all the world in an age when no nation can live alone. For the sharp social and political issues of the recent past—housing, wages, health, civil rights, all the matters that have seemed most urgently to affect justice and freedom under the laws of men—may, quite possibly, be fought to victorious conclusions within another generation. A host of hundreds of millions of human beings might, then, be ready to reach for what champions of justice have ever wished for them: "the good things of life." Then Christianity will be asked, with an urgency never known before in History, two questions: What are the "good" things? And why are they "good"?

Thus, as never before in History, may the voice of Christianity be heard as it seeks to teach History.

The final mark of this moment in Christian History is its secularized society—not the curse of it, but the challenge of it. This age, for the first time since Christianity became the officially accepted religion of the Roman Empire, is a time when no man need be a Christian because of political force, because of social fashion, or economic advantage, or

DR. PAUL J. TILLICH

Prussian-born Paul Tillich, professor of theology at Harvard, believes that "the kingdom of God is the fulfillment intended in history and implied in the ultimate." "God is creating now out of the past into the future," he says. "He creates always out of eternity into time." God works through men, who are "spontaneous and free agents." Dr. Tillich, a great systematic theologian of modern times, has long tried to relate religion to contemporary man's spirit.

CHRISTIANITY

by EMMET JOHN HUGHES

is a question that deeply concerns famous theologians as well as thoughtful Christians

because of prevailing intellectual habit around him. There is, in this society, no pressure or sanction to spur a man to be a Christian. There is nothing—but the force and the conviction of the faith itself. This age is neither congenial to sanctity nor hospitable to the practice of virtue. Yet, for this very reason, it is an age in which the fortitude of Christianity is sternly tested, its faith unmixed with base alloys.

It marks an age of Christianity that could be the most critical, the most anxious, the most exciting and the most meaningful since Constantine. It is not a time merely of darkness: for in that darkness the Light could be seen to shine most brilliantly. It might even be comprehended.

AS CHRISTIANITY stands thus in History, what does it teach of History? It teaches three things above all else: the nature of man, the pride of nations, and the end of History. These things sound banal and simple, when, of course, they are not. The story of Christ Himself follows few such supremely simplified patterns—harsh and precise—as men so often like to read into their lives. One of His chosen Twelve was Judas. Peter, the Rock, was he who denied Christ thrice. And Paul, missionary to the Gentiles, was also Saul, who helped to stone Stephen, the first of His martyrs. Such a faith can never—if true to itself—teach History with the pitiless simplicity of bold labels and brisk judgments.

This teaching begins with the nature of man: a creature of God, endowed with an immortal soul, whose destiny lies not in History but,

DR. REINHOLD NIEBUHR

Best known U.S. theologian, Reinhold Niebuhr of Union Seminary holds the view that "the mystery of history cannot be resolved except in the divine mercy." Man, as a creature of time, must approach his problems piecemeal. Yet each moment in history gives man the chance for some new achievement. Bourgeois liberalism and Marxist utopianism have mistakenly introduced "new forms of injustice into history in the very attempt of abolishing old ones."

through History, in eternity. Upon this teaching the whole Christian meaning of freedom and of justice rests: for the rights of man and the respect due him depend not upon any worldly status or worldly society —orderly or riotous, abundant or impoverished, cultivated or primitive —but upon this divine, changeless quality and purpose of human life.

What does this declaration matter within History? It matters decisively. It defines the source and the nature of the dignity and the sanctity of human life. Nor should men of the 20th Century have to grope long to see why this matters. For if the individual is not of eternal moment, he may then legitimately be made the slave of any moment. If he is committed to the service of no higher end, then he surely can properly be called to serve any larger end than his own contentment: state or empire—Third Reich or World Revolution. And once such claims are admitted, the "free world" must find its struggle with a Hitler or a Stalin reduced to a purely technical dispute over the relative prudence or efficacy of their methods or aims. If man be no more than just another product of the same natural forces that rust iron and ripen corn, why should he not be used as they are? If the ovens at Hitler's Buchenwald cremated efficiently, what was wrong with them beyond their awful novelty? And if the words "soul" and "sin" are stricken from men's speech, by what names may they call and know the ultimate good they cherish, the ultimate evil that besets them?

These same truths of man's destiny rule in an America of peace and abundance, as much as in a world of war and ruin. Sixteen million Negro Americans have challenged the rationalizations and excuses of the ruling white population of the South. A quarter of a century ago the Protestant theologian Reinhold Niebuhr, explaining the prejudices of privilege throughout society, wrote what reads like a contemporary diagnosis of the tragedy of the South: "Since inequalities of privilege are greater than could possibly be defended rationally, the intelligence of privileged groups is usually applied to the task of inventing specious proofs for the theory that universal values spring from . . . the special privileges which they hold." And to such specious proofs, no more damning indictment could be given than the flat declaration of Archbishop Joseph F. Rummel of New Orleans: "Racial segregation as such is morally wrong and sinful because it is a denial of the unity and solidarity of the human race as conceived by God in the creation of man in Adam and Eve . . . [and] because it is a denial of the unity and universality of the Redemption."

Such an instance illustrates the first Christian teaching on History: neither processes nor masses, neither cultures nor civilizations, are its measure and its meaning—but man alone. For in him alone are invested rights that are inalienable, truths everlasting. Beyond these, all else may be subject to the demands or pretensions of society.

Thus the fulfillment of man's destiny cannot fully be secured within any community. The individual sees, senses and judges beyond this community. Even as his life is shorter, as his impact upon History may be less than that of his community, yet his memory, his knowledge and his anticipations range far above and beyond it. For he, not it, faces final judgment. It is this truth—the eternal moment of the individual and his destiny in eternity—that so sternly condemns the pride of nations, the belief that any state, any society, any civilization has achieved the final, imperishable good. This is the great blasphemy of History, the grand and awful equivalent, in society, of the individual's moral forgetfulness, his denial of dependence upon God and his deification of his own will. Thus did Ezekiel decry the folly of an Egypt that dared boast of its Nile, "My river is mine own, and I have made it for myself."

What does this matter within History? This age, more than most, should glimpse the harsh answer quickly. All men of the West know how false would be any pretense of theirs to perfect virtue. They must know that both Naziism and Communism matured in no bizarre spiritual vacuum, but in a Western world that had everywhere witnessed and tolerated the scorn of prideful nations for the Christian concept of man. And all men of the West must know, too, that the trials they bear in Asia and Africa are little more than present retribution for past sins.

The West has, indeed, even less reason for a sense of righteousness than most of its peoples may admit. For only the most awesome self-righteousness can explain the willful self-deception of Western peoples during World War II in assessing the intent and integrity of their ally-by-accident, Soviet Russia. They lacked the humility to say the plain truth—that they welcomed any assistance in confronting an immediate

MSGR. WILLIAM R. O'CONNOR

A practicing theologian who heads a big Manhattan parish and also teaches at Columbia, Monsignor O'Connor states: "The world may well indeed have been an eternally existing world, but it is always a contingent world since it always owes its existence to the creative act of God." No created intellect, not even "the human intellect of Christ," is able "to know every single thing and event," but the more a man knows of God, the more he desires to know.

hardly have been sensed at the moment by the decimated Gallic tribes or the Saxons who fell with Harold at Hastings. It is ever thus in History. A Fire of London brings death and pain—and a new city. The bloodiest religious strife may yield, in its exhaustion, a sense of tolerance never known before. Nothing can so quicken man's love of peace as war. And through this strange rhythm of History, repeated again and again, one senses that the sparing of tragedy for one generation has come to pass only through the vicarious suffering of another.

At almost any given moment in History, strength and suffering, creativeness and destruction, seem bound together in strange and intricate union. From the insight of the ancient Hebrews or the courage of the martyrs to the simpler level of the music of the Negro or the poetry of the Irish—the grander (and the gentler) attainments of men seem inseparable from their bearing of some loss or pain. Each such glory bespeaks a kind of triumph wrought in defeat, a good wrested from evil. Through the chronicles of nations the creative triumph often seems to rise, glowing, in the shadow of danger or the darkness of decay, as Augustine cast his spell upon future ages while the Roman world around him fell to the Vandals. And in all such things, the Christian sees some of the works of Providence in History.

Relentless and ever-present seems that moral force of gravity, ever pulling men down as they reach for the stars. Between the purpose and the event there falls the shadow. The most impassioned 16th Century reformers rarely if ever foresaw what secular forces their words and deeds would unleash. The romantic revolutionaries of 1789 never imagined that, a few years later, they would be seen as the indispensable forerunners of the dictatorship of Napoleon. That most practical of the 19th Century statesmen, Bismarck, vividly sensed the presence of forces over which no man could be sovereign: "We can advance the clock," he answered, when asked why he did not hasten the day of German unification, "but time itself does not move any more quickly for that." In this 20th Century, a generation had a chance to mature with clear-eyed knowledge of the blunders and follies of Versailles—only to proceed to draw such a map of Europe as was drawn at Yalta and Potsdam. And, in all this, the Christian perceives the sternest of the terms and conditions of the fall of man. He senses, too, that the great "mistakes" of History

enemy. They insisted, instead, upon exalting themselves by endowing any ally sharing their trials with virtues that, in their hearts, they knew did not exist. For such fabulous pride, they have paid a bitter price.

Such instances, striking and true, justify no inference that, in the Christian's understanding, History meticulously metes out rewards and punishments. The Christian perceives no such thing. He sees, rather, the rude and jarring pilgrimage that has been the lot of Adam ever since his banishment: the flawed judgment of man, the darkened will, the corrupting pride. This, the Christian holds, is not only true doctrine—but accurate History. "Those who do not believe in the doctrine of the Fall," writes Herbert Butterfield, Professor of Modern History at the University of Cambridge, "can hardly deny that human history has always been history under the terms and conditions of the Fall."

What—in the Christian conception—are these "terms and conditions" of History? They include at least the following:

Progress in History is not a fiction, but it can be a deception. Sheer knowledge accumulates: a student of a 20th Century high school may know more about physics than an Aristotle. Wealth and resources, too, may accumulate; they cannot fail to grow with man's insight into the forces of nature. Yet knowledge does not mean wisdom. The capacity to do may steadily grow—but the capacity to do good need not. And this, indeed, may be the expression in History of original sin: the demonstrated inability of any one human generation to start with the heritage of the accumulated wisdom of another.

Final moral judgment, upon the living man or the historical moment, cannot be found within History—for History mirrors such truth only in the fickle fashion of the restless surface of a moving river, reflecting the misshapen images of shore and sky. In History, time tempers, if it does not twist, all judgment. The Norman conquest of England or Caesar's conquest of Gaul brought a "good" to later generations that could

DR. GEORGES FLOROVSKY

Father Florovsky, noted Orthodox theologian who is now at Harvard, finds "a divine pattern of human history" that is "much more than an abstract scheme or just a plan." History is based on divine rule, not on "human planning and desire." But "man should become the Son of God and behave as a son, and not as a hireling," for God gives us hope and "Christian hope is intrinsically a call to action . . . to justify or to manifest our hope in our deeds."

might more precisely be called sins—of pride, or of presumption, of greed or of despair—hovering, like omen-clouds, above the fields of all the Waterloos of History.

Thus the meaning and the measure of all things in History remain ever man, the individual, the image of God. This being true, Christianity perceives the falseness of any doctrine of progress that thinks of each generation as a mere steppingstone to the next. Past generations were not mere rehearsals for subsequent dramas of human fulfillment. There are no rehearsals, and, in History, there is no fulfillment.

This is the truth glimpsed in Leopold von Ranke's statement that all generations are equidistant from eternity. For in each, all men, ever of the same flawed human nature, are summoned to strive with all their moral strength to meet moral tests that, in their nature, are no different after the smashing of the atom than before the discovery of gunpowder. Paradoxically, precisely because the end of History is to be found only in eternity, the measure and meaning of human life are truly found not in the future of History, but in the present. For the living man now is as close as History can ever get to eternity. And so the Christian knows that he—like his faith—is, ultimately, in History, yet not of it. He knows that History is to mankind what to himself is his own body, of which he says: This body is not me, but mine. He knows that the most spectacular triumph in History cannot assure his personal salvation—yet his least deed may find some lasting echo in eternity.

If the Christian so believes, what does this fate matter within History? It matters much, for it spares him the gravest of men's follies. It enables him to scorn the false prophets promising fulfillment in a History where it cannot be. It enables him to scorn the deadliest idolatries—of a state, of a culture, of an abstract noun. It arms him against despair. For the Christian memory is crowded with the remembrance of dark things, of timeless shadows upon men and ancient curses upon nations. So even the cloud shaped like a mushroom cannot paralyze the spirit or atrophy the will. It arms him against self-righteousness: the sin that divides man from man, and nation from nation. For he knows that he and all men are sons not only of God, but also of Adam. And it reminds him—by denying all hope of a paradise in this world—that the accent of his responsibilities falls heavily, urgently, always upon the living moment.

JOHN COURTNEY MURRAY S. J.

Father Murray is editor of the quarterly *Theological Studies* and teaches at Woodstock College in Maryland. A powerful religious and intellectual call led him to the Jesuits. To him the Church is essential to human history, since it possesses "a spiritual authority which, while remaining spiritual, may reach into the temporal order there to lay the protective grasp of its authoritative moral judgments on those elements of secular life which have a sacred aspect."

THIS, then, is the meeting of History and eternity, as witnessed by Christianity. It is no peaceful encounter. And Christ duly warned all men: "I came not to send peace, but a sword." The ancient world knew no such dualism of temporal and spiritual, no distinction between Church and State. The conflict comes only with the Christian gospel. Origen, a great early Christian theologian, expressed the truth bluntly: "Before the preaching of the Word of God, all was peace; as long as the sound of the trumpet had not rung out, there was no conflict."

The medieval world, at times, seemed tempted to forget this. In that era many a Christian seemed to sense the settling of a Christian peace upon the world, and a tranquil future of devout contemplation. "We may well think fortunate (or perhaps simply lacking in awareness?)," writes the French Jesuit Henri de Lubac, "these men who thought that henceforth they would have nothing else to do . . . but give themselves over peacefully in the serene heights of the soul to the contemplation of the Holy Scriptures." This pious dream was rudely ended.

All ages since have decried, as they have tried to escape, the calls of Christ and of Caesar. Rousseau eloquently mourned the existence of "two laws, two leaders, two motherlands," appealing for "a reduction of all to political unity." And Rousseau's words have echoed loudest in 20th Century totalitarianism which, like paganism of old, has deplored Christians as "destroyers of unity."

It can never be otherwise: not since the Word was spoken, the sword drawn. "We do not come to Christ by way of repose and delight," Origen explained, "but through all kinds of tribulations and temptations."

This, then, is the clear commission of Christ. It is spoken to man in His image and to the Church upon His mission. And its instruction to both is the same: to be at war with the world. For with no things of the world may man make peace or find contentment—least of all with himself. Through History, there awaits the end in eternity: to come to Christ.

CANON HOWARD A. JOHNSON

The Rev. Howard Johnson is Canon Theologian of New York's Episcopal cathedral and a Columbia professor. To him "the dangling Christian" is one "who has not remotely grasped the central fact that the Word became flesh, that eternity has intersected time." At the present stage of history, many try "reducing man to the single dimension of his social value," leaving man and nature "instead of the ancient and orthodox trilogy 'Nature, Man and God.'"

EUROPE'S CATHEDRALS

Glorifying religion in stone, they stand as timeless testimonies to Christendom's faith

BLITZED COVENTRY, lofty English cathedral whose 1940 bombing by Nazis shocked the world, forms a 14th Century Gothic background for a wedding. A new church is being built alongside the old, but the ruins will remain with an altar made of rubble and the inscription, "Father Forgive."

As Christendom has expanded over the centuries from Asia Minor through Europe to the whole earth, it has put a lasting mark on the world in the form of innumerable testimonies to its faith. The Scriptures (*pages 260–76*) are the foremost of these enduring records. There are also many physical monuments of Christianity, none more marvelous than the great European cathedrals which embody religion in stone, sculpture, mosaic and stained glass.

"The Lord," exclaimed a 14th Century Burgundian monk, marveling at what he had seen in France, "seems to have snowed churches on the land." These eight pages show some of the shrines that still dominate Europe's horizons from English meadows to frowning northern cities to sunlit Italian squares, everywhere testifying to the surge of faith that swept across the medieval world.

Europe is still building churches. A new cathedral, with both its architecture and stained glass contemporary in design, is now rising in Coventry (*left*). And Europe's churches serve 450 million Christians, more than half of the world's total. However the figure is deceptive. Europe is split not only politically and economically but also religiously, between those who have denied God and those who still, in some fashion, keep their faith in a Supreme Being. No one knows how many of the continent's Christians are devout, or even among how many sects they are scattered.

Historically the stronghold of Christendom, Europe sent out missionaries to make Christianity the most widespread of religions. But now in the Eternal City itself, at the very gates of the Vatican, the majority of Romans do not regularly attend Mass. In Sweden less than five percent of the people are steady churchgoers, and Lutheran Archbishop Brilioth says, "It is uncertain if today one would dare call Sweden a Christian country. The Christian clothing it wears is an illusion."

Some Europeans are now questioning not Christianity's moral values so much as its actual relevance to present problems. There is a danger that the churches are becoming politely tolerated institutions in which traditional rituals take place but from which neither great light nor leadership is expected or forthcoming. Millions of industrial workers and young people are indifferent to religion.

Yet there are grounds for optimism as well. Many Europeans 20 years ago put their faith in stock political ideologies, good or bad, but today there is a growing interest in religion. Christian laymen have started vigorous spiritual movements in many lands. In Britain and France religious books and essays reach a far wider audience than ever before and religion is reviving at the universities. In West Germany, where Christianity was critically endangered under Hitler, both the Catholic and Protestant churches are resurgent. The coming years may see a new upswing of the religious fervor and civic pride which raised the great cathedrals. Their glory has for generations drawn pilgrims from all over the globe. Today the worshiper within their walls still finds in the lofty vaults and inspired ornaments a perennial summation of the Christian faith that created them.

FLOODLIT IN GREEN, the cathedral of Ulm thrusts its tower 528 feet into the night sky, far above the old city wall and ancient houses on which yellow spotlights play. The view is from the south across the Danube River. Work on the cathedral was begun under the Papacy in the 14th Century. It was interrupted when the city was drawn into Martin Luther's revolt, but was resumed after the citizens had voted in 1530 to have Protestant minister as their priest.

ULM Its towering spire is a monument to zeal of citizens

Like a giant filigree needle, the spire of the Lutheran cathedral at Ulm, in Germany, rises above a city of which it used to be said in the Middle Ages, "The gold of Ulm rules over the whole world." When in 1377 Ulm laid the foundation stone—which the mayor and townspeople covered with gold and jewels— Ulm had 11 churches, 14 monasteries and 31 chapels; but all stood on papal land, a circumstance unsatisfactory to the burghers. The plan was for a simple structure but the church kept on growing—it is now the second largest in Germany—and even after Ulm's fortunes had begun to decline, the citizens continued to build the cathedral, crowning it in the 19th Century with the tallest steeple in the world. Some of this spirit persists: West Germany today is a bulwark of European Christianity.

GLITTERING in the Venetian sunlight, the façade of St. Mark's looks upon a square which always is alive with pigeons and tourists. Like a colorful storybook, the arches of the façade are decorated with mosaics, mostly of 17th Century workmanship, which illustrate legends of St. Mark and stories from the Bible. In the gilt-roofed shrines above are Gothic carvings of saints, with St. Mark himself over the central arch. At far right is the Doge's palace.

254

POISED above the main entrance to St. Mark's, the famous four bronze horses still bear traces of gilding. Venetians believe that whenever the horses are taken down from their gallery, disaster will follow. In this century they have been moved twice, in the First and again in the Second World War.

ST. MARK'S Venice's prize possession blends arts and treasures of many countries

For 900 years the dazzling, domed Cathedral of St. Mark has rested like an Oriental diadem on the brow of Christian Venice. The city's proudest possession, it has provided a brilliant backdrop for princes and painters, sultans and sailors, traders, troubadours and tourists. Like Venice itself, for centuries the crossroads of the known world, it displays a miraculous mingling of the art and cultures of many lands. A Byzantine resplendence dominates the church—it was designed by a Greek architect inspired by the Byzantine Church of the Holy Apostles in Constantinople—but within, Gothic sculpture adjoins Roman capitals, Eastern arches and Saracen ornament.

This architectural extravaganza was begun in the 11th Century, when Venice determined to enlarge the shrine for the bones of its saint, whose body had been stolen from Alexandria by three Venetians about two hundred years before. Though the Church today must combat skepticism everywhere in Italy, Venetians still like to brag about the abduction and to claim that when a storm threatened the vessel which was bearing the relics, St. Mark roused himself miraculously and counseled the skipper. To make the church as magnificent as possible, every captain in Venice's fleet had to bring back beautiful materials for the builders. Soon the basic brickwork of St. Mark's was covered with marbles from Byzantium, alabaster from Arabia, porphyry from Egypt and carved capitals from Greece.

Almost as lavish were the trophies which the Venetians claimed during the Crusades. Most famous are the four bronze horses over the entrance of the church. Apparently Hellenistic Greek in origin, the statues were shipped to Constantinople about 330 by the emperor Constantine. In 1204 during the Fourth Crusade, they were seized by a doge who claimed them for Venice. Except for brief periods, they have since remained on St. Mark's, watching out over the bustling pageantry of the square.

TOOTHACHE VICTIM on a capital is probably a tribute to Bishop Bytton, whose own teeth were still perfect when his tomb was opened in 1848.

WELLS Placid water enhances serene beauty of church that knew war

The poetic setting of trees and a placid pond invests the Anglican cathedral of Wells with the pastoral beauty that characterizes the majority of great churches of England. For most of the 800 years since the cathedral was begun—it was dedicated in its entirety on October 23, 1239—the setting has been as peaceful as it is today, but now and then its quiet sanctity has been disturbed by rude intrusions. In the 12th Century, when the cathedral was just going up, a market threatened to take over the church, crowding the vestibule with vegetable stalls.

In the 13th Century a battery of local sculptors was employed to populate the west façade of the church with 386 statues of saints, clergymen and nobles (*opposite*), some of which have since been destroyed either by iconoclasts during the time of the Reformation or by time and weather. Within the cathedral other carvings (*above*) paid homage to native legends and to local worthies like Bishop Bytton, who was so famous for his beautiful teeth that his tomb was visited for centuries by people hoping to be relieved of toothaches.

In the 16th Century the peace of Wells was shattered again by Protestant vandals who pillaged and desecrated the church. In 1685 it was used as a stable by the rebel Duke of Monmouth whose soldiers set up their kegs of beer on the high altar. But, weathering these ravages, the cathedral always settled back into its calm, stately ways. This placidity continues, even though a searching survey of life in England today reports: "Despite the devoted adherence to the churches of millions of ordinary men and women who make up church membership, it remains true that in the lives of a large majority of people of all classes of the community, the church is no longer relevant."

STURDY TOWER and east end of the cathedral are mirrored in the flower-lined pond, which is fed by the ancient wells that gave the town its name.

NOTABLES IN NICHES are arrayed on exterior. At top is Roger, Bishop of Salisbury, and below him, King Henry I. Both lived in the 12th Century.

BOURGES Plain people's

Long before the Cathedral of St. Stephen reared its giant frame above the city of Bourges in central France, other Christian churches had occupied the hill on which the great edifice now rests. The earliest was built in the waning years of the Roman Empire and was followed by three other churches, each incorporating something of its predecessor. In the 12th Century the people of Bourges began the process again over the remains of a Romanesque church. The cathedral they erected contains in the heavy masonry of its crypt stones that served in walls built soon after Julius Caesar conquered the town in 52 B.C. And its graceful Gothic porches overshadow austere, sculptured doorways salvaged from an 11th Century church. The people of Bourges had to make do: money

LIKE A GILDED CROWN, the illuminated cathedral of Bourges in all its majesty projects against the evening sky. It extends 394 feet from the west façade (*left*) to the choir (*right*), its famous Butter Tower rising behind roof

toil built massive St. Stephen's

was scarce. But the guilds and the plain people—with a unanimity of piety that is not to be found in cynical France today—contributed both their labor and the cost of whatever materials had to be bought.

In 1506 a great calamity befell the church when the northwest tower collapsed. This time building funds were more easily available, for town and church were growing rich. By 1545 builders finished the famous Butter Tower, put up with money paid to the church by parishioners for the privilege of eating butter during Lent, and the cathedral was complete once more. Soon after, in 1562, iconoclastic Protestants smashed some statues and even tried to blow the church up, but the revolt was quickly put down and Bourges was preserved in all its massive grandeur.

in the center of the picture. The cathedral contains some of the world's finest stained glass. The example at upper left shows Christ with the Sword of the Spirit. The one at right depicts the Banquet of Dives, a rich man of the Bible.

OVERLOOKING THE DEAD SEA, this ruin at Qumran, Jordan was home of a pre-Christian Jewish sect which practiced a kind of baptism, ate communally with religious ceremonial, held property in common, believed in a Teacher of Righteousness who had been persecuted by a wicked High Priest, and awaited the coming of the Messiah. Members of this sect, who put up the main building between 135 and 76 B.C. and occupied the site until 68 A.D.,

CLUES TO

New discoveries from the Dead Sea shores

The Bible (from the Greek *biblia*, books) is for all Christians the most sacred of books, the source of truth, the revelation of God's word. No other book has been so lovingly reproduced. Yet precisely because it is held so sacred, the Bible has been the subject of unending debate.

The Bible was written during some 1,400 years (1300 B.C.–100 A.D.). Few of its many authors have been identified. No original manuscripts are known to exist—only copies of copies and translations into which errors have inevitably crept. Until recently scholars depended on Hebrew

AMERICAN SCHOLAR, Msgr. Patrick Skehan uses tweezers to pick up scroll fragment from under glass at a museum in Old Jerusalem. Found caked with mud, fragments were cleaned with camel's-hair brushes and castor oil.

OLDEST HEBREW TEXT discovered to date is made up of the above Dead Sea scroll fragments—the photograph is of three bits pieced together—which date probably from 225–200 B.C. These segments are from I Samuel 23:9–16.

secreted the Dead Sea Scrolls in nearby cliff caves. The sect is believed to have had links to the Essenes, who unlike the Sadducees and Pharisees—the two other major divisions of Judaism at the time—were never criticized by Jesus.

THE BIBLE

have spurred world interest in Scriptures

manuscripts of the Old Testament dating from the 9th to 11th Centuries A.D. The earliest complete New Testament manuscripts date from the Fourth Century A.D., though a Second Century bit of the Gospel of St. John exists (*right*).

But in 1947 the first of a series of discoveries relating to an ancient Jewish community at Khirbet Qumran in the Holy Land (*above*) was made in a group of Jordanian cliff caves near the Dead Sea. The most sensational archaeological treasure to be uncovered in modern times,

OLDEST GOSPEL TEXT in scholars' possession is the papyrus fragment (*right*) from John 18:31–33. Written in Greek, probably early in the Second Century, this passage describes the arraignment of Jesus before Pontius Pilate.

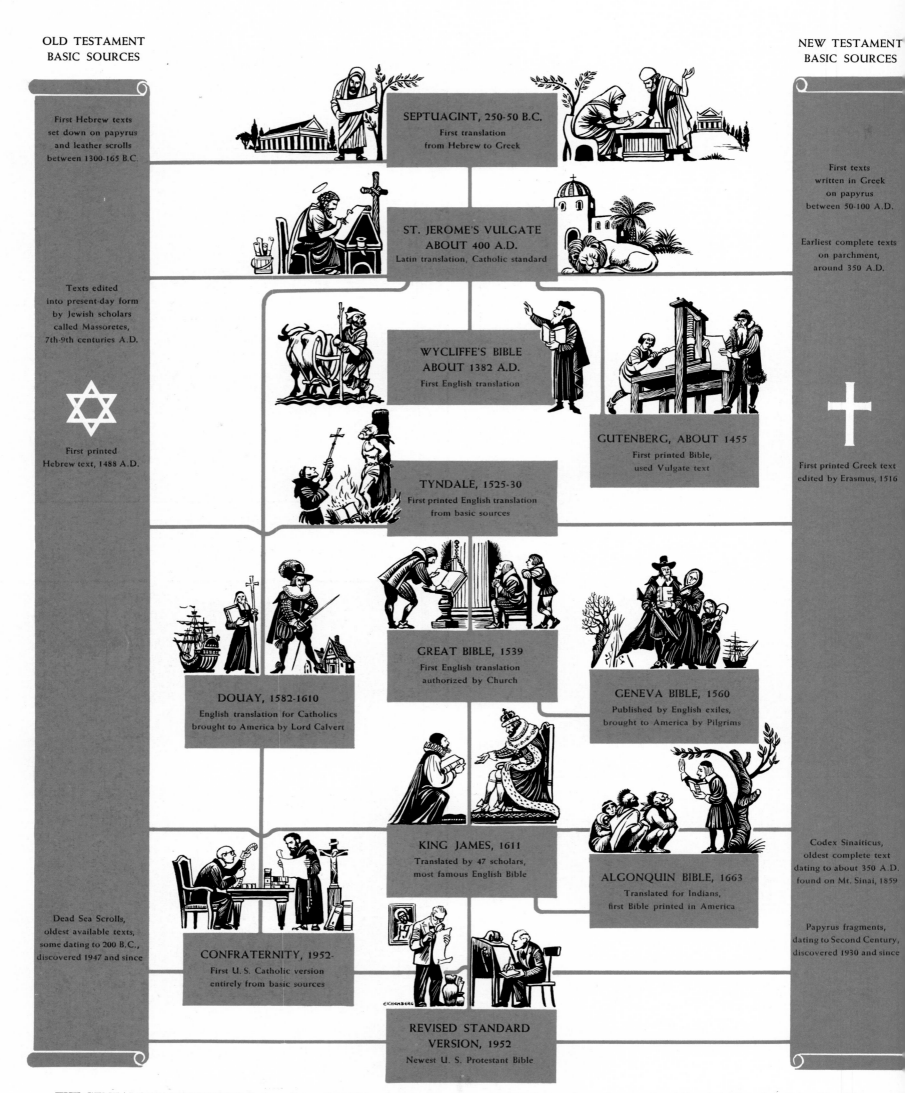

First Hebrew texts
set down on papyrus
and leather scrolls
between 1300-165 B.C.

Texts edited
into present-day form
by Jewish scholars
called Massoretes,
7th-9th centuries A.D.

First printed
Hebrew text, 1488 A.D.

Dead Sea Scrolls,
oldest available texts,
some dating to 200 B.C.,
discovered 1947 and since

First texts
written in Greek
on papyrus
between 50-100 A.D.

Earliest complete texts
on parchment,
around 350 A.D.

First printed Greek text
edited by Erasmus, 1516

Codex Sinaiticus,
oldest complete text
dating to about 350 A.D.
found on Mt. Sinai, 1859

Papyrus fragments,
dating to Second Century,
discovered 1930 and since

SEPTUAGINT, 250-50 B.C.
First translation
from Hebrew to Greek

ST. JEROME'S VULGATE
ABOUT 400 A.D.
Latin translation, Catholic standard

WYCLIFFE'S BIBLE
ABOUT 1382 A.D.
First English translation

GUTENBERG, ABOUT 1455
First printed Bible,
used Vulgate text

TYNDALE, 1525-30
First printed English translation
from basic sources

DOUAY, 1582-1610
English translation for Catholics
brought to America by Lord Calvert

GREAT BIBLE, 1539
First English translation
authorized by Church

GENEVA BIBLE, 1560
Published by English exiles,
brought to America by Pilgrims

KING JAMES, 1611
Translated by 47 scholars,
most famous English Bible

ALGONQUIN BIBLE, 1663
Translated for Indians,
first Bible printed in America

CONFRATERNITY, 1952-
First U. S. Catholic version
entirely from basic sources

REVISED STANDARD
VERSION, 1952
Newest U. S. Protestant Bible

THE GENEALOGY OF THE BIBLE, from the earliest Hebrew to the latest American versions, is given in the chart above which illustrates the most famous Greek, Latin and English translations. The long panels at the sides list some of the basic texts, written in Hebrew and Greek, which were available at the time of each translation. Radiating lines indicate whether the translation was based on these sources, on a previous translation, or on both. Some of the Bible's translators have suffered for their devotion. John Wycliffe was among the first of many Englishmen to incur the Church's wrath for producing unauthorized translations of the Scriptures, as well as for his heretical writings. William Tyndale, another English translator who was persecuted by the Church, fled to the Low Countries, where he was strangled. Henry VIII had copies of the Great Bible chained in order to foil overzealous worshipers.

262

the finds are principally time-brittled leather scrolls and bits of scrolls, carefully inscribed in Hebrew, Greek and Aramaic, the last being the language of Jesus. Dating as far back as the Third Century B.C., they include a virtually complete text of the Book of Isaiah, and they provide scholars for the first time with pre-Christian fragments from every book of the Hebrew Bible except Esther.

They include also a number of heretofore unknown works—one of them called *War of the Children of Light Against the Children of Darkness*—which draw attention to a Jewish sect that lived at Qumran almost a century before Christ's birth. Whether this sect influenced Jesus and John the Baptist is a matter of both study and dispute among theologians.

In 1953 an international team made up of eight scholars, among them Msgr. Patrick W. Skehan of Catholic University and Dr. Frank M. Cross Jr. of Chicago's McCormick Theological Seminary, began investigation of the discoveries. Though their work will take many years, it already has shed much new light on the life, thought and language of the world into which Jesus was born. Simultaneously, much new knowledge of the Bible is becoming available as a result of the microfilming of 2,700 ancient manuscripts in relatively inaccessible Holy Land libraries.

Through the centuries study of the Bible has attracted many of the diligent minds of each generation. The chart opposite illustrates the most famous versions which such scholarship has produced. The earliest Old Testament translation was the Septuagint, or "Version of the Seventy." Its name derives from the 72 Jewish scholars who did their work in Egypt.

The first rendering of the entire Bible into Latin was St. Jerome's Vulgate, a name deriving from *vulgatus*, meaning for common use. For a thousand years St. Jerome's was the only authoritative Bible in Western Europe, but it was seldom read by the common people. Two famous translations were produced by English exiles. The Geneva or Breeches Bible, a Puritan version, thus rendered Genesis 3:7, ". . . they sewed fig leaves together and made themselves breeches." The Douay Bible was translated in Douai and Rheims, France, by Roman Catholics fleeing Queen Elizabeth. It has remained the favorite of English-speaking Catholics ever since. The most popular version among Anglicans and Protestants has been the King James, whose grand style has influenced all English prose. An odd one is the "Wicked Bible" of 1631, which through typographical error instructs: "Thou shalt commit adultery."

Two recent translations may well supplant both the Douay and King James versions in popularity. They are the American Revised Standard Version, which sold four million copies in the U.S. and Canada in the first three years after its publication in 1952, and the Catholic Confraternity Bible, the first volume of which also was published in 1952. In one recent year the American Bible Society distributed 15 million Bibles or parts of the Scriptures in 64 countries, while commercial firms the same year are believed to have sold more than six million copies. The Book continues to be by far the most popular of books.

MODERN BIBLES are shown being turned out at the A. J. Holman Bible Co. Inc. of Philadelphia, where workman is pasting in the end covers of a Bible which, like most other Bibles, was made largely by hand. Holman is oldest and largest U.S. firm devoted solely to publishing the Scriptures.

ANCIENT BIBLE, the beautifully bound book above, called Codex Aureus, was produced for Charles the Bald of France in 870 A.D. In Latin, it belonged to a monastery at Regensburg until 1803, is now owned by the Bavarian state.

WHERE THE SCROLLS WERE FOUND is shown in view of cliffs near Qumran. Cave Number Four, small triangular opening in foreground, has yielded 362 fragmentary manuscripts. In scholars' eyes, it is far richer than the caves in background, although some of latter held almost complete texts. Why the writings were hidden is not known, but one theory is that they were put aside in accord with Jewish law, which forbids the destruction of sacred works.

CHRISTIAN SCRIPTURES

The New Testament has shaped Western civilization more decisively than anything else ever written. Its 27 varied documents, largely compiled between the years 50 and 100 A.D., tell the beginnings of Christianity. The birth, teaching, death and Resurrection of Jesus Christ are narrated in the four Gospels. Then come: the Acts of the Apostles, a history of the early Christian movement; the Epistles, or letters to the church groups that soon spread around the Mediterranean; and the Book of Revelation, a visionary portrayal of the final triumph of God's purpose.

The new religion that was to affect mankind so deeply was first preached in Jerusalem just after Christ's Ascension. It grew so fast that a thriving church existed even before the first parts of the New Testament, probably some of Paul's Epistles, were put down in colloquial Greek for the benefit of his congregations. Soon the Gospels and the Acts were written, though centuries passed before the whole book was assembled in its finally agreed-on form. Not until 1560 was an English translation divided into verses; the selections below, all from the famous King James version, are printed in paragraphs for easier reading. Where more than one book or chapter is quoted, the combined sources are listed at the end of the passage.

The fullest account of the conception, birth and infancy of Jesus is given in Luke's Gospel.

THE BIRTH OF JESUS

THE angel Gabriel was sent from God unto a city of Galilee, named Nazareth, to a virgin espoused to a man whose name was Joseph, of the house of David; and the virgin's name was Mary. And the angel came in unto her, and said, Hail, thou that art highly favored, the Lord is with thee; blessed art thou among women. And when she saw him, she was troubled at his saying. . . . And the angel said unto her, Fear not, Mary: for thou hast found favor with God. And, behold, thou shalt conceive in thy womb, and bring forth a son, and shalt call his name JESUS. He shall be great, and shall be called the Son of the Highest; and the Lord God shall give unto him the throne of his father David: and he shall reign over the house of Jacob for ever; and of his kingdom there shall be no end. Then said Mary unto the angel, How shall this be, seeing I know not a man? And the angel answered and said unto her, The Holy Ghost shall come upon thee, and the power of the Highest shall overshadow thee: therefore also that holy thing which shall be born of thee shall be called the Son of God. And, behold, thy cousin Elisabeth, she hath also conceived a son in her old age: and this is the sixth month with her, who was called barren. For with God nothing shall be impossible. And Mary said, Behold, the handmaid of the Lord; be it unto me according to thy word. And the angel departed from her.

And Mary arose in those days, and went into the hill country with haste, into a city of Juda; and entered into the house of Zacharias, and saluted Elisabeth. And it came to pass, that, when Elisabeth heard the salutation of Mary, the babe leaped in her womb; and Elisabeth was filled with the Holy Ghost: and she spake out with a loud voice, and said, Blessed art thou among women, and blessed is the fruit of thy womb. And whence is this to me, that the mother of my Lord should come to me? For, lo, as soon as the voice of thy salutation sounded in mine ears, the babe leaped in my womb for joy. And blessed is she that believed; for there shall be a performance of those things which were told her from the Lord. And Mary said,

My soul doth magnify the Lord, and my spirit hath rejoiced in God my Saviour. For he hath regarded the low estate of his handmaiden: for, behold, from henceforth all generations shall call me blessed. For he that is mighty hath done to me great things; and holy is his name. And his mercy is on them that fear him from generation to generation. He hath showed strength with his arm; he hath scattered the proud in the imagination of their hearts. He hath put down the mighty from their seats, and exalted them of low degree. He hath filled the hungry with good things; and the rich he hath sent empty away. He hath holpen his servant Israel, in remembrance of his mercy; as he spake to our fathers, to Abraham, and to his seed for ever. . . .

And it came to pass in those days, that there went out a decree from Caesar Augustus, that all the world should be taxed. . . . And all went to be taxed, every one into his own city. And Joseph also went up from Galilee, out of the city of Nazareth, into Judaea, unto the city of David, which is called Bethlehem; (because he was of the house and lineage of David) to be taxed with Mary his espoused wife, being great with child. And so it was, that, while they were there, the days were accomplished that she should be delivered. And she brought forth her firstborn son, and wrapped him in swaddling clothes, and laid him in a manger; because there was no room for them in the inn.

And there were in the same country shepherds abiding in the field, keeping watch over their flock by night. And, lo,

Abbreviation for Jesus, in Greek, is a frequent church decoration

the angel of the Lord came upon them, and the glory of the Lord shone round about them: and they were sore afraid. And the angel said unto them, Fear not: for, behold, I bring you good tidings of great joy, which shall be to all people. For unto you is born this day in the city of David a Saviour, which is Christ the Lord. And this shall be a sign unto you; Ye shall find the babe wrapped in swaddling clothes, lying in a manger. And suddenly there was with the angel a multitude of the heavenly host praising God, and saying, Glory to God in the highest, and on earth peace, good will toward men.

And it came to pass, as the angels were gone away from them into heaven, the shepherds said one to another, Let us now go even unto Bethlehem, and see this thing which is come to pass, which the Lord hath made known unto us. And they came with haste, and found Mary, and Joseph, and the babe lying in a manger. And when they had seen it, they made known abroad the saying which was told them concerning this child. And all they that heard it wondered. . . . But Mary kept all these things, and pondered them in her heart. And the shepherds returned, glorifying and praising God for all the things that they had heard and seen, as it was told unto them. . . .

—LUKE 1, 2

The four Gospels—Matthew, Mark, Luke and John—all tell the same story but differ both in countless details and in style. The first three, often called the "Synoptics" (from a Greek word meaning "seen with the same eyes"), follow a fairly similar sequence of events. As for the fourth, Clement of Alexandria made a comment about 200 A.D. which has found wide support since: "After the other evangelists had written the facts of the history, John wrote a spiritual Gospel." John opens with a wonderful hymn praising the Word of God: "In the beginning was the Word, and the Word was with God, and the Word was God. The same was in the beginning with God. All things were made by him; and without him was not any thing made that was made. In him was life; and the life was the light of men. . . . That was the true Light, which lighteth every man that cometh into the world."

Each Gospel has its own special insights and felicities, and narrates much that would otherwise be lost. Only Matthew, for example, tells us of Peter's walking on the water, and only Luke gives Christ's words of comfort to the penitent thief or the parable of the good Samaritan.

INFANCY OF JESUS

NOW when Jesus was born in Bethlehem of Judaea in the days of Herod the king, behold, there came wise men from the east to Jerusalem, saying, Where is he that is born King of the Jews? for we have seen his star in the east, and are come to worship him. When Herod the king had heard these things, he was troubled, and all Jerusalem with him. And when he had gathered all the chief priests and scribes of the people together, he demanded of them where Christ should be born. And they said unto him, In Bethlehem of Judaea. . . .

Then Herod, when he had privily called the wise men, enquired of them diligently what time the star appeared. And he sent them to Bethlehem, and said, Go and search diligently for the young child; and when ye have found him, bring me word again, that I may come and worship him also. When they had heard the king, they departed; and, lo, the star, which they saw in the east, went before them, till it came and stood over where the young child was. When they saw the star, they rejoiced with exceeding great joy. And when they were come into the house, they saw the young child with Mary his mother and fell down, and worshipped him: and when they had opened their treasures, they presented unto him gifts; gold, frankincense, and myrrh.

Globe with Cross is an emblem of Christ's sovereignty

And being warned of God in a dream that they should not return to Herod, they departed into their own country another way. And when they were departed, behold, the angel of the Lord appeareth to Joseph in a dream, saying, Arise, and take the young child and his mother, and flee into Egypt, and be thou there until I bring thee word: for Herod will seek the young child to destroy him. . . . Then Herod . . . sent forth, and slew all the children that were in Bethlehem, and in all the coasts thereof, from two years old and under. . . . Then was fulfilled that which was spoken by Jeremy the prophet, saying, In Rama was there a voice heard, lamentation, and weeping, and great mourning, Rachel weeping for her children, and would not be comforted, because they are not.

But when Herod was dead, behold, an angel of the Lord appeareth in a dream to Joseph in Egypt, saying, Arise, and take the young child and his mother, and go into the land of Israel: for they are dead which sought the young child's life. . . . And he came and dwelt in . . . Nazareth: that it might be fulfilled which was spoken by the prophets, He shall be . . . a Nazarene.

—MATTHEW 2

John the Baptist, the cousin and forerunner of Jesus, proclaimed judgment in the tradition of the fiery Hebrew prophets. He used the old Jewish ritual of baptism, but gave it a fresh emphasis. Jesus had a high esteem for John and once said, "Among those that are born of women there is not a greater prophet than John the Baptist." Before He started His own active ministry, Jesus was baptized by John and went out into the wilderness for 40 days and nights to fast and to prepare Himself.

BAPTISM, TEMPTATION

NOW in the fifteenth year of the reign of Tiberius Caesar, Pontius Pilate being governor of Judaea, and . . Annas and Caiaphas being the high priests, the word of God came unto John the son of Zacharias in the wilderness. And he came into all the country about Jordan, preaching the baptism of repentance for the remission of sins; as it is written in the book of the words of Esaias the prophet, saying, The voice of one crying in the wilderness, Prepare ye the way of the Lord, make his paths straight. Every valley shall be filled, and every mountain and hill shall be brought low; and the crooked shall be made straight, and the rough ways shall be made smooth. . . . Then said he to the multitude that came forth to be baptized of him, O generation of vipers, who hath warned you to flee from the wrath to come? Bring forth therefore fruits worthy of repentance. . . . And the people asked him, saying,

What shall we do then? He answereth and saith unto them, He that hath two coats, let him impart to him that hath none; and he that hath meat, let him do likewise. . . . And as the people were in expectation, and all men mused in their hearts of John, whether he were the Christ, or not; John answered, saying unto them all, I indeed baptize you with water; but one mightier than I cometh, the latchet of whose shoes I am not worthy to unloose: he shall baptize you with the Holy Ghost and with fire . . . and he will . . . purge . . . and will gather the wheat into his garner; but the chaff he will burn with fire unquenchable. And many other things in his exhortation preached he unto the people. . . . Then cometh Jesus from Galilee . . . unto John, to be baptized of him. But John forbade him, saying, I have need to be baptized of thee, and comest thou to me? And Jesus answering said unto him, Suffer it to be so now: for thus it becometh us to fulfil all righteousness. Then he suffered him. And Jesus, when he was baptized, went up straightway out of the water: and, lo, the heavens were opened unto him, and he saw the Spirit of God descending like a dove, and lighting upon him: and lo a voice from heaven, saying, This is my beloved Son, in whom I am well pleased.

Then was Jesus led up of the Spirit into the wilderness to be tempted of the devil. And when he had fasted forty days and forty nights, he was afterward ahungered. And when the tempter came to him, he said, If thou be the Son of God, command that these stones be made bread. But he answered and said, It is written, Man shall not live by bread alone, but by every word that proceedeth out of the mouth of God.

Then the devil taketh him up into the holy city, and setteth him on a pinnacle of the temple, and saith unto him, If thou be the Son of God, cast thyself down: for it is written, He shall give his angels charge concerning thee: and in their hands they shall bear thee up, lest at any time thou dash thy foot against a stone. Jesus said unto him, It is written again, Thou shalt not tempt the Lord thy God.

Again, the devil taketh him up into an exceeding high mountain, and showeth him all the kingdoms of the world, and the glory of them; and saith unto him, All these things will I give thee, if thou wilt fall down and worship me. Then saith Jesus unto him, Get thee hence, Satan: for it is written, Thou shalt worship the Lord thy God, and him only shalt thou serve. Then the devil leaveth him, and . . . angels . . . ministered unto him. . . .

—LUKE 3; MATTHEW 3, 4

Herod imprisoned John the Baptist and later had him beheaded. Meanwhile, Jesus began His own ministry, called His first disciples (known as the major apostles), and performed His first miracle. His rejoinder to His mother at the Cana marriage feast may have been part of His doctrine that all mankind was His family. Later He said, "Who is my mother? and who are my brethren?" Joseph is not mentioned during the period of Jesus' active ministry, and Mary is thought to have been a widow by then. In the passage below a sentence is added from the Roman Catholic Douay Bible (page 262) as its translation differs somewhat.

THE MINISTRY BEGINS

NOW when Jesus had heard that John was cast into prison, he departed into Galilee; and leaving Nazareth, he came and dwelt in Capernaum, which is upon the seacoast. . . . From that time Jesus began to preach, and to say, Repent: for the kingdom of heaven is at hand.

And Jesus, walking by the sea of Galilee, saw two brethren, Simon called Peter, and Andrew his brother, casting a net into the sea: for they were fishers. And he saith unto them, Follow me, and I will make you fishers of men. And they straightway left their nets, and followed him. And going on from thence, he saw other two brethren, James the son of Zebedee, and John his brother, in a ship with Zebedee their father, mending their nets; and he called them. And they immediately left the ship and their father, and followed him. . . .

There was a marriage in Cana of Galilee; and the mother of Jesus was there: and both Jesus was called, and his disciples, to the marriage. And when they wanted wine, the mother of Jesus saith unto him, They have no wine. Jesus saith unto her, Woman, what have I to do with thee? [Douay: Woman, what is that to me and to thee?] mine hour is not yet come. His mother saith unto the servants, Whatsoever he saith unto you, do it. And there were set there six waterpots of stone, after the manner of the purifying of the Jews, containing two or three firkins apiece. Jesus saith unto them, Fill the waterpots with water. And they filled them up to the brim. And he saith unto them, Draw out now, and bear unto the governor of the feast.

Anchor has long meant both hope and steadfastness to Christians

And they bare it. When the ruler of the feast had tasted the water that was made wine, and knew not whence it was (but the servants which drew the water knew), the governor of the feast called the bridegroom, and saith unto him, Every man at the beginning doth set forth good wine; and when men have well drunk, then that which is worse: but thou hast kept the good wine until now. This beginning of miracles did Jesus in Cana of Galilee, and manifested forth his glory; and his disciples believed on him. . . .

—MATTHEW 4; JOHN 2

In His preaching and healing Jesus soon ran afoul of an influential Jewish group, the Pharisees, who had a complex interpretation of the laws of Moses called "the tradition of the elders" (see page 161). His discussions with the Pharisees gave Jesus, Who believed that the spirit of a law was more important than its letter, the chance to explain and justify many key points in His message. The Pharisees were especially insistent on strict observance of the Sabbath.

THE PHARISEES

BUT so much the more went there a fame abroad of him: and great multitudes came together to hear and to be healed by him of their infirmities. And he withdrew himself into the wilderness, and prayed. And it came to pass on a certain day, as he was teaching, that there were Pharisees and doctors of the law sitting by, which were come out of every town of Galilee, and Judaea, and Jerusalem: and the power of the Lord was present to heal them. And, behold, men brought in a bed a man which was taken with a palsy: and . . . when they could not find by what way they might bring him in because of the multitude, they went upon the house top, and let him down through the tiling with his couch into the midst before Jesus. And when he saw their faith, he said . . . Man, thy sins are forgiven thee.

And the scribes and the Pharisees began to reason, saying, Who is this which speaketh blasphemies? Who can forgive sins, but God alone? But when Jesus perceived their thoughts, he answering said unto them, What reason ye in your hearts? Whether is easier, to say, Thy sins be forgiven thee; or to say, Rise up and walk? But that ye may know that the Son of man hath power upon earth to forgive sins, (he said unto the sick of the palsy,) I say unto thee, Arise, and take up thy couch, and go into thine house. And immediately he rose up before them, and took up that whereon he lay, and departed to his own house, glorifying God. . . .

And he said unto them, The sabbath was made for man, and not man for the sabbath. . . . For the Son of man is Lord even of the sabbath day. And when he was departed thence, he went into their synagogue: and, behold, there was a man which had his hand withered. And they asked him, saying, Is it lawful to heal on the sabbath days? that they might accuse him. And he said unto them, What man shall there be among you, that shall have one sheep, and if it fall into a pit on the sabbath day, will he not lay hold on it, and lift it out? How much then is a man better than a sheep? Wherefore it is lawful to do well on the sabbath days. Then saith he to the man, Stretch forth thine hand. And he stretched it forth; and it was restored whole. . . .

Then came together unto him the Pharisees, and . . . scribes, which came from Jerusalem. And when they saw some of his disciples eat bread with defiled, that is to say . . . unwashen, hands, they found fault. For the Pharisees, and all the Jews, except they wash their hands oft, eat not, holding the tradition of the elders. And when they come from the market, except they wash, they eat not. And many other things there be, which they have received to hold, as the washing of cups and pots, brazen vessels, and of tables. Then the Pharisees and scribes asked him, Why walk not thy disciples according to the tradition of the elders, but eat bread with unwashen hands? . . . But he answered and said unto them, Why do ye also transgress the commandment of God by your tradition? . . .

Then went the Pharisees, and took counsel how they might entangle him in his talk. And they sent out unto him their disciples with the Herodians, saying, Master, we know that thou art true, and teachest the way of God in truth, neither carest thou for any man: for thou regardest not the person of men. Tell us . . . What thinkest thou? Is it lawful to give tribute unto Caesar, or not? But Jesus perceived their wickedness, and said, Why tempt ye me, ye hypocrites? Show me the tribute money. And they brought unto him a penny. And he saith unto them, Whose is this image and superscription? They say unto him, Caesar's. Then saith he unto them, Render therefore unto Caesar the things which are Caesar's; and unto God the things that are God's. When they had heard these words, they marvelled, and left him, and went their way. . . .

—LUKE 5; MARK 2; MATTHEW 12;
MARK 7; MATTHEW 15, 22

Three terms used in the New Testament for the followers of Jesus are "apostles," "disciples" and "evangelists." In the Gospels the word "apostles" ("those sent") is limited to the twelve men Jesus chose for His intimate band—according to Mark "that they should be with him, and that he might send them forth to preach, and to have power to heal sicknesses, and to cast out devils." In the later books of the New Testament the apostles include other leaders such as Paul and Matthias.

The word "evangelists" ("heralds of the good news") refers to those who preach Christ's message, and at present is sometimes used to refer to the authors of the four Gospels. The term "disciples" ("learners") is also used for the apostles, but in a broader sense is used throughout the New Testament for believers in Christ.

CHOOSING THE TWELVE

AND it came to pass in those days, that he went out into a mountain to pray, and continued all night in prayer to God. And when it was day, he called unto him his disciples and . . . chose twelve, whom also he named apostles; Simon (whom he also named Peter), and Andrew his brother, James and John, Philip and Bartholomew, Matthew and Thomas, James the son of Alphaeus, and Simon called Zelotes, and Judas the brother of James, and Judas Iscariot, which also was the traitor. . . .

These twelve Jesus sent forth, and commanded them, saying . . . As ye go, preach, saying, The kingdom of heaven is at hand. Heal the sick, cleanse the lepers, raise the dead, cast out devils: freely ye have received, freely give. Provide neither gold, nor silver, nor brass in your purses, nor scrip for your journey, neither two coats, neither shoes, nor yet staves: for the workman is worthy of his meat. And into whatsoever city or town ye shall enter, enquire who in it is worthy; and there abide till ye go thence. And when ye come into an house, salute it. And if the house be worthy, let your peace come upon it: but if it be not worthy, let your peace return to you. And whosoever shall not receive you, nor hear your words, when ye depart out of that house or city, shake off the dust of your feet. . . .

Behold, I send you forth as sheep in the midst of the wolves: be ye therefore wise as serpents, and harmless as doves. But beware of men: for they will deliver you up to the councils, and they will scourge you in their synagogues; and ye shall be brought before governors and kings for my sake, for a testimony against them and the Gentiles. But when they deliver you up, take no thought how or what ye shall speak: for it shall be given you in that same hour what ye shall speak. For it is not ye that speak, but the spirit of your Father which speaketh in you. And the brother shall deliver up the brother to death, and the father the child: and the children shall rise up against their parents, and cause them to be put to death. And ye shall be hated of all men for my name's sake: but he that endureth to the end shall be saved. But when they persecute you in this city, flee ye into another. . . .

And he that taketh not his cross, and followeth after me, is not worthy of me. He that findeth his life shall lose it: and he that loseth his life for my sake shall find it. He that receiveth you receiveth me, and he that receiveth me receiveth him that sent me. . . . And it came to pass, when Jesus had made an end of commanding his twelve disciples, he departed thence to teach and to preach in their cities. . . .

And they went out, and preached that men should repent. And they cast out many devils, and anointed with oil many that were sick, and healed them. . . .

—LUKE 6; MATTHEW 10, 11; MARK 6

The most famous of all Christ's discourses is the Sermon on the Mount, which fills three whole chapters of Matthew. Among many other notable passages, it includes the Beatitudes ("Blessed are . . .") and the Lord's Prayer. Some authorities think it is too long to have been a single sermon, and is rather a collection of Jesus' sayings at various times. In any case, it is a wonderful exposition of the message of Jesus as Teacher and Savior.

SERMON ON THE MOUNT

AND seeing the multitudes, he went up into a mountain: and when he was set, his disciples came unto him: and he opened his mouth, and taught them, saying,

Blessed are the poor in spirit: for theirs is the kingdom of heaven. Blessed are they that mourn: for they shall be comforted. Blessed are the meek: for they shall inherit the earth. Blessed are they which do hunger and thirst after righteousness: for they shall be filled. Blessed are the merciful: for they shall obtain mercy. Blessed are the pure in heart: for they shall see God. Blessed are the peacemakers: for they shall be called the children of God. Blessed are they which are persecuted for righteousness' sake: for theirs is the kingdom of heaven. Blessed are ye, when men shall revile you, and persecute you, and shall say all manner of evil against you falsely, for my sake. Rejoice, and be exceeding glad: for great is your reward in heaven: for so persecuted they the prophets which were before you.

Ye are the salt of the earth: but if the salt have lost his savor, wherewith shall it be salted? it is thenceforth good for nothing, but to be cast out, and to be trodden under foot of men. Ye are the light of the world. A city that is set on a hill cannot be hid. Neither do men light a candle, and put it under a bushel, but on a candlestick; and it giveth light unto all that are in the house. Let your light so shine before men, that they may see your good works, and glorify your Father which is in heaven. . . .

Ye have heard that it was said by them of old time, Thou shalt not kill; and whosoever shall kill shall be in danger of the judgment: but I say unto you, That whosoever . . . shall say, Thou fool, shall be in danger of hell fire. Therefore if thou bring thy gift to the altar, and there rememberest that thy brother hath aught against thee; leave there thy gift before the altar, and go thy way; first be reconciled to thy brother, and then come and offer thy gift. Agree with thine adversary quickly,

Pelican giving blood to chicks recalls Jesus' own sacrifice

while thou art in the way with him; lest at any time the adversary deliver thee to the judge, and the judge deliver thee to the officer, and thou be cast into prison. . . .

Ye have heard that it was said by them of old time, Thou shalt not commit adultery: but I say unto you, That whosoever looketh on a woman to lust after her hath committed adultery with her already in his heart. And if thy right eye offend thee, pluck it out, and cast it from thee: for it is profitable for thee that one of thy members should perish, and not that thy whole body should be cast into hell. And if thy right hand offend thee, cut it off, and cast it from thee: for it is profitable for thee that one of thy members should perish, and not that thy whole body should be cast into hell. It hath been said, Whosoever shall put away his wife, let him give her a writing of divorcement: but I say unto you, That whosoever shall put away his wife, saving for the cause of fornication, causeth her to commit adultery: and whosoever shall marry her that is divorced committeth adultery. . . .

Ye have heard that it hath been said, An eye for an eye, and a tooth for a tooth: but I say unto you, That ye resist not evil: but whosoever shall smite thee on thy right cheek, turn to him the other also. And if any man will sue thee at the law, and take away thy coat, let him have thy cloak also. And whosoever shall compel thee to go a mile, go with him twain. Give to him that asketh thee, and from him that would borrow of thee turn not thou away.

Ye have heard that it hath been said, Thou shalt love thy neighbor, and hate thine enemy. But I say unto you, Love your enemies, bless them that curse you, do good to them that hate you, and pray for them which despitefully use you, and persecute you; that ye may be the children of your Father which is in heaven: for he maketh his sun to rise on the evil and on the good, and sendeth rain on the just and on the unjust. For if ye love them which love you, what reward have ye? do not even the publicans the same? And if ye salute your brethren only . . . do not even the publicans so? Be ye therefore perfect, even as your Father which is in heaven is perfect.

Swift dolphin, for resurrection, bears souls of dead to heaven

Take heed that ye do not your alms before men, to be seen of them: otherwise ye have no reward of your Father which is in heaven. Therefore when thou doest thine alms, do not sound a trumpet before thee. . . . Let not thy left hand know what thy right hand doeth . . . and thy Father which seeth in secret himself shall reward thee openly.

And when thou prayest, thou shalt not be as the hypocrites are: for they love to pray standing in the synagogues and in the corners of the streets, that they may be seen of men. . . . But thou, when thou prayest, enter into thy closet, and . . . pray to thy Father which is in secret; and thy Father which seeth in secret shall reward thee openly. But when ye pray, use not vain repetitions, as the heathen do: for they think that they shall be heard for their much speaking. Be not ye . . . like unto them: for your Father knoweth what things ye have need of, before ye ask him.

After this manner therefore pray ye: Our Father which art in heaven, hallowed be thy name. Thy kingdom come. Thy will be done in earth, as it is in heaven. Give us this day our daily bread. And forgive us our debts, as we forgive our debtors. And lead us not into temptation, but deliver us from evil. . . . Amen.

For if ye forgive men their trespasses, your heavenly Father will also forgive you: but if ye forgive not men their trespasses, neither will your Father forgive your trespasses. . . . When ye fast, be not, as the hypocrites, of a sad countenance: for they disfigure their faces, that they may appear unto men to fast. . . . But thou, when thou fastest, anoint thine head, and wash thy face; that thou appear not unto men to fast, but unto thy Father which is in secret: and thy Father . . . shall reward thee openly.

Lay not up for yourselves treasures upon earth . . . but lay up for yourselves treasures in heaven, where neither moth nor rust doth corrupt, and where thieves do not break through nor steal: for where your treasure is, there will your heart be also. . . . No man can serve two masters: for either he will hate the one, and love the other; or else he will hold to the one, and despise the other. Ye cannot serve God and mammon. Therefore I say unto you, Take no thought for your life . . . nor yet for your body, what ye shall put on. Is not the life more than meat, and the body than raiment? Behold the fowls of the air: for they sow not, neither do they reap, nor gather into barns; yet your heavenly Father feedeth them. Are ye not much better than they? . . .

Consider the lilies of the field, how they grow; they toil not, neither do they spin: and yet I say unto you, That even Solomon in all his glory was not arrayed like one of these. Wherefore, if God so clothe the grass of the field, which today is, and tomorrow is cast into the oven, shall he not much more clothe you, O ye of little faith? . . . But seek ye first the kingdom of God . . . and all these things shall be added unto you. Take therefore no thought for the morrow: for the morrow shall take thought for the things of itself. Sufficient unto the day is the evil thereof.

Judge not, that ye be not judged. For with what judgment ye judge, ye shall be judged: and with what measure ye mete, it shall be measured to you again. And why beholdest thou the mote that is in thy brother's eye, but considerest not the beam that is in thine own eye? Or how wilt thou say to thy brother,

Let me pull out the mote out of thine eye; and, behold, a beam is in thine own eye? Thou hypocrite, first cast out the beam out of thine own eye; and then shalt thou see clearly to cast out the mote out of thy brother's eye. Give not that which is holy unto the dogs, neither cast ye your pearls before swine, lest they trample them under their feet, and turn again and rend you.

Ask, and it shall be given you; seek, and ye shall find; knock, and it shall be opened unto you: for every one that asketh receiveth; and he that seeketh findeth; and to him that knocketh it shall be opened. Or what man is there of you, whom if his son ask bread, will he give him a stone? Or if he ask a fish, will he give him a serpent? . . . Therefore all things whatsoever ye would that men should do to you, do ye even so to them: for this is the law and the prophets. . . .

Beware of false prophets, which come to you in sheep's clothing, but inwardly they are ravening wolves. Ye shall know them by their fruits. Do men gather grapes of thorns, or figs of thistles? Even so every good tree bringeth forth good fruit; but a corrupt tree bringeth forth evil fruit. A good tree cannot bring forth evil fruit, neither can a corrupt tree bring forth good fruit. . . . Wherefore by their fruits ye shall know them. Not every one that saith unto me, Lord, Lord, shall enter into the kingdom of heaven; but he that doeth the will of my Father which is in heaven. Many will say to me in that day, Lord, Lord, have we not prophesied in thy name? and in thy name have cast out devils? and in thy name done many wonderful works? And then will I profess unto them, I never knew you: depart from me, ye that work iniquity.

Therefore whosoever heareth these sayings of mine, and doeth them, I will liken him unto a wise man, which built his house upon a rock: and the rain descended, and the floods came, and the winds blew, and beat upon that house; and it fell not: for it was founded upon a rock. And every one that heareth these sayings of mine, and doeth them not, shall be likened unto a foolish man, which built his house upon the sand: and the rain descended, and the floods came, and the winds blew, and beat upon that house; and it fell: and great was the fall of it.

And it came to pass, when Jesus had ended these sayings, the people were astonished at his doctrine: for he taught them as one having authority, and not as the scribes.

—MATTHEW 5–7

Throughout His relatively brief ministry on earth, which may have lasted only a year and was certainly no more than four years, Jesus worked an astonishing number of miracles. Some 35 are described in the Gospels, while many more are mentioned without details. He did not perform them to win followers, or to impress important people, but in compassion and in response to simple faith in Him. Even among Christians, attitudes toward His miracles have varied greatly, but these stories have played a large part in the spread of Christianity.

MIRACLES

NOW when he had ended all his sayings in the audience of the people, he entered into Capernaum. And a certain centurion's servant, who was dear unto him, was sick, and ready to die. And when he heard of Jesus, he sent unto him the elders of the Jews, beseeching him that he would come and heal his servant. And when they came to Jesus, they besought him instantly, saying, That he was worthy for whom he should do this: for he loved our nation, and he hath built us a synagogue. Then Jesus went with him. And when he was now not far from the house, the centurion sent friends to him, saying . . . Lord, trouble not thyself: for I am not worthy that thou shouldest enter under my roof: wherefore neither thought I myself worthy to come unto thee: but say in a word, and my servant shall be healed. For I also am a man set under authority having under me soldiers, and I say unto one, Go, and he goeth; and to another, Come, and he cometh; and to my servant, Do this, and he doeth it. When Jesus heard these things, he marvelled at him, and turned him about, and said unto the people that followed him, I say unto you, I have not found so great faith, no, not in Israel. And they that were sent, returning to the house, found the servant whole that had been sick.

And it came to pass the day after, that he went into a city called Nain; and many of his disciples went with him, and much people. Now when he came nigh to the gate of the city, behold, there was a dead man carried out, the only son of his mother, and she was a widow. . . . And when the Lord saw her, he had compassion on her, and said unto her, Weep not. And he came and touched the bier. . . . And he said, Young man, I say unto thee, Arise. And he that was dead sat up, and began to speak. And he delivered him to his mother. And there came a fear on all: and they glorified God. . . . Then Jesus answering said unto them, Go your way, and tell . . . how that the blind see, the lame walk, the lepers are cleansed, the deaf hear, the dead are raised, to the poor the gospel is preached. . . .

After these things Jesus went over the sea of Galilee. . . . And a great multitude followed him, because they saw his miracles which he did on them that were diseased. And Jesus went up into a mountain. . . . When Jesus then lifted up his eyes, and saw a great company come unto him, he saith unto Philip, Whence shall we buy bread, that these may eat? . . . Philip answered him, Two hundred pennyworth of bread is not sufficient for them, that every one of them may take a little. One of his disciples, Andrew, Simon Peter's brother, saith unto him, There is a lad here, which hath five barley loaves, and two small fishes: but what are they among so many? And Jesus said, Make the men sit down. Now there was much grass in the place. So the men sat down, in number about five thousand.

And Jesus took the loaves; and when he had given thanks, he distributed to the disciples, and the disciples to them that were set down; and likewise of the fishes as much as they would. When they were filled, he said unto his disciples, Gather up the fragments that remain, that nothing be lost. Therefore they gathered them together, and filled twelve baskets with the fragments of the five barley loaves, which remained over and above unto them that had eaten. Then those men, when they had seen the miracle that Jesus did, said, This is of a truth that prophet that should come into the world. . . .

Now a certain man was sick, named Lazarus, of Bethany, the town of Mary and her sister Martha. . . . Therefore his sisters sent unto him, saying, Lord, behold, he whom thou lovest is sick. . . . When Jesus came, he found that he had lain in the grave four days already. . . . Then said Martha unto Jesus, Lord, if thou hadst been here, my brother had not died. But I know that even now, whatsoever thou wilt ask of God, God will give it thee. Jesus saith unto her, Thy brother shall rise again. Martha saith unto him, I know that he shall rise again in the resurrection at the last day. Jesus said unto her, I am the resurrection, and the life: he that believeth in me, though he were dead, yet shall he live: And whosoever liveth and believeth in me shall never die. Believest thou this? She saith unto him, Yea, Lord: I believe that thou art the Christ, the Son of God, which should come into the world. . . . Then when Mary was come where Jesus was, and saw him, she fell down at his feet, saying unto him, Lord, if thou hadst been here, my brother had not died. When Jesus therefore saw her weeping, and the Jews also weeping which came with her, he groaned in the spirit, and was troubled, and said, Where have ye laid him? They said unto him, Lord, come and see. Jesus wept.

Grapes symbolize the blood of the martyred Savior

Then said the Jews, Behold how he loved him! And some of them said, Could not this man, which opened the eyes of the blind, have caused that even this man should not have died? Jesus therefore again groaning in himself cometh to the grave. It was a cave, and a stone lay upon it.

Jesus said, Take ye away the stone. Martha, the sister of him that was dead, saith unto him, Lord, by this time he stinketh: for he hath been dead four days. Jesus saith unto her, Said I not unto thee, that, if thou wouldest believe, thou shouldest see the glory of God? Then they took away the stone from the place where the dead was laid. And Jesus lifted up his eyes, and said, Father, I thank thee that thou hast heard me. . . . And when he thus had spoken, he cried with a loud voice, Lazarus, come forth. And he that was dead came forth, bound hand and foot with graveclothes: and his face was bound about with a napkin. Jesus saith unto them, Loose him, and let him go. Then many of the Jews which came to Mary, and had seen the things which Jesus did, believed on him. . . .

—LUKE 7; JOHN 6, 11

An ancient form of instruction (see pages 38 and 67 for Hindu and Buddhist examples) is the parable, which has been called "an earthly story with a heavenly meaning." Jesus told more than 40 parables in the course of His teachings, and no one else has ever used this ancient method of instruction so effectively.

PARABLES

THE same day went Jesus out of the house, and sat by the sea side. And great multitudes were gathered together unto him, so that he went into a ship, and sat; and the whole multitude stood on the shore. And he spake many things unto them in parables, saying, Behold, a sower went forth to sow; and when he sowed, some seeds fell by the way side, and the fowls came and devoured them up: some fell upon stony places, where they had not much earth: and forthwith they sprung up, because they had no deepness of earth: and when the sun was up, they were scorched; and because they had no root, they withered away. And some fell among thorns; and the thorns sprung up, and choked them: but other fell into good ground, and brought forth fruit, some an hundredfold, some sixtyfold, some thirtyfold. Who hath ears to hear, let him hear.

And the disciples came, and said unto him, Why speakest thou unto them in parables? He answered and said unto them, Because it is given unto you to know the mysteries of the kingdom of heaven, but to them it is not given. . . . Therefore speak I to them in parables: because they seeing see not; and hearing they hear not, neither do they understand. . . . Another parable put he forth . . . saying, The kingdom of heaven is likened unto a man which sowed good seed in his field: but while men slept, his enemy came and sowed tares among the wheat, and went his way. But when the blade was sprung up, and brought forth fruit, then appeared the tares also. So the servants of the householder came and said unto him, Sir, didst not thou sow good seed in thy field? From whence then hath it tares? He said unto them, An enemy hath done this. The servants said unto him, Wilt thou then that we go and gather them up? But he said, Nay; lest while ye gather up the tares, ye root up also the wheat with them. Let both grow together until the harvest: and in the time of harvest I will say to the reapers, Gather . . . the tares, and . . . burn them: but gather the wheat into my barn. . . .

Then Jesus sent the multitude away . . . and his disciples came unto him, saying, Declare unto us the parable of the tares of the field.

He answered and said unto them, He that soweth the good seed is the Son of man; the field is the world; the good seed are the children of the kingdom; but the tares are the children of the wicked one; the enemy that sowed them is the devil; the harvest is the end of the world; and the reapers are the angels. As therefore the tares are gathered and burned in the fire; so shall it be in the end of this world. The Son of man shall send forth his angels, and they shall gather out of his kingdom all things that offend, and them which do iniquity; and shall cast them into a furnace of fire: there shall be wailing and gnashing of teeth. Then shall the righteous shine forth as the sun in the kingdom of their Father. Who hath ears to hear, let him hear. . . .

And, behold, a certain lawyer . . . said unto Jesus, And who is my neighbor? And Jesus answering said, A certain man went down from Jerusalem to Jericho, and fell among thieves, which stripped him of his raiment, and wounded him, and departed, leaving him half dead. And by chance there came down a certain priest that way: and when he saw him, he passed by on the other side. And likewise a Levite . . . passed on the other side. But a certain Samaritan, as he journeyed . . . had compassion on him, and went to him, and bound up his wounds, pouring in oil and wine, and set him on his own beast, and brought him to an inn, and took care of him. And on the morrow when he departed, he took out two pence, and gave them to the host, and said unto him, Take care of him; and whatsoever thou spendest more, when I come again, I will repay thee.

Which now of these three . . . was neighbor unto him that fell among the thieves? And he said, He that showed mercy on him. Then said Jesus unto him, Go, and do thou likewise. . . .

Then drew near unto him all the publicans and sinners for to hear him. And the Pharisees and scribes murmured, saying, This man receiveth sinners, and eateth with them. And he spake this parable unto them, saying, What man of you, having an hundred sheep, if he lose one of them, doth not leave the ninety and nine . . . and go after that which is lost. . . ? And when he hath found it, he layeth it on his shoulders, rejoicing. And when he cometh home, he calleth together his friends and neighbors, saying unto them, Rejoice with me; for I have found my sheep which was lost. I say unto you, that likewise joy shall be in heaven over one sinner, that repenteth, more than over ninety and nine just persons, which need no repentance. . . .
—MATTHEW 13; LUKE 10, 15

Every religious leader is confronted with the problem of sin. Christ was continually concerned with it, since His opponents often tried to trap Him in its manifold complexities. Thus, in the case of the adulterous woman, if Jesus had—inconceivably—urged stoning, He would have challenged Roman authority which did not allow the Jews to execute people, while if He had condoned her act, He would have offended the Jewish religion. Just as He used such dilemmas to clarify His own message, so He used the welcoming of little children to teach profound truths.

FORGIVENESS AND LOVE

AND the scribes and Pharisees brought unto him a woman taken in adultery; and when they had set her in the midst, they say unto him, Master, this woman was taken in adultery, in the very act. Now Moses in the law commanded us, that such should be stoned: but what sayest thou? This they said, tempting him, that they might have to accuse him. But Jesus stooped down, and with his finger wrote on the ground, as though he heard them not. So when they continued asking him, he lifted up himself, and said unto them, He that is without sin

Eagle is for courage and faith, fish for baptism and for Jesus

among you, let him first cast a stone at her. And again he stooped down, and wrote on the ground. And they which heard it, being convicted by their own conscience, went out one by one . . . even unto the last: and Jesus was left alone, and the woman standing in the midst. When Jesus . . . saw none but the woman, he said unto her, Woman, where are those thine accusers? hath no man condemned thee? She said, No man, Lord. And Jesus said unto her, Neither do I condemn thee: go, and sin no more. . . .

And they brought young children to him, that he should touch them; and his disciples rebuked those that brought them. But when Jesus saw it, he was much displeased, and said unto them, Suffer the little children to come unto me, and forbid them not; for of such is the kingdom of God. Verily I say unto you, Whosoever shall not receive the kingdom of God as a little child, he shall not enter therein. And he took them up in his arms, put his hands upon them, and blessed them. . . .
—JOHN 8; MARK 10

During Christ's earthly ministry, Peter was His leading apostle. He was the first actually to name Jesus as the Messiah, and was always close to Him except for his brief denial the night before the Crucifixion. The Gospels have many vivid pictures of him as he followed Jesus.

PETER

AND straightway Jesus constrained his disciples to get into a ship, and to go before him unto the other side, while he sent the multitudes away. And when he had sent the multitudes away, he went up into a mountain apart to pray: and when the evening was come, he was there alone. But the ship was now in the midst of the sea, tossed with waves: for the wind was contrary. And in the fourth watch of the night Jesus went unto them, walking on the sea. And when the disciples saw him walking on the sea, they were troubled, saying, It is a spirit; and they cried out for fear. But straightway Jesus spake unto them, saying, Be of good cheer; it is I; be not afraid. And Peter answered him and said, Lord, if it be thou, bid me come unto thee on the water. And he said, Come. And when Peter was come down out of the ship, he walked on the water, to go to Jesus. But when he saw the wind boisterous, he was afraid; and beginning to sink, he cried, saying, Lord, save me. And immediately Jesus stretched forth his hand, and caught him, and said unto him, O thou of little faith, wherefore didst thou doubt? . . .

When Jesus came into the coasts of Caesarea Philippi, he asked his disciples, saying, Whom do men say that I, the Son of man, am? And they said, Some say that thou art John the Baptist; some, Elias; and others, Jeremias, or one of the prophets. He saith unto them, But whom say ye that I am? And Simon Peter answered and said, Thou art the Christ, the Son of the living God. And Jesus answered and said unto him, Blessed art thou, Simon Bar-jona: for flesh and blood hath not revealed it unto thee, but my Father which is in heaven. And I say also unto thee, That thou art Peter, and upon this rock I will build my church; and the gates of hell shall not prevail against it. And I will give unto thee the keys of the kingdom of heaven: and whatsoever thou shalt bind on earth shall be bound in heaven; and whatsoever thou shalt loose on earth shall be loosed in heaven. Then charged he his disciples that they should tell no man that he was Jesus the Christ.

From that time forth began Jesus to show unto his disciples, how that he must go unto Jerusalem, and suffer many things of the elders and chief priests and scribes, and be killed, and be raised again the third day. Then Peter took him, and began to rebuke him, saying, Be it far from thee, Lord: this shall not be unto thee. But he turned, and said unto Peter, Get thee behind me, Satan: thou art an offense unto me: for thou savorest not the things that be of God, but those that be of men.

Then said Jesus unto his disciples, If any man will come after me, let him deny himself, and take up his cross, and follow me. For whosoever will save his life shall lose it: and whosoever will lose his life for my sake shall find it. For what is a man profited, if he shall gain the whole world, and lose his own soul? or what shall a man give in exchange for his soul? . . . And after six days Jesus taketh Peter, James, and John his brother, and bringeth them up into a high mountain apart, and was transfigured before them: and his face did shine as the sun, and his raiment was white as the light. And, behold, there appeared unto them Moses and Elias talking with him. Then answered Peter, and said unto Jesus, Lord, it is good for us to be here: if thou wilt, let us make here three tabernacles; one for thee, and one for Moses, and one for Elias. While he yet spake, behold, a bright cloud overshadowed them: and behold, a voice out of the cloud, which said, This my beloved Son, in whom I am well pleased; hear ye him. And when the disciples heard it, they fell on their face, and were sore afraid. And Jesus came and touched them, and said, Arise, and be not afraid. And when they had lifted up their eyes, they saw no man. . . . Jesus charged them . . . Tell the vision to no man. . . .

—MATTHEW 14, 16, 17

The haloed "Lamb of God" holds Latin cross for atonement

Jesus came to Jerusalem shortly before His Crucifixion at the time of the Passover. For several days He stayed just outside Jerusalem, entering the city daily and returning each evening. His first triumphal entrance was on Palm Sunday. Later in the week He drove the money changers out of the Temple and had a series of sharp discussions with the chief priests, elders and Pharisees. On Thursday He came into Jerusalem for the Last Supper, and during the night was arrested in the Garden of Gethsemane outside the walls (see map on page 189). On Friday, before dawn, He was charged by the Jewish Sanhedrin, sentenced by the Roman governor Pilate that morning and then crucified.

THE LAST WEEK

ON the next day much people that were come to the feast, when they heard that Jesus was coming to Jerusalem, took branches of palm trees, and went forth to meet him, and cried, Hosanna: Blessed is the King of Israel that cometh in the name of the Lord. . . .

And some of the Pharisees from among the multitude said unto him, Master, rebuke thy disciples. And he answered and said unto them, I tell you that, if these should hold their peace, the stones would immediately cry out. . . .

And Jesus went into the temple of God, and cast out all them that sold and bought in the temple, and overthrew the tables of the money changers, and the seats of them that sold doves, and said unto them, It is written, My house shall be called the house of prayer; but ye have made it a den of thieves. And the blind and the lame came to him in the temple; and he healed them. . . .

And he taught daily in the temple. But the chief priests and the scribes and the chief of the people sought to destroy him, and could not find what that they might do: for all the people were very attentive to hear him. . . .

When the Pharisees had heard that he had put the Sadducees to silence, they were gathered together. Then one of them, which was a lawyer, asked him a question, tempting him, and saying, Master, which is the great commandment in the law?

Jesus said unto him, Thou shalt love the Lord thy God with all thy heart, and with all thy soul, and with all thy mind. This is the first and great commandment. And the second is like unto it, Thou shalt love thy neighbor as thyself. On these two commandments hang all the law and the prophets. . . .

And Jesus sat over against the treasury, and beheld how the people cast money into the treasury: and many that were rich cast in much. And . . . a certain poor widow . . . threw in two mites, which makes a farthing. And he called unto him his disciples, and saith unto them, Verily I say unto you, That this poor widow hath cast more in, than all they which have cast into the treasury: for all they did cast in of their abundance; but she of her want did cast in all that she had, even all her living. . . .

And it came to pass, when Jesus had finished all these sayings, he said unto his disciples, Ye know that after two days is the feast of the passover, and the Son of man is betrayed to be crucified. Then assembled together the chief priests, and the scribes, and the elders of the people, unto the palace of the high priest, who was called Caiaphas, and consulted that they might take Jesus by subtilty, and kill him. But they said, Not on the feast day, lest there be an uproar among the people. . . . Then one of the twelve, called Judas Iscariot, went unto the chief priests, and said unto them, What will ye give me, and I will deliver him unto you? And they covenanted with him for thirty pieces of silver. And from that time he sought opportunity to betray him. . . .

And the first day of unleavened bread . . . his disciples went forth, and came into the city, and found as he had said unto them: and they made ready the passover. And in the evening he cometh with the twelve. . . .

Jesus . . . riseth from supper, and laid aside his garments; and took a towel, and girded himself. After that he poureth water into a basin, and began to wash the disciples' feet, and to wipe them with the towel. . . . So after he had washed their feet . . . he said unto them . . . If I then, your Lord and Master, have washed your feet; ye also ought to wash one another's feet. . . . The servant is not greater than his lord; neither he that is sent greater than he that sent him. . . .

When Jesus had thus said, he was troubled in spirit, and testified, and said, Verily, verily, I say unto you, that one of you shall betray me. . . . He it is, to whom I shall give a sop, when I have dipped it. And when he had dipped the sop, he gave it to Judas Iscariot. . . . He then, having received the sop, went immediately out; and it was night. . . .

And as they did eat, Jesus took bread, and blessed, and brake it, and gave to them, and said, Take, eat; this is my body. And he took the cup, and when he had given thanks, he gave it to them: and they all drank of it. And he said unto them, This is my blood of the new testament, which is shed for many. Verily I say unto you, I will drink no more of the fruit of the vine, until that day that I drink it new in the kingdom of God. . . .

And he said, I tell thee, Peter, the cock shall not crow this day, before that thou shalt thrice deny that thou knowest me. . . . But [Peter] spake . . . If I should die with thee, I will not deny thee in any wise. Likewise also said they all.

And they came to a place which was named Gethsemane: and he saith to his disciples, Sit ye here, while I shall pray. And he taketh with him Peter and James and John . . . and saith unto them, My soul is exceeding sorrowful unto death: tarry ye here, and watch. And he went forward a little, and fell on the ground, and prayed that, if it were possible, the hour might pass from him. And he said, Abba, Father, all things are possible unto thee; take away this cup from me: nevertheless, not what I will, but what thou wilt. And he cometh, and findeth them sleeping, and saith unto Peter, Simon, sleepest thou? couldest not thou watch one hour? Watch ye and pray, lest ye enter into temptation. The spirit truly is ready, but the flesh is weak. And again he went away, and prayed, and spake the same words. And when he returned, he found them asleep again. . . . And he cometh the third time, and saith unto them, Sleep on now, and take your rest . . . the hour is come; behold, the Son of man is betrayed into the hands of sinners. . . .

And immediately, while he yet spake, cometh Judas, one of the twelve, and with him a great multitude with swords and staves [and] . . . goeth straightway to him, and saith, Master, Master; and kissed him. And they laid their hands on him . . . and bound him, and led him away to Annas first; for he was father-in-law to Caiaphas, which was the high priest that same year. Now Caiaphas was he, which gave counsel to the Jews, that it was expedient that one man should die for the people. . . .

Then all the disciples forsook him, and fled . . . but Peter followed him afar off unto the high priest's palace, and went in, and sat with the servants, to see the end. . . . And a damsel came unto him, saying, Thou also wast with Jesus of Galilee. But he denied before them all, saying, I know not what thou sayest. And when he was gone out into the porch, another maid saw him, and said unto them that were there, This fellow was also with Jesus of Nazareth. And again he denied with an oath, I do not know the man. And after a while came unto him they that stood by, and said to Peter, Surely thou also art one of them; for thy speech betrayeth thee. Then began he to curse and to swear, saying, I know not the man. And immediately the cock crew. And Peter remembered the word of Jesus, which said unto him, Before the cock crow, thou shalt deny me thrice. And he went out, and wept bitterly.

When the morning was come, all the chief priests and elders of the people took counsel against Jesus to put him to death: and when they had bound him, they led him away, and delivered him to Pontius Pilate the governor.

Then Judas, which had betrayed him, when he saw that he was condemned, repented himself, and brought again the thirty pieces of silver to the chief priests and elders, saying, I have sinned in that I have betrayed the innocent blood. And they said, What is that to us? . . . And he cast down the pieces of silver in the temple . . . and went and hanged himself. . . .

And Jesus stood before the governor: and the governor asked him, saying, Art thou the King of the Jews? And Jesus said unto him, Thou sayest. . . . Now at that feast the governor was wont to release unto the people a prisoner, whom they would. And they had then a notable prisoner, called Barabbas. Therefore when they were gathered together, Pilate said unto them, Whom will ye that I release unto you? Barabbas, or Jesus which is called Christ? . . . They said, Barabbas. Pilate saith unto them, What shall I do then with Jesus which is called Christ? They all say unto him, Let him be crucified. And the governor said, Why, what evil hath he done? But they cried out the more, saying, Let him be crucified. When Pilate saw that he could prevail nothing, but that rather a tumult was made, he took water, and washed his hands before the multitude, saying, I am innocent of the blood of this just person: see ye to it. . . . Then the soldiers of the governor took Jesus into the common hall, and gathered unto him the whole band of soldiers. And they stripped him, and put on him a scarlet robe. And when they had plaited a crown of thorns, they put it upon his head, and a reed in his right hand: and they bowed the knee before him, and mocked him, saying, Hail, King of the Jews! And they spit upon him, and took the reed, and smote him on the head. . . .

And they bring him unto the place Golgotha, which is, being interpreted, The place of a skull. And they gave him to drink wine mingled with myrrh: but he received it not. . . . And with him they crucify two thieves; the one on his right hand, and the other on his left. And the Scripture was fulfilled, which saith, And he was numbered with the transgressors. And they that passed by railed on him, wagging their heads. . . . Likewise also the chief priests mocking said among themselves with the scribes, He saved others; himself he cannot save. Let Christ the King of Israel descend now from the cross, that we may see and believe. And they that were crucified with him reviled him.

And when the sixth hour was come, there was darkness over the whole land until the ninth hour. And at the ninth hour Jesus cried with a loud voice, saying, Eloi, Eloi, lama sabachthani? which is, being interpreted, My God, my God, why hast thou forsaken me? And some of them that stood by, when they heard

Crown of thorns and three nails mean Christ's Passion on Cross

it, said, Behold, he calleth Elias. And one ran and filled a sponge full of vinegar, and put it on a reed, and gave him to drink, saying, Let alone; let us see whether Elias will come to take him down. And Jesus cried with a loud voice, and gave up the ghost. And the veil of the temple was rent in twain. . . . And when the centurion, which stood over against him, saw that he so cried out, and gave up the ghost, he said, Truly this man was the Son of God. . . .

When the even was come, there came a rich man of Arimathea, named Joseph, who also himself was Jesus' disciple. He went to Pilate, and begged the body of Jesus. Then Pilate commanded the body to be delivered. And when Joseph had taken the body, he wrapped it in a clean linen cloth, and laid it in his own new tomb, which he had hewn out in the rock: and he rolled a great stone to the door of the sepulchre. . . . Now the next day, that followed the day of the preparation, the chief priests and Pharisees came together unto Pilate, saying, Sir, we remember that that deceiver said, while he was yet alive, After three days I will rise again. Command therefore that the sepulchre be made sure until the third day, lest his disciples come by night, and steal him away, and say unto the people, He is risen from the dead: so the last error shall be worse than the first. Pilate said unto them, Ye have a watch: go your way, make it as sure as ye can. So they went, and made the sepulchre sure, sealing the stone, and setting a watch.

—JOHN 12; LUKE 19; MATTHEW 21; LUKE 19; MATTHEW 22; MARK 12; MATTHEW 26; MARK 14; JOHN 13; MARK 14; LUKE 22; MARK 14; JOHN 18; MATTHEW 26, 27; MARK 15; MATTHEW 27

The Christian religion is founded on the conviction of the disciples that Jesus rose from the dead the third day and appeared to many of them in various places.

THE RESURRECTION

AND when the sabbath was past, Mary Magdalene, and Mary the mother of James, and Salome, had bought sweet spices, that they might come and anoint him. And very early in the morning, the first day of the week, they came unto the sepulchre at the rising of the sun. . . . And when they looked, they saw that the stone was rolled away: for it was very great. And entering into the sepulchre, they saw a young man sitting on the right side, clothed in a long white garment. . . . And he saith unto them, Be not affrighted: ye seek Jesus of Nazareth, which was crucified: he is risen; he is not here: behold the place where they laid him. But go your way, tell his disciples and Peter that he goeth before you into Galilee: there shall ye see him. . . . And they . . . fled from the sepulchre. . . .

Then arose Peter, and ran unto the sepulchre; and stooping down, he beheld the linen clothes laid by themselves, and departed, wondering in himself at that which was come to pass. And, behold, two of them went that same day to a village called Emmaus, which was from Jerusalem about threescore furlongs. And they talked together of all these things which had happened. And it came to pass, that, while they communed together and reasoned, Jesus himself drew near, and went with them. But their eyes were holden that they should not know him. . . . And it came to pass, as he sat at meat with them, he took bread, and blessed it, and brake, and gave to them. And their eyes were opened, and they knew him; and he vanished out of their sight. . . . And they rose up the same hour, and returned to Jerusalem, and found the eleven gathered, and them that were with them, Saying, The Lord is risen indeed. . . .

And as they thus spake, Jesus himself stood in the midst of them, and saith unto them, Peace be unto you. But they were terrified and affrighted, and supposed that they had seen a spirit. And he said unto them, Why are ye troubled? and why do thoughts arise in your hearts? Behold my hands and my feet, that it is I myself: handle me, and see; for a spirit hath not flesh and bones, as ye see me have. And when he had thus spoken, he showed them his hands and his feet. And while they yet believed not for joy, and wondered, he said unto them, Have ye here any meat? And they gave him a piece of broiled fish, and of a honeycomb. And he took it, and did eat before them. . . . Then opened he their understanding, that they might understand the Scriptures, and said unto them, Thus it is written, and thus it behooved Christ to suffer, and to rise from the dead the third day: and that repentance and remission of sins should be preached in his name among all nations, beginning at Jerusalem. And ye are witnesses. . . .

But Thomas . . . was not with them when Jesus came. The other disciples therefore said unto him, We have seen the Lord. But he said unto them, Except I shall see in his hands the print of the nails . . . and thrust my hand into his side, I will not believe. And after eight days again his disciples were within, and Thomas with them: then came Jesus, the doors being shut, and stood in the midst, and said, Peace be unto you. Then saith he to Thomas, Reach hither thy finger, and behold my hands; and reach hither thy hand, and thrust it into my side; and be not faithless, but believing. And Thomas answered and said unto him, My Lord and my God. Jesus saith unto him, Thomas, because thou has seen me, thou hast believed: blessed are they that have not seen, and yet have believed. . . .

—MARK 16; LUKE 24; JOHN 20

Clover leaf was used by St. Patrick to explain Trinity to the Irish

In the first decades after Jesus' Ascension into Heaven, 40 days after His Resurrection, Christianity spread swiftly from a small movement within Judaism to a far-flung church. In the same period Jesus, Whose followers had first thought of Him as the Jewish Messiah, came to be regarded as the Redeemer of the whole world.

This almost explosive expansion of Christianity is narrated in the Acts and the Epistles. Peter, the one disciple who had denied Jesus with oaths and before witnesses, became now the militant leader of the fellowship. Soon, as Jesus had promised, the Holy Ghost (or Holy Spirit, the third member of the Trinity) descended on the little band with a gift of tongues and energy that sent them into all parts of the known world as powerfully persuasive evangelists to spread the word of Christ.

The mightiest of all these missionaries—even though not a member of the original band—was Paul, the outstanding figure in the second half of the New Testament. He began as Saul, a feared persecutor of Christians, and after his vision of Christ on the road to Damascus he also became known as Paul (for more on Peter and Paul, see pages 195–7). His forceful leadership against compelling Gentile converts to be circumcised and to follow Jewish dietary and other laws immensely broadened the field of Christian evangelism. Paul labored long in Asia Minor and later established the first known Christian churches in Europe. During a long imprisonment in Rome, before he was executed, he actively continued his work by preaching and by writing many of his great epistles.

The book of Acts was written by Luke and, like his Gospel, is addressed to Theophilus, otherwise unknown.

ACTS OF THE APOSTLES

THE former treatise have I made, O Theophilus, of all that Jesus began both to do and teach, until the day in which he was taken up, after that he through the Holy Ghost had given commandments unto the apostles whom he had chosen: to whom also he showed himself alive after his passion by many . . . proofs, being seen of them forty days, and speaking of the things pertaining to the kingdom of God: and, being assembled together with them, commanded them that they should not depart from Jerusalem, but wait for the promise of the Father, which, saith he, ye have heard of me. For John truly baptized with water; but ye shall be baptized with the Holy Ghost not many days hence. When they therefore were come together, they asked of him . . . Lord, wilt thou at this time restore again the kingdom to Israel? And he said unto them, It is not for you to know the time or the seasons, which the Father hath put in his own power. But ye shall receive power, after that the Holy Ghost is come upon you: and ye shall be witnesses unto me both in Jerusalem, and in all Judaea, and in Samaria, and unto the uttermost part of the earth.

And when he had spoken these things, while they beheld, he was taken up; and a cloud received him out of their sight. And while they looked steadfastly toward heaven as he went up, behold; two men stood by them in white apparel; which also said, Ye men of Galilee, why stand ye gazing up into heaven? this same Jesus, which is taken up from you into heaven, shall so come in like manner as ye have seen him go into heaven. . . . And when the day of Pentecost was fully come, they were all with one accord in one place. And suddenly there came a sound from heaven as of a rushing mighty wind, and it filled all the house where they were sitting. And there appeared unto them cloven tongues like as of fire, and it sat upon each of them. And they were all filled with the Holy Ghost, and began to speak with other tongues, as the Spirit gave them utterance.

And there were dwelling at Jerusalem Jews, devout men, out of every nation under heaven. . . . And they were all amazed and marvelled, saying one to another, Behold, are not all these which speak Galileans? And how hear we every man in our own tongue, wherein we were born? Parthians, and Medes, and Elamites, and the dwellers in Mesopotamia, and in Judaea . . . and Asia, Phrygia, and Pamphylia, in Egypt, and in the parts of Libya about Cyrene, and strangers of Rome, Jews and proselytes, Cretes and Arabians, we do hear them speak in our tongues the wonderful works of God. And they were all amazed, and were in doubt, saying . . . What meaneth this? . . .

But Peter, standing up with the eleven, lifted up his voice, and said unto them . . . Ye men of Israel, hear these words; Jesus of Nazareth . . . ye have taken, and by wicked hands have crucified and slain: Whom God hath raised up, having loosed the pains of death. . . . Therefore let all the house of Israel know assuredly, that God hath made that same Jesus, whom ye have crucified, both Lord and Christ.

Now when they heard this, they were pricked in their heart, and said unto Peter and to the rest of the apostles, Men and brethren, what shall we do? Then Peter said unto them, Repent, and be baptized every one of you in the name of Jesus Christ for the remission of sins. . . . They that gladly received his word were baptized: and the same day there were added unto them about three thousand souls. . . .

As for Saul, he made havoc of the church, entering into every house, and haling men and women committed them to prison. . . . And Saul, yet breathing out threatenings and slaughter against the disciples of the Lord, went unto the high priest, and desired of him letters to Damascus to the synagogues, that if he found any of this way, whether they were men or women, he might bring them bound unto Jerusalem.

And as he journeyed, he came near Damascus: and suddenly there shined round about him a light from heaven: and he fell to the earth, and heard a voice saying unto him, Saul, Saul, why persecutest thou me? And he said, Who art thou, Lord? And the Lord said, I am Jesus whom thou persecutest: it is hard for thee to kick against the pricks. And he trembling and astonished said, Lord, what wilt thou have me to do? And the Lord said unto him, Arise, and go into the city, and it shall be told thee what thou must do. . . . And Saul arose from the earth; and when his eyes were opened, he saw no man. . . .

There was a certain disciple at Damascus, named Ananias; and to him said the Lord in a vision . . . Arise, and go into the street which is called Straight, and inquire in the house of Judas for one called Saul, of Tarsus: for, behold, he prayeth, and hath seen in a vision a man named Ananias. . . .

And Ananias went his way, and entered into the house; and putting his hands on him said, Brother Saul, the Lord, even Jesus, that appeared unto thee in the way as thou camest, hath sent me, that thou mightest receive thy sight, and be filled with the Holy Ghost. And immediately there fell from his eyes as it had been scales: and he received sight forthwith, and arose, and was baptized. And when he had received meat, he was strengthened. Then was Saul certain days with the disciples which were at Damascus. And straightway he preached Christ in the synagogues, that he is the Son of God. But all that heard him were amazed, and said; Is not this he that destroyed them which called on this name in Jerusalem, and came hither for that intent, that he might bring them bound unto the chief priests? But Saul increased . . . in strength, and confounded the Jews which dwelt at Damascus, proving that this is very Christ. And after that many days were fulfilled, the Jews took counsel to kill him: but their laying wait was known of Saul. And they watched the gates day and night to kill him. Then the disciples took him by night, and let him down . . . the wall in a basket. . . .

And the apostles and brethren that were in Judaea heard that the Gentiles had also received the word of God. And when Peter was come up to Jerusalem, [those] that were of the circumcision contended with him, saying, Thou wentest in to men uncircumcised, and didst eat with them. But Peter rehearsed the matter from the beginning. . . . When they heard these things, they held their peace, and glorified God, saying, Then hath God also to the Gentiles granted repentance unto life. . . .

Then tidings of these things came unto the ears of the church which was in Jerusalem: and they sent forth Barnabas. . . . Then departed Barnabas to Tarsus, for to seek Saul: and when he had found him, he brought him unto Antioch. And . . . a whole year they assembled themselves with the church, and taught much people. And the disciples were called Christians first in Antioch. . . .

Then Saul (who is also called Paul), filled with the Holy Ghost . . . stood up, and beckoning with his hand said, Men of Israel, and ye that fear God, give audience. The God of this people of Israel chose our fathers, and exalted the people when they dwelt as strangers in the land of Egypt, and with a high arm brought he them out of it. . . . God, according to his promise, raised unto Israel a Saviour, Jesus. . . . Men and brethren, children of the stock of Abraham, and whosoever among you feareth God, to you is the word of this salvation sent. . . . Be it known unto you therefore, men and brethren, that through this man is preached unto you the forgiveness of sins: and by him all that believe are justified from all things, from which ye could not be justified by the law of Moses. . . .

And when the Jews were gone out of the synagogue, the Gentiles besought that these words might be preached to them. . . .

And the next sabbath day came almost the whole city together to hear the word of God. But when the Jews saw the multitudes, they were filled with envy, and spake against those things which were spoken by Paul, contradicting and blaspheming. Then Paul and Barnabas waxed bold, and said, It was necessary that the word of God should first have been spoken to you: but seeing ye put it from you, and judge yourselves unworthy of everlasting life, lo, we turn to the Gentiles. For so hath the Lord commanded us, saying, I have set thee to be a light of the Gentiles, that thou shouldest be for salvation unto the ends of the earth. And when the Gentiles heard this, they were glad, and glorified the word of the Lord: and as many as were ordained to eternal life believed. . . .

And Paul chose Silas, and departed, being recommended by the brethren unto the grace of God. And he went through Syria and Cilicia, confirming the churches. . . . Now when they had gone throughout Phrygia and the region of Galatia, and were forbidden of the Holy Ghost to preach the word in Asia, after they were come to Mysia, they assayed to go into Bithynia: but the Spirit suffered them not. And they passing by Mysia came down to Troas. And a vision appeared to Paul in the night; There stood a man of Macedonia, and prayed him, saying, Come over into Macedonia, and help us. . . .

And they that conducted Paul brought him unto Athens: and receiving a commandment unto Silas and Timotheus for to come to him with all speed, they departed. Now while Paul waited for them at Athens, his spirit was stirred in him, when he saw the city wholly given to idolatry. Therefore disputed he in the synagogue with the Jews, and with the devout persons, and in the market daily with them that met with him. . . .

Then Paul stood in the midst of Mars' hill, and said, Ye men of Athens . . . ye are too superstitious. For as I passed by, and beheld your devotions, I found an altar with this inscription, TO THE UNKNOWN GOD. Whom therefore ye ignorantly worship, him declare I unto you. God that made the world and all things therein, seeing that he is Lord of heaven and earth, dwelleth not in temples made with hands; neither is worshipped with men's hands, as though he needed any thing, seeing he giveth to all life, and breath, and all things; and hath made of one blood all nations of men for to dwell on all the face of the earth . . . for in him we live, and move, and have our being; as certain also of your own poets have said, for we are also his offspring. Forasmuch then as we are the offspring of God, we ought not to think that the Godhead is like unto gold, or silver, or stone, graven by art and man's device. . . . God . . . now commandeth all men every where to repent . . . he hath appointed a day, in the which he will judge the world in righteousness by that man whom he hath ordained; whereof he hath given assurance . . . in that he hath raised him from the dead.

Lily, for purity, has become the flower of the Virgin Mary

And when they heard of the resurrection of the dead, some mocked: and others said, We will hear thee again of this matter. So Paul departed from among them. Howbeit certain men clave unto him, and believed. . . .

—ACTS 1, 2, 8–9, 11, 13, 15–17

The Epistles occupy almost one-third of the New Testament and contain some of its most familiar teachings. Less familiar today are the apocalyptic writings (Revelation and certain Gospel chapters such as Mark 13, Matthew 24 and Luke 21), which do not seem as urgently important to most present-day Christians as they did to the first-century followers of Christ who thought the world would soon end.

Of the 21 epistles, 13 are ascribed to Paul. These depict his amazing ability to organize and supervise new churches in many lands, his great endurance and determination, and above all the deep spiritual vitality which did so much to shape world Christianity. The word "charity" (often translated "love"), in his most famous utterance, signifies the active love of one's fellow man because of union in Christ.

EPISTLES OF PAUL

THOUGH I speak with the tongues of men and of angels, and have not charity, I am become as sounding brass, or a tinkling cymbal. And though I have the gift of prophecy, and understand all mysteries, and all knowledge; and though I have all faith, so that I could remove mountains, and have not charity, I am nothing. And though I bestow all my goods to feed the poor, and though I give my body to be burned, and have not charity, it profiteth me nothing. . . .

Charity never faileth: but whether there be prophecies, they shall fail; whether there be tongues, they shall cease; whether there be knowledge, it shall vanish away. For we know in part, and we prophesy in part. But when that which is perfect is come, then that which is in part shall be done away. When I was a child, I spake as a child, I understood as a child, I thought as a child: but when I became a man, I put away childish things. For now we see through a glass, darkly; but then face to face: now I know in part; but then shall I know even as also I am known. And now abideth faith, hope, charity, these three; but the greatest of these is charity. . . .

For the love of Christ constraineth us; because we thus judge, that if one died for all, then were all dead: and that he died for all, that they which live should not henceforth live unto themselves, but unto him which died for them, and rose again. . . . And all things are of God, who hath reconciled us to himself by Jesus Christ, and hath given to us the ministry of reconciliation; to wit, that God was in Christ, reconciling the world unto himself, not imputing their trespasses unto them; and hath committed unto us the word of reconciliation. . . .

We then, as workers together with him, beseech you also that ye receive not the grace of God in vain. . . . But in . . . patience, in afflictions, in necessities, in distresses . . . by pureness, by knowledge, by long-suffering, by kindness, by the Holy Ghost, by love unfeigned, by the word of truth, by the power of God . . . as unknown, and yet well known; as dying, and, behold, we live; as chastened, and not killed; as sorrowful, yet alway rejoicing; as poor, yet making many rich; as having nothing, and yet possessing all things. . . .

Of the Jews five times received I forty stripes save one. Thrice was I beaten with rods, once was I stoned, thrice I suffered shipwreck, a night and a day I have been in the deep; in journeyings often, in perils of waters, in perils of robbers, in perils by mine own countrymen . . . in hunger and thirst, in fastings often, in cold and nakedness. Beside those things that are without, that which cometh upon me daily, the care of all the churches. Who is weak, and I am not weak? who is offended, and I burn not? . . . I will glory of the things which concern mine infirmities. . . .

For the law of the Spirit of life in Christ Jesus hath made me free from the law of sin and death. . . . God sending his own Son in the likeness of sinful flesh, and for sin, condemned sin in the flesh. . . . For to be carnally minded is death; but to be spiritually minded is life and peace. . . . And if Christ be in you, the body is dead because of sin; but the Spirit is life because of righteousness. . . . The Spirit itself beareth witness with our spirit, that we are the children of God: And if children, then heirs; heirs of God, and joint-heirs with Christ. . . . The sufferings of this present time are not worthy to be compared with the glory which shall be revealed in us. . . . If God be for us, who can be against us? . . . For I am persuaded, that neither death, nor life, nor angels, nor principalities, nor powers . . . nor height, nor depth, nor any other creature, shall be able to separate us from the love of God. . . .

Bless them which persecute you: bless, and curse not. Rejoice with them that do rejoice, and weep with them that weep. . . . Therefore if thine enemy hunger, feed him; if he thirst, give him drink: for in so doing thou shalt heap coals of fire on his head. Be not overcome of evil, but overcome evil with good. . . .

Bear ye one another's burdens, and so fulfil the law of Christ. . . . But let every man prove his own work . . . for every man shall bear his own burden. . . . Be not deceived; God is not mocked: for whatsoever a man soweth, that shall he also reap. For he that soweth to his flesh shall of the flesh reap corruption; but he that soweth to the Spirit shall of the Spirit reap life everlasting. And let us not be weary in well doing. . . .

Rejoice in the Lord always: and again I say, Rejoice. . . . And the peace of God, which passeth all understanding, shall keep your hearts and minds through Christ Jesus. . . . Whatsoever things are true, whatsoever things are honest, whatsoever things are just, whatsoever things are pure, whatsoever things are lovely, whatsoever things are of good report; if there be any virtue, and if there be any praise, think on these things. . . .

Be strong in the Lord, and in the power of his might. Put on the whole armor of God, that ye may be able to stand against the wiles of the devil. . . . And take the helmet of salvation, and the sword of the Spirit, which is the word of God: praying always with all prayer and supplication in the Spirit, and watching thereunto with all perseverance and supplication. . . .

But of the times and the seasons, brethren, ye have no need that I write unto you. For yourselves know perfectly that the day of the Lord so cometh as a thief in the night. For when they shall say, Peace and safety; then sudden destruction cometh upon them, as travail upon a woman with child; and they shall not escape. But ye, brethren, are not in darkness, that that day should overtake you as a thief. Ye are all the children of light, and the children of the day: we are not of the night, nor of darkness. Therefore let us not sleep, as do others; let us watch and be sober. For they that sleep sleep in the night; and they that be drunken are drunken in the night. But let us, who are of the day, be sober, putting on the breastplate of faith and love; and for a helmet, the hope of salvation. For God hath not appointed us to wrath, but to obtain salvation by our Lord Jesus Christ, who died for us, that, whether we wake or sleep, we should live together with him. . . .

For I am now ready to be offered, and the time of my departure is at hand. I have fought a good fight, I have finished my course, I have kept the faith: henceforth there is laid up for me a crown of righteousness, which the Lord, the righteous judge, shall give me at that day: and not to me only, but unto all them also that love his appearing. . . .

—1 CORINTHIANS 13; 2 CORINTHIANS 5, 6, 11;
ROMANS 8, 12; GALATIANS 6; PHILIPPIANS 4;
EPHESIANS 6; 1 THESSALONIANS 5; 2 TIMOTHY 4

Said the Lord, "I am Alpha and Omega, the beginning and the ending . . ."

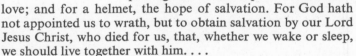

All the teachings of Jesus' followers are authorized by the resurrected Christ's final words to His disciples, uttered just before He ascended into heaven.

THE FINAL BIDDING

THEN the eleven disciples went away into Galilee, into a mountain where Jesus had appointed them. And when they saw him, they worshiped him: but some doubted. And Jesus came and spake unto them, saying, All power is given unto me in heaven and in earth. Go ye therefore, and teach all nations, baptizing them in the name of the Father, and of the Son, and of the Holy Ghost: teaching them to observe all things whatsoever I have commanded you: and, lo, I am with you alway, even unto the end of the world. Amen.

—MATTHEW 28

GOING FORTH, as Jesus commanded, Father Enrique Salazar sets out on one of his regular muleback rides over the steep hillsides of central Mexico. A priest to 35 villages of Indians in a 900-square-mile parish, Father Salazar, who was raised in Mexico City and trained in Rome, gives medicine and engineering advice to his parishioners in addition to spiritual counsel. Few of them can understand his Spanish, but all are thankful for the help he gives them.

CHRISTIANITY TODAY

More people are now trying to lead Christian lives than at any time since the Resurrection. The final section of this book reports some stirring aspects of the Christian present. One is the mighty effort toward ecumenical (*i.e.*, world-wide) unity being made by so many churches (*right*). Then there are the multitude of Christian sights and sounds across the U.S., largest Christian land, and equally heartening developments in the Church of South India. The final pages show how the Christian life is practiced in the sacraments Jesus inspired.

CHRISTIAN UNITY is the goal of the World Council of Churches, whose 1954 Assembly drew 125,000 adherents to an impressive demonstration (*above*) in Chicago's Soldier Field. The Council, federation of Protestant, Orthodox and Anglican churches, links 162 communions in 47 countries.

VILLAGE UNITY has been achieved by Trinity Lutheran Church (*left*) in Freistatt, Mo., where religion guides daily life. The church, of which W. J. Stelling (*in pulpit*) is pastor, has village's only school and is a major reason Freistatt has had only one divorce and no arrests in 20 years.

THE CHURCHGOING U.S.

America's spectacular religious upsurge both heartens and challenges Christian leaders

In the U.S. nearly 100 million people belong to Christian churches—far more than in any other land on earth. Religion commands the attention and the energy of Americans more thoroughly than at any time since the days of the country's first devout settlers. In the U.S., Protestants have 299,586 ordained ministers and the Roman Catholics have 48,349 priests, 159,545 nuns and 8,868 lay brothers. Seminary enrollments are at an alltime high. Up to 60 million Americans attend church each Sunday. More than 36 million are enrolled in Sunday schools, including 13 million adults who agree with Baptist Minister G. Beauchamp Vick of Detroit when he says, "I never met anyone who knew too much about the Bible."

To accommodate such huge numbers, a record volume of religious building (estimated at $970 million for Protestants and $500 million for Catholics in 1956) is under way, creating new structures which themselves often reflect

INTERRACIAL AMITY prevails in Methodist Church at Old Mystic, Conn., where the congregation is white and the minister, the Rev. Simon P. Montgomery (*above, singing the offertory*), is a Negro. One member expressed the sense of many: "It was the work of the Lord that sent him here." INTERPARISH COOPERATION (*below*) helps the Monadnock Congregational Church in Colebrook, N.H., whose members, shown rising to

SERVICE FOR MIGRANTS who work in the bean fields at Belle Glade, Fla. is facilitated by the National Council of Churches, which reaches some 200,000 of the country's 2 million itinerant farm laborers. The organization would like to expand its migrant work but lacks necessary funds.

sing "Holy, Holy, Holy!" are served by a circuit-riding preacher. He travels 24,000 miles a year, ministering to as many as five scattered churches.

the freshness and vitality of American religion. All across the U.S., new and sometimes surprising shapes mark the greatest revolution in church architecture since the Renaissance.

The varieties of American religious expression seem endless, from boisterous all-night gospel sings in jammed civic auditoriums to the stately unfolding of ancient ritual in cathedrals. U.S. Christians range from Orthodox who still use the original Greek of the New Testament to the Mennonites, established in Switzerland in 1525, to new groups such as the Church of the Foursquare Gospel organized by Aimee Semple McPherson in 1927.

The Rev. Billy Graham has reached more people, both at home and abroad, than any U.S. evangelist. The most famous Catholic

and Protestant preachers of this generation, Bishop Fulton J. Sheen and Dr. Norman Vincent Peale, command tremendous audiences through church sermons, published writings and, above all, television and radio appearances. Nor is it all a matter of one-man shows. Trade publishers issue an average of two religious books daily, many of which have become best sellers. In Atlanta five Protestant sects and several related bodies jointly run a radio-television center whose programs are used by some 1,300 stations. Catholic magazine and newspaper circulation in the U.S. has grown to almost 24 million.

The Christian note of contrition is, however, often lacking in U.S. religious life. Many Americans think that churchgoing makes them

EVANGELICAL HYMN, "Are You Washed in the Blood of the Lamb?" stirs an Assembly of God congregation in Mexico, Mo. who keep time with handclaps as they sing. The Assemblies of God are among the fast-growing Pentecostal sects whose believers often show great spiritual ardor.

281

better than their neighbors. And racial discrimination has prompted a leading Negro to note that "11 o'clock Sunday morning is the most segregated hour of American life." Some Protestants seem to seek within Christianity only a convenient "cult of reassurance," trying to use God instead of wanting God to use them. Certain churches even tend to neglect central Christian doctrines in order to stress obvious virtues like morality, honesty, thrift or patriotism as reasons why people should support them. The result, according to Theologian Jerald C. Brauer of the University of Chicago: "As more and more people are won into the churches, the faith may actually have less and less influence on their total lives."

Roman Catholicism, though far more definite than Protestantism in its teaching and doctrine, has been similarly affected by the American scene. Within the structure of its 130 U.S. dioceses the faithful are born, guided, taught, healed, married, sheltered and consoled; to them the Church is at once teacher, ruler and sanctifier. American Catholicism has shared the general growth of U.S. churches, and the Catholics have greatly expanded their parochial school system to make sure that Catholic children are properly educated and indoctrinated. Thoughtful leaders, however, now fear that many American Catholics have adapted themselves almost too comfortably to the world around them.

But the threads of doubt that are woven into the fabric of U.S. religious expansion, together with the very readiness of American believers to ask themselves searching questions, are in themselves a measure of Christian vitality in the U.S. and the faith's capacity for growth. America has made eloquent contributions to the religious heritage of the world,

SISTER OF CHARITY who works at a Roman Catholic settlement house on Chicago's West Side dresses a small boy both of whose parents have to go to work. The Chicago archdiocese, largest in U.S., operates 58 charitable agencies including 26 hospitals, 14 orphanages and 11 homes for aged.

DEVOUT OF ALL AGES, 75,000 strong, crowd New York's Polo Grounds for a Roman Catholic service during which they recite the rosary in unison. The rally pictured is part of world-wide campaign by Father Patrick Peyton.

SLUM PRIEST, Rev. C. Kilmer Myers (*opposite*), serves Episcopal mission parishes in rundown urban areas. With his colleagues he has brought new hope to minority groups, concentrating first on the children and then adults.

from the work of great theologians (*see pages 248–51*) to new church movements, to widespread introduction of such noble spirituals as "Swing Low, Sweet Chariot." Today more than two-thirds of the Protestant foreign missionaries in the world are from the U.S. and Canada. U.S. Catholicism today actively supports more than 5,000 missionaries in other parts of the world, though as late as 1908 the Vatican considered the U.S. a mission field.

Another hopeful sign for the future is the greater depth of religious interest shown by Americans under 25. A recent Cornell survey of 7,000 students in 12 colleges and universities showed that eight out of ten felt they need a religious faith; only one percent described themselves as atheists. Many churches have tackled the problem of Christian illiteracy at its root by greatly improving their Sunday-school courses and training better teachers for them. The next American generation may well have not only the largest but the best-informed group of Christians of any country in history.

FACTORY FELLOWSHIP, a devotional session in lunch period every Friday at the Douglas Aircraft plant in Long Beach, Calif., draws anywhere from 150 to 200 employees to the assembly-line room. Men and women sometimes have to sit in unfinished planes to listen as they eat their meal.

FRIENDSHIP CIRCLE, with all present joining hands, concludes a meeting of teen-agers who belong to the Oneonta Congregational Church of South Pasadena, Calif. Church keeps youngsters busy not only Sunday but all week.

CAMPUS WORSHIP at Massachusetts Institute of Technology emphasizes the resurgence of religion among U.S. students. Striking cylindrical chapel, 50 feet in diameter, uses "halo" illumination over metal screen hung on rods.

SYMBOL OF ONENESS in the South Indian service is the "Kiss of Peace," now widely used by interfaith groups around the world. In it each worshiper clasps his neighbor's hands and says: "The peace of God be with you."

A TRIUMPH OF UNITY

Five groups in unprecedented merger form the Church of South India

Tradition says that after witnessing the risen Christ, Thomas the Apostle preached in India and founded the Mar Thoma Syrian Church of Malabar which still exists there. The Jesuit Francis Xavier led a mission to India in 1542 and the first Protestants, two young men from Denmark, arrived in 1706. The first missionaries from the United States reached India in 1812 and others from many countries have followed. Despite this long, devoted evangelism, Christians remain a tiny minority of the Indian people. One great problem is described thus by Douglas Webster: "A Brahmin in the train professed faith in Christ, but, asked why

he did not join the Church, replied *Which?* Those who in Hinduism had been united soon began to find themselves in Christ divided."

Out of this background has come a daring and imaginative Christian experiment, by far the most promising effort yet made by Protestantism toward church unity. In 1947 five denominations merged to form the Church of South India and a leading Presbyterian, Dr. Henry Sloane Coffin, was moved to call it the "most significant event in ecclesiastical history since the Reformation." And in an era when the traditional sort of "foreign" missions is ending—because so many nations and peoples

ANGLICAN POMP at the laying of a school cornerstone (*left*) is a concession to local member churches, which may retain their old rituals for thirty years from the date of union.

SISTERS IN WHITE on preaching tour belong to a women's order which is one of the few in Protestantism to practice celibacy. The members operate village schools and dispensaries.

BAPTISM IN COW TROUGH is performed by Bishop Lesslie Newbigin, a former Presbyterian who often visits villages of his dusty Madurai-Ramnad diocese afoot. Son of a British shipowner, the bishop gets $1,560 per year.

consider it a kind of religious colonialism—South India also offers a hopeful new example of local Christian initiative. What distinguishes it from other church mergers is that the Church of South India embraces Methodist, Presbyterian, Congregationalist and Reformed churches and four Anglican dioceses. For the first time an "episcopal" church with its bishops and ritual has joined with non-hierarchical denominations.

Some Christians fear the union may result in a "watered-down" doctrine. But with more than a million members, most of them resembling the group at the right, the church is building up new disciplines and liturgy and a corps of unpaid lay preachers who have displayed a verve

CEREMONIAL TOUR of lush tropical Travancore is made by Bishop C. K. Jacob (*extreme right*) in a canoe because monsoon has flooded countryside. Bishop, an Indian, comes of a family that once belonged to Syrian Church.

JOYOUS HARVEST FESTIVAL in the village of Sachiapuram—the spot where Bishop Newbigin performed cow trough baptism (*top, left*)—attracts 3,000 worshipers, who sit on meeting-hall floor as sunlight through a matted

LAY PREACHER named Jesudason ("Servant of Jesus"), who is a convert to Christianity, studies his Bible by lamplight. The night after this picture was taken, hostile Hindus burned his home and those of 23 other Christians.

roof dapples the women's bright saris. The ceremony, which lasts three days, was instituted by Anglican missionaries over half a century ago as Christian equivalent of similar Hindu festivals and Church of South India has kept it.

ROADSIDE SERMON is preached to a bullock-driver by Jesudason, who tours the countryside on weekends. Jesudason gets 15 cents a day as a farm laborer. His evangelism is most successful among the Hindu "untouchables."

AN EXAMPLE to farmers, the Rev. Joseph John (*left*) starts his day by plowing. "The man behind the plow is as sacred as the pastor behind the pulpit," says the Rev. Mr. John, whose cooperative farm has inspired other villages.

reminiscent of the early Christians. Likely to affect its policies greatly is an experiment in practical Christianity conducted by the Rev. Joseph John and his doctor wife, Ranjitham. On 56 acres, which they bought for about $100 in the near-wilderness at Deenabandupuram in what is now Andhra state, they have created a model village. It includes a successful cooperative farm, a clinic, an elementary school, an orphanage and an agricultural school that also teaches carpentry and tailoring.

From this school youths go out to build houses, dig compost pits, mend clothes, conduct classes—and preach Christianity. The combination of Christian message and the Gandhian principles of rural uplift is an appealing one to many Indians. A Communist named Ponnusamy, sent to sabotage the work, stayed to become one of Mr. John's devoted assistants, teaching illiterate adults.

But the path of the Church of South India is already rocky. Not all Anglicans support the merger. India's national government, pressed by Hindu extremists, has restricted entry of missionaries. Some state governments have taken stern steps against Christianity, and individual Hindus sometimes burn the homes of Christian Indians. Yet "by its very existence," Anglicanism's bishops have said, "the Church of South India presents a challenge to the whole of the rest of Christendom."

PETITION FOR HELP in starting a school is presented to the Rev. Mr. John on the veranda of his house by a deputation from Anjalam, three miles off. Sitting on floor in front of him is Ponnusamy, his ex-Communist assistant.

GOOD SAMARITAN to the farmers and villagers for miles around, the presbyter's wife, Dr. Ranjitham John (the only M.D. in the area), examines patient outside dispensary. Nearly 200 lepers visit her weekly for treatment.

BLESSING OF BREAD by the Rev. Mr. John emphasizes the sacredness of food. He also blesses elements needed for a good harvest—land, water and grain—before breaking off part of each woman's bread to share with flock.

WORSHIP IN PADDIES is reminiscent of Millet's painting, The Angelus. At noon each day the bell of the community center at Deenabandupuram is rung and everyone, whether working in the fields or at home, stops to pray.

PATHWAYS
TO GOD'S GRACE

The sacraments mark key stages of a Christian's worship

For an overwhelming majority of the world's Christians the essence of religious experience is summed up in the sacraments. From infancy to death the sacraments (*see p. 203*) mark the key stages of Christian worship and sustain the individual worshiper. A sacrament, in St. Augustine's words, is the "visible form of an invisible grace." It is an outward act, derived from something Christ did or said, by whose performance and observation the individual receives God's grace. How the sacraments are observed by various Christian groups is shown on these and the next 12 pages.

Catholics (Roman and Eastern Orthodox) and many Anglicans count seven—Baptism, Confirmation, Communion, Marriage, Unction, Penance and Ordination—and Catholics believe that sacraments validly administered provide grace necessarily and at once. Other Anglicans—including some of their brethren in the U.S., the Episcopalians—and a majority of Protestants accept only Baptism and Communion as divinely instituted and hold with Luther that a "sacrament without testament [words to convey it] is the case without the jewel." A minority (Quakers, Unitarians and others) accept no sacraments as such, saying no external act should come between God's will and the believer. But in all Christianity's branches, though arguments over the sacraments have split Christendom, the faithful incorporate in their beliefs or practices what the sacraments express. "There has never been a week," says a Presbyterian minister, "perhaps not a day, since Pentecost that the sacraments have not witnessed to the Christian faith."

BAPTIST: Minister lifts a candidate after immersing her in the tank. A Baptist must be old enough (usually 12 to 14) to understand the sacrament.

RUSSIAN ORTHODOX: Priest anoints a baby with oil, then immerses him in font. Parents do not take part, baby being held by its godmother.

CONGREGATIONAL: With mother holding baby and father watching, minister sprinkles water from a silver bowl on the baby's forehead and says, "I baptize thee in the name of the Father, and of the Son, and of the Holy Ghost."

BAPTISM The individual formally enters Christ's church

"And it came to pass in those days, that Jesus came from Nazareth of Galilee, and was baptized of John in Jordan" (Mark 1:9). Baptism, based on that event, has always been considered the sacrament of initiation into the Christian church. It represents the individual's first act of faith and it seals him as a follower of Christ, washing away previous and original sin (derived from Adam's sin). With Communion, Baptism is recognized by all churches who accept the sacraments at all. While procedures differ from sprinkling (*above*) to total immersion (*opposite*), all use water and all have the deepest spiritual effect on the baptized. Martin Luther was frequently tried in his faith, but in his darkest hours he would repeat the words, "*Baptizatus sum*"—"I have been baptized."

ROMAN CATHOLIC: After blessing baby's mouth with salt (for wisdom) and anointing its breast and back with oil (for fortitude), priest pours water containing holy oil three times in the form of a cross on baby's forehead.

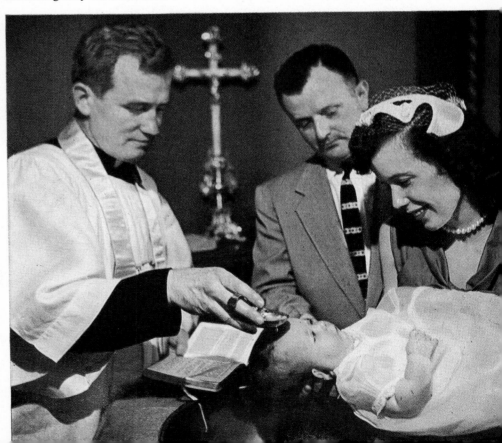

CONFIRMATION The soul receives the Holy Ghost

Confirmation completes the work of Baptism and permits the individual, who is usually between 7 and 14 years old, to assume greater spiritual responsibilities. The sacrament stems from the early evangelistic work of Christ's apostles. "Now when the apostles . . . heard that Samaria had received the word of God, they sent unto them Peter and John: Who . . . prayed for them, that they might receive the Holy Ghost. . . . Then laid they their hands on them, and they received the Holy Ghost" (Acts 8:14–17). For Roman Catholics (*above*) and for Episcopalians

(*opposite, top*), Confirmation is ordinarily administered by a bishop. Orthodox babies are confirmed immediately after they are baptized.

Because they regard its origin as apostolic and not divine, Protestants do not recognize Confirmation as a sacrament, although Episcopalians call it a "lesser" sacrament. The Lutherans once claimed it detracted from the efficacy of Baptism. But soon after the Reformation they reintroduced it, not as a sacrament but a rite which reminds children of the covenant made at Baptism and prepares them for their first Communion.

294

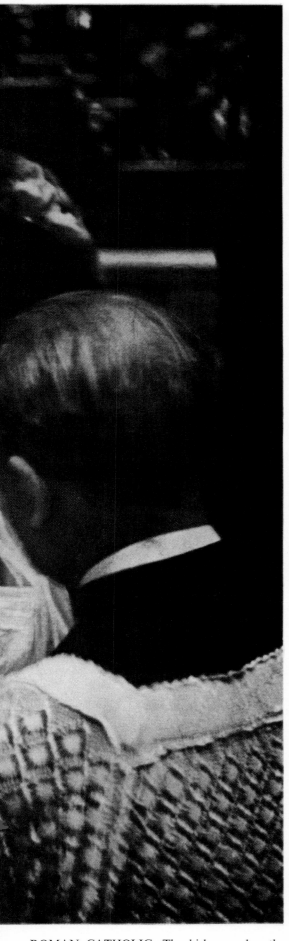

EPISCOPAL: His hands laid on her head, the bishop blesses a candidate, saying, "Defend, O Lord, this thy Child with thy heavenly grace; that she may continue thine for ever. . . ." White for girls and blue for boys are traditional colors for Confirmation, but rule is not followed strictly.

ROMAN CATHOLIC: The bishop makes the sign of the cross on the girl's forehead with chrism (olive oil and balm), saying, ". . . I confirm thee with the chrism of salvation," and blesses her. Then he pats her on the cheek and says, "Peace be with thee." Girl's sponsor stands behind her.

LUTHERAN: A girl kneels at the altar rail as the minister, who has examined her for doctrine, puts his hand on her head and says, ". . . for Jesus' sake, renew and increase in thee the gift of the Holy Ghost. . . ." He then declares to those present that she is a member of the congregation.

ARMENIAN APOSTOLIC: Kneeling by altar and holding a chalice of wine and wafers in his hand, the priest takes a wafer particle from chalice and places it upon the tongue of the communicant, who stands before him. Bread and wine have already been blessed and consecrated by the priest.

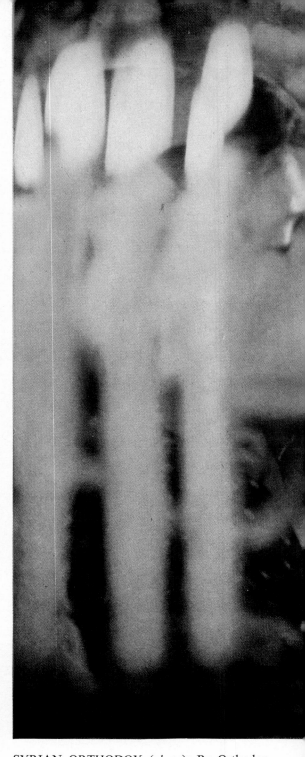

SYRIAN ORTHODOX (*above*): By Orthodox custom children receive Communion immediately after Confirmation, taking it directly from priest.

LUTHERAN: After receiving unleavened wafers passed to them on a small tray, communicants kneeling at altar rail take wine from silver chalice held by the minister, who wipes it after each one finishes. "Take and drink," he says, "this is the Blood of the New Testament, shed for thy sins."

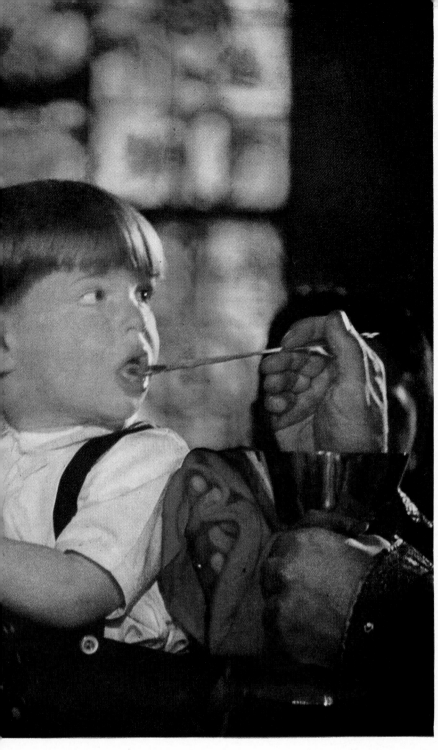

PRESBYTERIAN (*below*): Members of congregation remain in their seats as elders of the church pass among them with trays containing small glasses of grape juice and cubes of bread which have been consecrated by the minister.

ROMAN CATHOLIC: Before transubstantiation takes place, the priest raises chalice of wine and water over altar, offering it to God. Only the priest will drink from it. Others come to altar rail to receive consecrated Hosts (wafers).

COMMUNION Man

partakes of the sacred presence

"This is my body," said Jesus at the Last Supper. And then, "... this is my blood of the new testament, which is shed for many for the remission of sins" (Matthew 26:26, 28). The noblest of the sacraments and the one around which all the others revolve, Holy Communion re-creates the climactic meal of Jesus' life and commemorates His sacrifice for mankind. Roman and Orthodox Catholics, who call the sacrament the Holy Eucharist, believe that when a priest consecrates the bread and wine they are transubstantiated: they become Christ's actual Body and Blood, their appearance alone remaining as before. Most Protestants believe the body and blood are represented only spiritually, and some regard Communion simply as a memorial act. Whether it is taken by young (*above, left*) or old, in wafers or cubes of bread, the sacrament always has immense significance. In partaking of Christ's presence the believer partakes of Christ Himself and nourishes his soul for eternal life.

MARRIAGE The union of man and woman is blessed

While Christ's authorization of Holy Matrimony as a sacrament has been endlessly debated, Catholics and others have traditionally pointed to His presence at the marriage in Cana, where He performed His first miracle, for the required divine sanction. St. Paul added ". . . even as Christ also loved the church, and gave himself for it . . . so ought men to love their wives as their own bodies. . . . This is a great mystery: but I speak concerning Christ and the church" (Ephesians 5:25–32). It is considered a sacrament by Roman Catholics and by the Eastern Orthodox Church, some of the latter's ceremonies being richly elaborate (*opposite*). Protestants, while not denying Marriage's importance, rank it as a ceremony or rite below the sacramental level.

Solemnizing the union of man and woman, Marriage sanctifies human love and the procreation and education of children. The churches have always felt some degree of responsibility for education, secular as well as religious. None is more vigilant than the Roman Catholic which operates an entire educational system of its own. Catholic belief has also led the Vatican to specify that in mixed marriages all children must be brought up within the Catholic faith.

The Roman and Orthodox Churches are also the strictest in their rules concerning divorce, the Roman Church forbidding it and permitting permanent separation only for extreme causes like adultery. An annulment declares a marriage invalid from the beginning. For non-Catholics the rules vary widely but are generally less stringent than for Catholics.

Whether it is performed as a sacrament or a simple religious ceremony, Marriage is one of the most beautiful of all church occurrences. Particularly lovely is the phraseology of the Episcopal Book of Common Prayer which some other churches have adapted for the ceremony and which describes Matrimony as "an honourable estate, instituted of God, signifying unto us the mystical union that is betwixt Christ and His Church." For many the most moving passage is the one from the 1662 Anglican Prayer Book: "With this ring I thee wed; with my body I thee worship, with all my worldly goods I thee endow," with which the marriage is formally sealed, the ring symbolizing both union and eternity.

METHODIST: Near the end of the ceremony the couple kneels at the altar as the minister leads them and the congregation in the Lord's Prayer. Then the minister raises his hands over them (*above*) and pronounces the blessing.

QUAKER: The Friends, some of whom describe Marriage as a "continuing religious sacrament," have unique ceremony in which the couple marry themselves. They rise during a special service and simply say vows to each other.

GREEK ORTHODOX (*opposite*): The best man holds crowns, symbols of equality and virtue, over bride and bridegroom. Placing them on heads signifies marriage is solemnized. Later priest leads couple three times around altar.

PENANCE A
helps sinful mankind

Mercy and compassion, stemming from the life and character of the Savior Himself, have always distinguished the Christian faith. These qualities are embodied in the sacrament of Penance, in which the Christian confesses his sins and is granted absolution, or forgiveness. Penance can be made for specific sins, as is done by Catholics who confess individually to a priest (*opposite, top and bottom*). Or it can be made generally, as it is by the Episcopalians (*below*) who include confession as a part of their regular church service. Other groups such as the Salvation Army (*left*) have spiritual meetings at which sins are admitted.

Penance originated partly from Christ's remarkable powers of healing. He performed miracles not simply to alleviate physical suffering but to demonstrate His greater mission on earth—to free mankind from the bonds of sin. When He healed a palsied man He said, "Thy sins be forgiven thee" (Matthew 9:2). The Christian yearning for such liberation is reflected not only in the sacrament of Penance but in the words "Forgive us our debts" (or "our trespasses") in the Lord's Prayer.

Sacraments exist, said Calvin, to "support the weakness of our faith." This is especially true of Penance which presupposes man's continuing sinfulness. Luther himself, who had gone through torment over his own feeling of

SALVATION ARMY: "Repentance," says the Army, "is the First Condition of Salvation," and while it does not accept sacraments, it maintains a "Mercy Seat" or "Penitent Form" to which, during the Army's religious meetings, members are encouraged to come and confess their sins.

EPISCOPAL: The minister kneels and leads the congregation in the Litany, beseeching the Lord "to give us true repentance; to forgive us all our sins." The Episcopal General Confession, used more often, includes well-known phrase, ". . . We have left undone those things which we ought to have done; And we have done those things which we ought not to have done. . . . But thou, O Lord, have mercy upon us." Minister then pronounces absolution for all.

thorough confession to sanctify the soul

sin before his revolt, was reluctant to give up Penance as a sacrament. He finally did so because he could not accept its divine institution and because he felt it had no visible sign or manifestation—which St. Augustine had required. Catholics say Penance's divine institution derives from Christ's own words, spoken to His disciples after the Resurrection: "... Receive ye the Holy Ghost; whose soever sins ye remit, they are remitted unto them, and whose soever sins ye retain, they are retained" (John 20:22-3). Protestants say that although Christ prescribed Penance He did not clearly institute it as a sacrament.

Either as a sacrament or as a ceremony, Penance is always compounded of two external acts: 1) the confession, which must be accompanied by contrition or sincere repentance, and 2) the absolution. Protestants have stressed repentance, some "fringe" sects making "Repent!" a battle cry. Catholics place an equal value on absolution, in fact allowing only those who have been absolved to receive Holy Communion. For Catholics, confession must be made individually to a priest because the priest has to know what sins have been committed before he can decide whether the Lord's forgiveness should be conferred and what restitution, in the form of extra prayers or contributions, the penitent should make.

ROMAN CATHOLIC: A priest leans forward to hear clearly the confession which is being made to him through the screened partition at left. Devout Catholics usually confess once a week. Under no circumstances may priest use knowledge gained in confession outside the confessional enclosure.

GREEK ORTHODOX: After penitent, kneeling at the front of the church with the priest beside him, has confessed and the priest has asked God for mercy, priest places his stole over penitent's shoulders and pronounces the absolution. Orthodox make confession four or five times a year.

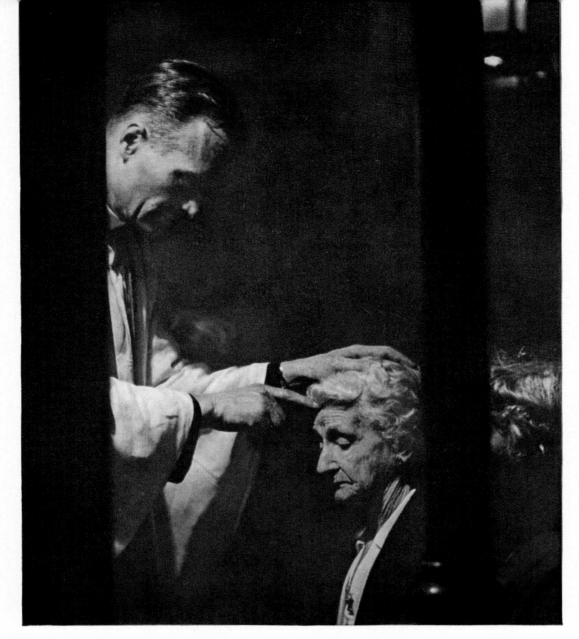

EPISCOPAL: At a weekly "Unction of the Sick" service, a priest, laying his hand on the head of an elderly woman, marks a cross on her forehead with holy oil and asks for mercy "that all thy pain and sickness of body being put to flight, the blessing of health may be restored unto thee."

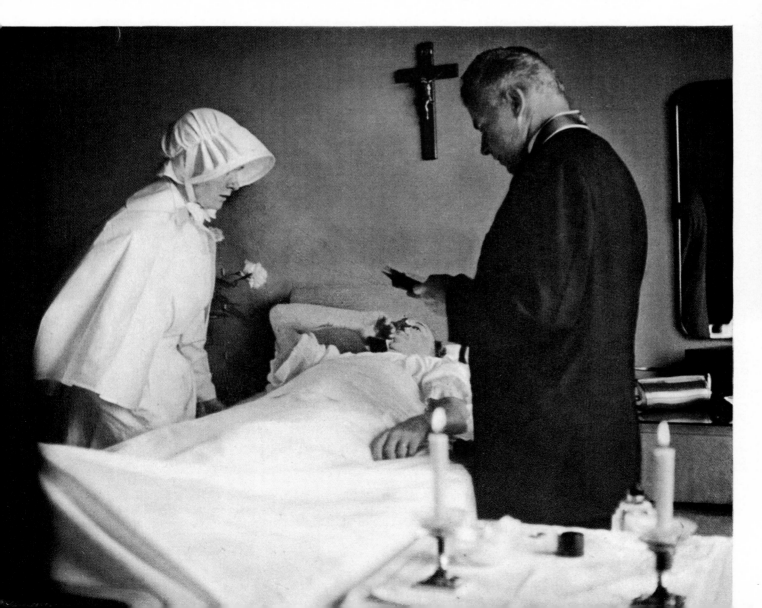

RUMANIAN ORTHODOX: In a home a priest, holding a cross, blesses an ailing woman. He anoints each person seven times and each time says prayer to God, "physician of souls."

ROMAN CATHOLIC (*left*): By a hospital bed a priest begins Extreme Unction while the patient holds a cross to his lips. The sacrament can be offered only once during same illness.

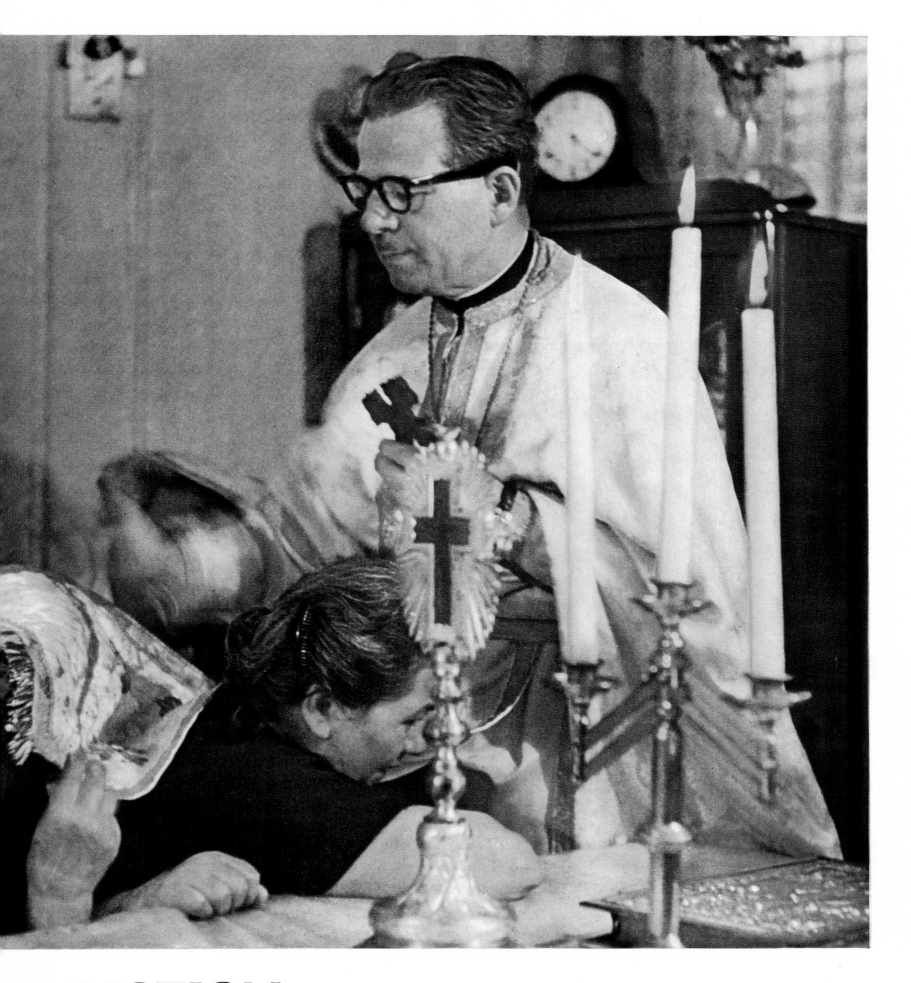

UNCTION The sick and dying are reassured of salvation

"Is any sick among you? let him call for the elders of the church; and let them pray over him, anointing him with oil. . . . And the prayer of faith shall save the sick, and the Lord shall raise him up; and if he have committed sins, they shall be forgiven him." So did the apostle James (5:14–15) set forth the sacramental basis for Unction.

Among Roman Catholics, Unction is administered only when there is danger of death and is called Extreme Unction (*opposite*, *bottom*). Completing the work of Penance, it assures the soul of grace during its last moments on earth, and although the individual should begin by making confession, this requirement is often waived if death is near. For the Eastern Orthodox, Unction is given as often as necessary to give comfort to the sick, and is frequently given in the home (*above*).

Protestants do not regard Unction as a sacrament. But the Episcopal Church has found increasing acceptance for its Unction service (*opposite*, *top*), given in cooperation with medical authorities. A "lesser" sacrament, the service has often helped to alleviate physical suffering.

ORDINATION The ministry perpetuates God's word

As a sacrament bestows something spiritual, the power to administer sacraments is sacred. In the Roman Catholic, Orthodox and Anglican Churches this power is conferred through the sacrament of Ordination, by which bishops or higher prelates make ministers or priests. "As my Father hath sent me," Christ said to His apostles, "even so send I you" (John 20:21). The apostles chose others to ordain and the process has continued in what is called Apostolic Succession. Ordination's decisive point is the laying on of hands. Even Protestants who deny Apostolic Succession use this gesture as a meaningful way of handing down the ministry, perpetuating both the church and God's word for all time.

METHODIST: A candidate is ordained a minister as five elders and a bishop (*white stole*) join in the laying on of hands. As with the Catholics, only the bishop need be there, but presence of others lends warmth to the ceremony.

EPISCOPAL: A great urban cathedral (*right*) arches above the ordaining of ten new members of the clergy, one of whom kneels in center of the chancel to receive the bishop's blessing.

ROMAN CATHOLIC: Robed in white, 36 candidates (*below*) prostrate themselves before the altar while a cardinal performs the Ordination. He will anoint their palms as part of the ritual.

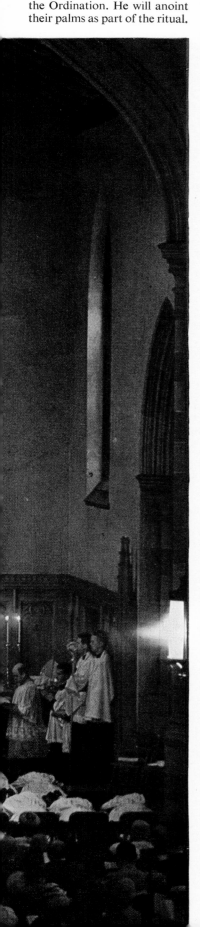

INDEX

*This symbol in front of a page number indicates that an illustration as well as mention of the subject is to be found on the page thus marked.

306

PICTURE SOURCES

Pictures on each page are listed from left to right and from top to bottom. Photographic listings are followed by the name of the photographer or agency

ENGRAVINGS AND COMPOSITION
BY R. R. DONNELLEY & SONS COMPANY, CHICAGO, ILLINOIS

LETTERPRESS PRINTING BY J. W. CLEMENT COMPANY, BUFFALO, NEW YORK
OFFSET PRINTING BY R. R. DONNELLEY & SONS COMPANY, CHICAGO, ILLINOIS

BINDING BY R. R. DONNELLEY & SONS COMPANY, CRAWFORDSVILLE, INDIANA

PAPER BY THE MEAD CORPORATION, DAYTON, OHIO